Italian Cinema and Modern European Literatures

1945–2000

Carlo Testa

Westport, Connecticut
London

Library of Congress Cataloging-in-Publication Data

Testa, Carlo.
    Italian cinema and modern European literatures, 1945–2000 / Carlo Testa.
      p. cm.
    Includes bibliographical references and index.
    ISBN 0–275–97522–3 (alk. paper)
    1. Motion pictures—Italy—History. 2. European literature—Film and video adaptations.
    3. Film adaptations.
    PN1993.5.I88T44   2002
    791.43'0945'09045—dc21   2001036708

British Library Cataloguing in Publication Data is available.

Library of Congress Catalog Card Number: 2001036708
ISBN: 0–275–97522–3

First published in 2002

Praeger Publishers, 88 Post Road West, Westport, CT 06881
An imprint of Greenwood Publishing Group, Inc.
www.praeger.com

Printed in the United States of America

The paper used in this book complies with the
Permanent Paper Standard issued by the National
Information Standards Organization (Z39.48–1984).

P

Contents

Acknowledgments

I wish to thank a number of colleagues without whose support my determination to complete this book would probably have foundered long ago: Peter Bondanella, Ben Lawton, Millicent Marcus, Lino Micciché, Àine O'Healy, and Pierre Sorlin. Further sincere thanks go to Alberto Bartolomeo at Casalini in Fiesole, Umberta Brazzini at the Mediateca Regionale Toscana in Florence, Valter Chierici at Videocavour in Milan, Alessandra Piovera and Graham and the friendly staff of Videomatica in Vancouver, as well as their counterparts at the Scuola Nazionale di Cinematografia (previously Centro Sperimentale di Cinematografia) in Rome and the Cineteca del Comune di Bologna.

A very special debt of gratitude is owed to the staff at the Interlibrary Loan Services of UBC, Keith Bunnell (Library Acquisitions), and Branko Peric (Arts Computing).

The appropriate parts of *Italian Cinema and Modern European Literatures* have benefited greatly from the UBC Hampton Fund's support for a Rossellini project. As for the book as a whole, it has drawn more than I can say from the encouragement I received from my wife, Daniela Boccassini, both while I was writing sections of it and when recovering from having done so.

This book is dedicated, with infinite gratitude, to all my teachers past and present.

Introduction

Cinema

Great cinema needs great issues.

Ettore Scola[1]

I don't know what the public "needs"—nor do I want to know. When the public sees films it likes, it just grabs them, and decrees their success.

Nanni Moretti[2]

Film and History

Film and society? A constant interaction, rather than a mere correlation.

Pierre Sorlin, *The Film in History*[3]

It is . . . not a question of repudiating interpretation but of situating its protocols within a broader historical inquiry. . . .

Some frameworks are more complex, precise, and nuanced than others; some reveal anomalies and counterexamples rather than mask them off.

The inferences produced by broad and nuanced frames of reference are thus more likely to capture fresh and significant aspects of the phenomenon.

A theoretically rigorous historical scholarship is at present a strong candidate for reinvigorating film study.

David Bordwell, *Making Meaning*[4]

Contexts

Culture as a whole can be considered as a text. It is, however, extremely important to underline that this is a text constructed in a complex way, made up of a hierarchy of "texts within texts," and forming a complex intertwining of texts.

Yurii Lotman, "Tekst v tekste"[5]

Long have we worked together for a wider and more humane history.

Marc Bloch, *Apologie pour l'histoire*[6]

Filmmakers, by definition, make films, but not just that. Like other common mortals, they engage in mundane activities linked, directly or otherwise, to their daily existence. They drive cars, talk to their drycleaner, buy—just possibly— groceries, and so on. One of the things they most demonstrably practice, how- ever, is reading. (Curiously, something they often claim *not* to do is watch movies, their own or someone else's.) Film directors' reading activities might, of course, be a matter of small consequence: they may read magazines, political or scientific, the maintenance manual for their Alfa Romeo, their children's homework, or the lottery numbers in the newspaper. Sometimes, however, what they read matters more. And it matters because what they read has a deep impact on the way they do what we consider them important for doing: making films.

   This is most frequently the case when film directors read literature. The reason seems simple enough: literature is a treasure trove of narrative subjects and techniques which, having grown steadily for about three thousand years as West- ern clocks tick, has by our time reached proportions that make it simply im- possible to ignore. Literature is a relatively (though only relatively) low-tech art; filmmaking, for its part, can occur only after the development of a con- siderably greater technological—and social—diversification in its host society. But, cinema's technical differences aside, the similarities between the two arts in telling their respective types of stories are otherwise overpowering. The phe- nomenon is, after all, not altogether unprecedented; an analogous process of fission occurred when Western theater split away from other genres in the Mid- dle Ages to become an autonomous field in its own right, yet remained a type of storytelling nonetheless. And it drew endlessly upon its predecessors from the times before the device called stage had been invented.[7] (Many of Shake- speare's dramas, to mention but one generally familiar name, can be described as theatrical re-creations of preexisting literary material.) Just as the rise of modern theater enormously broadened the means and the scope of storytelling, so too did cinema in its own time—to be sure, "with differences in the object and manner of its imitation of reality" to adapt to our context Lessing's sharply chosen terms.[8]

   Having said this, I want to emphasize that the goal of *Italian Cinema and*

Modern European Literatures is not to focus on the general theoretical question of the parallelism or interaction between film and literature. Many books, excellent and less excellent, have been doing so for a long time now, and readers seeking guidance on the subject already have a wide range of options before them.[9] The 1990s were an especially rich period in this sense for the English-reading public.[10] As for recent works that examine the literature-to-film re-creative process in a specifically Italian context, they include Sandro Bernardi's *Storie dislocate*, Cristina Bragaglia's *Il piacere del racconto*, Sara Cortellazzo and Dario Tomasi's *Letteratura e cinema*, Millicent Marcus's *Filmmaking by the Book*, and Giuliana Nuvoli and Maurizio Regosa's *Storie ricreate*. My own forthcoming *Masters of Two Arts*, which concentrates on nine major Italian films of the postwar period, offers a further contribution to the ever-expanding field of research that deals with the ways directors might re-create certain literary texts with which they feel a particular existential affinity.[11]

Since in *Masters of Two Arts* I sketch in greater detail my own position on re-creation as a theoretical issue, with a view to eschewing duplication here I will simply give a working definition of the term as I use it. For my purposes, *re-creation* is a concept which takes us beyond that of "adaptation" (the latter being tainted by the old "fidelity" prejudice). Re-creation can occur on the basis of cultural homologies between cultural-historical moments; it is, in practice, carried out by means of cinematographic devices equivalent to their literary counterparts. May I refer readers specifically interested in more details on the matter to *Masters of Two Arts*.[12]

In a very real sense, *Italian Cinema and Modern European Literatures* can be described as an inquiry into *diagonal contexts*. The first reason is a general theoretical one that holds within each art form; the concept was long familiar to the Russian formalists, who expressed it on a number of occasions. Viktor Shklovskii wrote as early as 1923: "By a law first ascertained—to the best of my knowledge—by myself, in the history of arts inheritance is transmitted not from father to son, but from uncle to nephew."[13] Diagonal transmission was also emphasized by Yurii Tynianov in his landmark book *Archaists and Innovators* (1929).[14]

Second, there is a specific diagonal quality that is unique to cinema as the most recently created of all arts. As Sergei Èizenshtein sharply puts it in his article "Pushkin and Cinema," "Cinema has no *direct* ancestors; its ancestors are all oblique."[15]

A third reinforcement of the "diagonal" concept obviously occurs to the extent that in the present book we are matching not only two different art forms with one another, but also *Italian* film with *European* literatures.

In the fourth and final place, *Italian Cinema and Modern European Literatures* is characterized by a diagonal slant in that it concerns itself systematically with other historical series outside the sphere of cinema. In other words, film-and-literature interaction is but one aspect of the issue I am about to examine. That interest cohabits here pervasively with a second and complementary one:

Why does a particular cinematic re-creation of literature occur instead of any other among the countless possible ones? On this subject I fully share the views embodied in the theoretical tradition of the Russian formalists, linguists, and semioticians, whose work was most recently continued by the Tartu school of semiotics. According to these scholars, artistic affinities operate in a dialectical relationship with historical circumstances—indeed, are comprehensible only within the broader historical contexts in which they occur.[16] It is comforting to see that this theoretical position is today shared by the most attentive and advanced segment in the field of film studies (Bordwell, Casetti, Stam).[17]

To summarize: alongside cinematic re-creation, the other main concern of *Italian Cinema and Modern European Literatures* is to analyze and describe what it was in the specific cultural situation of each moment in Italian history that made it attractive for film directors to have recourse to certain older texts in order best to articulate, in new texts, the issues of their own time.

Because of its greater emphasis on diachronic developments in Italian society, *Italian Cinema and Modern European Literatures* is structured differently from *Masters of Two Arts*: its chapters are arranged in chronological order and grouped according to a periodization of Italian history which I think is most functional to highlight similarities and differences, and in general to stress the *condition historique* of human artifacts. Most visibly, *Italian Cinema and Modern European Literatures* aims at covering a cultural territory many times broader: *Masters of Two Arts* covers nine films, whereas *Italian Cinema and Modern European Literatures* analyzes, in a more condensed manner, a much greater number of titles. Being exhaustive is, here as elsewhere, necessarily impossible, but coverage is indeed one of the avowed goals of this book—a book which amounts to a history of Italian cinema viewed from a particular angle.[18] Conversely, I am not in no way duplicating here the in-depth analysis carried out in *Masters of Two Arts*, to which I refer readers more specifically interested in any one of the nine films discussed there. In a nutshell, *Masters of Two Arts* and *Italian Cinema and Modern European Literatures* complement one another: the former privileges depth and individual artistic relations; the latter, breadth and historical context. A conceptual overlap occurs in their field of application: Italian post–World War II cinema in its interaction with French, German, and Russian literature. (To avoid duplication, the films of *Masters of Two Arts* appear here in cameo roles that can do only limited justice to the amount of attention they would otherwise have received.)[19]

There are a few exceptions within the strictly chronological structure of this book, and these occur where, within a given chapter, I place films with a strong mutual link (the same director and/or subject matter) into neighboring slots. At the cost of a slight aesthetic disruption, this aims at improving the logical continuity and readability of my argument.

As a further comment on this book's style of presentation, I should add here a few marginalia—not because I presume observant readers would not notice them on their own, but simply to give everyone an advance synopsis of what to expect.

The historical introductions are followed by a brief survey of contemporaneous filmmaking and a corresponding list of the most important Italian films of the period. Each chapter then usually begins with a general presentation or transition that leads to the discussion of individual films. The latter may be introduced by more specific presentations or transitions of their own, followed by the name of the director, the film's title (in English, then in Italian) and its date. If the title of the film and that of its prior text translate identically into English, I usually set them apart by using their respective original names.

Each film analysis contains a plot summary—generally of the film itself, rather than of its generative text, though on a few occasions I have thought it more effective to proceed otherwise. No plot summaries (or, indeed, notes) are given here for the nine items examined in *Masters of Two Arts*.

In the course of my discussion, specific footnotes comment on topics I am touching upon in the text; one final note, which acts as a transition to the next entry, generally collects the residual bibliographic references that I believe can be useful to my readers. Finally, each chapter is concluded by some generalizations on Europhile filmmaking in Italy during the period under consideration.[20]

The reason why I do not focus on the relationship between Italian cinema and *Italian* literature is altogether straightforward: there already are a number of books on this subject, and there is little I could add to their findings at this time. Where breadth is concerned, readers ought to consult Bragaglia and Nuvoli; for depth, Marcus's *Filmmaking by the Book*. On the other hand, since my personal history—or whatever entity controls that—has caused me, over time, to take a particular interest and pursue my research in the cultures of modern France, Germany, and Russia, it is fairly obvious that the comparative usefulness of my work will be greatest in the exploration of those areas.[21]

Of course, from Japan to Patagonia, there would be many different possible combinations of national influences (although, it seems to me, none as overwhelming as that bringing together the three traditions I am collating here). This is a field of inquiry that is well-nigh inexhaustible—certainly inexhaustible for a single researcher. I can find, however, grounds for comfort in the fact that many areas in the literatures of the world are far from unknown to the practitioners of Italian cinema; there is no reason to assume that intercultural links between Italy and other countries will not be soon explored as thoroughly.

Incidentally, not the least of the bonus features offered by a diagonal focalization on European literatures is a perception of the history of Italian cinema that is both different from those which came before it and complementary to them. By virtue of its different and complementary approach, I would argue, *Italian Cinema and Modern European Literatures* can avoid rounding up for the hundredth time only the usual candidates for glory, and instead adds to existing lists a number of deserving new names. These can be of interest to the public because of some historic-cultural feature they demonstrably share, rather than a common canonic status that may well evaporate as readers' and viewers' positions shift in time and space.

There are, needless to say, infinite types of intertextuality; here I will be working within a model based on several broad categories.

At one extreme of an ideal scale, I suggest the term *homological* to indicate re-creations that have a strong intellectual link to a prior text, but do no more than allude to it. These films are narratively independent from their prototypes and re-create them in manners which are appropriate for their twentieth-century contexts.

A type of film that is more imbued with actual diegetic material[22] from its prior text makes up the group of what I would call inscriptional or *epigraphic* re-creations. Here, the prior text is directly evoked, although only isolated icons from it are brought to fruition by the director.

Other films lie farther along the scale of the assimilation of prior material. These I would term *coextensive* re-creations. Here rightfully belong film-and-literature textual pairs that move from Beginning to Middle to End—or, if one will, from exposition to complication to peripety to retardation to dénouement—by retaining a significant set of functionally equivalent devices. Such devices include, variously combined, characters, plot, social background, point of view, and stylization. These films may have an embedded, shorter subunit with a strong coextensive link to a literary text; in that case they maintain what I suggest we call a *partially* coextensive relationship with that text. Or they may be *totally* coextensive with their predecessors.

Another possibility can be observed in a group of *mediated* re-creations. Among these I subsume films whose relation to their respective prior texts is filtered—and to a large extent controlled—by their choice to operate via an intermediate epiphany, be it from the theater, the opera, or the cinema itself. (I am, though, excluding mere filmed theater and filmed opera from consideration). Here, a triangular dialectic is visibly at work.

Finally, we have what may well be the least frequently attempted and most ambitious kind of all: *hypertextual* re-creations, in which directors deliberately strive to incorporate into their cinematic work a plurality of narrative texts by the same author. (Such cases, however, are so complex that they often deserve close-up scrutiny. Accordingly, I devote two chapters of *Masters of Two Arts* to Rossellini's *Vanina Vanini* and Visconti's *Morte a Venezia*.)[23]

In *Italian Cinema and Modern European Literatures* I link Italian cinema to the history of the nation that produced it—not to history as an *object* of representation, but as a *subject* of it. In the films I am considering here, Italian history—political, economic, cultural—is not (or not only) inside the frames; it is, in the first place, behind the camera. To each of the six major phases in the more than fifty years to date of the Italian Republic, there corresponds one chapter of *Italian Cinema and Modern European Literatures*.[24]

CHAPTERS ONE AND TWO

Chapter One covers the years 1946 through 1956, the peak time of the Cold War: a time, in Italy, of open conflict between the morally engaged great neorealist directors and conservative governments that considered such a position politically subversive. Chapter Two (1956–63) examines the later time when the class conflict in the peninsula became less systematically acute, in part due to Nikita Khrushchev's post-Stalinist revelations at the XX Congress of the CPSU, but perhaps primarily because by then the Italian economic miracle had seriously gotten under way.[25] I have chosen 1963 as a terminus ad quem because during that year an economic downturn set in—the euphemistically called *congiuntura*—which interrupted the years of the "boom," and also because the relatively continuous conservative political leadership of the previous period was at that time superseded by a new center-left coalition. (In 1963 the Socialists became junior tenants in the "room with the control buttons" of political power.)

CHAPTERS THREE AND FOUR

Chapter Three (1963–73) charts the years of a very rapid democratization, unfortunately accompanied by a no less sharp increase in the level of political and social conflict in Italian society. I identify 1973 as the year of the caesura, in acknowledgment of the rise of the first terrorist activities around that time and—decisively—in recognition of the cultural impact of the first global oil crisis. An additional advantage in my causing the clock to tick for a decade after 1963 is, I believe, that this allows us to avoid the common rhetoric of putting the social turmoil of the year 1968 on a pedestal for either idolatry or abomination; 1968 was a product of causes and effects, of which it, in turn, produced more. It was a year of acceleration, not an absolute turning point.

Chapter Four of *Italian Cinema and Modern European Literatures* deals with the most painful period in the history of the Italian Republic, 1973 to 1982, marked by the two opposite, yet in some bizarre way similar, phenomena of consumerist massification and political terrorism of various stripes. From both the political and the commercial end, individuals were threatened by totalitarian discourses that mirrored one another in their warnings to conform, "or else." Again, it was a deliberate choice that led me to position the assassination of Aldo Moro (1978) at the center of a phase of Italian history: in itself, the incident began nothing and ended nothing, it merely sped up the further evolution of longer-term processes.

CHAPTERS FIVE AND SIX

Chapter Five, which I reckon to run from 1982 to 1989, is sliced in such a way as to have at its zenith the star of Bettino Craxi. I view the year 1982 a watershed, insofar as it marks the intersection between the rapidly falling curve of terrorist attacks and the no less presto rising fortunes of the Socialist leader.

From then on, the Italian Socialists became guilty of the crime of hubris (and of a long list of others), assuming themselves to be eternally indispensable to Italian democracy as a buffer between the centrist Christian Democrats and the Communists. Paradoxically, they were caught wrong-footed by the collapse of their most redoubtable competitors: shortly after the Berlin Wall came down in 1989, the entire system in which the Socialists held the balance of power was swept out of Parliament—and, in dozens of cases, into court for all manners of administrative misconduct. Hence 1989 as the concluding year for this period of Italian history.

The sixth and last chapter (1989–2000) of *Italian Cinema and Modern European Literatures* starts at a time when the cracks caused in the Italian establishment by German unification translated into powerful shock waves for the entire peninsula. The republic born of the *Resistenza* against the Nazi-Fascists in 1943–45 lost, one after the other, its founding parties, which renamed themselves, split, or were voted out of existence. The magistrates engaged in the appropriately nicknamed Clean Hands investigations, particularly those of the Milanese Procura, succeeded in slapping long-overdue jail terms on the protagonists of some of the worst cases of corruption and embezzlement of public money during the 1980s. Meanwhile, the rise of new political actors unencumbered by what was perceived (by themselves) as obsolete ideological ballast added to the volatility of the system: the regional political associations calling themselves Northern Leagues and Silvio Berlusconi's privately owned party, Forza Italia, entered the fray, making it necessary for Italians to redefine the identity of their fifty-year-old republic precisely at the exciting, though awkward, time when Maastricht's Europe was knocking at the door.

The year 1996—the fiftieth anniversary of the referendum that generated the Republic of Italy on 2 June 1946—at first promised to be a turning point in the process of Italy's political rejuvenation: with a new, first-past-the-post majoritarian system in place, fresh elections for the first time gave parliamentary majority to a left-of-center democratic coalition. Yet hopes that Italy could complete a swift transition to a functional "Second Republic" akin to older western and northern European democracies were quickly dashed. In 1998, negotiations between Romano Prodi's government and Berlusconi's opposition over the necessary constitutional changes were sunk by the tycoon; Prodi's own government foundered amid old-style internal squabbling. As of 1999, Italy entered the Euro currency area, but with enormous sacrifices in terms of fiscal pressure and slow growth. While Berlusconi anointed himself as the one and only solution to Italy's many problems, Prodi's center-left successors, Massimo D'Alema and then Giuliano Amato, took the view that a better alternative was to play them down—or (for example, in the case of what could be called the "Northern question") to deny that they existed at all. At the dawn of the new century, Italy's long-standing political stalemate remained unresolved.

Just as I do not presume to know exactly what pitfalls await Italy on her path to less fettered development and closer integration with her European neighbors, so I have no way either of extrapolating from the past record what specific paths the cultural interaction between Italian filmmakers and their European interlocutors will take in the future. Only one thing is certain: during the past half century, the symbiosis between the two groups has been enormously rich and fruitful, and in a democratic, integrated political entity it will continue to offer us the fruits of mutual illumination. Over time, I hope, many more books like *Italian Cinema and Modern European Literatures* will pay homage to such intercultural works of art.

NOTES

1. "Il grande cinema ha bisogno di grandi problemi" (Ettore Scola, private communication to the author, Purdue University, October 1995).

2. "Non so di che cosa 'abbia bisogno' il pubblico; né lo voglio sapere. Quando il pubblico vede dei film che gli piacciono, li acchiappa, li fa suoi, e ne decreta poi il successo" (Nanni Moretti, private communication to the author, Rome, 18 December 1995).

3. Pierre Sorlin, *The Film in History: Restaging the Past* (Oxford: Basil Blackwell, 1980), p. 138.

4. David Bordwell, *Making Meaning: Inference and Rhetoric in the Interpretation of Cinema* (Cambridge, Mass.: Harvard University Press, 1989), p. 266.

5. Kul'tura v tselom mozhet rassmatrivat'sia kak tekst. Odnako iskliuchitel'no vazhno podcherknut', chto èto slozhno ustroennyi tekst, raspadaiushchiisia na ierarkhiiu "tekstov v tekstakh" i obrazuiushchii slozhnye perepleteniia tekstov. Yurii M. Lotman, "Tekst v tekste," *Trudy po znakovym sistemam* 14 (1981): 18. I have been unable to locate an English translation of this article. An Italian version of it appeared in Lotman, *La semiosfera*, ed. Simonetta Salvestroni (Venice: Marsilio, 1992 [1985]), p. 265.

6. Marc Bloch, *Apologie pour l'histoire: Or, The Historian's Craft*, trans. Peter Putnam (New York: Knopf, 1963), p. v. "Longuement nous avons combattu de concert, pour une histoire plus large et plus humaine" (Marc Bloch, *Apologie pour l'histoire, ou Métier d'historien* [Paris: Armand Colin, 1949], p. vii).

7. I am drastically simplifying the situation: the stage was, of course, invented in ancient Greece, and modern European theater—the theater of the appropriately named Renaissance—could never have become what it did, had it not grafted onto its medieval roots this particular piece of classical heritage. This not particularly revolutionary concept bears recalling here due to its great relevance for our present concerns: it eloquently brings home the importance of the re-creation of art in germane art forms over successive historical epochs.

8. The sentence, a quote from Plutarch, appears as the epigraph of Gotthold Ephraim Lessing, *Laokoon: Oder Über die Grenzen der Malerei und Poesie* (1766), vol. 5, pt. 2 of Lessing's *Werke und Briefe in zwölf Bänden*, ed. Wilfried Barner (Frankfurt am Main: Deutscher Klassiker Verlag, 1990).

9. Among the most important critical works on film and literature for the general public are Vito Attolini, *Storia del cinema letterario in cento film* (Recco): Le Mani, 1998); Wendell Aycock and Michael Schoenecke, eds., *Film and Literature: A Comparative Approach to Adaptation* (Lubbock: Texas Tech University Press, 1988); André

Bazin, *Le cinéma et les autres arts*, vol. 2 of his *Qu'est-ce que le cinéma?* (Paris: Editions du Cerf, 1959); George Bluestone, *Novels into Film* (Berkeley: University of California Press, 1966); Ben Brady, *Principles of Adaptation for Film and Television* (Austin: University of Texas Press, 1994); Gian Piero Brunetta, ed., *Letteratura e cinema* (Bologna: Zanichelli, 1976); Seymour Chatman, "What Novels Can Do That Films Can't (and Vice Versa)," *Critical Inquiry* 7: 1 (Autumn 1980): 121–40; Seymour Chatman, *Coming to Terms: The Rhetoric of Narrative in Fiction and Film* (Ithaca, NY: Cornell University Press, 1990); Jeanne-Marie Clerc, *Littérature et cinéma* (Paris: Nathan, 1993); Keith Cohen, *Film and Fiction: The Dynamics of Exchange* (New Haven, CT: Yale University Press, 1979); Roumiana Deltcheva, "Literature-Film Relations: Selected Bibliography (1985–1996)," in *Literature and Film: Models of Adaptation*, special issue of *Canadian Review of Comparative Literature/Revue Canadienne de Littérature Comparée* 23: 3 (September 1996): 853–71; Andrew Horton and Joan Magretta, eds., *Modern European Filmmakers and the Art of Adaptation* (New York: Frederick Ungar, 1981); Gerald Mast, "Literature and Film," in Jean-Pierre Barricelli and Joseph Gibaldi, eds., *Interrelations of Literature* (New York: MLA, 1982), pp. 278–306; Stuart Y. McDougal, *From Literature to Film* (New York: Holt, Rinehart and Winston, 1985); Lino Micciché, "Cinema e letteratura," in his *La ragione e lo sguardo: Saggi e note sul cinema* (Cosenza: Lerici, 1979), pp. 147–77; and Gabriel Miller, *Screening the Novel: Rediscovered American Fiction in Film* (New York: Frederick Ungar, 1980).

    10. Of the most recent publications, some that stand out are the following: Deborah Cartmell and Imelda Whelehan, eds., *Adaptations: From Text to Screen, Screen to Text* (London: Routledge, 1999); James Griffith, *Adaptations as Imitations: Films from Novels* (Newark: University of Delaware Press, 1997); Brian McFarlane, *Novel to Film: An Introduction to the Theory of Adaptation* (Oxford: Clarendon Press, 1996); James Naremore, ed., *Film Adaptation* (New Brunswick, N.J.: Rutgers University Press, 2000); and John Orr and Colin Nicholson, eds., *Cinema and Fiction: New Modes of Adapting, 1950–1990* (Edinburgh: Edinburgh University Press, 1992).

    11. Sandro Bernardi, ed., *Storie dislocate* (San Miniato: Edizioni ETS, 1999); Cristina Bragaglia, *Il piacere del racconto: Narrativa italiana e cinema (1895–1990)* (Florence: La Nuova Italia, 1993); Sara Cortellazzo and Dario Tomasi, *Letteratura e cinema* (Rome and Bari: Laterza, 1998); Millicent Marcus, *Filmmaking by the Book: Italian Cinema and Literary Adaptation* (Baltimore: Johns Hopkins University Press, 1993); Giuliana Nuvoli and Maurizio Regosa, *Storie ricreate: Dall'opera letteraria al film* (Turin: UTET, 1998); and Carlo Testa, *Masters of Two Arts: Re-creation of European Literatures in Italian Cinema* (Toronto: University of Toronto Press, 2002).

    The most valuable general works on Italian cinema—with or without a literary ascendancy—are Peter Bondanella, *Italian Cinema from Neorealism to the Present* (New York: Continuum, 1991 [1983]); Gian Piero Brunetta, *Storia del cinema italiano*, 4 vols. (Rome: Editori Riuniti, 1993 [1982]); Fernaldo Di Giammatteo, *Lo sguardo inquieto: Storia del cinema italiano 1940–1990* (Florence: La Nuova Italia, 1994); Marcia Landy, *Italian Film* (Cambridge: Cambridge University Press, 2000); Mira Liehm, *Passion and Defiance: Film in Italy from 1942 to the Present* (Berkeley: University of California Press, 1984); Millicent Marcus, *Italian Film in the Light of Neorealism* (Princeton, N.J.: Princeton University Press, 1986); and Pierre Sorlin, *Italian National Cinema 1896–1996* (London and New York: Routledge, 1996).

    12. A few words, though, regarding "fidelity." First, literary language and cinematic language are not directly convertible into one another, so "fidelity" is, in an extreme

sense, impossible to begin with. Second, who will measure it? "Fidelity" is, except perhaps in limit cases, to a large extent in the eye of the beholder. Third, who says that "fidelity"—if and when detected, proven, and measured—is necessarily a good thing? In fact, there are excellent reasons to suspect that absolute "fidelity" of a film to a work of literature would be an absolute terrible thing, a guarantee of cinematic mediocrity. Fourth, directors are rarely slaves to the "fidelity" myth; it would clearly be absurd to test their work against a criterion that had not guided them in the first place.

On the inconvertibility of literary language into cinematic language in a direct manner, see above all Jean Mitry, *The Aesthetics and Psychology of the Cinema*, trans. Christopher King (Bloomington: Indiana University Press, 1997); *Esthétique et psychologie du cinéma*, vol. 1 (Paris: Editions Universitaires, 1963).

On the ever-active dialogism between cultures and within each culture, see my references below to Russian formalists, linguists, and semioticians.

The notion of homology was brought into focus with particular sharpness by Marcello Pagnini in his *Semiosi: Teoria ed ermeneutica del testo letterario* (Bologna: Il Mulino, 1988), pp. 61–66.

13. Po zakonu, ustanovlennomu, naskol'ko ia znaiu, vpervye mnoi, v istorii iskusstv, nasledovanie proiskhodit ne ot ottsa k synu, a ot diadi k plemianniku. Viktor Shklovskii, *Literatura i kinematograf* (Berlin: Russkoe Universal'noe Izdatel'stvo, 1923), p. 27. The translation is mine.

14. See above all the essay "Dostoevskii and Gogol," repr. in *Texte der russischen Formalisten*, ed. Jurij Striedter, vol. 1 (Munich: Fink, 1969).

15. Net *priamykh* predkov kino, a predki vse kosvennye. Sergei Èizenshtein, "Pushkin i kino" [1939], in *Izbrannye proizvedeniia v shesti tomakh* (Moscow: Iskusstvo, 1964), vol. 2, p. 307. The translation is mine.

16. On the correlation between artistic (literary, cinematographic) and other historical (cultural-historical and social) series, see Yurii Tynianov, "On Literary Evolution" ("O literaturnoi èvoliutsii") and Boris Èichenbaum, "Literary Environment" ("Literaturnyi byt"), both translated into English in Ladislav Matejka and Krystyna Pomorska, eds., *Readings in Russian Poetics: Formalist and Structuralist Views* (Ann Arbor: Michigan Slavic Publications, 1978). A ringing manifesto for the establishment of a definitive (neither impressionistic nor mechanically deterministic) approach to the issue can also be found in Yurii Tynianov and Roman Jakobson, "Problemy izucheniia literatury i iazyka" (1928), in *Texte der russischen Formalisten*, vol. 2.

Much of this hoped-for work came to fruition with Mikhail Mikhailovich Bakhtin—on whom film studies specialists can consult Robert Stam's *Subversive Pleasures: Bakhtin, Cultural Criticism, and Film* (Baltimore: Johns Hopkins University Press, 1989)—and, above all, the Soviet school of semioticians trained in Bakhtin's theories and clustered around Yurii Lotman. Unfortunately, among Lotman's works relevant to this subject very little has been translated into English: essentially only *Universe of the Mind: A Semiotic Theory of Culture*, trans. Ann Shukman (London and New York: I. B. Tauris, 1990). For more details on publications in other languages, including my own article "Dalla letteratura al cinema: Adattamento o ri-creazione?," see the thematic bibliography at the end of this volume.

17. Even without counting the recent books on cinematographic "adaptation" from the 1990s already referred to, a definite closing of the chasm between research on theoretical series and that on sociocultural series can be detected, as of this writing, in such

important works as the following: Bordwell, *Making Meaning*; Francesco Casetti, *Theories of Cinema: 1945–1995,* trans. Francesca Chiostri et al. (Austin: University of Texas Press, 1999); *Teorie del cinema 1945–1990* (Milan: Bompiani, 1994); Francesco Casetti, "Lo sguardo novecentesco," in Bernardi, ed., *Storie dislocate,* pp. 17–26; and Robert Stam, *Film Theory: An Introduction* (Oxford: Blackwell, 2000).

18. Unfortunately, some of the earlier filmic material proved difficult or impossible to locate and view. In particular, I wish I could have done more to cover the 1940s, a period that—if nothing else, to bolster receipts at the box office—was more Europhile than we realize today. For practical reasons, I have chosen to concentrate on material that is, if not always easily, at least reasonably, available commercially or in media libraries in Italy or North America; but this was at times a painful option for me.

Indeed, a book of respectable size could perhaps be written on the cross-media intertextuality of many French-, German- and Russian-inspired films made in Italy during the first few years I take into consideration. Using Roberto Chiti and Roberto Poppi, *I film dal 1945 al 1959,* vol. 2 of *Dizionario del cinema italiano* (Rome: Gremese, 1991), I ran a control test for 1945–1948 and retrieved no fewer than thirteen items. Seven such entries are for Italian cinema proper:

1946. Riccardo Freda's *Black Eagle (Aquila nera),* from Pushkin's novella *Dubrovsky;* and Mario Soldati's *Eugenia Grandet,* from Balzac.

1947. Mario Camerini's *The Captain's Daughter (La figlia del capitano),* from Pushkin; Riccardo Freda's *Les Miserables (I miserabili),* from Hugo; Giacomo Gentilomo's *The Brothers Karamazov (I fratelli Karamazoff),* from Dostoevsky; and Gennaro Righelli's *The King's Messenger (Il corriere del re),* from Stendhal's *Red and Black.*

1948. Giorgio Pàstina's *Wilhelm Tell, the Archer of the Black Forest (Guglielmo Tell, l'arciere della Foresta Nera),* from Schiller.

Three further items are co-productions (all with France and in 1947): Jacques de Baroncelli's *Rocambole,* from Ponson du Terrail; Pierre Billon's *Ruy Blas,* from Hugo; and Christian-Jaque's *The Charterhouse of Parma (La Certosa di Parma),* from Stendhal. Finally, we have three filmed operas:

1946. Mario Costa's *Il barbiere di Siviglia,* from Rossini.

1947. Max Calandri's *Lohengrin,* from Wagner.

1948. Carmine Gallone's *The Legend of Faust (La leggenda di Faust),* a potpourri from Charles Gounod and Arrigo Boito.

The extant secondary literature on all these titles is scarce. Not untypical is the situation of *Rocambole* and *The Charterhouse of Parma,* which are briefly mentioned in Aldo Bernardini, "Le collaborazioni internazionali nel cinema europeo," in Gian Piero Brunetta, ed., *L'Europa. Miti, luoghi, divi,* vol. 1, pt. 1 of his *Storia del cinema mondiale* (Turin: Einaudi, 1999), p. 1037. Soldati's *Eugenia Grandet* gets two pages in Attolini, *Storia del cinema letterario,* pp. 107–09. As for the films themselves, among the few acceptably available ones at the time of this writing are *Eugenia Grandet* and Camerini's *The Captain's Daughter* (both were aired on afternoon TV in the 1990s and thereby acquired by at least some media libraries) and Freda's *Les Miserables* (commercial video). *The Charterhouse of Parma* is, given sufficient time, means and luck, retrievable in France.

Having mentioned co-productions, I wish to specify here that the criterion I have applied to discriminate for or against including any of them in *Italian Cinema and Modern European Literatures* is the nationality of the director. Thus, for example, ceteris paribus, Carmine Gallone's *Michael Strogoff* is in, while Christian-Jaque's *Charterhouse* is out.

19. To the extent that the key term here is "history," I feel it is my duty to operate in the same way as conventional historians would—and, just as they would, to articulate for readers my own methodological presuppositions. Historiography, to my mind, can most accurately be metaphorized as a fishing expedition:

> The facts are really not at all like fish on the fishmonger's slab. They are like fish swimming about in a vast and sometimes inaccessible ocean; and what the historian catches will depend partly on chance, but mainly on what part of the ocean he chooses to fish in and what tackle he chooses to use—these two factors being, of course, determined by the kind of fish he wants to catch. By and large, the historian will get the kind of facts he wants. History means interpretation. (Edward Hallett Carr, *What Is History?* [London: Macmillan, 1986], p. 18

To wit: on the one hand, what one catches depends largely on what one has equipped him/herself to catch. On the other hand, within such bounds, one will, first, catch fish that *are there* (i.e., that in fact materially exist); and, second, one will *not* be able to catch fish that are *not* there, making them up ex nihilo. In sum, historiography is to me a two-faced, subjective-objective, middle-way process eschewing both the ontological claims typical of nineteenth-century *Geistesgeschichte* and some more contemporary, solipsistic ones according to which there is nothing more to culture than a consistent Will to Power of Hegemonic Discourse.

20. Some discrepancies in English translations of titles or dates of release may occur due to differences in distribution in Italy and other countries.

21. Many are the important groups of films which my personal circumstances force me to leave to one side. A nonexhaustive list, chronologically and geographically arranged, of the material that could have been included by scholars with a background different from mine follows:

Antiquity. Ancient Greece: Pasolini's *Oedipus Rex (Edipo re*, 1967; from Sophocles) and *Medea* (1970; from Euripides); and Martone's *Theater of War (Teatro di guerra*, 1998; from Aeschylus's *The Seven Against Thebes*). Rome: Fellini's *Satyricon* (1969; from Petronius Arbiter's *Satyricon*). To these one could add all of Rossellini's and Olmi's films inspired by Judeo-Christian Scriptures.

Middle Ages. Europe: Pasolini's *Canterbury Tales (I racconti di Canterbury*, 1972; from Chaucer). Outside Europe: Pasolini's *Arabian Nights (Il fiore delle mille e una notte*, 1974; from the collection of Arab and South Asian tales); and Cavani's *Milarepa* (1974; from the Tibetan Buddhist text *The Life of Milarepa*).

Renaissance. Zeffirelli's *The Taming of the Shrew (La bisbetica domata*, 1967); and the many *Romeo and Juliets* from Shakespeare (Castellani, 1954; Freda, 1964; and Zeffirelli, 1968).

Nineteenth and twentieth centuries (outside Europe). Anglo-American literature: Visconti's *Ossessione* (1943; from James Cain's *The Postman Always Rings Twice*); Fellini's *Toby Dammit* (1968; from Edgar Allan Poe's *Never Bet the Devil Your Head*); and Bertolucci's *The Sheltering Sky (Il té nel deserto*, 1990; from Paul Bowles's *The Sheltering Sky*). Hispano-American: Antonioni's *Blow-Up* (1967; from Cortázar's *The Devil's Drool/Las babas del diablo*); and Bertolucci's *The Spider's Stratagem (La strategia del ragno*, 1970; from Borges's *The Theme of the Traitor and the Hero/Tema del traidor y del héroe*). Japan: Brass, *The Key (La chiave*, 1983; from Tanizaki's novel of the same title); and Cavani, *The Berlin* [sic] *Affair (Interno berlinese*, 1985; from Tanizaki's *The Buddhist Cross*).

Even for the nineteenth and twentieth centuries within Europe, a number of examples could be adduced to gauge the distance separating this book from full exhaustiveness. Among the items that come to my mind as victims of my own ignorance in the matter of—for example—British culture, the first are Comencini's *Misunderstood (Incompreso,* 1967; from Florence Montgomery's novel of the same title); Amelio's *Young Archimedes (Il piccolo Archimede,* 1979); from Aldous Huxley's homonymous short story); and Zeffirelli's *Jane Eyre* (1996; from Charlotte Brontë). A deserving Dutch entry inevitably denied its due in this book is Jona Oberski's *Childhood (Kinderjaren),* re-created by Faenza in *Jonah Who Lived Inside the Whale (Jona che visse nella balena,* 1993).

(However, for Amelio's reservations about the genesis of *Young Archimedes,* see his interview with Mimmo Rafele collected in Lucilla Albano, ed., *Il racconto tra letteratura e cinema* (Rome: Bulzoni, 1997), esp. p. 143.

22. Diegetic (from Greek *diêgêsis* meaning narration) relates to narration or plot; narrative.

23. For a survey of alternative possible classifications, see those listed and described in McFarlane, *Novel to Film,* pp. 10–11.

I particularly regret the absence of any specific categorization of literature-to-cinema re-creation in Gérard Genette's otherwise admirable *Palimpsests: Literature in the Second Degree,* trans. Claude Doubinsky and Channa Newman (Lincoln: University of Nebraska Press, 1997); *Palimpsestes: La littérature au second degré* (Paris: Seuil, 1982). (Genette uses the term *hypertext* to indicate any *"upstream"* text—a practice which has by and large been abandoned by subsequent scholarship.)

24. Again, in response to a question as to whether my history is going to be "objective" or not, I can only answer: of course it is, and of course it isn't. I must repeat that I consider objectivity to be an impossible ideal. Italian culture is not fond of the attempts, routinely made by neopositivistic hermeneutics, at presenting "facts" purely and simply; facts are, alas, rarely simple, and in any case never pure. (That said, my quote from E. H. Carr in note 19 indicates that Anglo-Saxon scholars are perfectly able to see eye to eye with a nonidealistic historiographic methodology.)

To rephrase the concept in more direct terms: my account of Italian history since 1945 develops out of the axioms of a consciously non-Berlusconian geometry. Yes, I *am* picking out certain sad facts in the history of Italian democracy while leaving out edifying ones (for example, the news of Berlusconi's willingness—abroad today in his hometown of Arcore—to offer free rent for life to very old farmers still operating on the prime building land the tycoon has purchased there for development). No, I do not think that Berlusconi was the best development that could happen to the Italian body politic since the good-natured Duce was foolishly taken in by an ever-scheming Führer.

For a condensed account in English of Berlusconi's fortunes, see "Berlusconi: An Italian Story," *The Economist,* 28 April 2001, 17–18, 23–28.

25. It goes without saying that the Cold War did not end on 31 December 1956, that the Italian "economic miracle" did not begin on 1 January 1957, and so on. Any such periodization is adopted here, as is customary in such cases, as a somewhat arbitrary conceptualization of certain phenomena that shape successive historical ages. In practice, features of each chronological segment overlap with those of the preceding one and the following one (or ones) for a long time before and after their own peak.

1

The Cold War (1945–56)

The "subject" of a work is what a bad one finally boils down to.
Paul Valéry[1]

The years 1945 and 1946 saw the gradual reestablishment of normalcy in Italy after the end of World War II and the civil war against the Nazis and Mussolini's puppet northern republic (Repubblica di Salò). Under Allied occupation, central rule emanated from a coalition government that, mirroring the makeup of the anti-Fascist insurrectional committee, the CLN (Comitato di Liberazione Nazionale), included all six anti-Fascist parties (Partito d'Azione, Comunista, Democrazia Cristiana, Liberale, Repubblicano, Socialista). The first Italian government after the fall of the regime was under the leadership of Ferruccio Parri, of the Partito d'Azione.

Quite apart from constitutional issues—establishing the guidelines for multiparty elections, drafting a new constitution, choosing between a monarchic or a republican state form—occupied Italy had to cope with a host of emergency situations: the purge and replacement of Fascist civil servants, the conflict with Yugoslavia over the new northeastern border, Sicilian separatism, massive pressure by landless peasants for agrarian reform in the countryside, inflation, the black market economy, currency devaluation. Soon political conflicts between left-wing and right-wing parties arose, particularly over the attempt to remove Fascist personnel from sensitive political positions. Echoing dissatisfaction harbored by the U.S. administration about the Italian government's political ambivalence, the Liberals and the Christian Democrats eventually withdrew their support from the coalition of national unity, so that Parri was forced to resign in November 1945.

In December 1945 a new, center-right government was sworn in under the leadership of Alcide De Gasperi, a Christian Democrat. (The next non-Christian Democrat prime minister would be Giovanni Spadolini in 1981, thirty-six years later.) De Gasperi adopted deflationary policies, reversed guidelines on dismissal of Fascists from the public administration, and proclaimed an amnesty for all political crimes committed under the former regime. The international situation, meanwhile, became ever more tense; Winston Churchill coined the expression "iron curtain."

On 2 June 1946, in a nationwide referendum Italians opted for a republican state form; they also elected representatives to a special assembly (Assemblea Costituente) in charge of drafting a new constitution. Slowly and painfully negotiated as a compromise between lay and Church desiderata, this document went into effect on 1 January 1948.

Taking advantage, during the interregnum, of the disarray of the previously Fascist-run film industry, Rossellini brought out two cinematic products of a novel and as yet undefinable theoretical status: *Rome, Open City* (1945) and *Paisan* (1946). The Italian public was at first underwhelmed by their artistic merits: they presented *reality*, not art. Fortunately, other audiences around the world opined differently, and eventually persuaded Italians that art and realism were far from being mutually exclusive concepts.

In 1947 Italy experienced a dramatic turning point: Harry Truman announced the launch of the Marshall Plan for U.S.-friendly countries of Western Europe. Against the backdrop of severe social and political unrest, Italy acceded to the plan; at the same time, the parties of the left were definitively excluded from government. Walter Lippmann described the new global situation as a "Cold War." Carrying out what would later turn out to be the first in a long string of political massacres in the story of the Italian Republic, the band of the Sicilian rebel Salvatore Giuliano attacked a peasants' rally at Portella della Ginestra and killed eight demonstrators.

Having fulfilled its mandate, in 1948 the Constituent Assembly resigned. Elections for the new Parliament took place in the explosive atmosphere of the Cold War. (Palmiro Togliatti, the secretary of the Italian Communist Party, was shot at and seriously wounded by a right-wing extremist.) The center-right parties obtained an absolute majority. In 1949, not without further conflict in Parliament and outside it, Italy joined NATO. The Vatican excommunicated all Communists and their supporters.

The year 1950 marked the beginning of the Korean War. In Italy, economic restructuring led to the onset of industrial recovery, accompanied, over the next few years, by increased unemployment, strikes, lockouts, occupations of uncultivated land by landless peasants, and bloodshed as the police repressed laborers' demonstrations. Emigration was encouraged by international agreements; a fund for special pilot projects in the South was created (Cassa per il Mezzogiorno).

The 1950s saw Italy turn from a prevalently agrarian country to one dominated by industry. In agricultural areas the population was depleted by mass migrations either to foreign countries or toward the northern regions of the *triangolo industriale*; in industrialized areas, the influx of millions of workers brought steady growth, but also a human toll in attendant social problems.

In politics, the Cold War continued throughout the 1950s: purges racked Eastern Europe, McCarthyism swept the United States, and with the "swindle bill" (*legge truffa*) of 1952–53 Italian centrist governments attempted to skew the rules of parliamentary representation by assigning bonus seats to the political majority (i.e., themselves). Giulio Andreotti castigated De Sica for persevering after *Bicycle Thieves* (*Ladri di biciclette*, 1948) and offering in *Umberto D.* (1952) yet another poverty-stricken, "unflattering" image of Italy to the world. State-controlled TV (RAI Radio Televisione Italiana) began broadcasting, and reached ever-growing audiences with variety shows imitating U.S. models.

In 1953, Stalin died. In 1956–57, Nikita Khrushchev's revelations at the Twentieth Congress of the Communist Party of the Soviet Union, and the repression of the Hungarian revolt which followed it, caused a deep crisis in the Italian Communist Party. Italian Socialists distanced themselves from the Communists; many Communists abandoned their party. As Italian society became more diversified, the decade-long polarity of the Cold War began to fray.

In cinema, the years between 1945 and 1956 were the heyday of neorealism: at first in its morally committed variant, and later also in its "pink," merely entertaining, one. To rephrase the concept in more sharply political terms, the peak of the Cold War largely coincided with the great season of neorealism proper—the latter eventually turning into one of the many political victims of the former.

Among the most important reference films of this time are Antonioni's *Chronicle of A Love* (*Cronaca di un amore*, 1950), *The Vanquished* (*I vinti*, 1952), *The Lady Without Camellias* (*La signora senza camelie*, 1953), and *The Girlfriends* (*Le amiche*, 1953); Comencini's *Bread, Love and Fantasy* (*Pane, amore e fantasia*, 1953); De Santis's *Tragic Hunt* (*Caccia tragica*, 1946), *Bitter Rice* (*Riso amaro*, 1949), and *No Peace Among the Olive Trees* (*Non c'è pace tra gli ulivi*, 1950); De Sica's *The Children Are Watching Us* (*I bambini ci guardano*, 1943), *Shoeshine* (*Sciuscià*, 1946), *Bicycle Thieves* (*Ladri di biciclette*, 1948), *Miracle in Milan* (*Miracolo a Milano*, 1951), *Umberto D.* (1952), and *The Gold of Naples* (*L'oro di Napoli*, 1954); Fellini's *The White Sheik* (*Lo sceicco bianco*, 1952), *The Loafers* (*I vitelloni*, 1953), and *The Road* (*La strada*, 1954); Germi's *In the Name of the Law* (*In nome della legge*, 1949), *The Path of Hope* (*Il cammino della speranza*, 1950), *The Brigand of Tacca del Lupo* (*Il brigante di Tacca del Lupo*, 1952), and *The Railroad Man* (*Il ferroviere*, 1956); Lattuada's *The Bandit* (*Il bandito*, 1946), *The Mill on the River Po* (*Il mulino del Po*, 1949), *Anna* (1952), *The Overcoat* (*Il cappotto*, 1952), *The She-Wolf* (*La lupa*, 1953), and *The Beach* (*La spiaggia*, 1953); Lizzani's *Beware! Bandits*

(*Achtung! Banditi*, 1951) and *Chronicle of Poor Lovers* (*Cronache di poveri amanti*, 1954); Maselli's *Breaking Ranks* (*Gli sbandati*, 1955); Monicelli's *Cops and Robbers* (*Guardie e ladri*, 1951); Pietrangeli's *The Sun in the Eyes* (*Il sole negli occhi*, 1953); Rossellini's *Rome, Open City* (*Roma, città aperta*, 1945), *Paisan* (*Paisà*, 1946), *Love* (*Amore*, 1948), *Germany Year Zero* (*Germania anno zero*, 1948), *Stromboli, Land of God* (*Stromboli, terra di Dio*, 1949), *Francis, Jester of God* (*Francesco, giullare di Dio*, 1950), *Europa '51* (1951), *Voyage to Italy* (*Viaggio in Italia*, 1953), *Joan of Arc Burned at the Stake* (*Giovanna d'Arco al rogo*, 1954), and *Fear* (*La paura*, 1954–55); Visconti's *Ossessione* (1943), *The Earth Trembles* (*La terra trema*, 1948), and *Senso* (1954).

Most directors of the immediate postwar period belonged to a generation brought up under the "calligraphic" mandates of the Fascist era: no politics, no violence, no real-life ugliness. They aimed at reaching large masses of people and generally cared little for the exploration of new paths in cinematographic expression or techniques. And they often drew upon preexisting literary texts whose plots they re-created for the screen with hardly any ambition beyond an illustrative one.[2]

Mario Soldati shared a few traits with this group. A gifted but not yet well-known literary author, in the 1930s Soldati, facing financial distress, had to seek employment in the film industry, at the time still largely based in his hometown of Turin. After making over two dozen films between 1938 and 1959—mostly re-creations from Italian nineteenth-century novels—he turned to TV productions with similar characteristics. His literary output, on the other hand, continued into the 1990s.

Soldati's *Eugenie Grandet* (*Eugenia Grandet*, 1946) is re-created from Balzac's novel of the same title.[3]

We are in the French provinces—the town of Saumur—shortly after the post-Napoleonic Restoration. The dreamy Eugenia lives a lonely life, kept on a tight leash by her avaricious father, the cooper-turned-speculator Grandet. Her lazy and morally worthless cousin Carlo suddenly comes to Saumur from Paris, where his father is about to commit suicide after going bankrupt.

Eugenia promptly falls for the foppish young man. Believing he will come back to her healthy, wealthy, wise, and above all in love, she gives him enough money to go to the Indies and start a new life there. The latter Carlo does successfully, but without giving Eugenia, over time, any sign of life or gratitude. Then new challenges spring up for the young woman: when old Grandet dies, she takes over the ownership and the management of the multimillion-franc-estate.

Carlo comes back after seven years. In a businesslike manner, he returns to Eugenia the borrowed sum, announcing to her that he intends to marry the daughter of the Marquise d'Aubrion . . . because, *chère cousine*, such is the way of the world. However, instead of being put off by Carlo's effrontery, Eugenia once more sacrifices herself for his sake: she fully settles the debts outstanding from her uncle's bankruptcy, thus for all intents and purposes making Carlo's marriage financially possible.

The marriage of Eugenia's faithful nanny, Nanon, chronologically coincides with Carlo's. Eugenia will henceforward live alone in her father's large and now empty home.

Particularly toward the end of the film, Soldati makes some deft rearrangements vis-à-vis the novel in the structure and chronology of the events he narrates. For example, he excises altogether the eventual marriage and widowhood of Balzac's Eugénie, concurrently delaying Nanon's definitive departure so as to maximize the traumatic impact that Carlo's betrayal has on Eugenia. The director is also skillful in manipulating the symbolism of certain objects. Thus, the almost comically decadent nightgown which le dandy initially leaves with his cousin as a token of his supposed eternal love later migrates to the shoulders of a more appropriate support—the Virgin—wrapped around whose statue Eugenia admires it, in the film's final images, transfixed in wistful contemplation.

Surely, Soldati's Eugenia Grandet responded to the aesthetics of a historical situation where little more than illustration was generally envisaged by directors or, indeed, expected of them. It was a production that, a decade later, could have been undertaken by RAI, the Italian TV corporation, for its programs aimed at cultural literacy among the general public. Yet this was, in itself, a far from undeserving goal—a goal that, sampling today's airwaves, one certainly wishes the Italian TV stations of the twenty-first century had the dignity to "go back" to.[4]

But melancholy provincial beauties remembering things past were only one—and by far not the main one—of the staples of the Italian cinema of the time. The next two items in our list, Freda's Les Miserables and Camerini's The Captain's Daughter, will require some substantial contextualization in this sense.

If there is any truth to the anonymous popular definition of cinema as a factory of illusions, rarely might Italian audiences have embraced such a view with more zeal than in the war-ravaged years following the end of the hostilities in 1945. Aside from gorging itself on American-made films, old and new, whose landing on the fatherland's shores Fascism had long forbidden, the Italian public of the time mainly flocked to view historical films able to take it to an escapist world of heroines and heroes wearing splendid costumes and roaming exotic, faraway lands.

The overwhelming majority of such cloak-and-dagger or sentimental products were made by filmmakers of Soldati's generation, who, having come of age under the Fascist regime, felt at ease with a time-tested, politically indifferent formula. Monicelli, who would become one of the most successful directors in the second half of the century but at the time was an obscure young scriptwriter, described the immediate postwar situation in no roundabout way:

The historical films of those years were aimed at a working-class public. Freda's films, such as Black Eagle and The Mysterious Knight, enjoyed an incredible success.[5]

Audiences grew passionate for the heroes of these films, which we invariably presented as absolutely upright—something we did in part to stay within the tradition of the cheap serial novel, and in part to humor what we knew to be the public's taste. In the wake of those hits, Camerini [shot] *The Captain's Daughter*, from Pushkin; then Righelli made *The King's Messenger*, from Stendhal's *Red and Black*; . . . and Gentilomo dared shoot *The Brothers Karamazov*.[6]

This style of production was very much in line with Europhile films that had routinely been made under Fascism until almost the very end of the war. One thinks, for example, of Renato Castellani's *A Pistol Shot* (*Un colpo di pistola*, 1942), from a novella by Pushkin (*The Shot*, from *Tales of Belkin; Vystrel*, from *Povesti Belkina*, 1831), or of Flavio Calzavara's *Resurrection* (*Resurrezione*, 1944), from Tolstoy (*Voskresenie*, 1899). Riccardo Freda's *Black Eagle* (*Aquila nera*, 1946), a re-creation of Pushkin's short story "Dubrovsky" (1832–33), fits seamlessly into this artistic—or, to put the matter more precisely, artistico-commercial—pattern.[7]

It is certainly curious to note how nonchalantly the cultural heritage of a supposedly enemy nation such as Russia could be appropriated first by the belligerently anti-Bolshevik Fascist regime, and after 1945 by an industry that was, by any standard of measurement, drenched in the culture of its Western military occupants. (Freda was a particularly zealous fan of the U.S. cinematic tradition, with which he deliberately aimed at competing.) It is difficult to assess today to what extent the films mentioned bracketed out any substantive Russianness from their treatment of their subject matter or, conversely, attempted to use it in order to question the legitimacy of the Communist dictatorship. Without any reasonable access to this abundant material, one certainly is left with a gnawing sense of curiosity about what traits could have been given to improbable personae such as, for example, a "Fascist" Tolstoy.

Freda's presence in the company just described comes as little surprise to those who are both familiar with the director's artistic inclinations and aware of how much of the old Fascist regime lived on in the Italy of 1945—not only politically but also culturally and, in particular, cinematographically. A fairly long string of quotations could be assembled by collating Freda's scathing judgments of his favorite bogeypersons: "the filthy stench" [*i fetidi miasmi*] of neorealism in cinema (the credo he swears by being "imagination");[8] a narrative focus on common people, such as we find in De Sica's works (Freda being all-out for hero worship); and cinematic intellectualism as practiced by the likes of Antonioni and Fellini (Freda's most fervent admiration going, rather, to Hollywoodian adventure films). It is almost painful to see how, even a long time after the events discussed, Freda could still argue as follows:

More than thirty years ago, everyone was delirious about *Rome, Open City*. People said *that* was the path which cinema had to take. I laughed about that, because I thought that this kind of filmmaking was accidental, absolutely uninteresting. I put forward this opinion often and on different occasions, and I know that as a consequence I am not much appreciated. But I still hold, and I say so openly, that realism in general is the worst possible form of artistic expression. . . . Realism is but a mechanical reproduction of real life. . . .

It is funny [*buffo*] that an aesthetics which [in painting] was already in a stage of advanced putrefaction should have been able to become a great new form of expression in cinema.[9]

The angle from which Freda perceives Fascism is not only altogether consistent with the above views, but is in itself revealing:

[D]uring the allegedly abominable twenty years of Fascism . . . there were, to be sure, a few problems of freedom for intellectuals; but I remember that one day, alluding to colleagues who ranted that they could not freely express their ideas, Vitaliano Brancati told me: "They should pray [to] God and be grateful to Him, because the day they will be free to express themselves, it will turn out that they had nothing to say!"[10]

As late as 1994, Freda still exhibited an almost pathetic insistence that Rossellini's fame was due to sheer good luck.[11] There is considerable consistency in this; no more need be said, I believe, on the extent to which art and politics can be two sides of the same coin.

The mere listing of selected titles from Freda's filmography between 1940 and 1980 is probably more eloquent than any metatextual commentary on them: *One Hundred Love Letters* (*Cento lettere d'amore*, as scriptwriter); *Don Cesare di Bazan; The Whole City Sings* (*Tutta la città canta*); *Black Eagle* (*Aquila nera); Les Miserables (I miserabili); The Mysterious Knight (Il cavaliere misterioso); Guarany; Count Ugolino (Il conte Ugolino*, from Dante's *Inferno); D'Artagnan's Son (Il figlio di D'Artagnan); The Betrayal, or The Past That Kills (Il tradimento, o passato che uccide)* . . . and more in the same vein: *The Vengeance of Black Eagle; Spartacus; Theodora, Empress of Byzanthium; Beatrice Cenci* (possibly from Stendhal's novella or Shelley's *The Cenci*, with Antonin Artaud's *The Cenci* as a very distant third candidate); *The Vampires; Ambushed in Tangier; In the Sign of Rome; Haji Murat* (i.e., *Agi Murad* [sic], the White Devil, from Tolstoy's novella by that title); *Caltiki the Immortal Monster; The Mongols; The Giants of Thessalia; Manhunt; Maciste at the Court of the Great Khan; Maciste's Descent to Hell; Dr. Hichcock's* [sic] *Horrible Secret; The Seven Swords of the Avenger; The Specter; The Magnificent Adventurer; Romeo and Juliet* (from Shakespeare); *Genevieve of Brabant; Coplan FX 18* (a.k.a. *Agente 777); Mission Summergame* (title in English); *Death Does Not Count Dollar Bills* (under the pseudonym "George Lincoln"); *The Fire-Tongued Iguana* (under the pseudonym "Willy Pareto"); and *Murder Obsession* (title in English).

In view of the above production, one must at least grant Freda a high degree of artistic consistency: as decade follows decade, he remains faithful to one and the same formula, reclothing it each time in the garb of the latest cinematic trend. Thus, in his production the historical costume film of the 1940s and early 1950s is superseded, in the late 1950s and early 1960s, by large-scale "peplum" (classico-mythological) productions, with an occasional nod to Tolstoy's Caucasus; then, around the mid-1960s, the ancient world yields—and in the 1970s gives way entirely—to the horror film and the pseudo-007 thriller. *Death Doesn't Count Dollar Bills* seems to have strong credentials as Freda's one and only contribution to the tradition of the spaghetti western. Clearly, all this amounts to an almost perfect map of the paths taken by Italian commercial cinematography over four decades of its history—a fact that somehow makes Freda highly representative in his own right. To be sure, while there is nothing inherently wrong with this kind of representativeness, one cannot help feeling skeptical about the director's praise of "imagination" (and his attendant dismissal of the neorealist revolution) when one holds up to it such a long list of repetitive formula films.

Freda's *Les Miserables* (*I miserabili*, 1947) is a film of James Bond-like deeds and frenzied manhunts that duplicates the plot (or, rather, parts of the plot) of Victor Hugo's novel of the same title.[12] The film consists of two parts: *Manhunt* and *Storm over Paris*.

Manhunt. In order to mend his past ways, Jean Valjean, a former convict in a penal colony, changes his identity along with his life. He becomes mayor of a small town and is a benefactor of his community. However, he is persecuted by the malign policeman Javert, who, through a ruse, corners him into revealing his past to the village. Valjean acts in accordance with his newly found sincerity; then, eluding Javert's surveillance, he flees to Paris with his adopted daughter, Cosetta.

Storm over Paris. The 1832 Paris uprising breaks out. Valjean saves the life of the revolutionary student Mario; Mario and Cosetta fall in love. The evil Javert, ever on the good man's heels, finds Valjean, yet cannot arrest him; in a fit of remorse, in fact, he jumps to his death in the Seine. Cosette and Mario get married, but Valjean is able to witness only the first few minutes of their happiness: he is shot and killed by a former fellow inmate.

There is no attempt in the film to reelaborate the original text; this is a "faithful" transposition of its prototype in the damning sense of the word—a would-be replacement of the book. It is an ancillary product whose basic paradox consists in the fact that the more it strives to complete with its original on an equal footing, the more it proves to be merely derivative from it.

Yet, as unrevealing as it might appear at first sight, Freda's double feature (together, the two episodes last for a total of over three hours) does nonetheless draw our attention to an important sociopolitical fact: that in certain cultural circumstances—for example, the early years of the Cold War, during which the film was shot—an escapist variant of filmmaking will take certain "attractive" (i.e., potentially lucrative) subjects and turn them into films *in a form purged of all critical social content.* However adventurous and fantastic Hugo's over-lengthy novel may be, there is more to it than a seemingly endless string of funambulist stunts; these are just a conduit for Hugo to convey a message of, to put the matter mildly, social awareness. (In a subtler way, there is a political dimension, too, in many of Pushkin's only apparently "romantic" stories.) No such luck in Freda's *Les Miserables*. Yet the very first scenes in the film feature the hungry young protagonist, Jean Valjean, stealing a loaf of bread from a baker's and being jailed for it. What more did we need in order to realize that we have here a major social issue on our hands? In the historical frame of the Italy of 1947, it might have been instructive to consult for feedback the landless southern peasants occupying untilled *latifondi*, or the Sicilian day laborers murdered at Portella della Ginestra by Salvatore Giuliano.

Yet no eyes are blinder than those that do not wish to see. In historical perspective, films such as Freda's *Les Miserables* are important documents that reveal, first and foremost, a deliberate will to blindness in the act of their production. The repression carried out in the film of an important political connection must—ironically—be described as the most obvious ideological feature of the very strategy that aims at hiding ideology.[13]

In sum, Freda's works embody in accomplished form the cinematic typology of the *romanzo popolare* or penny dreadful. They are a historical continuation of the productions that in the first half-century after the invention of cinema in 1895 served as a substitute for literature for people who were barely, or not at all, able to read.

Mario Camerini was easily, along with Alessandro Blasetti, the best director of the 1930s in Italy: soft-spoken, inward-looking, with a keen eye for psychology—and definitely as un-Fascist a filmmaker as one could afford to be in the circumstances. (Not coincidentally, he more than once worked with De Sica and Zavattini.) It should thus not be surprising if, appearances notwithstanding, Camerini's *The Captain's Daughter* (*La figlia del capitano*, 1947) turns out to be much more than the usual run-of-the-mill adventure story. Of course, the film's prototype was a good place to look for psychological subtlety.[14]

In Pushkin's *Kapitanskaia dochka* (1836), the calendar marks the year 1773; Pugachëv's rebellious Cossacks, Tatars, and land-hungry serfs are coming. A small, exposed fort in the steppe is held by a few Russians: peasant families, the soldiers of the garrison, captain Mironov, his wife, his angelic daughter Masha, and a few young officers stranded there either for want of better luck or in punishment for their past misbehavior. Shvabrin, the villain, has been thrown out of the Imperial Guard in the capital for killing a man in a duel; Grinëv, the hero, has to contend with a particularly strict father.

Both Shvabrin and Grinëv are in love with Masha; but Masha loves Grinëv.

There are a couple of good reasons for this: Shvabrin is ugly—and he speaks French with too much gusto to be a reassuring figure to the shy girl.

The bearded and mustachioed Pugachëv storms the fort, takes it, and executes almost the entire garrison, captain and wife included. Masha hides. To save his skin, Shvabrin joins the self-proclaimed czar. Pugachëv recognizes Grinëv as the young lord who a few months before had saved his life during a deadly blizzard by offering him one of his own fur coats. Chivalrous to a fault, the good savage, the rebel hero untainted by civilization, heeds the call of honor: he spares Grinëv and sets him free.

Pugachëv then puts Shvabrin in charge of the fort and moves on in his campaign. Masha is now in the villain's hands. Grinëv rushes to the nearest walled city, Orenburg, to whip up support there for an expedition to retake the fort. His plan, however, fails. Meanwhile, Orenburg itself is besieged. Worse, Masha writes that Shvabrin wants her to marry him, failing which he threatens to deliver her as a prostitute to the rebels' encampment. Horrified, Grinëv leaves Orenburg and flies to Masha's defense—and in so doing he technically defects to the enemy.

Grinëv soon stands again before the upright rebel, and in less than no time puts his cards down: he tells Pugachëv that there is a young woman at the fort, his fiancée, who is being mistreated. The gamble pays off. Pugachëv does not bat an eyelash: "You should have told me sooner," he cheerfully cries. "Justice must reign in my wide lands. As soon as circumstances permit, we'll marry the two of you, and throw in a banquet to boot." Until such time Pugachëv once more allows Grinëv—now in Masha's company—to go free.

The two immediately set out to reach the Russian side. Grinëv sends Masha to Orenburg, then dutifully joins the army's campaign against the rebels. The war rages on until the summer of 1774, when Pugachëv is defeated and captured.

Is this the end of our heroes' trials? Quite the opposite: Pushkin now describes how they have to face their enemies in a context no less dangerous than the previous one.

With the peace comes bad news: Grinëv, suspected of treason, is arrested and put on trial for leaving his post. At the trial, for fear of exposing Masha to the unpleasantness of cross-examination, he avoids mentioning her. Without her testimony, his version of the events is unsupported. Furthermore, Shvabrin, who appears as a witness, accuses his rival of having actively collaborated with the rebels. Grinëv is sentenced to death by the military court.

Having learned this, Masha rushes to St. Petersburg and attempts to meet the Empress Catherine II at her summer residence in Tsarskoe Selo. In the park that surrounds the palace, Masha encounters a mysterious lady, who listens to her story intently. This is none other than the empress, herself. Soon Masha obtains Grinëv's release. Pushkin's two lovers can now marry and proliferate happily ever after on their estate near Simbirsk.

There is much to praise in certain aspects of Camerini's film, the protagonists' characterization first and foremost (Pugachëv's measured grandeur, Shvabrin's crystalline shamelessness, Masha's chaste devotion). Yet there is something which interests me even more. The question I wish to raise here is, To what extent is all this relevant to the Italy of 1947? To a remarkably large extent, in fact—less in the historical facts of the plot than in the cultural connotations of the way in which it is presented. The following is likely to have had little to do with Camerini's conscious choices as an artist and everything to do with the context in which he lived.

At the precise time of the conflict over the contested eastern border with Yugoslavia, and in the period immediately before the elections of April 1948 that were to define whether Italy would lock in with the American-led Western bloc or with the pro-Soviet Eastern one, the frenzy of political propaganda in Italy was such that the rhetoric of the "Westernizers" did not shrink from describing the "Slavophile" hordes as anthropophagous barbarians likely to eat Italian children at the first sign of the red votes approaching 51 percent. Without denying that on the Italo-Yugoslav border a large number of hate crimes did in fact occur at the end of the war—crimes triggered in the first place by the aggression unleashed by the Fascist regime against its eastern neighbor—most historians today would probably consider the charge of anthropophagy leveled at the would-be invaders as exaggerated. Stereotypes, however, thrived in the late 1940s—and what better stereotypes to apply to Pushkin's Russians than the very ones attributable to their distant descendants in 1947?

Hence, in Camerini's retelling of *Kapitanskaia dochka*, a great number of elements do not merely convey a generic exoticism, but specifically suggest its gory Russianness. The following are a few narrative details in *La figlia del capitano*—substantially modifying Pushkin's plot rendered above—that in retrospect strike one as functional to the foregrounding of the threatening, irrational, uncontrollable, or in any way dangerous traits of Russians:

Russians as drunkards and gamblers. On the eve of his accession to the Imperial Guard, young Grinëv gets smashed and gambles away his new uniform. He is sent to the steppe as punishment.

Russians as weirdly subverting the decorum of civilized society. Camerini's Vasilisa Egorovna Mironova, the captain's wife, receives the newcomer Grinëv while puffing on her pipe and bossing around the soldiers of the garrison, as her husband ought to do (but doesn't).

Russians as cruel and barbaric. The Bashkir freedom fighter who falls into the Russian army's hands has already had such a distinction before (during the insurrection of 1741)—and had already been rewarded for it by having his nose, ears, and tongue cut off. The film displays the maimed outlaw's face in full, graphic detail. And during the rebels' festive meal that follows the occupation of the fort, the renegade Shvabrin advises Pugachëv to have Grinëv's tongue cut out, it being appropriate "to punish only that part of his body which, in refusing to hail you as Czar Peter III, has offended you."

Russia as a despotic country, the empress as a vapid tyrant. Camerini's empress twice refuses to believe Masha's version of the the events. The first time, she is incognito in the park of her palace. On the second occasion, Masha elbows her way past crowds of soldiers and courtiers, and confronts a suzerain deeply engrossed in the preparation of a fashionable soirée. However, her plea fails (in part, perhaps, because it is rambling and unfocused; in the Italy of 1947, a short, sharp plea about social injustice would have endowed the story with politically subversive implications—something the film wishes to avoid like the plague. For Grinëv, thus, death it will be. Only Pugachëv's testimony will persuade the empress to pardon Grinëv at the last moment.

Also deserving of mention is the film's particular effort to reproduce simple costumes (the rebels' fur-lined leather coats, hats, and so on) and interiors (log huts with unfinished walls and a vividly authentic steppe look).

How does all of the above appear in Pushkin? In similar form, one might have thought, extrapolating from the fact that a sizable amount of the original dialogue is retained in Camerini's film almost verbatim. In fact, the opposite is true. A brief inspection of Pushkin's text shows how substantially a given narrative can be reaccentuated to say something altogether different in a different context, even if the modifications it undergoes are technically minor.

Russians as drunkards and gamblers. There indeed is a reference in Pushkin to Grinëv indulging in an excessive intake of spirits; but that is only to oblige his (lower-class) comrades-in-arms. Anyway, this occurs *after* the young man's father has dispatched him to the fort in the steppe—a decision the father takes for reasons entirely unrelated to alcohol:

Petrusha is not going to Petersburg. What would he learn if he did his service there? To be a spendthrift and a rake? No, let him serve in the army and learn the routine of it, and know the smell of powder and be a soldier and not a fop in the Guards![15]

The original Grinëv—who has never served in Petersburg—thus does *not* end up in rebel territory as punishment for rowdy behavior.

Russians as weirdly subverting the decorum of civilized society. In Pushkin, the captain's wife does *not* smoke a pipe. She is presented and characterized instead in the following manner:

An elderly lady, dressed in a Russian jacket and with a kerchief on her head, was sitting by the window. She was winding yarn which a one-eyed old man in an officer's uniform held for her on his outstretched hands. "What do you need, *batyushka?*" she asked me, going on with her work.[16]

Clearly, she is an unrefined woman from the country, but not the quasi virago she is made out to be in the film. This is Pushkin, after all, not Gogol.

Russians as cruel and barbaric. Pushkin's narrator prepares for the presentation of the maimed Bashkir insurgent through some strongly worded comments on the cruelty of torture and against the reluctance of some judges of the "old times" to apply a "beneficent law which abolished it." (If this sounds insufficiently incendiary today, we should remember that in 1773 Beccaria's *An Essay on Crimes and Punishments* [*Dei delitti e delle pene* 1764], had been in print for less than a decade.) Only then is the old man's appearance described. After that is done, the narrator provides a final wrap-up of his own:

When I recall that this happened in my lifetime, and that now I have lived to see the gentle reign of Emperor Alexander, I cannot but marvel at the rapid progress of enlightenment and the diffusion of humane principles. Young man! If my notes ever fall into your hands, remember that the best and most permanent changes are those due to the softening of manners and morals and not to any violent upheavals.[17]

While there is every reason to suspect that the praise of Czar Alexander ought to be taken rather antiphrastically (he had exiled Pushkin to the Caucasus), it would be arbitrary to conclude that *therefore* the point made in the last sentence quoted is not "really" meant by the novel's narrator.

Clearly, Camerini's cinematic re-creation does not apply with equal thoroughness to the duplication of all narrative elements in Pushkin's novel. The film's re-creation of its prototype is altogether selective (i.e., it follows a discernible ideological pattern).

And as for Shvabrin's suggestion at the banquet that Grinëv be hauled in, questioned, cornered, and merrily detongued, in Pushkin Shvabrin is, quite simply, not present at the dinner table.[18]

Russia as a despotic country, the empress as a vapid tyrant. In the novel, shortly after Masha has met the mysterious lady in the Tsarskoe Selo park, an imperial carriage stops to pick up the girl at the inn where she is lodged, and takes her to the palace. Pushkin describes in rapid tempo what happens to her next. Trembling with emotion, Masha walked up the stairs. She was led through a number of deserted, spacious, luxuriously furnished rooms. Finally, the doors to the empress's dressing room were flung open, revealing to Masha the lady to whom she had been talking just a few minutes before.

The empress called her to her side and said, with a smile: "I am glad that I have been able to keep my promise to you, and to grant your request. Your case is settled. I am convinced that your betrothed is innocent. Here is a letter, which please take yourself to your future father-in-law."

Mar'ia Ivanovna took the letter with a trembling hand and fell, weeping, at the feet of the empress, who lifted her up, kissed her and engaged her in conversation. "I know you are not rich," she said, "but I am in debt to Captain Mironov's daughter. Do not worry about the future. I will provide for you."[19]

No guards here, no crowds, no elbows, no melodramatic pleas, no partying at court, no death warrant—but imperial pardon, and an unexpected dowry. It is astonishing to measure, upon examination, to what an extent Camerini's Catherine modifies Pushkin's. An enlightened, providential dea ex machína was clearly not an acceptable figure with which to close a film that needed to represent things Russian through the negative prism typical of a particular cultural-historical moment in Italian history.[20]

All this is well and good, one might think, but aren't we arguing after the fact about the logic of a development which anyway cannot be experimentally falsified? Where is the argument's counterproof?

In nonexperimental sciences, this is always a ponderous objection; yet it turns out that this time there is something very close to a counterproof. Just over a decade after Camerini's, not-so-subconscious tocsin about the dangers of voting for semibarbaric tyrants with large mustaches, Lattuada reinterpreted *Kapitanskaia dochka* in his *The Storm*. He did so from a viewpoint entirely different from Camerini's, yielding a very differently oriented *kolossal* (large-scale production). But it was by then 1958; under the protection of a NATO nuclear umbrella, the Italian *miracolo economico* had taken firm roots; and *Sputnik* was warming up its engines for an entirely unbarbaric takeoff from the launching pad. Stalin had been dead for a while, and the world was then perceivable with a wide angle and in bright Technicolor. Only eleven years after Camerini's black-and-white Pushkin, the Italians who viewed Lattuada's *The Storm* lived in a different world than they used to; even when the same prototext was re-created for them in a film, they watched a different world on the screens of their cinemas.[21]

In the 1940s and 1950s, Roberto Rossellini, one of the most important directors in the history of Italian cinema, repeatedly drew on European literary traditions for his filmmaking. He made three such works in the period under scrutiny: *A Human Voice, Joan of Arc Burned at the Stake*, and *Fear*.

Rossellini's *A Human Voice* (*Una voce umana*, 1947) was shot with Jean Cocteau—who was both a playwright and a film director. Combined with *The Miracle (Il miracolo)* (written by Fellini, who also played a role in it), the film was released the following year under the collective title *Love (L'amore)*.

A Human Voice duplicates the text of Cocteau's one-act monologue, *The Human Voice (La voix humaine*, 1930).[22]

A young woman, jilted by her lover, in a telephone conversation clings to the most tenuous trace of attention on his part. Following, for over half an hour, the capricious convolutions of the departed lover's mood, the female protagonist covers the entire gamut of postamorous feelings, from renewed hope to self-conscious dignity to utter dejection.

Cocteau's text is a tour de force that fully exploits the scenic potential of a technology relatively exclusive before the 1930s, the telephone, and requires superior ability from the actor impersonating—so to speak—two parts at once. Anna Magnani, whose relationship with Rossellini began around the time the film was made, gave just such a performance—a performance made all the more remarkable, one could argue, by the fact that it went against the grain of her commonly accepted filmic persona (to say nothing of her empirically verifiable personality).

In 1947, what could be called the avant-garde or experimental aspect of Cocteau's play was a thing of the past; surrealism, in vogue throughout the 1930s, had by then been replaced by a stunned meditation over the silence of a couple of continents' worth of rubble. In the transition from book to film, the new historical situation gave Cocteau's piece a new context, and thus inevitably a new meaning. What now stood out was no longer its experimental or technical aspect, but its content emphasizing solitude—a solitude brought about by a breakdown in communication. Indeed, hardly any expository structure would seem able to render the sullen atmosphere of the late 1940s more fully than a performance centered entirely on the inability of a human voice to elicit any response whatever from its presumed counterpart. In *A Human Voice*, the *other* voice has become a noumenon, a thing-in-itself that the subject's consciousness can only postulate, but not verify.

Although one should be wary of facile sociologisms in extrapolating between contiguous yet separate realms of human experience, one cannot avoid confronting the fact that, with the onset of the Cold War, an abrupt breakdown in communication appears as the single obvious feature of the years 1947–48, not only in Italy but across the globe as well. In view of this, the theme of *A Human Voice* seems ideal to transcribe onto the human register events and motions occurring in the political and social sphere. Aprà is entirely correct in arguing that in this film Rossellini focuses "on irrational residues, on the global condition of the human being during the postwar period, in Italy as well as in Europe. His is not necessarily a criticism. As ever, Rossellini wants to know rather than to judge."[23]

It can be no coincidence either that, in the passage from Cocteau's play to Rossellini's film, *"La" voix humaine* becomes *"A" human voice*. With the transition from the definite to the indefinite article, universal representativeness is cast aside and a minor, contingent status is embraced. The Western mind can no longer claim to embody, under whatever guise, *the* voice of humanity; the one, often stammering, voice we do apprehend now is merely one in a vast plurality. No one who, in 1947, had gone through the experience of the war could doubt that, for better or worse, human existence is a collective affair, and each person's voice is but one among millions.

The film marked the beginning of increasingly violent attacks on Rossellini, carried out especially by left-leaning critics who, after having too hastily hailed *Rome, Open City* and *Paisan* as engaged in a directly political sense, in this case accused the director of slipping into unpolitical "whateverism" (*qualunquismo*). It would take conservative and Catholic observers just a few more years—and, above all, Rossellini's relationship with Ingrid Bergman—to join the Rossellini-bashing troops from the opposite end of the political spectrum.[24]

In 1948 Ingrid Bergman had starred in Fleming's *Joan of Arc*—but with what qualifications for martyrdom? Hardly any, it would seem, compared to those she had developed by 1954, after years of savage attacks—by critics, intellectuals, politicians, holier-than-thou conservatives, the tabloid press—on herself and her companion Rossellini, guilty of having betrayed the best and brightest from one end of the gamut (Hollywood, in Hollywood's eyes) to the opposite one (the Lukácsian left, in the eyes of the Lukácsian left).

On the path to some ultimate human truth ensconced beyond volcano tops and ancient archaeological finds, Rossellini and Bergman had, in *Stromboli*,

Land of God (*Stromboli, terra di Dio*, 1949) attempted to find, and deliberately avoided spelling out, what in the 1920s the poet Eugenio Montale had called by the felicitous term "*the* formula to open worlds for you." But the refusal to propose or accept any ready-made answers to resolve one's *mal du siècle*, though good enough when it came from Montale, was evidently not good enough from Rossellini and Bergman, against whom it was viciously held.[25] It seems as though in those years McCarthy-style witch-hunts were not happening only in politics; art clearly came neck and neck in the contest. Not until Antonioni's star surfaced, in the entirely different historical atmosphere of the early 1960s, would film critics—slowly at first—begin to intuit that the issues Rossellini had pursued more than a decade earlier possessed an intrinsic philosophical value (quite apart from their potential commercial value to the film industry). By then, however, it was too late; well before the applause started, Rossellini had, typically, changed tack once more, building upon his voyage to India in 1957 to develop an almost exclusive interest in the cultivation of didactic filmmaking. Thus it was that in Rossellini's Joan of Arc film Ingrid Bergman landed on the stake in more ways than one.

Rossellini's *Joan of Arc Burned at the Stake* (*Giovanna d'Arco al rogo*, 1954) is derived from a well-received theatrical tour in which Bergman brought to stages throughout Europe the oratorio *Joan of Arc Burned at the Stake* (*Jeanne d'Arc au bûcher*, composed in 1935, first performed in 1938), written by Paul Claudel and set to music by Arthur Honegger.[26] The production we see in the film is that of the Teatro San Carlo in Naples.

The rotating spheres of Heaven appear, and against their dark backdrop we witness shining cohorts of angels and saints. Alone at the center of the stage, Giovanna engages in lyrical dialogue with Saint Dominic, who welcomes her among the ranks of the blessed.

In flashback, major episodes from Giovanna's life are evoked and reenacted around her: merry village life, intrigue at the court, her manipulated trial—conducted not by human beings but by animals in men's garb. We then see Giovanna sentenced, the stake prepared, and the young woman (who has all the while been proclaiming her innocence) eventually chained to it.

When the flames are lit, the end of the film coincides with the end of Giovanna's earthly life—the end of her death, and the beginning of her life eternal. As she ascends to Heaven, she cries: "Here I am! Here! Love is strongest! God is strongest!" (*Eccomi! Ecco! L'amore è il più forte! Dio è il più forte!*)

Rossellini used black backdrops and a multilevel scene to dramatic effect, contravening at his own peril Claudel's original preference for a virtually motionless stage. In the end, however, the director half-charmed, half arm-twisted Claudel into accepting the final product as the best conduit for what even the irritable author had to acknowledge was Bergman's superior acting.

While there could be no question, due to Claudel's personality, of Rossellini deviating from his master text, the film nonetheless has a brilliant life of its own, if only because the mimetic component it can afford as a cinematic artifact is able to bring out the brutish animality of Joan's judges in a way that will ever remain inimitable for the written page. Claudel may well inscribe as the Court of Law's motto "We have no judge other than the Pig"[27] and instate the Pig as Judge, the Sheep as Jury, and the Jackass as Secretary; none of that can come close to our seeing with our eyes "sheep," "pigs," and "jackasses" skillfully displayed on the screen, identified in their respective dignities by appropriate signs.

Bergman and Rossellini must have derived at least some comfort from meditating on the fate that, since time immemorial, tends to befall prophets in their respective fatherlands. Their regret may well have been that historical verisimilitude had prevented Claudel from appointing film critics to a prominent incarnation in the tribunal's animal farm.[28]

Shortly after *Giovanna d'Arco*, the history of Italian cinema records Rossellini's *Fear (La paura*, 1954–55), re-created from Stefan Zweig's novella of the same title (*Die Angst*, 1925). The theoretical premises on which the film was based were very much the same as those underpinning *Giovanna d'Arco*: we cannot forever shoot films in cities reduced to debris, he attempted to explain to those who only expected of him sequels to *Rome, Open City, Paisan*, and *Germany Year Zero*. He could have been even more precise and argued as follows: it is exactly because my detractors so vehemently espouse the tenets of realism that they ought to take into account the transformations in the decade after World War II; far from condemning our quest for new themes, they ought instead to *impel* us directors toward a "realism" defined not in the terms of a season now bygone, but in those of the present, alive one.

Yet how many times can artists be told by all and sundry that they are in the wrong (or worse) before they lose self-assurance and, with it, the lightness of touch that alone can disprove their critics' charges? Moreover—a far from unrelated question—how often is it possible for film directors to obtain the material means necessary to produce a work of art that fully corresponds to their artistic persuasion? Such were the problems Rossellini had to contend with in making *Fear*.

Irene is the wife of Alberto, a pharmaceutical industrialist, and works with her husband in the factory's laboratory. Deeply unhappy in her marriage, she has long had a lover, Enrico, without suspecting that her husband, aware of her relationship, has for just as long been observing her behavior. Both Irene's sense of guilt and her admiration for her husband's apparent equanimity are thus sorely misplaced.

Johanna, a woman who claims to have been Enrico's lover in the past, blackmails Irene into making ever-higher payments for her silence. When the stakes become unaffordable, Irene, in despair, calls the bluff—and discovers that Johanna has actually been in cahoots with Alberto all along.

Deeply shaken by this discovery, Irene goes to the lab, where she prepares to commit suicide. Moments before she takes poison normally used in scientific experiments, Alberto arrives, confessing to having masterminded this other experiments of sorts. When

Irene admits to her own misconduct, the two spouses acknowledge their respective errors and pledge to attempt a fresh start for their marriage.

The film, with obvious conceptual similarities to the earlier *Voyage to Italy*, was made quickly, and no less quickly tampered with by the producer when its failure at the box office became obvious. A doctored version of it was eventually rereleased, but did no better—a fate, judging by his reaction (or lack thereof), of no concern to the director. Just as the philosophical possibility of movement can most effectively be proven by walking, so *Fear* seems resoundingly to bring home the reality of an individual's alienation from his environment not by stating it but, performatively, by practicing it. In this sense, the film has the merit of developing to the utmost a feature which had characterized *A Human Voice*: that of embodying its conflictual *Zeitgeist* less by what it says than by what it is. It might be only at a second, cultural-historical level that we can make sense of what *Fear* is and of how it came to be just that.

Did Rossellini, artistically speaking, believe in *Fear*, or did he not? He does not seem to have expressed himself on this particular film. Exceptionally, however, he once commented on a later, equally unsuccessful one, *Black Soul* (*Anima nera*, 1962), that it was "inconsistent with the very essence of [his] work"— and, even more straightforwardly, that he was "ashamed" of it.[29] Granted, things may be more complex than they seem: according to Rossellini, *Black Soul* shares its creator's peculiar badge of shame with only one other film, *General Della Rovere*. And *General Della Rovere* was awarded a Golden Lion at Venice in 1959, going then from height to height with both the critics and the public. Thence it is only one step to the suspicion that in Rossellini's self-slandering comment a great portion of shame may also accrue to us, the public—who, unable to distinguish adequately between one movie and the next, damn the one and extol the other as inspired simply on the basis of our preconceived judgment about what ideas Roberto Rossellini (and Ingrid Bergman) should be allowed to put forward. Are the two so dangerous, then? Perhaps *we* are the ones who fear them.[30]

Two more works, as different from one another as one can imagine, were inspired by nineteenth-century Russia around this time: Lattuada's *The Overcoat* and Gallone's *Michael Strogoff*. Having devoted a chapter in *Masters of Two Arts* to a detailed analysis of Lattuada's *The Overcoat* (*Il cappotto*, 1952), a milestone in the final phase of Italian neorealism, I will avoid repetition here and simply point out that in this film the neorealist heritage acquires, perhaps for one last time, a supratemporal hue, intriguingly succeeding in encompassing both the historical and the perennial. This is germane to Lattuada's own artistic sensitivity, as well as to his permanently "political" program.

How does Lattuada achieve this? The most obvious of the modifications carried out in *Il cappotto* vis-à-vis Gogol's story of the same title (*Shinel'*, 1842) consists in rendering the boorish Russian protagonist in Petersburg, Akaki Akakievich, as the meek Carmine De Carmine, a Southerner employed as a humble scribe in a northern Italian town. That town happens to be Pavia, on the banks of the Ticino River—which the film, however, is careful to present as simply a cold location in a snow-clad northern landscape.

In 1952, at the height of the Cold War, Lattuada's film captures to perfection the social antagonism typical of the time. Gogol's grotesque characters and events live on in a slightly altered form, as the Russian locale is replaced by a background of social problems, and the subject matter is recast by Lattuada so as to convert into material objects and tangible rapports (an overcoat, theft, physical chill) sensations circulating through the body politic in the guise of collective emotions.

What is humane and compassionate in one film can become sentimental and corny in the next. Just how much more sugary a place Russia is in Gallone's *Michael Strogoff* (*Michele Strogoff*, 1956) should stand out from the following account.

The Tartars are, literally, up in arms against the czarist empire: they are putting Siberia to fire and sword, and—thorough rebels that they are—have cut telegraph lines from the capital. How to get a vital message through to the emperor's loyal troops in Irkutsk? A heroic officer is called for, able to disguise himself as a merchant, ride unscathed through thick and thin, shoot down threatening wild bears, stay clear of the ambiguous charms of strangely benevolent Gypsy beauties, steer log rafts along raging rivers, survive torture in detention camps, unmask homicidal traitors, and in the end deliver the dispatch. Having been put in charge of the task, Strogoff accomplishes all of the above with panache, ease, sangfroid, facility, and utterly martial self-assurance.

He even manages, without batting an eye, the most challenging part of the mission: unwaveringly posing as the husband of Nadia, his (needless to say) young and intensely attractive blonde guide. Or, rather, he manages this until the very last thirty seconds of the film, when—without saying a word or losing his accustomed military grin—Michael suddenly kisses Nadia and exchanges with her, this time for real, the make-believe marriage rings supplied to them by the czarist secret service.

If all of this sounds like a papier-mâché Russia plagiarized from the surface of Pushkin's *The Captain's Daughter*, my readers may rest assured: so, too, does the rest that I am not mentioning.

The Italian components of this bombastic *kolossal* (large-scale production) are one of the co-producing companies, a number of actors and operators, and—obviously—the director, Carmine Gallone, better known in the history of Italian cinema for the classico-mythological "peplum" films he assembled under and for the Fascist regime (e.g., *Scipione Africano*, 1937), a few filmed operas, and some items in the postwar Don Camillo series.[31]

As an extenuating circumstance for the poor quality (up to and including the faded, reddish colors) of this Hollywood-aping wide screen production, one could of course cite the equally exasperating level of its literary prototype, Jules Verne's *Michel Strogoff* (1876), which casts the first stone in rehashing, without originality, themes and situations from Pushkin.[32]

Compared to Gallone's *Strogoff*, even Lattuada's later Pushkinian efforts in *The Storm* are an improvement: both films are graced by hordes of Yugoslav cavalrymen disguised as Tartar rebels, bear dances at county fairs by the Danube, and such—but, if nothing else, Lattuada's film is based on a better story. *Michele Strogoff* is one of the (many) brilliant examples of how in cinema size, if not accompanied and supported by other qualities, can matter decisively: the bigger, the worse.[33]

The last re-creation in this chapter is Gassman's *Kean—Disorder and Genius (Kean—genio e sregolatezza,* 1956), a film whose diegetic (narrative) makeup is unusually multilayered.

Phase one of our story is set in England in the 1810s, 1820s, and early 1830s. The actor Edmund Kean attains immense fame and success for his genial performances of Shakespeare, as well as for his bohemian lifestyle outside the theater.

In phase two, we are in Paris in the 1830s, where Alexandre Dumas *père* writes the play *Kean ou Désordre et génie* (1836).[34] This work emphasizes the conflict between the spiritual nobility of the artist (a position with which Dumas identifies) and the knavish, philistine mores of well-to-do society, aristocratic as well as bourgeois. Since Kean is an actor, and the play stages him as he practices his trade, Dumas is able to produce some captivating moments when his protagonist, falling out of the Romeo role assigned to him in a play-within-the-play, persuasively accuses his public of hypocrisy. Dumas's drama is nowhere near as dense or tragic as Vigny's analogous, and earlier, *Chatterton* (1835), but it offers the reader sufficient cause for interest.

Kean's third avatar also materialized in France, where, in the twentieth century, Jean-Paul Sartre substantially reworked and adapted the play to the circumstances of very different times.[35] The philosopher accentuates the socially critical aspects of Kean's marginal position—and must, therefore, adjust his Shakespearean quotes accordingly. In Act IV, Kean no longer declaims a climactic impromptu tirade against his worldly persecutors as he wears the clothes of Romeo; he does so in those of Othello. The difference between the two roles accurately measures, and ideally exemplifies, the difference in tone and taste between the Parisian audiences of 1836 and those of 1954. Sartre's re-creation is shrewd, and in itself warrants detailed commentary; what remains open to debate is, of course, whether it was an optimal use of Sartre's intellectual resources to attempt grafting serious social commentary onto Dumas's plot, a fundamentally old-fashioned amorous triangle.

Kean's fourth, cinematographic stage consists in a revised version of the play directed by Gassman in 1956, with Gassman in the lead role.

Kean is the quintessential bohemian: a lover of wine, women, and debts, he lives a passionate and irregular life. He has no qualms about vying with the Prince of Wales, up to this time his comrade-in-revelry and protector, for the love of Countess Elena, the Danish ambassador's wife. Elena seems to prefer the actor, whom she goes to visit in his dressing room. Someone else does, too: the wealthy Anna (Dumas also has an impecunious Ketty), the young daughter of a cheesemaker from Ireland, who is both in love with Kean and persuaded of her talent as an actress.

Kean and the countess plan to rendezvous in a pub before the evening performance, but she fails to show up. Anna turns up in her stead, begging Kean to help her deflect the undesired advances of a spurned aristocratic lover. The nobleman follows hard on her heels—and a shouting match with Kean ensues, during which the lord refuses to engage in duel with the actor because the latter is so far below his own station in society. Piqued by the episode, Elena now redirects her benevolence toward the Prince of Wales.

The lead actress's sudden refusal to play Desdemona in *Othello* (in Dumas, Juliet in *Romeo and Juliet*) forces Kean, despite his misgivings, to accept Anna's prompt self-nomination.

However, Anna is in fact inexperienced, and proves not to be up to the challenge. The performance disappoints the audience. Seeing Elena and the Prince of Wales in their box, apparently pleased by the flop, Kean interrupts his Shakespearean perorations and bursts into passionate rhetoric against the cruel hypocrisy of the ruling class.

After the show, things take an ugly turn for Kean: he is accused of *lèse-majesté*, and his creditors throng around him, clamoring for their money. Yet, zenith follows nadir in a manner that is as sweeping as it is unexpected: an enthusiastically supportive public has collected enough money to pay Kean's debts; the prince is a good friend again; Anna remains determined to become an actress—and is as enamored of her idol as ever. The money she has offered Kean will now be considered by him, in the actor's emotional words to her, "no longer alms, but a dowry!"

Gassman's histrionic ability, which serves him so well on many other occasions, is here at loggerheads with Sartre's committed, critical rewriting of Dumas: the playwright goes one way, and the *mattatore* (winner-take-all) actor constantly pulls in the opposite one. It is difficult to see Gassman's Kean as a victim of philistinism, however defined; more likely, viewers will experience him as an inexhaustibly narcissistic male logomachist.[36]

That is a pity, because with a performance matching Sartre's intentions, the more recent version of the drama would at least have had a fair chance of putting its topicality to the test in the new medium of cinema.[37]

The phenomenon that most immediately stands out in the history of Italian cinema during the Republic's first period, 1945–1956—the age of the Cold War—is the overwhelming preponderance of totally coextensive re-creations from French and from Russian.

No fewer than six such items can be identified in the French area: Soldati's *Eugenie Grandet* (1946), from Balzac; Freda's *Les Miserables* (1947), from Hugo; Rossellini's *A Human Voice* (1947), from Cocteau; Rossellini's *Joan of Arc Burned at the Stake* (1954), from Claudel; Gallone's *Michael Strogoff* (1956), from Verne; and Gassman's *Kean* (1956), from Dumas and Sartre.

Two make up the Russian area: Camerini's *The Captain's Daughter* (1947), from Pushkin; and Lattuada's *The Overcoat* (1952), from Gogol. More could be added to this category, however—first in line is Freda's *Black Eagle* (1946), also from Pushkin—were the relevant material to become available for viewing.

In contrast, the picture is only barely sketched in when it comes to German literature: here, only one item occurs (Rossellini's *Fear*, 1954–55, from Stefan Zweig).

Adventure cinema of a strictly commercial nature predominates at this time and within the cultural and economic bounds of this market. Only *The Overcoat* and Rossellini's triad (*A Human Voice, Joan of Arc, Fear*) envisage, in different ways, bringing to their public anything other than diversion. It is, however, revealing that all the films identified in this period are coextensive re-creations of the total kind. In other words, the more demanding films last mentioned are, from a formal point of view, no less willing than their unproblematic counterparts to adopt a standard pattern in re-creating cinema from literature. Half a century after the fact, such an immediately visible lack of differentiation cannot fail to strike us.

The war is over; it is time to rebuild. To bring home the bread, the butter, and if at all possible the sugar, too, the film industry goes for tried-and-tested ways to produce money spinners. Re-creations from European literatures that aim for mere entertainment often succeed at the box office; thus, more difficult ones adopt similarly conventional narrative techniques. Yet, as a number of such films show, those techniques are not free from artistic problems; innovative filmmaking might need to produce its own, appropriately innovative forms.

NOTES

1. Paul Valéry, *Analects*, trans. Stuart Gilbert, vol. 14 of Valéry's *Collected Works* (Princeton, N.J.: Princeton University Press, 1970), p. 239. "Le sujet d'un ouvrage est à quoi se réduit un mauvais ouvrage" (Paul Valéry, "Autres rhumbs," in his *Tel Quel* [Paris: Gallimard, 1943], vol. 2, p. 159).

2. "Calligraphism" was by no means synonymous with a pro-Fascist outlook; in fact, for a number of auteurs, the cultivation of *l'art pour l'art* formal perfection was a primary way of avoiding any explicit endorsement of the regime. While some directors (e.g., Freda, on whom see more below) had no qualms of this nature, such was indeed Soldati's problem—and, as prominently, Lattuada's.

3. Tackling Balzac's *Eugénie Grandet* with any degree of seriousness would be a multiple-bookshelf affair hardly justified in Soldati's context. Among the best editions currently available are Honoré de Balzac, *Eugénie Grandet*, trans. Marion Ayton Crawford (London: Penguin, n.d. [1955]); *Eugénie Grandet*, in *Scènes de la vie de province*, ed. Pierre Barbéris et al., vol. 3 of *La Comédie humaine*, ed. Pierre-Georges Castex (Paris: Gallimard Pléiade, 1976).

4. The video of *Eugenia Grandet*, recorded from a long-ago airing by RAI, is available only in a few media libraries; one review and one article on the film were published in 1946—and then virtually nothing until Vito Attolini's *Storia del cinema letterario* (Recco: Le Mani, 1998), pp. 107–09.

For a general coverage of Soldati's films, one can usefully consult the following:

Giovanna Ioli, ed., *Mario Soldati: Lo specchio inclinato* (San Salvatore Monferrato: Edizioni della Biennale Piemonte e Letteratura, 1999); and Giorgio Barberi Squarotti et al., eds., *Mario Soldati: La scrittura e lo sguardo* (Turin: Museo Nazionale del Cinema-Lindau, 1991).

5. For the large box office receipts reaped by *Aquila nera*, see Christopher Wagstaff, "Il nuovo mercato del cinema," in Gian Piero Brunetta, ed., *L'Europa: Miti, luoghi, divi,* vol. 1, pt. 1 of his *Storia del cinema mondiale* (Turin: Einaudi, 1999), p. 859.

6. Monicelli's retrospective account of the films of the early postwar years can be found in Franca Faldini and Goffredo Fofi, eds., *L'avventurosa storia del cinema italiano raccontata dai suoi protagonisti: 1935–1959* (Milan: Feltrinelli, 1979), p. 104. For more details on this little-studied time and segment of Italian cinema production, see also Gian Piero Brunetta, *Storia del cinema italiano*, vol. 3 (Rome: Editori Riuniti, 1993 [1982]), pp. 296–302.

For some of the (scant) information available on Castellani's *A Pistol Shot*, see the director's own statements, in Faldini and Fofi, eds., *1935–1959*, pp. 54–55. On Calzavara's *Resurrection*, all I have been able to locate is in Faldini and Fofi, eds., *1935–1959*, p. 17; and Roberto Chiti and Enrico Lancia, eds., *I film dal 1930 al 1944*, vol. 1 of *Dizionàrio del cinema italiano* (Rome: Gremese, 1993), pp. 284–85.

7. At this time, none of the films here mentioned is available on the Italian market or in public video libraries.

While it seems impossible today to view Freda's *Black Eagle*, we fortunately have a reasonable amount of information on it in French and Italian books. See Stefano Della Casa, *Riccardo Freda* (Rome: Bulzoni, 1999), pp. 24–29; Faldini and Fofi, eds., *1935–1959*, pp. 103–04, 149, 151, 181; Riccardo Freda, *Divoratori di celluloide: Cinquanta anni di memorie, cinematografiche e non* (Milan: Emme Edizioni/Edizioni del Mystfest, 1981), pp. 79, 112–13; and Éric Poindron, ed., *Riccardo Freda: Un pirate à la caméra. Entretiens* (Arles: Institut Lumière/Actes Sud, 1994), pp. 144–58.

In his interview with Poindron, Freda enters into a specific discussion of Pushkin—whose "Dubrovsky" can be found in English in volumes of collected short stories such as Alexander Pushkin, *The Captain's Daughter and Other Stories*, trans. Natalie Duddington (London: Dent; New York: Dutton, 1961), pp. 147–216. The standard edition of the original is Aleksandr Sergeevich Pushkin, "Dubrovskii," in vol. 8, pt. 1 of *Polnoe sobranie sochinenii* (Moscow and Leningrad: Izdatel'stvo Akademii Nauk SSSR, 1948), pp. 159–223.

8. Freda, *Divoratori di celluloide*, p. 79.

9. Freda, *Divoratori di celluloide*, pp. 91–92.

10. Freda, *Divoratori di celluloide*, pp. 134–35.

11. See Freda's statements in Poindron, ed., *Riccardo Freda*, passim, esp. pp. 132–35.

12. An extensive English-language rendition of Hugo's novels can be found in *The Works of Victor Hugo*, trans. Isabel F. Hapgood et al. (New York: Kelmscott Society, 1887), of which *Les Miserables* takes up two and a half volumes (4, 5, and 6a). The most recent edition is Victor Hugo, *Les Miserables*, (London: D. Campbell, 1998). As for the original, a commendably compact yet complete edition is *Les Misérables*, vol. 2 of Hugo's *Romans* (Paris: Seuil Intégrale, 1963).

13. For references to Freda's *I miserabili*, see Della Casa, *Riccardo Freda*, pp. 29–31; Faldini and Fofi, eds., *1935–1959*, p. 104; Freda, *Divoratori di celluloide*, pp. 111–12; and Poindron, ed., *Riccardo Freda*, pp. 159–72.

On Freda's poetics and general modus operandi, see Faldini and Fofi, eds., *1935–1959*, pp. 103–04, 147, 149, 176, 184, 276, 356, 358, 392.

14. A convenient English translation of Pushkin's novel is in the 1961 edition cited in note 7. In the original *Polnoe sobranie sochinenii*, too, *Kapitanskaia dochka* is in the same volume as "Dubrovskii" (vol. 8, pt. 1).

15. Pushkin, *The Captain's Daughter*, p. 6; *Romany i povesti*, ch. 1, p. 282.

16. Pushkin, *The Captain's Daughter*, p. 21; *Romany i povesti*, ch. 3, p. 295.

17. Pushkin, *The Captain's Daughter*, p. 47; *Romany i povesti*, ch. 6, pp. 318–19.

18. Pushkin, *The Captain's Daughter*, pp. 60, 59; *Romany i povesti*, ch. 8, pp. 330, 329.

19. Pushkin, *The Captain's Daughter*, pp. 115–16; *Romany i povesti*, ch. 14, pp. 373–74.

20. As mentioned, more changes, all pointing in the same direction, were involved; I have focused only on the macroscopic ones.

21. Camerini has long been described as a forerunner of Italian cinematic neorealism, with a particular predilection for the plight of the "little person" (in this instance, Masha). See, among many concurring opinions, Monicelli's particularly qualified one, in Faldini and Fofi, eds., *1935–1959*, p. 32.

The most thorough English-language treatment of Camerini's prewar movies is in James Hay, *The Passing of the Rex: Popular Film Culture in Fascist Italy* (Bloomington: Indiana University Press, 1987). In Italian, and for coverage of the director's entire career, see Sergio Grmek Germani, *Mario Camerini* (Florence: La Nuova Italia, 1980).

Very little exists in the way of critical literature on *La figlia del capitano*—mere one- or two-liners scattered in histories of Italian cinema. A small gem consists in a frank avowal by Vittorio Gassman (who played Shvabrin) that, between the beginning of his career and *Big Deal on Madonna Street* (*I soliti ignoti*, 1958), *La figlia del capitano* is one of the few films of which he does not feel ashamed (Faldini and Fofi, eds., *1935–1959*, p. 396).

22. Jean Cocteau, *The Human Voice*, trans. Carl Wildman (London: Vision Press, 1951); *La voix humaine*, in vol. 7 of Cocteau's *Oeuvres complètes* (Geneva: Marguerat, 1948), pp. 53–77. For a good general introduction to Cocteau's play in English, see Bettina L. Knapp, *Jean Cocteau* (Boston: Twayne, 1989 [1970]), pp. 69–70.

23. "[Rossellini si interessa] dei residui irrazionali, della condizione globale dell'uomo nel dopoguerra italiano e poi europeo. La sua non è immediatamente una critica. Si tratta sempre di conoscere prima [che] di giudicare." Adriano Aprà, "Rossellini oltre il neo-realismo," in Lino Micciché, ed., *Il neorealismo cinematografico italiano* (Venice: Marsilio, 1999 [1978;1974]), p. 296.

24. On Rossellini's *A Human Voice*, see further: Guido Aristarco, *Neorealismo e nuova critica cinematografica: Cinematografia e vita nazionale negli anni quaranta e cinquanta: Tra rotture e tradizioni* (Florence: Nuova Guaraldi, 1980), pp. 55–68; Peter Bondanella, *The Films of Roberto Rossellini* (Cambridge: Cambridge University Press, 1993), p. 15; Peter Brunette, *Roberto Rossellini* (New York: Oxford University Press, 1987), pp. 87–91; Faldini and Fofi, eds., *1935–1959*, pp. 198–200; José Luis Guarner, *Roberto Rossellini* (New York: Praeger, 1970), pp. 25–28; Stefano Masi and Enrico Lancia, *I film di Roberto Rossellini* (Rome: Gremese, 1987), pp. 37–39; Gianni Rondolino, *Roberto Rossellini* (Florence: La Nuova Italia, 1974), pp. 68–70; Gianni Rondolino, *Roberto Rossellini* (Turin: UTET, 1989), pp. 121–28; Roberto Rossellini, *Il mio metodo*, ed. Adriano Aprà (Venice: Marsilio, 1987), pp. 7, 64–65—neither passage is included in

the English edition, *My Method*, trans. Annapaola Cancogni (New York: Marsilio, 1992); Roberto Rossellini, *Quasi un'autobiografia*, ed. Stefano Roncoroni (Milan: Mondadori, 1987), p. 67; and Mario Verdone, ed., *Roberto Rossellini* (Paris: Seghers, 1963), p. 191.

25. Eugenio Montale, *Cuttlefish Bones (1920–1927)*, trans. William Arrowsmith (New York: Norton, 1992), p. 41; "la formula che mondi possa aprirti," *Ossi di seppia*, in *L'opera in versi*, ed. Rosanna Bettarini and Gianfranco Contini (Turin: Einaudi, 1980), p. 27.

On Rossellini's politics, see in particular Geoffrey Nowell-Smith, "North and South, East and West: Rossellini and Politics," in David Forgacs et al., eds., *Roberto Rossellini: Magician of the Real* (London: British Film Institute, 2000), pp. 7–19.

26. Paul Claudel, *Jeanne d'Arc au bûcher*, in his *Théâtre*, ed. Jacques Madaule and Jacques Petit, vol. 2 (Paris: Gallimard Pléiade), 1965, pp. 1215–42.

27. "Non habemus alium judicem nisi Porcum" (Claudel, *Jeanne d'Arc au bûcher*, p. 1222).

28. On *Giovanna d'Arco*, see Pio Baldelli, *Roberto Rossellini* (Rome: Samonà e Savelli, 1972), pp. 242–44, 298–99; Bondanella, *The Films of Roberto Rossellini*, p. 22; Brunette, *Roberto Rossellini*, pp. 177–82; Alessandro Cappabianca, *Il cinema e il sacro* (Recco: Le Mani, 1998), pp. 62–64; Guarner, *Roberto Rossellini*, pp. 68–70; Stephen Gundle, "Saint Ingrid at the Stake: Stardom and Scandal in the Bergman-Rossellini Collaboration," in Forgacs et al., eds., *Roberto Rossellini*, pp. 64–79; Masi and Lancia, *I film di Roberto Rossellini*, pp. 67–70; Rondolino, *Roberto Rossellini* (1974), pp. 85–86; Rondolino, *Roberto Rossellini* (1989), pp. 211, 223; Rossellini, *Il mio metodo*, p. 8 (not included in the English edition); and Rossellini, *Quasi un'autobiografia*, pp. 68–70.

29. Rossellini's self-deprecating statement on *Black Soul* can be found in Baldelli, *Roberto Rossellini*, pp. 231–32. *Fear* is discussed on pp. 146–47 and 231–34.

30. On *Fear*, see further Bondanella, *The Films of Roberto Rossellini*, pp. 22; Brunette, *Roberto Rossellini*, pp. 183–91; Faldini and Fofi, eds., *1935–1959*, pp. 338–39; Guarner, *Roberto Rossellini*, pp. 71–73; Masi and Lancia, *I film di Roberto Rossellini*, pp. 70–72; Rondolino, *Roberto Rossellini* (1974), pp. 86–88; Rondolino, *Roberto Rossellini* (1989), pp. 222–27; and Michel Serceau, *Roberto Rossellini* (Paris: Editions du Cerf, 1986), pp. 223–30.

31. The following are good, informative discussions of Gallone's *Scipione* and the director's prewar career in general: Guido Aristarco, *Il cinema fascista: Il prima e il dopo* (Bari: Dedalo, 1996), passim; Peter Bondanella, *Italian Cinema from Neorealism to the Present* (New York: Continuum, 1991 [1983]), pp. 18–19; Hay, *The Passing of the Rex*, pp. 155–61; and Marcia Landy, *Italian Film* (Cambridge: Cambridge University Press, 2000), pp. 55–60.

32. The novel can be found in English as Jules Verne, *Michael Strogoff: The Courier of the Czar*, in vol. 8 of Verne's *Works*, ed. Charles F. Horne (New York and London: Vincent Parke, 1911), pp. 143–396. In French, there are literally dozens of Strogoffs; the most recent is Verne, *Michel Strogoff* (Evry: Editions Carrefour, 1998); see also Verne's *Les oeuvres*, ed. Gilbert Sigaux (Paris: Hachette, 1978).

33. The film is available in two editions on videocassette: a French one as *Michel Strogoff* and an Italian one as *Michele Strogoff*. On the other hand, no such luxury—in fact, absolute starvation—accompanies the film on its would-be journey to scholarly immortality. One can, at most, glean some raw facts on it from film dictionaries.

In 1970 Eriprando Visconti directed a remake of the film, giving it the title *Strogoff*.

34. An English-language version of *Kean* is in Alexandre Dumas *père*, *The Great*

Lover and Other Plays, adapted by Barnett Shaw (New York: Frederick Ungar, 1979), pp. 73–162. (This version includes a short biographical note on Edmund Kean.) In French, see Alexandre Dumas [*père*], Kean ou Désordre et génie [1836]), in vol. 5 of his *Théâtre complet* (Paris: Calmann-Lévy, n.d. [ca. 1866]), pp. 101–212. Useful information on the author can be gleaned from Richard S. Stowe, *Alexandre Dumas père* (Boston: Twayne, 1976). Stowe discusses *Kean* on pp. 55–58.

35. Jean-Paul Sartre, *Kean: Disorder and Genius*, trans. Kitty Black (London: Hamish Hamilton, 1973[1954]). The French original appeared in 1954 (Gallimard) and included Dumas's text in appendix. An excellent multipurpose edition, which combines Dumas's original play (in French), Sartre's remake (in French), and an introduction and copious notes (in English), is Jean-Paul Sartre, *Kean*, ed. David Bradby (Oxford: Oxford University Press, 1973).

36. The logomachy cheerfully carried on, most recently, with Kean's phase five: Gassman's own and further reelaborated version of the comedy under the title *Sincere Lies*. See Vittorio Gassman, *Bugie sincere* (Milan: Longanesi, 1997).

37. The film is briefly treated in Tullio Kezich's "Vittorio fra i tromboni," in Fabrizio Deriu, ed., *Vittorio Gassman: L'ultimo mattatore* (Venice: Marsilio, 1999), esp. pp. 54–55. Limited, but usefully factual information on Gassman's *Kean* can also be found in Sandra Teroni and Andrea Vannini, *Sartre e Beauvoir al cinema* (Florence: La Bottega del Cinema, 1987), p. 65.

2

The Economic Miracle (1956–63)

Since the inception of the Cold War, Italy had been characterized by capital-friendly political stability, open market policies, and the low wages that a labor movement weakened by a large surplus of workers reluctantly had to accept. As of the mid-1950s, such capitalistic virtues began to pay off, and the so-called *miracolo economico* took off in earnest.

GDP grew at an average yearly rate of over 5 percent; inflation stayed low. Unemployment gradually decreased (from over 10 percent to 3 percent nationwide). Italy became firmly integrated within the European economy thanks to the free-trade area created by the CECA (Comunità Europea del Carbone e dell'Acciaio, European Coal and Steel Community), later expanded into the CEE (Comunità Economica Europea, European Economic Community). The first skyscrapers went up in Milan, *autostrade* were built at a rapid pace, and Fiat launched the mass-produced 600 and 500 models. Visconti's *Rocco and His Brothers* (1960) depicted manual workers recently immigrated to Milan who struggle to make ends meet and to cope with intercultural problems; Fellini's *La dolce vita* (1960) portrayed their would-be intellectual counterparts fluttering about Roman studios, streets, and cafés.

After 1958, under the ecumenical papacy of John XXIII (Angelo Roncalli), Italian Catholics—more specifically, the Christian Democrats—started debating the possibility of cooperation with moderate Socialists. On the other hand, in 1960 a quasi-insurrectional situation occurred when the neo-Fascist party MSI (Movimento Sociale Italiano) called a national meeting at Genoa, and the Tambroni government bloodily repressed the ensuing protests and general strike.

The early 1960s saw the peak of the *miracolo economico* and of its cultural repercussions. Pope John XXIII's Second Ecumenical Council brought to the Catholic world a long-outstanding *aggiornamento* (update) with respect to the changes that had occurred in modern Western societies after the industrial revolution. Starting from an admittedly small base, the Italian economy grew briskly; not only sales of cars and home appliances, but also the book industry, TV, pop music (*cantautori* or author-singers), and cinematic *commedia all'italiana* boomed. Italians indulged in sweet historical revenge against centuries of foot travel—or outright stasis—by practicing reckless, fast-lane driving (Dino Risi's *Overtaking/Il sorpasso*, 1962), and could even enjoy their newly acquired status of modern Europeans by suffering from a Scandinavian-like inability to communicate with one another (Antonioni's tetralogy: *L'avventura*, 1960; *La notte*, 1961; *L'eclisse*, 1962; *Deserto rosso*, 1964).

During the same years, however, many chickens were on the way home to roost: starved for capital, Italian agriculture stagnated; a growing shortage of workers gradually put inflationary pressure on wages; the economic and cultural disequilibrium between North and South was only temporarily alleviated, rather than structurally addressed, by money transfers from emigrants; the Cassa per il Mezzogiorno wastefully drained financial resources, dissipating them in capital-intensive projects in the South that enriched well-connected contractors— and those they were connected to—while creating few jobs for everyone else. Worst of all, perhaps, throughout the country there were overcrowded working-class dormitory neighborhoods. Combined with the Italian state's chronic inefficiency in providing indispensable services (urban planning, transportation, medical care, schools, day care, universities, telecommunications), this gradually exacerbated the living conditions of millions, and would eventually ignite the sparks of a smoldering discontent.

By the mid-1950s, neorealism as such was rarely practiced—but many films of those years aimed for "realism" *tout court* either by means of critical historical reconstructions or via a committed glance into present conditions. It is revealing of a major historical transformation that socially or morally critical films and mass-consumed *commedia all'italiana* would coexist without friction during the period 1956–1963, to the point that in many instances the two categories smoothly blended. Though somewhat counterintuitive, this was a typical characteristic of the Italian cinema of and around the 1960s, testifying to its uniquely important social role at this time.

Among the most noteworthy titles produced at this time are Antonioni's *The Scream (Il grido,* 1957), *L'avventura* (1960), *La notte* (1961), and *L'eclisse* (1962); Bertolucci's *The Grim Reaper (La commare secca,* 1962); Bolognini's *Handsome Antonio (Il bell'Antonio,* 1960), *The Rough Path (La viaccia,* 1961), and *Agostino* (1962); Comencini's *Everyone Go Home (Tutti a casa,* 1960) and *Bube's Girlfriend (La ragazza di Bube,* 1963); De Sica's *Two Women (La ciociara,* 1960), *The Condemned of Altona (I sequestrati di Altona,* 1962), and *The Boom (Il boom,* 1963); Fellini's *The Nights of Cabiria (Le notti di Cabiria,*

1957), *La dolce vita* (1960), and *8 ½* (1963); Germi's *The Straw Man (L'uomo di paglia*, 1958), *Divorce—Italian Style (Divorzio all'italiana*, 1961), and *Seduced and Abandoned (Sedotta e abbandonata*, 1963); Lattuada's *The Storm (La tempesta*, 1958), *Sweet Delusions (I dolci inganni*, 1960), *Letters by a Novice (Lettere di una novizia*, 1960), *The Mishap (L'imprevisto*, 1961), *Mafioso* (1962), and *The Steppe (La steppa*, 1962); Maselli's *Heirs Apparent (I delfini*, 1960); Lizzani's *The Verona Trial (Il processo di Verona*, 1962); Loy's *One Day as Lions (Un giorno da leoni*, 1961) and *The Four Days of Naples (Le quattro giornate di Napoli*, 1962); Monicelli's *Big Deal on Madonna Street (I soliti ignoti*, 1958), *The Great War (La grande guerra*, 1959), and *The Organizer (I compagni*, 1963); Olmi's *Time Stood Still (Il tempo si è fermato*, 1959) and *The Job* (a.k.a. *The Sound of Trumpets) (Il posto*, 1961); Pasolini's *The Scrounger (Accattone*, 1961), *Mamma Roma* (1962), and *RoGoPaG* (1963); Petri's *The Teacher from Vigevano (Il maestro di Vigevano*, 1963); Pietrangeli's *Adua and Her Workmates (Adua e le compagne*, 1960) and *The Woman from Parma (La parmigiana*, 1963); Dino Risi's *Poor yet Good-Looking (Poveri ma belli*, 1956), *A Difficult Life (Una vita difficile*, 1961), *Overtaking (Il sorpasso*, 1962), and *The Monsters (I mostri*, 1963); Rosi's *The Challenge (La sfida*, 1957), *The Swindlers (I magliari*, 1959), *Salvatore Giuliano* (1961), and *Hands over the City (Le mani sulla città*, 1963); Rossellini's *General Della Rovere (Il generale Della Rovere*, 1959), *India* (1959), *Viva l'Italia!* (1960), *Vanina Vanini* (1961), and *RoGoPaG* (1963); Paolo and Vittorio Taviani's *A Man to Be Burned (Un uomo da bruciare*, 1962); Vancini's *The Long Night of 1943 (La lunga notte del '43*, 1960); and Visconti's *White Nights (Le notti bianche*, 1957), *Rocco and His Brothers (Rocco e i suoi fratelli*, 1960), *Boccaccio '70* (1962), and *The Leopard (Il gattopardo*, 1963).

The first filmmaker whose work concerns us in this chapter is Lattuada, who directed the Russophile *The Overcoat* (1952). Twice in the period under consideration he figuratively returns to Russia: first with *The Storm*, then with *The Steppe*.

Despite the title, Lattuada's *The Storm (La tempesta*, 1958) is based neither on Pushkin's novella *The Blizzard (Metel'*), from *Tales of Belkin (Povesti Belkina*), nor on his poem "The Storm" ("Buria"); it combines instead two separate Pushkin works, *A History of Pugachëv's Rebellion (Istoriia Pugachëva*, 1834) and the novel *The Captain's Daughter*.

The plot of *The Storm* moves back and forth between that of *The Captain's Daughter*, already discussed, and the historical military framework in the capital and on the battlefield.

The title alludes both to the real storm during which Pugachëv and the narrator of the novella first meet and to the metaphorical storm unleashed by the Cossacks' and peasants' rebellion in the south of Catherine's empire.

Lattuada has stated that the film intends to harmonize the fictional and the historical sides of Pushkin's two works into something new and—presumably—preferable to either. However, the reality is that the internal narrative balance of Pushkin's prose (to say nothing of Camerini's *La figlia del capitano*) is torn apart by Lattuada for no better purpose than that of posing as an Italian John Wayne discovering new Monument Valleys out east. The following is an account of just why *The Storm* may deserve the label of a doubtfully Pushkinian "spaghetti eastern."

In Pushkin (and Camerini), Pugachëv has considerable psychological depth, as he alternates moments of folksy naïveté with others of fatalism and tragic grandeur. His speech is simple but sharp, his justice cruel but honest; his behavior is ever bound by a quasi-chivalric sense of honor. A strange cross between a slim, long-bearded Russian peasant and a Shakespearean hero, Pushkin's (and Camerini's) Pugachëv is, overall, a dignified pretender to the throne to which he so ardently aspires.

In Lattuada, Pugachëv is an awkward, heavyweight blusterer who sports a well-trimmed beard and behaves as one would in a saloon of the Far West. His lines are banal and miserably delivered, and make a mockery of the character's claim to imperial rank. Amedeo Nazzari had been perfectly cast as Pugachëv by Camerini; one wonders by virtue of what lottery Van Heflin was picked for Lattuada's film and this particular role.

In Camerini, Vittorio Gassman is an impeccable Shvabrin: devious, cynical, manipulative, immensely hedonistic, and, by the end of the story, committedly evil for evil's sake. By contrast, one does not even remember if Lattuada's film has a Shvabrin at all. To add insult to injury for the spectator, Lattuada does round up Gassman, but he uses him as the crown prosecutor at Grinëv's trial, a very minor and inflexible role that straitjackets Gassman into insignificance.

Pushkin's (and Camerini's) Masha can be likened to the comparatively calm space at the center of a tornado; a simple, brave, self-reliant country girl, she possesses no more and no less than the power of innocence. In Lattuada, Masha becomes a personage best characterized as a mysterious vamp: Silvana Mangano plays her as she later played the bourgeois wife, Lucia, in Pasolini's *Teorema* (1968), or Tadzio's mother in Visconti's *Morte a Venezia* (1971)—a beauteous, unfathomable sphinx. On the one occasion in *The Storm* when she breaks that mold, she does so in the most incongruous circumstances: during her final showdown with the empress, when she attempts to browbeat Catherine into submission by ominous allusions to the unaddressed real causes of Pugachëv's rebellion. (The legal issue is, in fact, whether or not Grinëv participated in the insurgency, a matter utterly unrelated to the bad, good, or excellent reasons behind the rebellion itself.) We see the two women peck away at each other at length, just after a full two minutes of lavishly dressed courtiers improbably dancing to music composed by Mozart some fourteen years after the events portrayed.[1]

One more element among *The Storm*'s crimes against plausibility and taste is the fact that Lattuada's Grinëv is a foppish airhead who *does* serve in the

Imperial Guard, *does* drink himself silly before service, and *does* get sent off to the steppe. How, exactly? One day, during a military review, he succumbs to his hangover, collapsing just about in the empress's arms. With a lascivious expression she blurts out: "Very good-looking! Who is he?" Then Grinëv is notified of the punishment.

Plausibility and taste also suffer in the film when public notices are posted, in English and pseudo-gothic font, for Pugachëv's capture; when the cannonade-cum-cavalry-charges of the decisive battle drag on for more than eight minutes (to say nothing of a number of undecisive ones); and when Soviet Ministry of Culture-style folk dances are inflicted on the viewers as a display of "local Technicolor."[2]

While Camerini's *La figlia del capitano* is unquestionably a more incisive film, it seems to me that we should nevertheless welcome the opportunity for comparative analysis that the existence of *The Storm* affords us. It would be in and of itself engrossing to carry out a detailed technical analysis (lenses, takes, framing, and so on) of corresponding sequences in the two films. For example, in *La figlia del capitano* the rolling of drums that precedes Pugachëv's execution is presented with a medium long shot of three old, almost worn-out, drums aligned on one diagonal across the screen. In contrast, Lattuada positions the gallows in the vanishing point, with a row of dozens of soldiers leading up to it from the right, and on the left (duplicating Camerini's diagonal) at least nine distinctly discernible tambours in an impeccably spanky outfit. If nothing else, one can see just how much richer a country Italy has become in such a short period of time.[3]

Of course, the purpose of carrying out such a critical exercise would not be to extol Camerini's hypothetical transmedia "fidelity" to Pushkin (we already saw that *La figlia del capitano* cannot aspire to this particular claim). Rather, one of the points of it might be to show in detail how *The Storm* undoes the internally balanced mechanisms of its cinematic predecessor—drifting farther and farther, in the process, not so much from Pushkin as from some basic mandates of artistic cohesion. And from those of fairness, too: despite countless borrowings from *La figlia del capitano*, which at times border on the cinematic quote, no one in *The Storm*'s team seems ever to have offered a public tribute to Camerini's efforts. Or, if this occurred, no echo of it has reached any of the publications I have been able to consult on the subject.[4]

Given its different scope and style, I would argue that Lattuada's *The Steppe* (*La steppa*, 1962) is a more balanced and successful film. It was inspired by Chekhov's *The Steppe: The Story of a Trip* (*Step': Istoriia odnoi poezdki*, 1888).[5]

Lattuada, who read Chekhov's story at the beginning of the 1950s, as he was making *The Overcoat*, gives us a firsthand, effective condensation of the film:

La steppa is [an] apparently simple story—the awakening of Iegorushka, a young boy who in the course of a trip through the steppe experiences the problems of life and sees important examples that disturb and anguish him. He witnesses disease, old age, religious zeal, greed for gold, the example of the two Jews (the philosophical one who burns his money in the stove, and the other, avaricious one—marvelous extremes of humanity's ambivalent nature), his mother's affection at the beginning, the power of nature, physical violence. . . .

Comprehending all this, comprehending that life is a struggle for survival, is an experience which takes the boy by the throat, and, by the end of the film, causes him to burst into cathartic tears.[6]

Russia being, as always, off-limits to capitalistic crews, *La steppa*, too, was made in Yugoslavia; rather than forging what he could not obtain, Lattuada embraced with enthusiasm—and great painterly finesse—what he did have.[7]

This is precisely what makes the film unique in a visual sense: Lattuada chose to project little Iegorushka's adventures onto a backdrop that straddles the southern Slav world and the Muslim world of central Bosnia. The final sequences of the film, in particular, capture the beauty and the medieval look of historic Mostar in a way than cannot but touch us now, at a time when the region has been torn by war and destruction. *La steppa* is not only Chekhov and it is not only Lattuada; today it is also—alas—a document of a recent past when hatred and intolerance, briefly, did not hold sway.

The year before *La steppa*, two films appeared in Italy that bore a strong imprint of European literatures: Rossellini's *Vanina Vanini* and Olmi's *The Job*. For the former, I must refer readers to the relevant chapter in *Masters of Two Arts*. However, I should at least point out that Rossellini's *Vanina Vanini* (1961), re-created from Stendhal's 1828 novella of the same title, was the director's last full-length fiction film for almost fifteen years—arguably because of some discomfiting lessons he had to learn from the making of it.

While the commercial potential was inevitably what most attracted the producer to the idea of a film from Stendhal, Rossellini eyed the project as a potential conduit for the new type of pedagogical cinema for which he had begun to yearn. Thus, the subject matter was intended to provide specific historical information for the masses and to educate them to understand the events to which they were being exposed. The director seems to have been sufficiently intuitive to grasp (though he never said so in such stark terms) that, having forged too far ahead with his misunderstood Ingrid Bergman films, it was advisable for him to go back to the drawing board and lead the general public to aesthetic appreciation by a gradual learning process. His *Vanina Vanini* arose from a desire to break the deadlock of self-centered contemporary books and films about incommunicability, and to roll into one the commercial, the poetic, and the didactic potentials of a love story inspired by one of the great classics of European literature. Combining all these promised to deliver the best of many worlds.

In practice, however, things turned out quite differently, and *Vanina Vanini* strikes one today as a well-meant but inevitably ill-fated early attempt to make the film industry work against its own priorities. The art of cinema could not hope to win out against the wrong producer, the wrong lead actor, the wrong sound track, the wrong team of advisers and scriptwriters, and, last but not least, Rossellini's wrong approach to Stendhal's deceiving simplicity. Although (and in a sense because) the director's views were in many respects some thirty years ahead of his time, *Vanina Vanini* was for him worse than an artistic error; it was a *strategic* one: an error he committed in the mistaken belief that compromise would allow him to enrich Italian cinema by an at least partial expression of his new ideas.

As for Olmi's *The Job/The Sound of Trumpets* (*Il posto*, 1961), it deserves inclusion here because of Olmi's deliberate reproduction of mechanisms typical of Kafka's novels.

If we define as Kafkaesque a world where an inscrutable machinery draws workers into pyramid-shaped institutions, each of whose levels, guarded by porters, is sealed off from the next; where paper-pushers endlessly deal with files of which they have no understanding; and where advancement typically means moving from the last to the penultimate desk when a colleague dies of old age, then Olmi's *The Job/The Sound of Trumpets* deserves to be called Kafkaesque indeed.

Domenico Cantoni is the adolescent child of a working-class family living in the countryside north of Milan. Introverted and subdued to the point of passivity, Domenico seeks a white-collar job in the city less out of personal ambition than because, in a booming economy, his parents believe this is the thing to do. Having applied for a job with an unspecified large company, he is called in for an interview.

On the appointed day, Domenico floats and flows along in a setting far too big for him: the city, the crowds, the shiny metal-and-glass headquarters of the unspecified company, the ancient palazzo where the stultifying, grotesque, inane "psychotechnic tests" are held. His only real interest is in a friendly young co-applicant, Antonietta. Large companies do not pay well, she argues, but once you get a job in one, it's guaranteed for life. Eventually, the awe-inspiring mechanism determines (without telling them, or us, why) that both young people are to be hired.

Domenico is shown around the Technical Section to which he has been assigned. The employees there, whose tasks are unspecified, sit behind long rows of desks, overseen by an accountant (*ragioniere*). The latter's raison d'être remains a mystery to Domenico, as it does to us. He certainly pays no heed to the doubtfully productive activities semi-openly practiced, in an eerie silence, by the clerks: fumbling with lightbulbs, cutting cigarettes in two, throwing crumpled papers around, combing themselves, clearing out drawers. However, before Domenico gets too depressed by the prospect of definitively joining this macabre ritual, the boss explains to him that he hadn't requested a clerk but an assistant errand boy (*fattorino d'anticamera*).

Any problems with starting from that level? "Of course not," is Domenico's reply. So the boss tells his secretary to have Domenico do something while he waits to become a clerk.

Domenico is entrusted to Sartori, the senior errand boy—and promptly advised by him to ignore the bell calls coming from despotic, whimsical administrators. The official company New Year's Eve party then takes place, steeped in a surrealistically stilted cheerfulness.

Sudden cut to a funeral-like scene: the clerks in the Technical Section circle around the camera.

This is a low-angle shot, with the camera positioned in such a way as to duplicate a corpse's viewpoint. The reasons for this take are real enough: the most senior employee has, in fact, died, and the accountant is sifting through his possessions, to sort out the company's from the deceased's. Among the latter, a thick manuscript surfaces whose top page bears the heading "Chapter Nineteen." After a moment of embarrassed silence, the *ragioniere* decrees: "Personal," assigning it to the appropriate pile. The dead man's belongings are finally put into a sack, and the sack is placed atop a tall cabinet.

Now a desk stands empty, and Domenico, promoted to clerk, occupies it. Not so fast, though: a mini-rebellion ensues among the employees. Bowing to them, the *ragioniere* reminds Domenico that, as a matter of seniority, he ought to be sitting farther back in the room. As everyone else slides toward the supervisor's desk by one slot, Domenico walks to the lowest-level position at the opposite end.

A ditto machine starts operating in the room; its clacking noise becomes louder and louder, eventually moving offscreen and starting to resemble the monotonous clanging of a train. Domenico sits down. Close-up of his face, as he rolls his eyes skyward—to heaven? to the dead man's manuscript in the the sack? End, and credits.

It is revealing that Domenico's story should unfold (or, more accurately, spin on itself) at the heart of modern capitalism in Italy: the city of Milan, to and from which the protagonist commutes with an effort that Olmi makes every effort to emphasize. Domenico comes from Meda in the Brianza region, perhaps twenty miles from the Milanese Duomo as the crow flies; yet, culturally speaking, the distance between Meda and downtown is great indeed.[8]

By the time *The Job/The Sound of Trumpets* appeared on screen, the never-ending debates as to just what movement ought to succeed neorealism as the critical flagship of Italian cinema had burned themselves out. The answer we can detect in the filmic production of the time is two-pronged: on the one hand, the facile (though not always superficial or unengaged) genre of the *commedia all'italiana*; on the other, intellectually committed films in the vein of Olmi's. This is the marker of a dramatic change: more than a decade after Rossellini's rejected attempts, incommunicability "in Antonioni's style" (whatever the accuracy of the perception) was finally becoming acceptable to the critics and the public at large.

In the course of the next decades, Bertolucci, Bellocchio, and many others explored with increasing tenseness the path of inward malaise characterized by clenching of fists, both in one's pockets and over one's head. The 1960s were triumphally marching on.[9]

Another master of Italian cinema who, in the early 1960s, tried his hand at the recreation of a major text of European literature was De Sica, whose Sartrean efforts yielded *The Condemned of Altona* (*I sequestrati di Altona*, 1962).

Jean-Paul Sartre's *Les séquestrés d'Altona* (1959), set at the end of the 1950s in an almost fully rebuilt Federal Republic of Germany, presents a story of incest, guilt, remorse, and a few more emotions in the same league, as they affect a family of industrialists from Altona, a wealthy suburb of Hamburg.[10] Despite some formal problems and a certain penchant for psychological typification, this committed drama is a brave and, in the cultural history of capitalistic Western Europe, early attempt at raising the issue of collective responsibility for the many holocausts which Nazi-Fascist dictatorships could, after a given moment, perpetrate without encountering opposition from the majority of their subjects.

At the end of World War II, Franz Gerlach, an officer of the Wehrmacht who has seen (or just possibly done) too much to be at ease with his own conscience, locks himself in the—very large—garret of his father's house in Altona, a wealthy suburb of Hamburg. His father, meanwhile, runs the Gerlach shipyards with capitalistic savvy. While Germany rebuilds after the war and embarks upon a long economic miracle, his father and his sister Leni, who believe he would otherwise be put on trial for war crimes, keep Franz in hiding, falsely telling him that Germany still lies in ruins.

When the elder Gerlach finds out he has cancer, he recalls to Altona his other son, Werner, and Werner's wife, Johanna, with whom he has always had an uneasy relationship.

This intergenerational difficulty is hardly surprising, since the two are left-leaning. The film shows us Johanna regularly playing Brecht in an avant-garde theater company.

Upon arriving in Altona, Johanna discovers Franz in his hideout, and she reveals to him that his father and Leni have been lying to him for over fifteen years: Germany is now fully reconstructed, though divided in two, and in the West, capitalism is again thriving.

One evening, Franz steals out of the attic; he goes downtown and sees for himself the consumeristic glory that has replaced—rather than exposed, questioned, and cleansed—the totalitarian horror of the past. Unable to cope with his guilt, and with the fact that, as he now realizes, he is just about the only one in the country who feels stuck with it, Franz sinks into even deeper depression and self-destructive rage. But he will not be the only one to go: to expiate more fully for Germany's misdeeds, on his next visit to the shipyard he joins his father atop a slipway frame—and pulls the industrialist with him as he hurls to the ground below.

The film's first scenario was written by Jules Dassin in collaboration with Sartre. However, the producer (Carlo Ponti) was dissatisfied with the result, and turned to De Sica. De Sica asked Zavattini to redo the job for him. The producer did not like this draft either, and put Abby Mann, an American, in charge. Having consulted with Sartre, Mann produced yet another scenario, which seems to have pleased neither the producer nor the original author. Sartre at this point asked that his name be removed from the credits of the film-to-be, which henceforward would be "freely inspired" by his drama. Mann then wrote a final version of the screenplay.[11]

Having thus been chopped, stretched, adjusted, and softened, Sartre's story acted as the basis for a film that left the critics, to put it mildly, befuddled as to why the Ponti-De Sica-Loren trio should have bothered at all with a subject matter so uncongenial to them. Charitable exonerations of the director are, of course, possible but, in a world of reasonably free will, had (and have) scant hope of ever proving persuasive. Gian Piero Brunetta goes from bland to blunt on this film, and with uncharacteristic exasperation argues that in *The Condemned of Altona* De Sica fully attains the level of his incompetence.[12]

The film includes excerpts from Bertolt Brecht's dramas *Terror and Misery of the Third Reich (Furcht und Elend des dritten Reiches*, 1935–38) and *The Resistible Rise of Arturo Ui (Der aufhaltsame Aufstieg des Arturo Ui*, 1941, first produced in 1958), in which Sophia Loren does her generous best to impersonate a Communist militant.

It is now time to consider three films made by perhaps the most important Italian filmmaker to re-create European literature during this period—indeed, perhaps, at any time. I am alluding to Visconti's *White Nights, Rocco and His Brothers*, and "The Job."

White Nights: A Sentimental Novel. From the Memoirs of a Dreamer (Belye nochi. Sentimental'nyi roman. Iz vospominanii mechtatelia, 1848) is the full title of Dostoyevsky's story that inspired Visconti's *White Nights (Le notti bianche*, 1957). Narrated in the first person, the fictional memoirs tell us about the impossible love of the appropriately defined Dreamer for a young woman he has met in the summer-long milky light of St. Petersburg's intricate net of canals.

Having befriended one another, the protagonist and the young woman, Nastenka, make the best of the great discrepancy between their fantastic means and their financial ones. As they roam around town, they entertain one another with sentimental daydreaming about all-time Romantic favorites such as Walter Scott, opera, and voyages to Italy.

Nastenka sincerely enjoys the Dreamer's company, but only up to a point—up to the point when her absent fiancé, of whom she feared (and the Dreamer hoped) that he might never come back to the capital, does return. Fulfilling a lifelong wish, Nastenka then elopes with her beloved, but not before having written a warm thank-you letter to the Dreamer. The experience nudges the defeated Dreamer, once again humiliated and offended by life, just a little farther into otherworldly distraction. He continues to fantasize, shedding an occasional tear of tenderness and blessing Nastenka, despite all, for what she has given him: "My God, a whole moment of happiness! Is that too little for the whole of a man's life?"[13]

Visconti, cinematically fresh (if that can be the word) from the efforts of *Senso* (1954), shifted the narrating agent outside the Dreamer's consciousness, dividing his attention more evenly between him (now Mario) and her (now Natalia); furthermore, he updated the plot by a century, transposing it to the Italian small town of Leghorn. Why Leghorn, rather than the obvious Italian equivalent of St. Petersburg, Venice? Because, I surmise, the decisive element in the story that Visconti wanted to retain was a resigned, low-class inwardness, to render which exotic Venice must have seemed out of the question to him. And Leghorn, too, has canals, sufficiently less splendid to have made it ideal for the director's purposes.[14]

Neither this geographical change nor the introduction of an episode in which Mario and Natalia, while bar-hopping, romantically dance together—and eventually witness a performance in rock-'n-roll contortions—strikes me as bearing out some critics' claim that Dostoyevsky's story line was dramatically changed by Visconti. Such departures, in fact, seem to me to lie entirely within the central band of what could be called the bell-shaped curve plotting normal practices of cinematic re-creation.

Of greater interest are critical comments aiming to show that *White Nights*, while not as overpowering as some of Visconti's masterpieces, was nonetheless an important marker both in the director's career and in the history of Italian cinema. The reason for this is clear: on the one hand, *White Nights* fell halfway between the two peaks of *Senso* in 1954 and *Rocco and His Brothers* in 1960, signaling Visconti's quest for a new aesthetics after the battles for cinematic realism of the previous ten years. On the other hand, and more generally, the film aptly symbolized the dysphoric mood of Italian democrats amid the many political disappointments of a country that, in 1957, still appeared stuck in impotent provincialism. Mario and Natalia can be said to represent Visconti's symbolic portrait of the quintessential Italians of those years: she, waiting for Prince Charming to liberate her; he, afloat in the escapist helplessness of a thousand velleities, and no determination to see any of them through.[15]

These circumstances make it possible and logical to apply to Visconti's *White Nights* much that is also true of Lattuada's *The Overcoat*. In *White Nights*, we have yet another little man endowed with a dreamer's soul; yet another dance for those to whom dance is but a forbidden desire; yet another female companion who suddenly vanishes (here, a real-life being, not just a garment); and yet another bitter delusion over the cruelty of the world. How much more Gogol do we need? Perhaps just the punch line from the *Tale of How Ivan Ivanovich Quarreled with Ivan Nikiforovich*: "It *is* a dreary world, gentlemen!"[16]

Are we thus back chez Gogol? Almost literally so. The author of *White Nights* was the *early* Dostoyevsky, the one who had not yet been exiled to Siberia, and for whom the *Notes from Underground* still lay in a distant future—the Dostoevsky, in other words, who (to paraphrase a famously spurious but also remarkably accurate quip) had not yet emerged from Gogol's overcoat.[17]

Emigration and enslavement in a foreign nation, love and strife among brothers, and the enduring hope for reunion in and with the Promised Land: no more is necessary to discern, in the biblical pattern newly mythicized by Thomas Mann in *Joseph and His Brothers* (*Joseph und seine Brüder*, 4 vols., 1933–48), the same structure that sustains Visconti's *Rocco and His Brothers* (*Rocco e i suoi fratelli*, 1960). By the further injection of substantial diegetic (narrative) components from Dostoyevsky's *The Idiot* (*Idiot*, 1868–69) and from Italian literature (Verga and above all Testori), *Rocco* no less epically thematizes the mass migration of Southerners to northern Italian cities during the 1950s.

Miracolo economico: train upon train from the South disgorges its human load at Milan's Central Station. Vincenzo Parondi, the eldest son of a widow from Lucania, has already made the trip. Now his mother joins him with her four other sons: Simone, authoritarian, coarse, capricious, and violent; Rocco, kind and dedicated to those he loves; Ciro, upright and hardworking; and Luca, just a boy. The group takes the least bad lodgings they can afford, in an unhealthy basement in the Lambrate neighborhood.

Simone, who seeks easy money and fame in the world of professional boxing, meets Nadia, a prostitute from a provincial town in the North, and becomes attached to her. After a brief relationship, however, she rejects him. Shortly afterward, she is arrested. Rocco, meanwhile, does his time in a not too dissimilar fashion: he is drafted into the army. When the two are discharged, the inevitable happens: on the way back to Milan, they coincidentally meet and fall in love.

This strikes old-fashioned Simone as insubordination, an ultimate slap in the face that cries for reversal—and revenge.

On a dark and stormy night, Simone beats up Rocco and rapes Nadia, thus reasserting his authority over both. And Rocco? Instead of rebelling, he feels guilty for the turn of events, and he leaves Nadia. No less selflessly, he determines to settle the wayward Simone's debts. To that end he, too, takes up boxing.

Yet even this fails to assuage Simone, who again seeks out Nadia at her "workplace" by the ill-reputed Milan Idroscalo, and insists that she come back to him. When she once more refuses, he kills her. As the family is celebrating one of Rocco's victories, Simone shows up, distraught, confessing to the murder.

What to do? Cover up for the brother, according to the archaic Southern law of complicitous silence in defense of one's kin, or denounce him, embracing the presumed Northern tradition of rationalism, democratic individualism, and responsible citizenhood?

While the mother is happy that Simone has finally "gotten rid of his curse," Ciro wants to turn Simone in, and Rocco in vain tries to stop him. Little Luca witnesses the scene in distress.

Three days later the police nab Simone. In front of the Alfa Romeo factory where Ciro works, Luca tells him what has happened, bearing a grudge against him for what he thinks was Ciro's mean attitude. Deeply moved, Ciro patiently explains to his youngest brother: "Unlike our native village, the city allows people to live without having to be anyone's serfs, making them aware of their rights and their duties. But Simone didn't understand that, and thus ended up giving everyone such a wretched example. Rocco, on the other hand, is a saint, who always forgives everyone for what they do. He may or may not succeed in going back to the village. More likely you, Luca, who will have grown up in the city, will be able to return there and have a better life—in many, many years from now."

The film thus applies in a complex way the concept of the Promised Land to its new location and its new century. Over the very long term, *Rocco*'s characters act in accordance with biblical tradition: they sustain a deep-seated desire to reinstate, one day, their long-abandoned roots. In the foreseeable future, however, the film functions in a film manner rather contrary to the Bible's model: by deflecting in a forward direction a thrust previously projected toward the past. The present-day Canaan lies not behind the Parondi family, in the Lucania they have abandoned, but ahead of them, in the North—a foreign country into which the youngest adult brother must become integrated, and which he intends to contribute to shaping politically. To Visconti the Communist aristocrat, in our day and age it is not the workers who must reach the Promised Land, but the Promised Land that must be brought among them.[18]

This revolution, cultural no less than economic, is bound to take some doing: in an ironic reversal of the biblical context, the chosen people have not migrated *to* Africa but are said by the Milanese, with contempt, to be *coming from* it— a statement destined to be proven particularly incorrect only in the 1980s and 1990s, with the equally massive (and equally disruptive) arrival of true Africans. The peculiar irony of this intercultural dynamic would not have been lost on the director of *Rocco and His Brothers*, easily the most Europhile among Italian filmmakers.[19]

Just how topical the economic subject of employment was in the Italy of these years can be gathered by considering that, albeit at the opposite end of the social spectrum, more on the subject of paid labor is contained in Visconti's "The Job" ("Il lavoro," from *Boccaccio '70*, 1962).

It is true, as Nietzsche's aphorism would have it, that "even concubinage has been corrupted—by marriage"?[20] If so, no better confirmation of that thesis could be found than the episode I am about to discuss, part of a collective film titled *Boccaccio '70*. (The other contributors were De Sica, Fellini, and Monicelli).[21]

Visconti expands for the screen Maupassant's dramatic sketch "On the Edge of the Bed" ("Au bord du lit," 1883).

In Maupassant, a physically exuberant count neglects his wife, preferring to offer sacrifices to the god of Love—or at any rate of Eros—on commercially available living altars, which he hires for considerable sums. When, one day, he feels capriciously attracted to his wife, the countess stops him dead and gives him a thorough dressing-down.

The minimum she will bargain for is a month's worth of services; and she demands for it a salary comparable to what he would pay for the best-qualified of his mistresses.

The count attempts to object that, she being his wife, to do so would be "stupid" and "ridiculous," but loses out against her cogent argument to the contrary:

"Nothing is more natural. We are strangers one to the other, are we not? Now, you desire me. You can't marry me, since we are already married. Therefore you buy me, perhaps somewhat less expensively than you would another woman.

"Consider the following. Instead of going to a wench who would waste it, this money will remain in your home, in your household. Besides, is there anything more amusing or original for an intelligent man than treating himself to his own wife? When it comes to illegitimate love, one only cares for whatever costs dear, very dear. You give our . . . legitimate love a fresh value, a taste of debauchery, an appetizing . . . dirty twist, if you . . . fix a price for it, as you would for a marketed affair. Don't you think?"

The count finally caves in and coughs up an advance payment for the first month.[22]

Visconti, who reconstructs an aristocratic ambiance in contemporary Italy with great wealth of details, puts flesh on the bones of Maupassant's brief anecdote by developing practical and psychological aspects latent in the original plot.

On the practical side, Pupe, the countess, and Ottavio, the count, have a third party intrude: the telephone—over which plenty of communication goes on, particularly with lawyers (in charge of the couple's impending divorce) and with Pupe's father (in control of her purse strings). Thus we become privy to Pupe's disenchanted comments to others about her belated realization that marriage is really about joining patrimonies, not people.

From the psychological viewpoint, Visconti transforms what Maupassant presents as an intellectual divertissement into a fairly dramatic exploration of the options open to Pupe as a second-best alternative to love after the disappointment of her sentimental illusions. With respect to the France of 1883, in the Italy of 1962 an epochal transformation has taken place such that remaining confined in one's home, luxurious though it may be, amounts to a self-inflicted prison term, with boredom and a sense of superfluousness looming large. (Moravia's enormously successful novel *Boredom/La noia* dates from 1960, a mere two years before the release of "Il lavoro.") No matter how wealthy, any self-respecting young woman thus owes it to herself to find a meaningful function in society. And is money not a measure of usefulness in a capitalistic society? I earn, therefore I am; and if I earn a lot, I must be useful indeed. While money is also at stake in Maupassant's story, it becomes a full-fledged psychological motif only eighty years later in Visconti, by way of Pupe's newly started career.

Hence the existential markers quite openly (and somewhat ironically) exhibited in "Il lavoro." Pupe reads a "difficult" book, a German edition of Giuseppe Tomasi di Lampedusa's *The Leopard* (Visconti's own film followed in 1963); and the utterly unintellectual Ottavio tackles—one would be hard put to say that he absorbs—the original edition of an even more difficult one: Robbe-Grillet's *Les gommes*, a *nouveau roman* for the times when novels are no longer possible.

We never do obtain a definitive answer to the riddle of the murder in Robbe-Grillet's quasi thriller, despite the promise extended by its Sophoclean motto: "Time, which looks after everything, has given the solution despite you."[23] In the end Pupe, too, finds an only partial solution to her predicament: contrary to her impassive literary prototype, she furtively hides a tear as she takes the coveted first check from her husband. As Marxists well know—and there can be no doubt that Visconti knew his Marx—however richly one is paid, commodification has its costs.[24]

The trends of the immediate postwar years continued into the period 1956–1963, when Italy experienced its *miracolo economico*. Again there is a very high proportion of totally coextensive re-creations from French and from Russian.

We have three items in the French area: Rossellini's *Vanina Vanini* (1961), from Stendhal; De Sica's *The Condemned of Altona* (1962), from Sartre; and Visconti's "The Job"/"Il lavoro" (in *Boccaccio '70*) (1962), from Maupassant.

Likewise, three originate from the Russian sphere: Visconti's *White Nights* (1957), from Dostoyevsky; Lattuada's *The Storm* (1958), from Pushkin; and Lattuada's *The Steppe* (1962), from Chekhov.

By comparison, German literature is again represented less frequently: we have Visconti's 1960 *Rocco*, related to Thomas Mann, and Olmi's 1961 *The Job/Il posto*, inspired by Kafka.

While almost all of the re-creations from French and Russian are *totally coextensive* (*The Storm* is the only exception: it is, or at any rate attempts to be, a *hypertextual* re-creation), those from Mann and Kafka aim for a significantly greater degree of conceptual reelaboration. The two German-inspired items in question for this period—both important, successful films—are *homological* re-creations. It may be an oversimplification to summarize this trend by saying that while France and Russia are easier places to go to make a quick lira with a straightforward adventure film, Germany can come into its own when the final product envisaged is more sophisticated and individually hand-crafted. Yet it would be an oversimplification containing more than a grain of truth.

The conclusions that can be drawn by analyzing the first two historical periods we are considering, 1945–56 and 1956–63, are thus largely similar.

For close to two decades, Italian cinema inspired by Russian literature—with the notable exception of *Il cappotto*—is a cinema of adventure films or at any rate of relatively unproblematic works. Totally coextensive re-creation seems to suit that condition well.

The films from French literature, on the other hand, are a more mixed bag: some aim at little more than diversion (*Les Miserables, Michael Strogoff, Kean*), some present themselves as entertaining but are at bottom very serious (*Eugenie Grandet, A Human Voice*, "The Job"/"Il lavoro"), some present themselves as very serious but are, or strive to be, mass products (*Altona, Vanina Vanini*); only one (*Joan of Arc*) is truly able to plumb depths of existential concerns. For them, too, total re-creation seems a suitable approach—suitable, that is, to cover the entire spectrum from the tragic with a satirical twist (*Joan of Arc*) to the ironic with a stern component ("The Job"/"Il lavoro").

As for the films from German, they tend to be both rarer and more "difficult"—which perhaps explains why only one of the three (*Fear*) follows its prototype relatively closely. Of course, both Mann's and Kafka's original texts could be effective because they eschewed flat-footed realism in the first place; therefore, a literal reproduction of their symbolic features would easily have entailed missing their point from the very start.

The years between 1945 and 1963 were politically stable in Italy (though far from conflict-free) and economically favorable; after decades of poverty, growing material well-being stoked the demand for consumption, including that for the products of the film industry. Italian cinema responded with a strong and increasing production, inspired by, among other things, a very substantial number of classics of European literatures—classics which were most often subjected to a process of totally coextensive recreation. Whether they are more or less dramatic, politically engagé, or creative in their attitude toward their literary counterparts, these items understandably share a concern for name recognition and tend to retain well-known original titles. Some exceptions occur in cases (Mann, Kafka) when directors feel that homological re-creations are most appropriate; here an influence from literature is clearly discernible, but only after a deep transmutation both in the subject matter of the film *and* in its title.

There is one curious thing about the films of the *miracolo economico*: in a very short interval (1961, 1962) two of them, otherwise unrelated, directly thematize employment—Olmi's *Il posto* and Visconti's *Il lavoro*. Other films in the same years (*Rocco*, most notably, in our group) show a similar interest in the labor market.[25] Another peculiarity characterizes the first two postwar decades taken as a whole: while—from Pugachëv's rebellion to the Risorgimento's endemic conspiracies—the films we examined portray plenty of social discomfort, none of them deals with the Russian Revolution or, more generally, treats a revolution in the twentieth century as a real possibility. On both counts, our corpus suggests a society which is in continuous, and some respects conflictual, transformation, but does not feel threatened by an immediate crisis, moral, political, or otherwise. What does this prove? Merely that however sharp an eye film directors may have for the society they live in, they cannot be expected to be able to predict the future with accuracy.

NOTES

1. Mozart's music is the minuet (third movement) in Symphony No. 40, composed in 1788.

2. To the works cited in the section of Chapter 1 devoted to Camerini's *La figlia del capitano*, one must add the following items on Lattuada's *The Storm*: Edoardo Bruno, *Alberto Lattuada* (Rome: Edizioni Cinecittà International, 1993); Claudio Camerini, *Alberto Lattuada* (Florence: La Nuova Italia, 1982), pp. 53–54; Callisto Cosulich, *I film di Alberto Lattuada* (Rome: Gremese, 1985), pp. 71–74; Alberto Lattuada, *La tempesta*, ed. Filippo M. De Sanctis (Bologna: Cappelli, 1958); and Alberto Lattuada, *Il mio set: Qualche*

sogno, qualche verità, una curiosità illimitata, ed. Vito Zagarrio (Ragusa: Libroitaliano, 1995).

3. It would be even more engrossing to be able to include in the analysis a further, recent film of Pushkinian inspiration: Aleksandr Proshkin's *The Russian Rebellion (Russkii bunt*, 1999).

4. On the removal of Camerini's name from the history of Italian cinema, at least as perceived by Dino De Laurentiis, the producer of *The Storm*, this is literally all the latter has to say on the issue:

One day, the *signori* from Bosna Film in Sarajevo asked me if I was interested in producing with them a film to be shot in Yugoslavia. . . . After a bit of reflection, it occurred to me to produce [Pushkin's] *The Captain's Daughter*. I watched the old film; I felt it was remote in time. (Mi vidi il vecchio film; lo sentii lontano nel tempo.) Quoted in Lattuada, *La tempesta*, p. 233

Among the historical alterations and narrative choices made in *The Storm* which I discuss here, many are also—though briefly—touched upon by De Sanctis ("Il lavoro per la sceneggiatura," in Lattuada, *La tempesta*, pp. 149–57). De Sanctis's prose engages in a tenacious, if stylistically turbid, work of self-congratulation aimed at proving that *The Storm* (a.) reinstates what Pushkin *really* meant to say about Pugachëv, but wasn't allowed to by czarist autocracy; (b.) visualizes the *real* psychological dynamics of the "four protagonists"; and (c.) reconstructs for modern viewers *really* normal and natural human behavior (as opposed to the abnormal, contrived behavior of Pushkin's times).

Autohagiography and cultural imperialism aside, the seven-page Pushkin-in-cinema filmography included in *La tempesta* (pp. 139–45) altogether omits Camerini's *La figlia del capitano*. Something strange is definitely going on here, not least considering that De Laurentiis had also produced Camerini's film.

5. The best English-language version of the text is Anton Pavlovich Chekhov, *The Steppe*, in his *Stories 1888–1889*, vol. 4 of *The Oxford Chekhov*, ed. and trans. Ronald Hingley (Oxford: Oxford University Press, 1980), pp. 13–95. The Russian standard edition for the original is *Step'*, in *Sochineniia 1888–1891*, vol. 7 of *Polnoe sobranie sochinenii i pisem* (Moscow: Nauka, 1977), pp. 13–104. For a general presentation of the story, see Ronald L. Johnson, *Anton Chekhov: A Study of the Short Fiction* (New York: Twayne, 1993), pp. 50–51. What Johnson writes about the loose narrative structure of Chekhov's work is no less true of Lattuada's film that re-creates it.

6. Lattuada's comments on *La steppa* are translated from Franca Faldini and Goffredo Fofi, eds., *L'avventurosa storia del cinema italiano raccontata dai suoi protagonisti: 1960–1969* (Milan: Feltrinelli, 1981), pp. 171–72. More of Lattuada's statements on the film are in Aldo Tassone, *Parla il cinema italiano* (Milan: Il Formichiere, 1980), vol. 1, p. 162.

7. For secondary literature on *La steppa*, see Camerini, *Alberto Lattuada*, esp. pp. 65–67; and Cosulich, *I film di Alberto Lattuada*, pp. 83–86. The screenplay is included in Alberto Lattuada, *La steppa*, ed. Franco Calderoni (Bologna: Cappelli, 1962).

8. On *The Job/The Sound of Trumpets*, see Peter Bondanella, *Italian Cinema from Neorealism to the Present* (New York: Continuum, 1991 [1983]), pp. 173–75; Jeanne Dillon, *Ermanno Olmi* (Florence: La Nuova Italia, 1985), pp. 24–29; Mira Liehm, *Passion and Defiance* (Berkeley: University of California Press, 1984), pp. 202–03; Lino Miccichè, ed., *Cinema italiano: Gli anni '60 e oltre* (Venice: Marsilio, 1995 [1975]), pp. 226–28; and Dario E. Viganò, ed., *Il cinema delle parabole*, vol. 1 (Cantalupa: Effatà Editrice, 1999), pp. 69–90.

Further important material on and by Olmi is in Tassone, *Parla il cinema italiano*, vol. 2, pp. 177–220. *The Job/The Sound of Trumpets* is discussed on pp. 201–03. Olmi specifically mentions Kafka, endorsing the Kafkaesqueness of the film, on pp. 202–03.

9. These allusions are to Bellocchio's *Fists in the Pocket (I pugni in tasca*, 1965) and *Triumphal March (Marcia trionfale*, 1976), on which more in the next chapters.

10. Sartre's original drama is *The Condemned of Altona: A Play in Five Acts*, trans. Silvia Leeson and George Leeson (New York: Vintage, 1961); *Les séquestrés d'Altona: Pièce en cinq actes* (Paris: Gallimard, 1960).

11. Some information on this film is contained in Sandra Teroni and Andrea Vannini, *Sartre e Beauvoir al cinema* (Florence: La Bottega del Cinema, 1987), pp. 73–74. (Brecht's correct title on p. 73 should be noted, however; far from being *Grandezza* [!] *e miseria . . .* , in Italian it is *Terrore e miseria del terzo Reich.*)

A useful report on the imbroglio that produced the film's hodgepodge is provided in Faldini and Fofi, eds., *1960–1969*, p. 108.

12. Gian Piero Brunetta, *Storia del cinema italiano* (Rome: Editori Riuniti, 1993), vol. 4, p. 356.

13. The Dreamer's resigned one-liner concludes the narration. Fyodor Dostoyevsky, *White Nights*, trans. Constance Garnett (New York: Macmillan, 1923 [1918]), p. 49; Bozhe moi! Tselaia minuta blazhenstva! Da razve ètogo malo khot' by i na vsiu zhizn' chelovecheskuiu? Fëdor Mikhailovich Dostoevskii, *Belye nochi*, in *Povesti i rasskazy 1848–1859*, vol. 2 of *Polnoe sobranie sochinenii v tridsati tomakh* (Leningrad: Nauka, 1972), p. 141.

14. *White Nights* was not shot in Leghorn at all; the canals were reconstructed in the Cinecittà studios.

15. On the film, see Guido Aristarco, *Neorealismo e nuova critica cinematagrafica* (Florence: Nuova Guaraldi, 1980), pp. 71–79; Guido Aristarco, *Su Visconti* (Rome: La Zattera di Babele, 1986), esp. pp. 47–52; Pio Baldelli, *Luchino Visconti* (Milan: Gabriele Mazzotta Editore, 1973), pp. 159–92; Alessandro Bencivenni, *Luchino Visconti* (Milan: Il Castoro, 1999), pp. 38–43 (pp. 34–39 in the 1982 edition); Sara Cortellazzo and Dario Tomasi, "Mario e i sognatori: Dostoevskij, Visconti e Bresson," in their *Letteratura e cinema* (Rome and Bari: Laterza, 1998), pp. 59–73; Caterina D'Amico de Carvalho, *Life and Work of Luchino Visconti* (Rome: Cinecittà International, n.d. [1998]), pp. 90–97; Luciano De Giusti, *I film di Luchino Visconti* (Rome: Gremese, 1985), pp. 69–76; Lino Micciché, *Luchino Visconti: Un profilo critico* (Venice: Marsilio, 1996), pp. 35–37; Geoffrey Nowell-Smith, *Luchino Visconti* (New York: Viking Press, 1973 [1967]), pp. 118–32; Veronica Pravadelli, *"Le notti bianche*: Natalia, o la luce dell'utopia," in Pravadelli, ed., *Il cinema di Luchino Visconti* (Rome: Fondazione Scuola Nazionale di Cinema, 2000), pp. 157–74; Renzo Renzi, *Visconti segreto* (Bari: Laterza, 1994), pp. 99–105; Gianni Rondolino, *Luchino Visconti* (Turin: UTET, 1981), pp. 375–82; and Alain Sanzio and Paul-Louis Thirard, *Luchino Visconti cinéaste* (Paris: Persona, 1984), pp. 83–84.

An English translation of the screenplay is in Luchino Visconti, *Three Screenplays: White Nights, Rocco and His Brothers, The Job*, trans. Judith Green (New York: Orion Press, 1970).

16. Nikolai Gogol, *The Tale of How Ivan Ivanovich Quarreled with Ivan Nikiforovich*, in vol. 2 of *The Complete Tales*, trans. Constance Garnett, ed. Leonard Kent (Chicago: University of Chicago Press, 1985) p. 214; Skuchno na ètom svete, gospoda! Nikolai Vasil'evich Gogol', *Povest' o tom, kak possorilsia Ivan Ivanovic s Ivanom Ni-*

kiforovichem, in *Mirgorod*, vol. 2 of *Polnoe sobranie sochinenii* (Moscow and Leningrad: Izdatel'stvo Akademii Nauk SSSR, 1937), p. 276.

17. On the alleged, but most likely unauthentic, statement by Dostoyevsky that "we have all emerged from under Gogol's overcoat," see F. C. Driessen, *Gogol as a Short-Story Writer: A Study of His Technique of Composition*, trans. Ian F. Finlay (The Hague: Mouton, 1965) p. 185.

18. In the vast bibliography on *Rocco and His Brothers*, see especially Aristarco, *Su Visconti*, esp. pp. 52–60; Baldelli, *Luchino Visconti*, pp. 193–216; Bencivenni, *Luchino Visconti*, pp. 43–50 (pp. 39–46 in the 1982 ed.); Valerii Bosenko, "Il senso della storia," in David Bruni and Veronica Pravadelli, eds., *Studi viscontiani* (Venice: Marsilio, 1997), pp. 251–59; Gianni Canova, *"Rocco e i suoi fratelli*: Visconti e le aporie anestetiche della modernità," in Pravadelli, ed., *Il cinema di Luchino Visconti*, pp. 175–86; Luigi Chiarini, *Arte e tecnica del film* (Bari: Laterza, 1962), p. 305; D'Amico de Carvalho, *Life and Work of Luchino Visconti*, pp. 104–11; De Giusti, *I film di Luchino Visconti*, pp. 77–86; Faldini and Fofi, eds., *1960–1969*, pp. 24–33; Micciché, *Luchino Visconti: Un profilo critico*, pp. 39–42; Nowell-Smith, *Luchino Visconti*, pp. 158–78; Renzi, *Visconti segreto*, pp. 130–38; Sam Rohdie, *Rocco and His Brothers (Rocco e i suoi fratelli)* (London: British Film Institute, 1992); Rondolino, *Luchino Visconti*, pp. 390–412; and Sanzio and Thirard, *Luchino Visconti cinéaste*, pp. 85–90.

The screenplay was published in Visconti, *Three Screenplays: White Nights, Rocco and His Brothers, The Job*; Luchino Visconti, *Rocco e i suoi fratelli*, ed. Guido Aristarco and Gaetano Carancini (Bologna: Cappelli, 1960; 2nd ed., 1978).

19. The concept of Visconti as the most Europhile among Italian filmmakers was put forward persuasively by Lino Micciché in "Visconti, artista europeo," a paper delivered at the conference European Cinemas, European Societies, 28 September 1995, at Indiana University, Bloomington, then further elaborated in his *Luchino Visconti: Un profilo critico*, pp. 85–88.

It might be interesting to consider whether Visconti's evident Europhilia was a factor in determining the director's hardly triumphal reception in North America—a sorry circumstance that brought great cultural damage in its wake. For a solid account of the relevant facts, see Peter Bondanella, "La (s)fortuna critica del cinema viscontiano in USA," in Bruni and Pravadelli, eds., *Studi viscontiani*, pp. 277–86. I further elaborate on the theoretical impact of this situation in my *Masters of Two Arts*.

20. Friedrich Nietzsche, *Beyond Good and Evil*, trans. Helen Zimmern, vol. 12 of his *Complete Works*, ed. Oscar Levy (New York: Russell and Russell, 1964 [1909–11]), p. 93. "Auch das Concubinat ist corrumpirt worden:—durch die Ehe." Friedrich Nietzsche, *Jenseits von Gut und Böse*, in vol. 5 of his *Sämtliche Werke: Kritische Studienausgabe in fünfzehn Einzelbänden*, ed. Giorgio Colli and Mazzino Montinari (Munich: Deutscher Taschenbuch Verlag; Berlin: de Gruyter, 1988), p. 94.

Given that (a.) *Beyond Good and Evil* was originally published in 1886, three years *after* "On the Edge of the Bed," and (b.) Nietzsche declared himself "particularly attached" ("besonders zugethan") to Maupassant (*Ecce Homo*, "Warum ich so klug bin" ["Why I Am So Smart"], part 3, vol. 6 of *Sämtliche Werke, Kritische Studienausgabe*, p. 285), even the most literal-minded *Philolog* will be hard pressed, I believe, to deny the possibility of Nietzsche's direct acquaintance with our story. His dictum can then be properly applied to Visconti via their common prototype in Maupassant.

21. The video version of *Boccaccio '70* currently distributed in North America has been reedited, and the Monicelli section dropped. See also note 25.

22. "Au bord du lit" is in Guy de Maupassant, *Contes et nouvelles (1875–1884)*, ed. Louis Forestier, vol. 1 (Paris: Gallimard Pléiade, 1974), pp. 1040–46.

Rien de plus naturel. Nous sommes étrangers l'un à l'autre, n'est-ce pas? Or, vous me désirez. Vous ne pouvez pas m'épouser puisque nous sommes mariés. Alors vous m'achetez, un peu moins peut-être qu'une autre.

Or, réfléchissez. Cet argent, au lieu d'aller chez une gueuse qui en ferait je ne sais quoi, restera dans votre maison, dans votre ménage. Et puis, pour un homme intelligent, est-il quelque chose de plus amusant, de plus original que de se payer sa propre femme? On n'aime bien, en amour illégitime, que ce qui coûte cher, très cher. Vous donnez à notre amour . . . légitime, un prix nouveau, une saveur de débauche, un ragoût de . . . polissonnerie en le . . . tarifant comme un amour coté. Est-ce pas vrai? (Maupassant, *Contes et nouvelles*, vol. 1, pp. 1045–46)

23. The original motto is "Le temps, qui veille à tout, a donné la solution malgré toi" (Alain Robbe-Grillet, *Les gommes* [Paris: Editions de Minuit, 1953.])

24. On *The Job*, see Baldelli, *Luchino Visconti*, pp. 217–24; Bencivenni, *Luchino Visconti*, pp. 50–53 (pp. 46–49 in the 1982 ed.); Vincenzo Buccheri, "*Il lavoro*: L'immagine al presente," in Pravadelli, ed., *Il cinema di Luchino Visconti*, pp. 187–98; D'Amico de Carvalho, *Life and Work of Luchino Visconti*, pp. 114–19; De Giusti, *I film di Luchino Visconti*, pp. 87–90; Faldini and Fofi, eds., *1960–1969*, pp. 256–57; Micciché, *Cinema italiano: Gli anni '60 e oltre*, pp. 257–58; Micciché, *Luchino Visconti: Un profilo critico*, pp. 43–44; Nowell-Smith, *Luchino Visconti*, pp. 69–77; Rondolino, *Luchino Visconti*, pp. 422–31; and Sanzio and Thirard, *Luchino Visconti cinéaste*, p. 91.

An English translation of the screenplay is in Visconti, *Three Screenplays: White Nights, Rocco and His Brothers, The Job*.

25. A thoroughly deserving item that could be added is Monicelli's *Renzo and Luciana*, a sweet-and-sour *commedia all'italiana* analysis of family problems arising from discrimination against mothers and from incompatible work shifts among married couples. This is the episode that was left out of the video version of *Boccaccio '70* distributed in North America.

3

Democratization and Conflict (1963–73)

The Italy of the post–World War II "boom" did not invent the economic cycle; but, much to its surprise, it discovered it—around 1963. At that time, low unemployment having translated into successful demands by workers for salary increases, the country became progressively gripped in the vicious cycle of a fast-growing internal demand, rising imports, widespread capital flight, a worsening balance of payments, a weakening of the currency, and a resurgence of long-tamed inflation. All of this, in turn, quite naturally led back to the beginning: pressure on employers for cost-of-living adjustments in salaries. And so on. It is impossible to apportion in a politically neutral manner the responsibilities for just such an inflationary development; blame could be laid at the door of the Italian labor unions for their newly found assertiveness, or at that of industry for having failed to respond to the incurred increase in labor costs with a corresponding technologically driven increase in productivity. What is certain is that the Italy of the economic miracle had based its success on cheap labor. When this particular historical circumstance proved to belong to the sphere of the contingent rather than to that of the eternal, the Italian bourgeoisie, industrial and otherwise, was caught off guard without a viable alternative to, on the one hand, granting pay increases where inevitable, raising prices, and wishing that the problem would go away (thus fueling the inflationary spiral just described)— and, on the other, hugging the old Fascist comrades back onto the stage in order to intimidate and discipline dangerous left-leaning subversives, such as the labor unions, back into line.

The period between 1963 and 1973 thus marked a very real widening of democratic opportunities for masses previously excluded from input into the guidance of society, but also a dramatic intensification of the reaction to it. Among the signs of democratization or, more generally, of modernization in Italian society one could count, in 1963, the accession of the Italian Socialist Party to the first government of the center-left and the awarding of the Nobel Prize for chemistry to Giulio Natta, an Italian researcher instrumental in the development of special plastics; in 1964, the opening of the first subway line in the country (in Milan), the merger and nationalization of telephone companies (power utilities had undergone the same process in 1962), and the election of the pro-center-left president Giuseppe Saragat with the decisive votes of the Communist Party; in 1965, the launch on a mass scale of paperback books, the opening of the tunnel under Monte Bianco, and of a state-of-the-art nationally owned steel mill in the South, at Taranto, and the beginning of construction on the last stretch of the *autostrada* to the tip of the peninsula (Naples to Reggio Calabria).

In 1966, Italians witnessed the acquittal of the Milanese students charged with obscenity for having run in their school's paper, *The Mosquito (La zanzara)*, a survey on sexual behavior among students; in 1967, the publication of Don Lorenzo Milani's *Letter to a Teacher (Lettera a una professoressa)*, as well as the first occupation of a university (the Università Cattolica in Milan)—both of these being protests against the growing loss of touch with a rapidly changing social reality on the part of century-old institutions, and the construction of an Alfa Romeo factory in the South, near Naples (Alfasud), the first attempt to bring automobile factories to the workers rather than the reverse; in 1968, the introduction of a more generous social security and pension plan funded by the state, as well as a wave of occupations and protest rallies at most major universities, a few *licei* (high schools), the Venice film festival, the opening night at La Scala, and even some churches (by Catholics dissenting from the Church's politically conservative positions).

The year 1969 was characterized, during the "hot autumn" (*autunno caldo*), by a series of local and general strikes for better economic and working conditions—and, as importantly, for structural social reforms, above all in public services and housing; 1970, by the approval by Parliament of a nationwide workers' statute which gave workers' rights a stronger legal basis, by the beginning of a timid decentralization with the devolution of limited powers to regionally elected assemblies, by the completion of the automatization of long-distance telephone calls within the country, and by the introduction of legislation permitting divorce; and 1972, by the approval in Parliament of bills legalizing conscientious objection to military draft and setting maximum limits to pretrial imprisonment, and by the (at least theoretical) enunciation by the Constitutional Court of a free-speech principle in political matters equivalent to the First Amendment in the United States.

If all this seems like progress—and most of it, in most ways, was—the obverse of the coin shows the enormous conflict and pain that the decade's advances entailed. In 1963, a long-foretold tragedy occurred in the eastern Alps when an entire mountain collapsed into the basin of the Vajont dam, washing away entire villages and killing almost 2,000, and countless demonstrations by labor unions were repressed by the police. In 1964, General Giovanni De Lorenzo, commander of the Carabinieri and previously head of the Italian secret service (SIFAR), attempted a right-wing coup with the implicit approval of President Antonio Segni. In 1966, over a dozen Italian emigrant workers died during an excavation in Switzerland (many more, over 200, had died in similar circumstances in Belgium in 1956); Paolo Rossi was the first student to be killed by right-wingers during clashes at Rome University; and nature, severely disrupted by deforestation and uncontrolled settlement, lashed back with a catastrophic flood in Florence and a devastating mudslide in Agrigento. In 1967, the first confrontations occurred in street demonstrations against the Vietnam war and the military coup in neighboring Greece; and, in Milan, marking a watershed in the history of Italian common criminality, the Cavallero band of bank robbers permanently changed the prevailing perception of what constituted a "normal" level of violence by spraying passersby with bullets, killing four.

In 1968, clashes between riot police and students and strikers continued—this was also the year of the May upheaval in Paris, the Black Panther movement in the United States, and the massacre at the Square of the Three Cultures in Mexico City—and the Italian police shot protesting day laborers in the agricultural town of Avola, killing two and wounding dozens. In 1969, Felice Riva, an industrialist and former president of Milan Football Club, was arrested for fraudulent bankruptcy; released on parole, he skied across the Alps into Switzerland and then flew to nonextraditing Lebanon; the police shot protesting workers in Battipaglia, killing two and wounding 200; and extraparliamentary groups began to theorize the use of revolutionary violence. Meanwhile, a brutal "strategy of tension" (*strategia della tensione*) was unleashed to scare middle-of-the-road citizens into the arms of right-wing, law-and-order parties: a bomb explosion, unclaimed by any group, killed almost 20 at the Banca dell'Agricoltura in Milan's Piazza Fontana; the police promptly arrested two anarchists, Pietro Valpreda (who would spend almost exactly three years in jail awaiting trial) and Giuseppe Pinelli (who following his arrest "accidentally" died after plunging—or being plunged—out of a window at the central police station). In 1970, more demonstrators were shot and killed by the police in Milan; the first political kidnapping by left-wing terrorists occurred; and the right-wing extremist Junio Valerio Borghese, a veteran of Mussolini's 1943–45 regime, attempted a military coup.

In 1971, riots exploded in southern regions over the devolution of power toward one rather than the other provincial capital; for the first time in the history of the Republic, a petition challenged an existing law: Catholic conservatives filed to take divorce off the books by means of a national referendum; and news of illegal financing of government parties by Montedison, a state-owned chemical giant, began to spread.

In 1972, the Red Brigades carried out their first, brief kidnapping; pensioners and students were killed by riot police during demonstrations, or died in custody shortly thereafter; the left-wing publisher Giangiacomo Feltrinelli was found dead in the countryside near Milan in unclear circumstances, the "official story" alleging that he was attempting to blow up a high-voltage pylon (a much-favored activity among German-speaking supporters of independence in the border region of South Tyrol, but never before or after practiced by revolutionists); and the police inspector in charge of questioning Pinelli on the night of his death was gunned down in Milan.

In 1973, political slayings, both on the left and on the right, both random and targeted, continued apace; the *strategia della tensione* continued, with a bomb that killed four outside the central police station in Milan; inflation became rampant: the lira was forced to fluctuate freely (i.e., was devalued) with respect to the monetary "snake" that linked the French, German, and Benelux currencies within a narrow band; successive governments attempted to impose price controls on essential goods—but these backfired, causing hoarding, mobs, and occasional episodes of black-marketeering; Naples and other major southern cities were struck by cholera (30 dead); for once, a politically charged play by Dario Fo was not censored, but he was arrested while rehearsing it; the Yom Kippur War triggered the first worldwide oil crisis, and a tangible austerity along with it: traffic, public lighting, evening shows were curtailed, and no-drive Sundays were introduced; the Red Brigades kidnapped again; the Italian secret services, though tipped off in advance, failed to forestall a Palestinian attack on Fiumicino Airport in Rome (30 dead).

Pace Pasolini's claim that the overarching conflict of this period pitched privileged bourgeois (to him, the demonstrating students) against exploited proletarian sons (the riot policemen), the years 1963–73 were in Italy the time of a social turbulence of an extremely complex nature, entailing many heterogeneous areas of clash and diverse flashpoints. With both unequivocal signs of democratization and a daily experience of bloodshed, it is not surprising that in 1973 Enrico Berlinguer, the secretary of the Italian Communist Party, in the face of mounting violence called for a truce, advocating cooperation among democratic parties. Simplified to the extreme, his suggestion was immediately referred to by just two words taken from his argument and labeled as the theory of "the historical compromise."

During the years 1963–73, political conflict reached a level of intensity that had not been experienced during the Republic for a long time—though, to be sure, one not quite as high as that measurable at the time in Greece, Vietnam, the Portuguese colonies in Africa, the Middle East, or Chile, ravaged by a military coup.

This was a time of continuing great vigor and inspiration in Italian cinema—and, no less importantly, of great public resonance for the themes which it took up. Not least, possibly because of the still insufficient maturity of the country's democracy, through the 1960s and 1970s Italy's cinema continued to act as a type of public forum where the nation's most pressing issues could, and would, be aired. Unsurprisingly, given this historical context, a vast number of films that left a lasting trace in the history of Italian cinema between 1963 and 1973 can be attributed to the category of a broadly defined *cinema politico*, while many among the others express a not too dissimilar existential malaise.

Among the most important titles of these years are Antonioni's *Red Desert (Deserto rosso,* 1964), *Blow-Up* (1967), and *Zabriskie Point* (1970); Bellocchio's *Fists in the Pockets (I pugni in tasca,* 1965), *China Is Nearby (La Cina è vicina,* 1967), and *In the Name of the Father (Nel nome del Padre,* 1971); Bertolucci's *Before the Revolution (Prima della rivoluzione,* 1964), *Partner* (1968), *The Spider's Stratagem (La strategia del ragno,* 1970), and *The Conformist (Il conformista,* 1971); Bolognini's *Metello* (1970); Citti's *Ostia* (1970) and *Wicked Stories (Storie scellerate,* 1973); Comencini's *The Old Lady's Money (Lo scopone scientifico,* 1972); De Sica's *Marriage, Italian Style (Matrimonio all'italiana,* 1964) and *The Garden of the Finzi-Continis (Il giardino dei Finzi-Contini,* 1970); Fellini's *Juliet of the Spirits (Giulietta degli spiriti,* 1965), *Satyricon* (1969), *The Clowns (I clown,* 1970) and *Roma* (1972); Ferreri's *The Queen Bee (L'ape regina,* 1963), *Dillinger Is Dead (Dillinger è morto,* 1969), *The Hearing (L'udienza,* 1971), *The She-Dog* (a.k.a. *Liza) (La cagna,* 1972), and *Blowout (La grande bouffe/La grande abbuffata,* 1973); Germi's *Ladies and Gentlemen (Signore e signori,* 1966); Lattuada's *The Mandrake (La mandragola,* 1965), *Don Juan in Sicily (Don Giovanni in Sicilia,* 1967), and *It Was I Who Did It (Sono stato io,* 1973); Leone's *A Fistful of Dollars (Per un pugno di dollari,* 1964) and *Once upon a Time in the West (C'era una volta il West,* 1968); Lizzani's *Bandits in Milan (Banditi a Milano,* 1968) and *Gramigna's Lover (L'amante di Gramigna,* 1969); Loy's *Inmate Held Awaiting Trial (Detenuto in attesa di giudizio,* 1971); Maselli's *Time of Indifference (Gli indifferenti,* 1964); Monicelli's *The Brancaleone Army (L'armata Brancaleone,* 1966); Montaldo's *Sacco e Vanzetti* (1970); and Olmi's *A Man Named John (E venne un uomo,* 1965) and *The Scavengers (I recuperanti,* 1969).

Further important titles are Pasolini's *The Gospel According to Matthew (Il Vangelo secondo Matteo,* 1964), *The Hawks and the Sparrows (Uccellacci e uccellini,* 1965), *Oedipus Rex (Edipo Re,* 1967), *Teorema* (1968), *Pigsty (Porcile,* 1969), *Notes for an African Orestes (Appunti per un'Orestiade africana,* 1970), *Medea* (1970), *The Decameron* (1971), and *The Canterbury Tales (I racconti di Canterbury,* 1972); Pietrangeli's *I Knew Her Well (Io la conoscevo bene,* 1965) and *How, When, Why (Come, quando, perché,* 1969); Petri's *Inquiry on a Citizen Above All Suspicion (Indagine su un cittadino al di sopra di ogni sospetto,* 1970), *The Working Class Goes to Heaven (La classe operaia va in paradiso,* 1971), and *Property No Longer Is Theft (La proprietà non è più un furto,* 1973); Pontecorvo's *The Battle of Algiers (La battaglia di Algeri,* 1966); Dino Risi's *In the Name of the Italian People (In nome del popolo italiano,* 1971); Nelo Risi's *Diary of a Schizophrenic Girl (Diario di una schizofrenica,* 1968); Rosi's *The Moment of Truth (Il momento della verità,* 1965), *Just An-*

other War (Uomini contro, 1970), *The Mattei Affair (Il caso Mattei*, 1972), and *Lucky Luciano* (1973); Rossellini's *The Rise of Louis XIV (La presa del potere da parte di Luigi XIV*, 1966); Scola's *The Most Exciting Evening in My Life (La più bella serata della mia vita*, 1972) and *Trevico-Turin: A Voyage to Fiat-Nam (Trevico-Torino, viaggio nel Fiat-Nam*, 1973); Paolo and Vittorio Taviani's *The Subversives (I sovversivi*, 1967), *Under the Sign of Scorpio (Sotto il segno dello Scorpione*, 1969), and *Saint Michael Had a Rooster (San Michele aveva un gallo*, 1971); Vancini's *Bronte* (1972) and *The Matteotti Murder (Il delitto Matteotti*, 1973); Visconti's *Sandra of a Thousand Delights (Vaghe stelle dell' Orsa*, 1965), *The Stranger (Lo straniero*, 1967), *The Damned (La caduta degli dèi*, 1969), *Death in Venice (Morte a Venezia*, 1971), and *Ludwig* (1973); and Wertmüller's *The Seduction of Mimi (Mimì metallurgico ferito nell'onore*, 1972) and *Love and Anarchy (Film d'amore e d'anarchia)*, 1973.

Being able to catch up on a few centuries of economic backwardness is a feat the Italians of the mid-1960s may have believed themselves able to perform— and to a certain extent were able to perform. But how about intellectual backwardness? Ignorance and provincialism cannot be dispelled as fast as a ravioli factory can be built. More than half a millennium ago, when Italy was the center of the civilized world, one could simply sit by the wayside and wait for cultural pilgrims to flock to the peninsula's promised land. Later, though, disaster struck. Theaters went up in London, the French built Fontainebleau and then Versailles, Peter the Great decided he needed a new capital, a group of intellectuals came up with the *Encyclopédie*, Goethe and Schiller started meeting in Weimar, and the Romantics, in Jena—and that's to say nothing of the universities, laboratories, museums, and libraries gradually sprouting up in the nineteenth and twentieth centuries throughout northern Europe and North America.[1] Since then, visiting foreigners no longer went to Italy to admire the achievements of the present, but to marvel at the vestiges of a remote past. Since then, Italians wishing to be citizens of the world have had to question a long-established pattern of complacency in their culture, and to look beyond the Alps for an update on the most current (though, granted, not invariably the wisest) social trends, theories, ideas, research stimuli, and worldviews. Indeed, much of the intellectual life of the 1960s in Italy was characterized by the desire to match material progress with cultural progress—and visibly marked by the effort expended in doing so.

That is certainly the case with the first film to be examined in the period between 1963 and 1973: Bertolucci's *Before the Revolution (Prima della rivoluzione*, 1964), which has a strong link to Stendhal's *The Charterhouse of Parma (La Chartreuse de Parme*, 1839).[2] Bertolucci is up to two things with *Before the Revolution*: first, re-creating Stendhal's infinitely energetic Italians in the far less adrenaline-filled mold of twentieth-century *incomunicabilità*; second, offering an explicit homage as a *parmigiano* to the literary artistry deployed in the *Charterhouse*, which Stendhal sets in Bertolucci's native city. That homage is conveyed by the film in three labels that amount to as many mimetic commitments to its prototype: "Gina," "Fabrizio," "Clelia."

Unlike Stendhal's Gina, in Bertolucci, Fabrizio's aunt is not a countess but a Milanese commoner undergoing psychoanalysis. (No prizes for detecting a strong correlation between neurosis and the city of Milan in the Italian cinema of the early 1960s.) She is told by her analyst to travel the world a bit in order to allay her phobias, and thus lands in the small provincial town of Parma. There, the local bourgeois habitually engage in just four activities: churchgoing, eating ravioli, talking about food, and (for the dangerously subversive among them) attending the single yearly "cultural" event of the area, the Festa dell'Unità—a sausages-cum-folksongs fair organized by the official daily paper of the Italian Communist Party. Understandably, Fabrizio is more than bored by such options; indeed, in his claustrophobia he is racked by feelings similar to what Vittorini's *Conversation in Sicily (Conversazione in Sicilia*, 1941) had called "abstract furies" (*astratti furori*).[3]

When Fabrizio attempts to identify an alternative in Communism, which has strong roots in the rural province of Parma, he can find only partial comfort in his conversations with a local teacher, Cesare. A cross, in appearance and philosophy, between Sartre and Cesare Pavese, Cesare is a father figure dear to Fabrizio, but is too existentially inclined to be able to pull the young man out of his spleen. An affair with Aunt Gina, begun on Easter night in the all-but-abandoned printing room of the family palazzo (there is, or rather there used to be, a commercial press in one of the wings of the building inhabited by the young man's ancestors), does not give Fabrizio the desired help either.

One is reminded, at this turn, of the protagonist in Chekhov's *The Schoolteacher*: seized by a paroxysmic sense of entrapment in provincial routine, the young man dejectedly writes in his diary: "Where am I, my God?! I am surrounded by nothing but narrow-mindedness and pettiness. Boring, inane people, small pots with sour cream, milk jugs, cockroaches, dull women. . . . There is nothing more terrible, more offensive, more depressing than pettiness. I must run away from here, I must run this very day—or else I will lose my mind!"[4]

The film now follows the precarious evolution of Fabrizio's and Gina's affair, alternating it with the presentation of Fabrizio's interaction with other friends (a film buff, a nostalgic country squire) who, for one reason or another, are unable to provide him with the guidance and deliverance he so eagerly seeks. Eventually, Fabrizio realizes that even his relationship with Cesare is based on a misunderstanding of a political nature: the Communists feed the people inferior cultural products, on the wrong assumption that "bad" can become "good" when supplied by a "good" source (the Communists themselves) for a "good" purpose (the advancement of their cause). In the park where the Festa dell'Unità is being organized, Fabrizio finally tells Cesare that, in his opinion, under Communist guidance the people are being groomed not to carry out a cultural and political revolution, but simply to ape the ruling class: "With you, the proletariat wishes to do nothing but become just like the bourgeois and don a bourgeois dress!"

After fruitless attempts at breaking ranks with his own class and acquiring new certainties, Fabrizio thus falls back into line. The off-screen voice of a first-person narrator fatalistically announces: "Ideology proved only a vacation for me. . . . My bourgeois future is determined by my bourgeois past. I thought I was living the years of the Revolution, whereas I was living the years *before* the Revolution."

What about Clelia? Clelia is the attractive, but not particularly interesting, young woman whom Fabrizio, having entirely caved in, agrees to marry in order to please his mother. In one of the most effective scenes in the film, Parma's opera theater is shown hosting a performance of Verdi's *Macbeth*. As the repulsive witches on stage go about their supernatural concoctions and wonder aloud as to when they ought to meet again, some of their (morally, at any rate) equally repulsive counterparts in the public offer comments about Fabrizio's reassuring turnaround. As Clelia acts her own part by staying put in her family's box and listening to the prescribed music, Fabrizio and Gina haunt the foyer and the corridors of the theater, laboriously—and, to an extent, liberatingly—working out the retrospective dynamics of their sentimental education. The story that started out with links to Stendhal thus winds up chronicling a modern defeat in a narrative style as powerful as Flaubert's.

This is not to accuse Bertolucci of arbitrariness for starting out with Stendhal. To be sure, the enormous gap between the adventurous, fast-paced, blue-skied Parma of Stendhal's *Charterhouse* and Bertolucci's sleepy, overfed, bigoted Parma remains; yet one of the director's main goals in *Before the Revolution* lies precisely in drawing our attention, in an ironic manner, to that gap. The film can in fact be regarded as a lucid denunciation of the distance between the Italians of the day and those of the past (as described in French Romantic literature, at any rate).

A dictum by Talleyrand appears on the screen immediately after the film's credits: "Those who haven't known life before the Revolution can have no conception of the sweetness of life." In view of the gap just discussed, what are we to make of this? Clearly, the statement is quoted with an ironic intention; it is a specimen of that apparently most importable of all ironies, a political-existentialist one. In Bertolucci's film, the human spirit feels trapped and nauseous in expectation of a revolution that will, in fact, never come; what we are—in Parma, in Italy, in the world—cannot be reconciled with that which, dreaming along in Stendhal's literary universe, we wish we could be. The gates of the imaginary Parma are closed, and there is no desirable real one in sight to take its place.[5]

In what would turn out to be the last decade of his activity, Visconti made two more films that drew upon European literatures for their inspiration: *The Stranger (Lo straniero*, 1967), and *Death in Venice*.

Visconti had known and cherished *L'étranger*, Camus's existentialist masterpiece, since 1942, the year it was published. However, circumstances long prevented the director from turning the novel into a film: World War II, then the political battles around neorealism, the pro- vs. anti-Communist diatribe, his own impulse cinematically to revisit Italian history during the 1950s and early 1960s, and eventually the war in Algeria for many years before it gained its independence in 1962.

Later on in the 1960s, the situation at last looked favorable for the project: not only did it again become possible to make films in Algeria, but the theme broached in the novel—estrangement from society and from one's own self—experienced an impressive comeback, gaining a high profile in public awareness. True, the sense of pointlessness and absurdity felt across Europe in the interwar period only partially coincided with its later counterpart; rather than signaling the incipient malaise of a consumerist society, that form of alienation had its roots in the anguishing sense of an individual's imprisonment between opposed, heavily armed continental nationalisms. But the two feelings were, in some sense, historically correlated; and for all practical purposes it was possible to perceive the two as one.

Meursault, a low-level clerk in the French colony of Algeria, betakes himself under a scorching sun to the nursing home where his mother has just died. He looks, he listens, he smokes—passively, without participation. The next day, he coincidentally meets Maria, a former colleague; he goes for a swim and then sleeps with her, simply because she is there. For the same nonreasons he teams up with a neighbor of his, the insignificant crook Raimondo. Raimondo abuses his Arab girlfriend; when the law inquires into this, Meursault testifies in Raimondo's favor, without holding any particular opinion of his acts, because he sees no reason not to.

The following Sunday, Meursault and Maria go with Raimondo to see friends of his who have a house at the beach. Some Arabs follow Raimondo and knife him in order to punish him for his recent crime against their kin. To avoid escalating the conflict, Meursault takes the gun which Raimondo is carrying.

Later in the day, wandering along the beach, Meursault sees the same group of Arabs. One of them again pulls a knife. With no particular recollection of this man, but blinded by the blade's blinking in the sun, Meursault draws the gun and fires repeatedly, killing the Arab.

Being "blinded by the sun" may seem to be a weak motive; and, indeed, it is. But that is the very point: planning a proper assassination is an ability that, like many others, eludes Meursault, who looks, feels, and acts like a sleepwalker.

At the trial, the judicial wheels start grinding. The characters in the story appear one after the other, ritually and monotonously. The exchanges with the prosecutor strike Meursault as unreal, something that does not really belong to his life. Not only is he being accused of murder, he is also faulted for his lifestyle and his alleged insensitivity toward his mother's death. Yet, however much he hears himself being described as a criminal, he does not feel he is one; it is someone else who is being described.

Alienated from the entire process, Meursault relinquishes his right to defend himself. After he is sentenced to death, he refuses the comforts of religion. Indifferent, open, shorn of all prejudices about any preestablished meaning of life—that is, free, and in particular free of any hope—Meursault readies himself for the execution.

A widespread opinion (not shared by this writer) holds that, despite certain features of the film which do justice to Visconti's talent, *Lo straniero* does not succeed as an autonomous work of art. Fingers are usually pointed in two directions: at Camus's widow and at fate.

Camus's widow painted Visconti into a corner by insisting that there be no deviation from her late husband's text. This made it impossible for the director to introduce the war for Algerian independence into the plot, a subject which he felt would have allowed him to illustrate more adequately the protagonist's otherwise peculiarly unexplained psychology. (Meursault's colonial condition is implied in the novel but never discussed explicitly; *L'étranger* eschews all rationalization, because its very point is to present its readers with the indecipherability of the world as an inescapable fact of human existence. If the heaviness of Being were psychologically explainable, it would cease to be intolerable, and thus absurd.) Stuck at the surface of things, Visconti—whose talents were altogether different from Antonioni's—could therefore do little better than engage in the cinematic equivalent of taking the body measurements of an ancient statue: useful if intending to tailor a good suit for it, but only marginally relevant when attempting to capture its essence and philosophical significance.

As for fate, its role is said to have consisted in causing Alain Delon, who had already played in *Rocco and His Brothers* and *The Leopard*, to be committed to another production at the time Visconti called upon him for his Camus. Visconti, so the argument runs, then had to fall back on his second preference, Marcello Mastroianni: an actor certainly willing and able to take on a difficult role, but with hindsight judged inadequate to give Camus's Meursault the necessary enigmatic aura. Instead of impersonating an impenetrable Stranger with many layers of meaning, Mastroianni confirmed the impression of being, in the words of Dino De Laurentiis, "as soft as home-baked bread."[6] Thus, his Stranger allegedly came across as not quite estranged enough from the world: at worst, just a bit lazy.

For the sake of fairness, one must acknowledge that Mastroianni has a partially different story to tell. According to him, it was *he* who picked Visconti, not the other way around.[7] Whatever the truth, Visconti himself was not satisfied with the final result of his efforts.

The director's understandable disappointment with the circumstances in which he had to work are merely the tip of the iceberg of a uniquely challenging film. "Unique" is certainly a fitting adjective to describe the quality of Camus's *L'étranger* as a work of literature—its extreme textual evasiveness. Laudably, Visconti did not allow himself to get trapped twice in the same dilemma: when, only four years after *Lo straniero*, he made *Morte a Venezia*, he ensured he could take all liberties necessary to progress from illustration to re-creation. Aschenbach in Italy—another Stranger on Mediterranean shores—then vindicated to the full Meursault's/Mastroianni's only apparent home-baked "laziness."[8]

I will not dwell here on Visconti's *Death in Venice* (*Morte a Venezia*, 1971), to which I devote the final chapter in *Masters of Two Arts*. Suffice it to say that by the beginning of the 1970s there undoubtedly was an urgent need, subjective as well as objective, to read Thomas Mann afresh if one wanted to turn his work into film. After publication of *Der Tod in Venedig*, almost sixty years had elapsed—a period of far-reaching upheavals in the global system of alliances, international cultural relations, and personal relationships. It was under the influence of such causes that Visconti chose to discard the outdated literary link between Italy and savage primeval drives which, in Mann, Greco-German rationality ought to tame and control. Undertaking some substantial innovations vis-à-vis Mann, Visconti made Aschenbach, the protagonist, a musician rather than a writer, and introduced germane material from Mann's *Doctor Faustus* (*Doktor Faustus*, 1947). He furthermore fortified the somewhat fragile persona of Mann's deuteragonist Tadzio, assigning to him a correspondingly larger portion of the film's attention and interest, with—as an entirely intended consequence—a noticeable intensification of the homosexual component in the story.

In this, *Morte a Venezia* was definitely a harbinger of new times: the 1970s in Italy were characterized by an acute public awareness that the personal or emotional aspect can never be separated out of any political issue, and vice versa. In that decade, the personal dimension of life came to be perceived by definition as an already political one ("the personal is political," *il privato è politico*); and Visconti's film opened new paths for this awareness.

There may be a thousand reasons why the year 1968 turned out memorable on the global stage; but a conspicuous additional one (connected to the first thousand by many links) guarantees that year's uniqueness in the thin slice of world history scrutinized in the present book. I am alluding to the fact that 1968 witnessed the release of two important Italian films, *each* of which was re-created on the basis of two literary works from different European literatures—the two literatures being, in both cases, the French and the Russian. In fact, in both cases the Russian work offered an extended narrative structure onto which the filmmakers grafted a certain feature of the French text, in whose light the original was ultimately reorganized, refashioned, and reinterpreted. The two Russian classics are, respectively, by Dostoyevsky and Tolstoy; their two French counterparts in the dialogue are by Artaud and Rimbaud; and the two Italian directors are Bertolucci and Pasolini.

One can tell that Bertolucci's *Partner* (1968) was made during the year which wished to give, as one slogan effectively put it, "all power to the imagination." Imagination in the film certainly there is aplenty, for its plot, derived from Dostoyevsky's *The Double* (*Dvoinik*, 1861–64 [1846]),[9] is inflected by copious inserts from Antonin Artaud's *The Theater and Its Double* (*Le théâtre et son double*, 1938),[10] and its action is transposed to an acting school in contemporary Rome.

Jacob (Pierre Clémenti), a Frenchman, teaches theater at the Accademia di Arte Dram-
matica. He is a rabid cinephile who strolls around town with a book on Murnau under
his arm, and a hyperintellectual as well: in his room, hiding behind precariously balanced,
wall-like piles of books, he declaims to himself excerpts from *The Theater and Its Double*. Doubleness is, as it were, second nature to him: his own name duplicates that of
Iakov Petrovich Goliadkin in *The Double*—as does that of his henchman Petrushka, who
is Petrushka in Dostoyevsky, too. Bertolucci's Petrushka certainly does not lag behind
his master in ratcheting up his own prototype by a few notches: a fantastic character, he
acts as both Jacob's servant and his landlord, and by his own incoherence substantially
contributes to keeping the chaos in the apartment at a maximum.

It doesn't seem that Jacob's life could become any more unstitched; yet it gloriously
does so when one day a person claiming to be Jacob's double (also played by Pierre
Clémenti) shows up on his doorstep and begins to usurp his place in interacting with
others.

Jacob I (true, in this, to his namesake in Dostoyevsky) falls in love with the coquettish
Clara but, being clumsy and anyway a conformist in such matters, does not know how
to approach her. Conversely, Jacob II is a no-holds-barred subversive. At home, he
dreams of social revolution, bit by bit builds a functioning guillotine, and papers the
room's walls with pseudo Vietnamese flags.[11] He teaches students how to make Molotov
cocktails. Finally, it is certainly he, rather than his logorrheic and action-averse original,
who, to the cheerful tune of an English pop song called "I Want to Be Your Dazzling
White Knight," drowns with a washing machine the cute (and sluttish) young woman
peddling her hypercapitalistic collection of Hosts, whiter-than-white laundry detergents,
door-to-door.

That said, Jacob I and Jacob II have enough in common to be able to engage
in prolonged confabulations on how best to prepare, implement, and act out the
Ultimate Spectacle, that is, the Revolution, whose final goal is "to give back to
people a sense of their own mortality." The following is a typical example of
how such surrealistic exchanges unfold: "How does *it* begin?"—"Theater."—
"How does *it* end?"—"Theater."—"Theater!"—"Theater!!"—"Theater!!!"—
"Theater!!!!"—"*Cinema!!!!!*"

The film's dénouement occurs in the guillotine room, on the adjoining windowsill, and
on the outside molding. Jacob II announces to Jacob I that he, Jacob I, has failed (no
further details offered); the Spectacle will therefore not take place. Or rather, it *will* take
place, but neither Jacob I nor Jacob II will be able to witness it. Despite having failed—
Jacob II elliptically carries on—"You really are a good partner; in fact, you are so good
I will spare your life. Had you succeeded, I would have killed you and taken your place;
but now that would be useless."

"Why, though, set up a guillotine for that?"

"Because I needed your head. Today, however, Public Enemy Number One is really
American imperialism. And this is only the beginning."

Having uttered these last words, Jacob II steps out of the window for a little
stroll. It seems he might, just possibly, decide to jump down to the sidewalk.
(No one in the street has noticed him yet).

Jacob I. "Wait for me, I'm going with you! . . . Anyway, are we one or two?"

Jacob II (off). "I don't know! It takes time!"

Jacob I (as he, too, steps across the window sill). "Jacob! I have a brilliant idea!"
Fade to white.

Bertolucci was quite specific in explaining both what he aimed for in *Partner* and why, four years after the defeat of revolution in Parma, he undertook this peculiarly Roman-looking and Parisian-sounding project. The following is the director's entirely cathartic explanation:

Partner catalyzed all the experiences I had made in the first half of the Sixties—mine but not only mine—and somehow released them, allowing me to move beyond them. The film came after four years of frustration, four years when I would write films that I would not be able to shoot because I could not find financing for them, or, conversely, I would be approached to shoot films I wasn't interested in. I had come to see myself as a martyr, attributing all fault to the production and distribution system. . . .

Partner is a very neurotic and somewhat hysterical film, with all the tics and twitchings of a certain approach to cinema. . . . With *Partner* I definitely had the perception of being in a tunnel, in a dead end.

The utopian thrust was deliberately pursued by the director in the film:

And then there was 1968. In *Partner* there was a tangle of various things. . . . *Partner* talks about Artaud, I came up with something of a pastiche between *The Double* and *The Theatre and Its Double*—the idea of the double is often present in my films. There was a school of theater, the actors were doing theater in the streets. It was May 1968, and my way of experiencing 1968 was to allow myself to be absorbed into the Utopia of 1968, just as it was contained in the slogans. But whereas one could notice all around the tendency to pretend that that was not Utopia, to me that's clearly what it was.[12]

In the history of Italian cinema, *Partner* is not nearly as disposable as many critics implicitly or explicitly make it out to be. For one, the film ideally embodies what the revolt of 1968 was all about in the performing arts: experimentation, intercultural and intertemporal collage, revolutionary and anti-imperialist slogans and punch lines, a passion for split personalities, a (Sade-inspired) view of life as a permanent spectacle, and vice versa; and utopianism by the handful.

The greatest works of art leave a mark on history; *Partner* did not go quite that far, but it suceeded in a no less important task—it was deeply marked by history. *Partner* is an exhaustive anthology of innovative Italian filmmaking during a dramatic transition and, to my mind, an invaluable document of that cultural juncture.[13]

Pasolini's *Teorema* (1968) questions conventional perceptions of reality from a different angle. The film's conceptual starting point is Tolstoy's novella *The Death of Ivan Ilich (Smert' Ivana Il'icha,* 1886),[14] which depicts the sudden collapse of self-assurance in a middle-aged bureaucrat obsessed by the notion of decorum upon the discovery that he has terminal cancer. What is even more devastating to Ivan Ilich is that death—more exactly, *his* death—seems a perfectly natural occurrence to everyone around him. (As Tolstoy sharply shows, the psychology of the bystanders is in fact not so simple: while they betray no particular compassion for Ivan's plight, they also go to great lengths to argue away the reality of his approaching departure, thereby showing that *it* terrifies them.)

The disease that saps the physical well-being of Tolstoy's protagonist undergoes a radical transformation in *Teorema*, and in the film it becomes an ailment of a moral nature: it is bereavement due to the sense of loss of the divine, the Numinous, in a materialistic bourgeois society. Pasolini illustrates this loss as it applies to the five dwellers in a luxury villa on the outskirts of Milan: Paolo, a wealthy industrialist; Lucia, his self-consciously classy wife; Pietro and Odetta, their adolescent children; and Emilia, their maid, a recent migrant from the surrounding countryside. In almost every sense, Tolstoy's Ivan is shaped and defined by the notion of propriety; Pasolini's Milanese family, by the fact of property.

How does Pasolini manage to multiply by five the sudden realization of inanity that so devastated Ivan? By embodying that experience in the physical presence of a mysterious visitor, and then making that visitor disappear as suddenly as he arrived.

Milan's suburbs, outside a factory. Blue-collar workers are interviewed by a journalist who wants to learn their reaction to unusual news: their boss has given up ownership of the business and transferred it to them, the proletarians. How did it happen? The rest of the film amounts to an elucidative flashback to this prologue.

A divine visitor shows up at the industrialist's elegant villa. The angelic guest seduces its five inhabitants and, in sequence, makes love to each one of them.

Upon meeting the heavenly visitor Paolo is so shocked that he falls ill and must take to his bed. Having picked up a volume of Tolstoy's short stories, he reads to the young man and Odetta a passage he particularly identifies with: "But just through this most unpleasant matter, Ivan Il'ich obtained comfort. Gerasim, the butler's young assistant, always came in to clean up. Gerasim was a clean, fresh peasant lad. . . ."[15] This is all Paolo reads out in Pasolini; and those curious enough to check the film against the original will be rewarded, for they will catch Pasolini re-creating Tolstoy in a highly charged manner.[16]

Later, the guest receives a mysterious summons and disappears. This leaves a sense of emptiness and loneliness in its wake. Lucia becomes a loose woman; Pietro attempts in vain a career as a painter; Odetta sinks into an apparently inexplicable autism. Emilia goes to the farm in her home village and performs miracles there, then comes back to Milan. There, she finally sacrifices her life, asking to be buried alive at the bottom of an open construction pit, so the hoped-for return can occur. As for Paolo, he strips himself of his bourgeois identity and moves to the absolute loneliness of the wilderness: reduced to nothing more than a voice crying in the desert, he takes to roaming, naked, the upper slopes of Mount Etna.

Whence the visitor who makes it possible to restructure *The Death of Ivan Ilich* into *Teorema*? The latter-day angel who suddenly appears among the industrial bourgeoisie does not at first seem to be the transcription of any modern literary prototype. If anything, he could be perceived as owing his epiphany more directly to Pasolini's interest in ancient myth, Christian and pre-Christian, to which the director devoted so much attention in the films of the last decade of his life (*The Gospel According to Matthew, Oedipus Rex, Notes for an African Orestes, Medea*). But in fact he hails from Rimbaud, perhaps the archetypal *poète maudit* of French Symbolism.[17]

More than once in *Teorema*, Pasolini—who was a poet long before he turned to cinema—offers a brotherly tribute to the author of *The Drunken Boat (Le bateau ivre*, 1871, published in 1883), *Illuminations (Les illuminations*, 1871–1873, published in 1886), and *A Season in Hell (Une saison en enfer*, 1873, published in 1873). The nucleus in Rimbaud that served as the starting point for Pasolini's cinematic rewriting, originally contained in *The Deserts of Love (Les déserts de l'amour*, presumed written in 1872), is read out aloud by the visitor upon being urged to do so by the ailing Paolo: "I understood that He was occupied with his daily life, and that the circuit of kindness would be longer in returning than a star. He did not return, and will never return, that Adorable man who came to my room—something I would never have supposed."[18]

Rimbaud's text is slightly different: "I understood that She was occupied with her daily life, and that the circuit of kindness would be longer in returning than a star. She did not return, and will never return, that Adorable woman who came to my room—something I would never have supposed."[19] Rimbaud's poetry reverberates from early on in *Teorema*—in fact, from the very first day that the celestial visitor installs himself in his host family and makes himself at home in their villa.

On that day, it is (according to the quasi screenplay published by Pasolini) "late spring, or early fall"; it is the afternoon, or perhaps it is the end of the morning. The beautiful young guest, of whom we know nothing because "it is unnecessary to,"[20] is sitting in a rattan chair in the garden, absorbed in his Rimbaud. Emilia works nearby, raking leaves (in the film) or mowing the lawn (in the book); while she does so, she is lost in adoration of the otherworldly youth. In his innocence, he remains oblivious to her presence, and reads on. We know from the quasi screenplay that the Rimbaud edition is "an inexpensive paperback one"; to our philological comfort, from the film we can gather that it is the bilingual edition (*Oeuvres/Opere*) most commonly circulating in Italy at the time.[21]

That sui generis angels from Hell have many a verse in common with sui generis angels from Heaven is doubtless the message established here by Pasolini. What may at first be less clear to us is why the supernal visitor in the chair should read "bound classnotes from lectures in medicine or engineering" immediately before turning to the French *maudit*.[22]

Having encountered no solution to the angelic riddle in the extant literature, I would suggest that the narrative contiguity between science and poetry points to some ultimate desirable coessentiality of the two in the Pasolinian universe. After all, the further developments in *Teorema* argue forcefully that the fallen (post-Numinous?) status experienced by humans in the industrialized society is due precisely to the divorce that has occurred between the technological and the spiritual, between the divine and the material. The overcoming of just such a conflict seems symbolically prefigured in the Angel's harmonization of the quantitative precision of science with the qualitative visionariness of Rimbaud's poetry.[23]

The year 1968 was marked by a third Italian film that shares with *Partner* and *Teorema* an almost unclassifiable originality: Nelo Risi's *Diary of a Schizophrenic Girl (Diario di una schizofrenica,* 1968). In another uncanny "double" from that year, a pathological turn similar to that taken by Odetta in *Teorema* undergoes here concentrated scrutiny and becomes the subject matter for a film of its own.

Nelo Risi's *Diario* is a film that one cannot easily forget, not despite but because of the linearity and the soberness of its thrust. Effectiveness and economy of means go hand in hand in *Diario* as the director charts the pain, conflicts, and self-destructive drives experienced by a young Italian woman.

Anna—the elder, adolescent daughter of the wealthy Zenos—suffers long years of inner torment before her struggle can finally be resolved in a positive manner thanks to the determination of Mme. Blanche, a Swiss psychiatrist practicing in Lucerne to whom Anna is entrusted. After a frustrating period of mixed results in her therapy, which Anna spends grappling with suicidal impulses of variously conscious levels (she does, on one occasion, wander autistically about a surreal-looking Lucerne, eventually attempting to drown herself in the lake), a breakthrough finally occurs when Mme. Blanche realizes that the only way to reconstruct Anna's ego is to start courageously from the point where it fell apart: her infancy.

Anna's enduring silence, and later her disconnected talk, are recognized by Mme. Blanche as an expression of Anna's need for maternal protection. Her recurring theft of apples from a tree at a nearby farm is correctly interpreted by the therapist as a symbolic plea for access to the breast that Anna's distant, selfish, aggressive mother denied her as a baby. Her inability to understand the underlying identity between herself and single parts of her body (a tooth, an arm, her mouth) suggests to Mme. Blanche the most effective way to rebuild Anna's personality: externalize her sense of self and project it onto a small "baby," the doll Candido. The two women's interaction eventually pays off, and Anna can at long last be reintegrated into reality as an autonomous, self-reliant person.

The basis for the film is provided by M.-A. Sèchehaye's *Journal d'une schizophrène,* first published in French in 1950[24]—an engrossing text which consists of a reconstruction and after the fact verbalization of the feelings experienced at the time of the events by Renée, a young woman diagnosed as schizophrenic, followed by a technical summary and commentary by the analyst. Although Renée's sensations are impalpable and located in a realm far beyond language, Sèchehaye, who edits them, has a concise, concrete, and powerfully evocative way of translating them into nonspecialist prose—a prose to which, it seems to me, only the most pedantic and insensitive classification would deny the essential qualities of a literary text. In fact, not only is the *Journal* literature, it is literature of precisely the kind that brings us closest to the liminal area where one encounters the ultimate question of what literature is all about. It cannot be a coincidence that the film's scriptwriters endowed the anonymous analyst of the *Journal*'s text (just "Maman" for Renée) with a highly charged historical last name, Blanche: the last name of the doctor who in the 1850s was in charge of the—for us—illustrious lunatic Gérard Labrunie alias de Nerval, by any standard one of the greatest figures in the history of French poetry.

Nelo Risi's *Diario*, to be sure, does not follow the *Journal* closely; and I shall now draw up a list of points, not necessarily in order of appearance or of importance, where the distance between book and film is most obviously measurable.

The person who in the *Journal* says "I" is called Renée; in the film, she becomes Anna. With respect to "Maman," something puzzling happens in the film: in becoming "Blanche," she loses all professional titles and becomes, emphatically, only Madame. Renée is a Francophone Swiss, and her hometown—possibly Geneva—is but a short walk from the border (though she utters in German one of her recurrent cries of distress, "Die Polizei!"). In modest economic circumstances, she has many younger siblings, for whom she struggles to care before she is hospitalized. We know nothing about her parents, and any implication that Renée's sufferings may be a consequence of their attitude and behavior is left entirely implicit in both the *Journal* proper and in the case history appended to it. By contrast, the film's Anna hails from a bourgeois family in what all circumstantial evidence suggests is northern Italy.[25] Anna's parents are presented to the viewers as the obvious, perhaps too obvious, cause of the young woman's self-destructive position: the mother more directly so, the father by way of his almost permanent business-related absence from home. In the film, Anna has only one sister (the relationship with her—like Renée's with her siblings—is a competitive, conflictual one). Furthermore, while Renée goes in and out of clinics and hospitals, Anna's story essentially takes place in Mme. Blanche's home and only one institution.

The *Journal* lines up a number of retrospective episodes that occurred while Renée attended primary school, illustrating how she gradually lost touch with her schoolmates' evolving abilities. The film converts these incidents into flashbacks related to Anna's life with her family. A similar narrative reshuffling occurs with the young woman's experiences in the clinic. The book has ample details about the variously violent abuse Renée suffers in her asylum's pavilion for *femmes agitées*, and it gives insight into the enormous "diplomatic" efforts—uncannily similar to those made familiar by Holocaust literature—necessary for the vulnerable patient to keep the guards on her side. No such negotiations appear in the cinematic re-creation; the Zenos are far too rich for *this* kind of trouble. Any push-and-pull psychodealings are dramatized in the film as going on behind Anna's back between the mother, the father, Mme. Blanche, and the clinic's director.

With great frequency, Renée mentions to her readers the orders, which she receives from what she calls The System, to hurt others, and then to hurt herself in punishment for having done so. Although Anna's behavior is analogous, we do not see or hear her being subject to such bombardment; we do not experience those injunctions along with her. How, then, does the film allow us to get inside her mind and share in her predicament? By reporting to us, step by step, the explanations jotted down by Mme. Blanche in her notes or recorded by her on a cassette player. In other words, the interpretation which the book presents at the end as a continuous commentary is segmented in the film and intercut with Anna's story at each appropriate narrative junction. The analyst's discourse undergoes little modification in the transition from one medium to another; what changes is the distribution of the textual blocks by which it is delivered.

Whereas the book consistently presents and describes the world as perceived from Renée's subjective viewpoint, the camera—as is often the case in similar instances—stands almost exclusively outside Anna's mind, showing her as objectively given. The *Journal* is conceived in the first person, whereas the *Diario* amounts to a third-person narration; it is, strictly speaking, less a diary than something akin to a chronicle. In a third-person narrative, we may learn that apples can symbolically represent breasts; in a first-person account, they *are* breasts. However, it is exclusively in the first of the two guises that the film presents them.

Despite this, we are, as viewers, fully able to sympathize with Anna; that is the point of Mme. Blanche feeding us her *explications de texte* in small increments, as we become able to absorb them. Yet, some regret does linger in our minds as we see the director unflinchingly embrace an external perspective. There are passages in the *Journal* where the world is described by Renée as surrealistically silent, empty, and flooded with a paralyzing electric light; in that world, people act like puppets operated by invisible strings, performing all manner of jerky, incomprehensible movements. Representing Anna's hallucinations *as seen by her eyes* might have fallen within the bounds technically accessible to cinema in the second half of the twentieth century; and exploiting at least a few of the opportunities available in this direction would certainly have enhanced the impact of an already powerful film. On the other hand, I would certainly agree that pathology may not mix easily with a second-degree objective diagnosis of the pathogenic sociopolitics that causes the very phenomenon one is denouncing.

Indeed, if ever there was a work that cannot be read in an interpretive vacuum, that work is *Diario*. The film came to fruition on a terrain long prepared by the seminal work carried out in Italy during the 1960s by the "alternative psychiatry" of Franco Basaglia and his circle in Trieste, and more widely accessible to the English-reading public by means of such a fundamental earlier work as R. D. Laing's *The Divided Self* (1959).[26] The increased sensitivity to this subject at the time the film was made could not, in turn, have been awakened without the cultural ferment of the second half of the 1960s, and in particular without its eruption in 1968.

Chronologically, *Journal d'une schizophrène* belongs to the Cold War years of Lattuada's *Il cappotto*. There it might have lain forever frozen, at least as far as the nonspecialist public is concerned, had cinema not offered it asylum in a subsequent cultural age—an age which the *Journal* contributed to prepare, and to which it more properly belonged.[27]

Bellocchio's *In the Name of the Father (Nel nome del Padre*, 1971) responds to very much the same cultural circumstances as the previous three films: it, too, questions the patriarchal structure of power as crystallized in the social and family pyramid.

Bellocchio had been at work on the subject for some time. His artistic trajectory had begun in the mid-1960s with a film about rebelliousness and conflict within a provincial bourgeois family, *Fists in the Pocket*. Then came *China Is Nearby*, which projected a quintessential case of social ambition against the backdrop of recent political ferment in Italy over Mao's revolutionary China. Later, *In the Name of the Father* depicted events from the end of the 1950s in a boarding school run by an imaginary order of Catholic brothers. In the second half of the 1970s, *Triumphal March*, set in Italian army barracks during those ebullient, questioning years, powerfully thematized the clash between a closed structure of power and its challengers. While all four films have an important mimetic component, they also forcefully aim at a metaphorical representation of society in their portrayal of repressive responses from above against those defying the status quo.

In the Name of the Father features a large number of spineless young bourgeois pupils in a Catholic boarding school who are aided and abetted in their mediocrity by the education they receive. Only two restless souls among them, Franc (pronounced *Frants*) and Angelo, show any sign of wanting to break the general mold. Angelo is the more subversive of the two; however, he also shows a perceptible penchant for technocracy that makes him politically available for unpredictable and, I would be inclined to argue, potentially dangerous drifts.

After staging a school play—on which more below—that amounts to an intellectual call to arms, the two attempt to organize a student rebellion in the school. However, they miss a golden opportunity for success when they spurn an alliance with the proletarian attendants employed there. Left to its own devices, the spark of the students' rebelliousness fizzles out, and business eventually resumes as usual. Victory would only have been within reach if (a grand if) the students had been able to cast off their bourgeois identity altogether and link up in strategic cooperation with the revolutionary working class.

Having rationalized this much from the only too obvious political content of the film, there remains to add a (political) consideration peculiarly neglected in the extant literature on *In the Name of the Father*: the entire story is told in flashback, and intercut with images of the ruin and abandonment that have befallen the school since the time of the events narrated. The conclusion is inescapable: over a decade later, the students *have* learned from their mistakes, and what they had failed to do during the school year 1958–59 they have now successfully implemented.

The central scene of the film, Bellocchio stresses, is the play—a play which, in a time-honored tradition, the older pensioners stage yearly for the benefit of their junior counterparts and the gratification of their teachers. This is the locus in *In the Name of the Father* where literary reminiscences are lavishly thrown in, creating a bizarre mixture. (The presumed author of the show, it should be remembered, is the character Angelo, not the film's implicit narrator.) The following is a rendering of the play's agitated plot:

1. We are in an operating room, where a bloodspattered surgeon, Dr. Faustulus, is busy spaying human-sized dogs.

2. A countess shows up with her six-foot-tall pet, begging the surgeon to operate on the animal.

3. The countess's dog turns out to be Satan in disguise, who, in exchange for the doctor's soul, promptly offers him the ability to wield demonic powers by kissing.

4. Faustulus readily accepts, since, as he puts it, "the soul does not exist in any case."

5. A profession of negative faith is sung, to full orchestra accompaniment, from Verdi and Arrigo Boito's *Otello* (1887): "I believe in a cruel God who created me" ("Credo in un dio crudel che m'ha creato").

6. The demonic dog abducts the countess and her children, taking them to Faustulus's secret dwelling.

7. The countess begs for mercy, but is rebuffed.[28]

8. Faustulus promises to free the countess if she agrees to be kissed by him; under duress, she accepts.

9. The cavalry comes to the rescue of the beleaguered heroes: Beato Contardo, the founder of the order to which the boarding school belongs, steps in. Echoing the rallying cry of the Christian emperor Constantine, he announces: *In hoc signo vinces*, "By this symbol [the Cross] thou shalt overcome"—but, unexpectedly, both Faustulus *and* the countess deride him for uttering these words.

10. Reinforcements are in order: inside a cloud of surgical cotton, and to the din of thundering music, God appears, urging Faustulus, the rebel spirit, to mend his ways.

11. Mozart and Da Ponte provide a suitably solemn finale, with God singing the part of the Commendatore and Faustulus that of Don Giovanni:

God: Tempo più non v'è!
Faustulus: Da qual tremore insolito
              Sento assalir gli spiriti. . . .

12. Finally, amid lightning and smoke, Faustulus is cast to the bottom of Hell. *Te Deum*. The good brothers of Beato Gontardo's order can now sigh with relief—at least as far as school recitals are concerned.

There are two main points to make about this show-within-the-show: one political, the other cultural. The political one was articulated with great clarity by Bellocchio himself in explaining his position on the inadequacy of "Angelo-Faust" 's approach:

If his discourse is not inscribed into a more general one—into a movement of ideas, a political strategy—it will immediately be resorbed. This is in accordance with the old rule practiced by the bourgeoisie in power, which can tolerate just anything, because it knows its own strength. The bourgeoisie knows well that the routine of daily life, played out to the tune of rules established by itself, will very quickly erase all anti-bourgeois impression, emotion, or reaction, even the most violent or radical one.[29]

As we saw, this is consistent with the political argument developed in the representational frame narration of the film.

With respect to Angelo's play in *In the Name of the Father*, its cultural relevance can be effectively summarized by stating that, for the hundredth time in literature or film, Faust's original figure is here used as an ingredient in a pastiche endowing him with, on the one hand, socially subversive traits and, on the other, a certain pro-scientific fanaticism. However, as I have attempted to show elsewhere, the alterity of Faust (of *the* famous Faust parodied by *In the Name of the Father*, Goethe's) is to be found first and foremost on the existential plane. This is a characteristic which makes him an improbable figurehead as a revolutionist, and an all but absurd one as a scientist.[30] I accept as a matter of course Bellocchio's observation that Angelo's collected fragments amount to a deliberately impressionistic assembly of high-school recollections. Whatever the artistic rationale, however, it is clearly via a questionable logic that one extracts from Goethe's drama a derivative persona utterly incompatible with its original. Any lesser, generic old devil would have been better suited for the task at hand. To be sure, Bellocchio may have been aware of this, and implied as much by calling his rebel not Faust but Faustulus.[31]

By a curious coincidence, *In the Name of the Father* creates a demonic-erotic combination of narratives similar to that present in Christian Dietrich Grabbe's tragedy *Don Juan and Faust (Don Juan und Faust*, 1829); there, however, the two heroes remain distinct co-protagonists, and are adversaries in matters of love.

While many, indeed most, of the films discussed in this chapter scrutinize and question structures of power, the task of articulating stories within a specifically and properly revolutionary setting falls to the next item in chapter 3: the Taviani brothers' *Saint Michael Had a Rooster*—a film that focuses on the plight of the lonely Great Man grappling with the intractability of history. Steeped in the almost literally revolutionary atmosphere of the early 1970s, Paolo and Vittorio Taviani, at the time close to the positions of the Italian Communist Party, re-created *Saint Michael Had a Rooster (San Michele aveva un gallo,* 1971) from a novella by Tolstoy, *The Divine and the Human (Bozheskoe i chelovecheskoe,* 1906).[32]

The film depicts the fate of a fictional nineteenth-century revolutionist, Giulio Manieri, who in vain attempts to foment a revolt in central Italy, is jailed for years, and by a skillful combination of discipline and fantasy successfully manages to withstand the trials of protracted isolation.

Manieri, however, collapses into utter despair when, during a transfer from one jail to another, he realizes, through a coincidental encounter with younger revolutionists, that the political line he clings to is superannuated and incompatible with that of the rising generation. When he sees the scorn the junior subversives pour upon his convictions, Manieri plunges to his death from the boat that is transporting him.

The film reelaborates Tolstoy substantially, first and foremost in considering *one* death only. The novella harks back instead to a parallelism already tested by the writer long before in *Three Deaths (Tri smerti,* 1859).

The three deaths examined in Tolstoy's *The Divine and the Human* are tightly intertwined. The story's first protagonist is Svetlogub, a revolutionist sentenced to death for giving logistic support to the terroristic activities of his group—a group headed by the iron-willed leader Mezhenetskii. Despite his involvement in a violent form of subversion, Svetlogub is mild-natured at heart. In jail, he meditates on the Gospel. He lives out the last few days before his execution peacefully, and when he dies, he dies in peace, making a profound impression on one of his elder prison mates. This prisoner is the second protagonist of *The Divine and the Human.* He is an Old Believer who, as befits one of his apocalyptic faith, views the present social state as a direct expression of the power of the modern Antichrist: the czar. Admiring and almost envying Svetlogub's inner calm, the Old Believer assumes that the lad must hold in his mind the doctrinal key to ineffable visions.

The third protagonist of the novella is Mezhenetskii. One day he, too, is captured; by coincidence, he is jailed in the same institution as the Old Believer. When the old man learns about this, he asks to meet the comrade of the deceased "luminous youth" ("svetlyi iunosha"). Needless to say, Mezhenetskii's thoroughly political reply to the Old Believer's questioning gives the old man no enlightenment whatever.

Mezhenetskii is sentenced to seven years' isolation in the Peter-and-Paul fortress; forced labor will follow that. In jail, his enormous willpower allows him to overcome moments of depression by creating inside his cell a fantasy double of the outside world. There, he fantasmatically meets friends and comrades, studies, dines comfortably, travels, and even carries on his terroristic activities—typically, for him, until these meet with victory and shower him with glory.

As in the Tavianis' film, a fortuituous transfer brings about Mezhenetskii's conflictual, crisis-laden encounter with revolutionists of the younger generation. In Tolstoy, however, the upset leader does not have an immediate chance to carry out his self-destruction. At the new prison, further delay awaits him: the Old Believer, by yet another coincidence held on the same premises, is dying and wants to see him once more. In fulfillment of St. John's apocalyptic prophecy, the old man dies seeing the Lamb triumph over evil and redeem all worldly suffering. By contrast, the comforts afforded by universal love are denied to the pragmatic Mezhenetskii; to him, failing in the face of world history is a failure without redemption. Hence his despair and, thereupon, his rapidly executed decision to hang himself. After his death, Mezhenetskii's body is brought to the morgue and juxtaposed to that of the Old Believer.

The strategy adopted by the Tavianis in re-creating Tolstoy can be described as one of diegetic (narrative) simplification as well as elaboration. Simplification is implemented by excising from the film the deaths of the Old Believer and of Svetlogub. Elaboration occurs, on the other hand, to the extent that Manieri is not a mere duplication of Mezhenetskii, but a more developed and humane character. The Tavianis endow him with the deeds of the iron-willed subversive as well as with Svetlogub's and the Old Believer's fundamental meekness— with traits, in other words, that are reassigned to him after originating in the personality of his deleted Tolstoyan co-protagonists. The overall result entails a considerable potential for the viewers to empathize with Manieri: a potential that in the case of Tolstoy's one-dimensional Mezhenetskii is simply not there.

A special mention must be made of the fundamental role played by the sound track in *Saint Michael Had a Rooster*: in particular, by Tchaikovsky's *Capriccio italien*, whose shockingly sudden extradiegetic[33] ons-and-offs[34] convey with indescribable power the psychological reality of Manieri's pendulum in and out of the imaginary world he is able to create inside his mind while doing time in jail.[35]

The paradox about *Saint Michael Had a Rooster* in cultural-historical perspective is that the film raises the issue of the relationship between the nineteenth-century "Romantic," anarchistic approach to political activity and the twentieth-century "scientific," mass-industrial version of it, at a time—1971— when it could seem deceptively obvious that the future belonged to the latter, while the former was but a quaint feature of a long-bygone time. Little did anyone suspect that between 1971 and 1981, the decade following the release of the film, the world would see something close to this very conflict being fought out, quite literally, in Italian factories and streets. During that time, the Red Brigades and similar groups would square off against labor unions and pro-democracy organizations, forcing these to seek the support (as well as endure the suffocating embrace) of an arch-conservative states's ubiquitous police forces. "The state's reaction against us is but a product of *your* terroristic activities"—how topical the younger militant's complaint against Manieri's political adventurism would have struck Italian viewers of nineteen *eighty*-one![36]

To be sure, by the time terrorism became a real factor effectively threatening to tear apart the fabric of Italian society, it also became ipso facto impossible for filmmakers (and for others as well) to tackle it openly and fully. It is fortunate that, in shooting *Saint Michael Had a Rooster* decades after the facts portrayed, the Tavianis also managed to slip it in a few years before the new, and at the time unpredicted, tragic events of the 1970s.

Another telling example of what the cultural turning point of 1968 could do to filmmakers is offered by the life work of Ettore Scola, who emerged from that historical juncture with a deeper—sharper and more society-conscious—artistic persona. Having written or directed a number of successful *commedie all'italiana* during the 1960s, at the turn of the decade Scola began to get involved in more complex filmmaking. Without altogether losing his earlier ability to elicit *nazional-popolare* laughter, Scola from then on began to coat that laughter with a more somber stain, creating the wry humor of films able to point out with impressive precision where and why the Italian polity born of the economic miracle left much (at times, very much) to be desired. This refocusing of his creative nous explains the great difference in conceptual weight, and long-term impact, between, for example, an early comedy such as *The Economic Downturn (La congiuntura*, 1963) and the post-1968 *We All Loved Each Other So Much (C'eravamo tanto amati*, 1974). Not that *The Economic Downturn* has a shallow subject matter; on the contrary, its ostensible theme is the illegal transfer of lire abroad in defiance of the strict capital controls in force at the time. Conversely, *We All Loved Each Other So Much* is—on the face of it, at any rate—just a love story, the story of a woman and her three best male friends over the three decades of their acquaintance. But it is the diversity in levels of discourse that makes all the difference between the two films: in *The Economic Downturn*, serious topics are but a pretext for what is hardly more than an entertaining road movie, whereas in *We All Loved Each Other So Much* sentimental interactions acquire a symbolic resonance that charts the profound social transformations undergone by the Italian Republic in its sequential "love affairs" with different political alternatives or possible models of development.

Scola's *The Most Exciting Evening in My Life (La più bella serata della mia vita*, 1972), re-created from Dürrenmatt's *The Car Breakdown (Die Panne*, 1955),[37] includes diegetic and stylistic features from both films just mentioned, and to that extent can be considered a transitional feature between the director's earlier artistic mode and his later, more complex one.

The social climber Alfredo Rossi, a tax-evading capitalist who lives in Milan, drives his fast sports car across the Swiss border with the intention to export 100 million lire illegally. However, having miscalculated his timing and arrived at his destination after the banks have closed, he is unable to convert his shaky savings into the rock-solid local currency and deposit them into his account. As he looks for a hotel for the night, he is fascinated and then challenged into some fast driving by an attractive, black-clad female motorcyclist. After a number of high-speed passes, Rossi's car suffers a breakdown on a mountain road. Rossi does not know where he is. A rough and grumpy highlander takes him on his cart to a forbidding nearby castle.

The castle is inhabited by four retired judges, whose favorite way of fighting off boredom is to keep their professional skills polished by adjudicating mock trials. Would Rossi be willing to humor their pastime? The Italian capitalist knows that his car has been repaired but, urged by the castle's beautiful waitress (the woman who was driving the motorcycle), he responds affirmatively, agreeing to stay for dinner and spend the night.

In a gesture of exquisite cultural conservatism that clashes with Rossi's crass effrontery, the four judges don formal nineteenth-century attire, with their plebeian counterpart having to follow suit. The dinner may now begin.

Refined courses and drinks alternate with an ever more pressing examination of Rossi's life by the judges. Half facetiously, half sternly, some embarrassing questions are fired at the self-made man: Why is he taking money out of his country? Why has he for years been using a professional title for which he does not qualify? Why did he deal on the black market during World War II? Why did he have an affair with his boss's wife? Why did his boss then die in unclear circumstances—opening the path for *him* to take over? Partly challenged, partly flattered by this sweeping exposure of his very special skills, Rossi defiantly plays along until the very end. Finally, the justices meet and, granting the prosecutor's request, hand down the capital punishment against Rossi. "Of course," Rossi asks, "this is all a game, is it not?" The court agrees to stay the judgment.

In the morning, Rossi wakes up from unpleasant dreams and finds that the setup was just a virtuoso feat of Swiss hostelry—an expensive entertainment for rich tourists, complete with a mock death sentence certificate. He happily pays the steep bill: this was definitely the most entertaining evening in his whole life. He drives off, but soon the woman on the motorcycle crosses his path again. Again Rossi starts racing with her—until the rolled-up parchment, tossed about in the vehicle, winds up under the pedals and causes him to lose control; he plunges to his death at the bottom of a ravine.

True to form, though, Rossi dies as he has always lived: laughing even though he is dying, laughing and not caring one iota.

In Dürrenmatt, a similar plot unfolds on a much more inward-looking register: the protagonist is, by textual default, Swiss; he does not export capital (where would he export it, anyway?); and having taken to heart the criticism he has heard during his hosts' game, early the next morning he commits suicide.

From the point of view of genre, *The Most Exciting Evening in My Life* can best be conceptualized as a tragicomedy. This, indeed, does not surprise, given its Dürrenmattian heredity: the Swiss dramatist cherishes just that type of textual ambiguity. But no surprise does not mean no novelty and no change. Seen from the angle of Italian society, *The Most Exciting Evening* is a telling sign of the transformations that had intervened since the exuberant 1960s of funny road movies: the *tragi-* has been added, a prefix destined to rise to a sorry fame in the further course of the 1970s. *The Most Exciting Evening* is no doubt one of the best examples of *tragicommedia all'italiana* of all times.[38]

Turning to the third epoch in the history of republican Italy, the ten years between 1963 and 1973, we find a picture by most standards substantially different from that during the first two decades after World War II.

The French grouping is again the largest one, with three exclusive items: Bertolucci's *Before the Revolution* (1964), from Stendhal; Visconti's *The Stranger* (1967), from Camus; and Nelo Risi's *Diary of a Schizophrenic Girl* (1968), from Sèchehaye.

Russian has one exclusive re-creation: the Tavianis' *Saint Michael Had a Rooster* (1971), from Tolstoy.

To the above we must add the two films that straddle the French and the Russian spheres: Bertolucci's *Partner* (1968), from Dostoyevsky and Artaud; and Pasolini's *Teorema* (1968), from Tolstoy and Rimbaud.

German now in effect fills the earlier times' gap, with three re-creations to its credit: Bellocchio's *In the Name of the Father* (1971), from Faustian legends by various authors; Visconti's *Death in Venice* (1971), from Thomas Mann; and Scola's *The Most Exciting Evening in My Life* (1972), from Dürrenmatt.

Not only is there a trend toward the reshuffling in the distribution by nation of the re-created films; the hierarchy between types of re-creation also has changed substantially.

While *homological re-creations (Before the Revolution)* and *epigraphic re-creations (In the Name of the Father)* continue to exist, *partially coextensive re-creations* become frequent (*Partner* and *Teorema; Saint Michael Had a Rooster*). This is in contrast to the fact that the number of *totally coextensive re-creations* drops to less than half (*The Stranger* and *Diary of a Schizophrenic Girl: Death in Venice; The Most Exciting Evening in My Life*).

In addition, as of the 1960s the concept of a strict taxonomy began to be insufficient to describe certain films. For example, the label *partially coextensive re-creation* can be applied only to *Saint Michael Had a Rooster* in an inadequate manner: the Tavianis' manipulation of Tolstoy's material is so sophisticated that one hardly notices any loss in the re-created story. And films such as *Partner* and *Teorema* are even more difficult to classify. These can be called *partially coextensive re-creations* in a technical sense: there are segments from Dostoyevsky and Artaud in Bertolucci, as there are from Tolstoy and Rimbaud in Pasolini. Yet there obviously is more to the two films than the mere co-presence in them of two literary authors. Bertolucci and Pasolini do not just put two texts side by side and then wait to see what the sum total will be; they have the two texts significantly interact with one another in shaping the identity of the film. Except for the fact that they do not focus on two works by the same author, *Partner* and *Teorema* could be considered outstanding *hypertextual re-creations*—and, as such, perhaps suggest the creation of yet more subcategories within the latter group. How far can the classificatory process be taken?

A new, more flexible attitude toward cinematic re-creation began to assert itself in the course of the 1960s. Clearly, during this period the theoretical picture became increasingly complicated, reflecting a more diverse cultural backdrop both in the audiences and in the filmmakers. To mention but one, it strikes as altogether symptomatic of a new epoch that in *Teorema* Pasolini did not even think of presenting or explaining Rimbaud to his viewers, but rather forged ahead and used him with no further ado. This presupposed the director's confidence that a sufficiently large part of his public would be familiar enough with Rimbaud to receive and decode his message. Twenty years before 1968, such a course of action would have been unthinkable.

That said, a growing complexity of narrative strategies is not the only phenomenon that strikes the observer of the Italian cinema between 1963 and 1973. Just as noticeable is a penchant to portray, in diverse guises, upheavals aimed at the establishment of social justice—not, that is, as historical events, but as very real working hypotheses for the present. It is the circumstances of *today*'s revolution, rather than Gavroche's or Pugachëv's, which are debated at this time.

NOTES

1. With a sudden conversion from the semifacetious to the semipedantic, I will here hasten to add that, from Shakespeare's *Romeo and Juliet* to the Berkeley campanile, in much of the superior cultural flourishing just alluded to, Italians could, in fact, recognize a strong Italian component—in a "double reversal" pattern that is normal in the historical phenomenon of dialogism (mutual interrelationship) between cultures.

2. See Stendhal, *The Charterhouse of Parma*, trans. C. K. Scott Moncrieff (London: Zodiac Press, 1980); *La Chartreuse de Parme*, ed. Ernest Abravanel, vols. 24–25 of his *Oeuvres complètes*, ed. Victor Del Litto (Geneva: Cercle du Bibliophile, 1969).

3. The expression "astratti furori," originally used by Elio Vittorini in *Conversation in Sicily*, was insightfully applied by Miccichè to Bertolucci's cinema in his *Cinema italiano: Gli anni '60 e oltre* (Venice; Marsilio, 1995 [1975]), p. 202. For *Before the Revolution*, see ibid., pp. 203–05, 208–09.

4. My translation from Chekhov's *The Schoolteacher*. For an alternative English version, see Anton Chekhov, *The Russian Master*, ed. and trans. Ronald Hingley, in vol. 7 of *The Oxford Chekhov* (Oxford: Oxford University Press, 1978), p. 130; and Anton Pavlovich Chekhov, *Uchitel' slovesnosti*, in *Sochineniia 1892–1894*, vol. 8 of *Polnoe sobranie sochinenii, i pisem* (Moscow: Nauka, 1977), p. 332.

5. For Bertolucci's (and others') comments on the film, see Ermelinda M. Campani, *L'anticonformista: Bernardo Bertolucci e il suo cinema* (Fiesole: Cadmo, 1998), pp. 19–24; Francesco Costa, *Bernardo Bertolucci* (Rome: Dino Audino Editore, n.d. [1995?]), pp. 17–18; Franca Faldini and Goffredo Fofi, eds., *L'avventurosa storia del cinema italiano . . . 1960–1969* (Milan: Feltrinelli, 1981), pp. 248–52, 438; Goffredo Fofi, *Il cinema italiano: Servi e padroni* (Milan: Feltrinelli, 1971), pp. 105–07; T. Jefferson Kline, *I film di Bernardo Bertolucci: Cinema e psicanalisi* (Rome: Gremese, 1994), pp. 35–50; Lino Miccichè, "Prima della rivoluzione," in Roberto Campari and Maurizio Schiaretti, eds., *In viaggio con Bernardo: Il cinema di Bernardo Bertolucci* (Venice: Marsilio, 1994), pp. 31–40; Stefano Socci, *Bernardo Bertolucci* (Milan: Il Castoro, 1996), pp. 7, 24–30; and Aldo Tassone, *Parla il cinema italiano*, vol. 2 (Milan: Il Formichiere, 1980), pp. 45–82, esp. 67–69.

6. "Un attore molle, tipo pane fatto in casa" (Dino De Laurentiis, in Costanzo Costantini, *Marcello Mastroianni: Vita, amori e successi di un divo involontario* [Rome: Editori Riuniti, 1996], p. 88).

Mastroianni's relation to Visconti is further discussed (among much else) in Enzo Biagi, ed., *La bella vita: Marcello Mastroianni racconta* (Rome: RAI-ERI; Milan: Rizzoli, 1996); and in Marcello Mastroianni, *Mi ricordo, sì, io mi ricordo*, ed. Francesco Tatò (Milan: Baldini e Castoldi, 1997), passim.

7. Visconti's comments on *Lo straniero*, along with Mastroianni's dissenting opinion, are drawn from Faldini and Fofi, eds., *1960–1969*, pp. 264–65.

8. *Lo straniero* is extremely difficult to view; only the Scuola Nazionale di Cinema in Rome (formerly Centro Sperimentale di Cinematografia) ownsa 35 mm copy of it.

The film is treated briefly in Pio Baldelli, *Luchino Visconti* (Milan: Gabriele Mazzotta Editore, 1973), pp. 257–60; Alessandro Bencivenni, *Luchino Visconti* (Milan: Il Castoro, 1999 [1994; 1982]), pp. 68–72 (same pages in the 1982 ed.); Caterina D'Amico de Carvalho, *Life and Work of Luchino Visconti* (Rome: Cinecittà International, n.d. [1998]), pp. 158–63; Luciano De Giusti, *I film di Luchino Visconti* (Rome: Gremese, 1985), pp. 112–14; Lino Micciché, *Luchino Visconti: Un profilo critico* (Venice: Marsilio, 1996), pp. 56–58; Angelo Moscariello, *Cinema e/o letteratura* (Bologna: Pitagora Editrice, 1981), pp. 6–8; Nowell-Smith, *Luchino Visconti* (New York: Viking Press, 1973 [1967]), pp. 179–85; Renzo Renzi, *Visconti segreto* (Bari: Laterza, 1994), pp. 183–86; Gianni Rondolino, *Luchino Visconti* (Turin: UTET, 1981), pp. 459–62; and Alain Sanzio and Paul-Louis Thirard, *Luchino Visconti cinéaste* (Paris: Persona, 1984), pp. 107–08.

In this context, a welcome recent contribution to *Lo straniero* scholarship is Leonardo De Franceschi, "Piccola storia di un film dimenticato: *Lo straniero*," *Bianco & Nero* 60, 2 (March–April 1999): 68–89; further expanded by the author into a full-sized monograph, *Il film* Lo straniero *di Luchino Visconti: Dalla pagina allo schermo* (Rome: Scuola Nazionale di Cinema-Biblioteca di Bianco & Nero, 1999); and echoed yet again in his "*Lo straniero*. Il mio caso," in Veronica Pravadelli, ed., *Il cinema di Luchino Visconti* (Rome: Fondazione Scuola Nazionale di Cinema, 2000), pp. 247–58.

9. A handy English edition of *The Double* is Fedor Dostoyevsky, *Notes from Underground. The Double*, trans. Jessie Coulson (Harmondsworth: Penguin, 1972). *Dvoinik* is contained, along with *Bednye liudi (Poor Folk)* and other stories, in vol. 1 of Fëdor Mikhailovich Dostoevskii, *Polnoe sobranie sochinenii* (Leningrad: Nauka, 1972).

10. Antonin Artaud, *The Theater and Its Double*, trans. Mary Caroline Richards (New York: Grove Press, 1958); *Le théâtre et son double* (Paris: Gallimard, 1964 [1938]). Also in vol. 4 of his *Oeuvres complètes*.

11. The flags in *Partner* have a white star in the center and a red and blue band—a cross between (North) Vietnam's and Panama's.

12. Bertolucci's quote translated here is drawn from Faldini and Fofi, eds., *1960–1969*, p. 448. On and by the director, see also Tassone, *Parla il cinema italiano*, vol. 2, pp. 45–82, esp. 69–71.

13. Lucid and detailed commentary on this generally too harshly judged film can be found in Ezio Alberione et al., eds., *Stefania Sandrelli* (Palermo: Edizioni Papageno, 1998), p. 44; Campani, *L'anticonformista*, pp. 25–32; Francesco Casetti, "Partner," in Campari and Schiaretti, eds., *In viaggio con Bernardo*, pp. 48–57; Kline, *I film di Bernardo Bertolucci*, pp. 51–65; Micciché, *Cinema italiano: Gli anni '60 e oltre*, pp. 205–09; and Socci, *Bernardo Bertolucci*, pp. 31–37.

There is also a careful, sympathetic technical analysis of *Partner* by Pier Paolo Pasolini (26 October 1968) included in the Pasolinian anthology *I film degli altri*, ed. Tullio Kezich (Parma: Guanda, 1996), pp. 84–88. At the opposite end of the spectrum, Fofi (*Servi e padroni*, p. 107) is as scathing toward *Partner* as he ever gets.

14. Leo Tolstoy, *The Death of Ivan Ilich*, trans. Louise Maude and Aylmer Maude, in vol. 15 of *Tolstoy Centenary Edition* (Oxford: Oxford University Press, 1934); Lëv Nikolaevich Tolstoi, *Smert' Ivana Il'icha*, in vol. 26 of his *Polnoe sobranie sochinenii* (Moscow and Leningrad: Khudozhestvennaia Literatura, 1936).

15. My translation from the film's dialogue. For full information on the sources, see note 16.

16. First, Pasolini's Tolstoy in the film: "Ma anche in questa sgradevole situazione Ivan Ilich trovò conforto. Veniva sempre *a fare le pulizie* Gerasim. Gerasim era un giovane contadino pulito, fresco. . . ." *Fare le pulizie* means to clean up, to do house chores. Thus, in Pasolini the young man's intervention is nonspecific; this implies that Paolo's "unpleasant situation" is simply a description of his general dyscrasia.

Second, Pasolini's Tolstoy in the quasi screenplay, which is slightly less elliptical: "Ma anche in questa sgradevole *funzione*, Ivàn Ilìch trovò un conforto. Veniva sempre *a portar via* il contadino cantiniere Geràsim. Geràsim era un giovane contadino pulito, fresco . . ." (Pier Paolo Pasolini, *Teorema* [Milan: Garzanti, 1974 (1968)], p. 64; emphasis added).

Third, Tolstoy's Tolstoy—whose wording is altogether explicit: the unpleasantness of the circumstances consists in the fact that the ever-dignified Ivan Ilich, having constantly repressed human creatureliness in himself and others, is now ashamed of seeing a stranger daily remove his feces—"carry the things out" (Tolstoy, *The Death of Ivan Ilich*, p. 49); "vynosit' za nim" (Tolstoi, *Smert' Ivana Il'icha*, p. 95)—or, in the Italian translation, "portar via le feci" (Lëv Tolstòj, *La morte di Ivàn Ilìch*, trans. Serena Prina, in vol. 2 of *Tutti i racconti*, ed. Igor Sibaldi [Milan: Mondadori, 1998 (1991)], p. 377).

This remark is not meant to accuse the director of being a cheat. The question is clearly one of recontextualization: in *Teorema* the issue of shame (or, indeed, of shame's collapse) is removed from the sphere of the excremental and readdressed via the sexual sphere. This explains why Pasolini, having quoted around the contentious point, then sticks all the more doggedly to Gerasim's other useful function in Tolstoy: raising Ivan's legs atop his own shoulders so as to alleviate the ill man's pain (to my mind a parasexual rather than merely "funny" business, *pace* the comments in Maurizio Viano, *A Certain Realism: Making Use of Pasolini's Film Theory and Practice* [Berkeley: University of California Press, 1993], p. 203).

17. The term was coined by Paul Verlaine, for a while Rimbaud's lover, for an anthology of "subversives" he edited.

18. Again, Pasolini's Italian first: "Egli apparteneva alla propria vita, ed il dono di un suo atto di bontà avrebbe messo più tempo a riprodursi che una stella. L'Adorabile che, senza che io lo avessi mai sperato, era venuto, non è ritornato, e non tornerà mai più." In the quasi screenplay, this passage is not quoted directly, but merely referred to as "the exact words [the young man] had by chance [!] arrived at" ("esattamente le parole a cui era per caso arrivato"; Pasolini, *Teorema*, p. 70).

19. Arthur Rimbaud, *Complete Works, Selected Letters*, ed. and trans. Wallace Fowlie (Chicago: University of Chicago Press, 1975 [1966]), p. 289. Nowhere in the vast secondary literature on Pasolini have I found an exact quote of the French original: "J'ai compris qu'elle était à sa vie de tous les jours, et que le tour

de bonté serait plus long à se reproduire qu'une étoile. Elle n'est pas revenue, et ne reviendra jamais, l'Adorable qui s'était rendue chez moi,—ce que je n'aurais jamais présumé" (Arthur Rimbaud, *Les déserts de l'amour II*, in his *Oeuvres*, ed. Suzanne Bernard and André Guyaux [Paris: Garnier, 1987 (1983)], p. 189).

20. Pasolini, *Teorema*, p. 24.

21. The Rimbaud edition used in the film appears to be the one in the collection Universale Economica Feltrinelli, recognizable because of the characteristic portrait of the author on its front cover.

22. The further references to the scene in the garden are from Pasolini, *Teorema*, pp. 25–27.

23. Publications on Pasolini are almost countless (and growing), but the following items on *Teorema* are reasonably complementary representatives of diverse trends: Alessandro Cappabianca, *Il cinema e il sacro* (Recco: Le Mani, 1998), pp. 119–22; René de Ceccatty, *Sur Pier Paolo Pasolini* (Le Faouët: Editions du Scorff, 1998), pp. 105–09; Luciano De Giusti, *I film di Pier Paolo Pasolini* (Rome: Gremese, 1983), pp. 92–99; Fofi, *Servi e padroni*, pp. 112–13; Naomi Greene, *Pier Paolo Pasolini: Cinema as Heresy* (Princeton, N.J.: Princeton University Press, 1990), pp. 130–36, 139–49 passim; Alberto Marchesini, *Citazioni pittoriche nel cinema di Pasolini (da* Accattone *al* Decameron*)* (Florence: La Nuova Italia, 1994), pp. 107–18; Italo Moscati, *Pasolini e il teorema del sesso. 1968: Dalla mostra del cine al sequestro . . .* (Milan: Il Saggiatore, 1995); Serafino Murri, *Pier Paolo Pasolini* (Milan: Il Castoro, 1994), pp. 97–105; Patrick Rumble, *Allegories of Contamination: Pier Paolo Pasolini's Trilogy of Life* (Toronto: University of Toronto Press, 1996), pp. 140–44; Piero Spila, *Pier Paolo Pasolini* (Rome: Gremese, 1999), pp. 79–82; and Viano, *A Certain Realism*, pp. 198–213.

Useful introductions to Pasolini's life work are the following: Ben Lawton, "The Evolving Rejection of Homosexuality, the Sub-Proletariat, and the Third World in the Films of Pier Paolo Pasolini," *Italian Quarterly* 82–83 (Fall 1980–Winter 1981): 167–73; Nico Naldini, *Pasolini, una vita* (Turin: Einaudi, 1989); Enzo Siciliano, *Pasolini: A Biography*, trans. John Shepley (New York: Random House, 1982); and Enzo Siciliano, *Vita di Pasolini* (Florence: Giunti, 1995 [1978]).

24. M. R. Sèchehaye's *Diary of a Schizophrenic Girl* appeared in English as early as 1951 (New York: Grune and Stratton). It has been republished many times since, most recently as *Autobiography of a Schizophrenic Girl: The True Story of "Renee,"* trans. Grace Rubin-Rabson (New York: Penguin Meridian, 1994). The original, reprinted eight times to date, is M.-A. Sèchehaye, *Journal d'une schizophrène: Auto-observation d'une schizophrène pendant le traitement psychothérapique* (Paris: Presses Universitaires de France, 1987 [1950]).

Though Sèchehaye's first name is entered in a number of library catalogs as "Marguerite Renée," the French original of her book indicates it as "M.-A."

25. In the film it remains unclear, from the purely linguistic point of view, just how the Italophone Anna can communicate in Lucerne.

26. The works of psychiatry alluded to here are Ronald David Laing, *The Divided Self: An Existential Study in Sanity and Madness* (Baltimore: Penguin, 1959); Franco Basaglia, *The Institution Denied (L'istituzione negata)* (Turin: Einaudi, 1968); and Franco Basaglia, *The Deviant Majority (La maggioranza deviante)* (Turin: Einaudi, 1971). So far, neither of Basaglia's books has been translated into English.

27. Surprisingly, the secondary literature on this important film amounts to little more

than a short entry in Lino Micciché, *Cinema italiano degli anni '70: Cronache 1969– 1979* (Venice: Marsilio, 1989 [1980]), pp. 24–27.

28. As one churchman in the audience observes, this episode is a remake of the chapter on the *Innominato* (Unnamed One) in Manzoni's novel *The Betrothed*.

29. Bellocchio's statements are quoted from Franca Faldini and Goffredo Fofi, eds., *Il cinema italiano d'oggi 1970–1984 raccontato dai suoi protagonisti* (Milan: Mondadori, 1984), pp. 133–35.

Further authorial comments on the film can be collected from Bellocchio's interview with Fofi that introduces the screenplay: Marco Bellocchio, *Nel nome del padre*, ed. Goffredo Fofi (Bologna: Cappelli, 1971), esp. pp. 31–34. An important source of material on and by the director is also Tassone, *Parla il cinema italiano*, vol. 2, pp. 7–44. Interestingly, Bellocchio mentions Marx and Freud among the thinkers who influenced him, but (at this stage in his life, anyway) not Lacan.

30. On a reading of Goethe's *Faust* alternative to that of some common clichés, at least some of which (Faust-the-scientist) seem to have been accepted by Bellocchio, see Carlo Testa, *Desire and the Devil: Demonic Contracts in French and European Literature* (New York: Peter Lang, 1991), pp. 15–28.

31. Insightful comments on *In the Name of the Father* are presented in Sandro Bernardi, *Marco Bellocchio* (Milan: Il Castoro, 1998 [1978]), pp. 62–70 (pp. 70–83 in the 1978 ed.); Laura Bertuzzi, *Il cinema di Marco Bellocchio* (Castelsangiovanni: Pontegobbo, 1996), pp. 89–100; Peter Bondanella, *Italian Cinema from Neorealism to the Present* (New York: Continuum, 1991 [1983]), pp. 339–41; Goffredo Fofi, *Capire con il cinema: Duecento film prima e dopo il '68* (Milan: Feltrinelli, 1971), pp. 235–37; Mira Liehm, *Passion and Defiance* (Berkeley: University of California Press, 1984), pp. 285– 87; Paola Malanga, ed., *Marco Bellocchio: Catalogo ragionato* (Milan: Edizioni Olivares, 1998), pp. 90–91, 152–57; and Micciché, *Cinema italiano: Gli anni '60 e oltre*, pp. 369–70.

A good collection from film journals is contained in Anita Nicastro, ed., *Marco Bellocchio: Per un cinema d'autore* (Florence: Ferdinando Brancato Editore, 1992), pp. 152–53, 230–40, 313–14, 413–14.

32. None of the classic editions of Tolstoy in English (most notably the Oxford *Tolstoy Centenary Edition*) includes the novella. For an early edition, see Leo Tolstoy, *The Divine and the Human and Other Stories . . .* (Christchurch, U.K.: Free Age, 1900 [?]). (In Italian the text has been in print since 1943.) The standard original is Lëv Nikolaevich Tolstoi, *Bozheskoe i chelovecheskoe*, in vol. 42 of *Polnoe sobranie sochinenii* (Moscow and Leningrad: Khudozhestvennaia Literatura, 1957), pp. 194–227.

33. "Extradiegetic" means outside the narration, unrelated (or at any rate, not directly related) to the events being described.

34. Suddenly, Tchaikovsky's music goes on in the soundtrack, and just as abruptly it goes off with no relation whatever to events—only to moods.

35. On *Saint Michael Had a Rooster*, see Fulvio Accialini and Lucia Coluccelli, *Paolo e Vittorio Taviani* (Florence: La Nuova Italia, 1979), pp. 68–82; Guido Aristarco, *Sotto il segno dello scorpione: Il cinema dei fratelli Taviani* (Messina and Florence: G. D'Anna, 1978), pp. 101–52; repr. as "*San Michele aveva un gallo*," in his *I sussurri e le grida: Dieci letture critiche di film* (Palermo: Sellerio, 1988), pp. 173–206; Pier Marco De Santi, *I film di Paolo e Vittorio Taviani* (Rome: Gremese, 1988), pp. 74–85; Faldini and Fofi, eds., *1970–1984*, pp. 127–30; Riccardo Ferrucci and Patrizia Turini, *Paolo e Vittorio Taviani: La poesia del paesaggio* (Rome: Gremese, 1995), pp. 119–23 (also in

the parallel English ed., *Paolo and Vittorio Taviani: Poetry of the Italian Landscape*); Jean A. Gili, ed., *Paolo et Vittorio Taviani: Entretien au pluriel* (Arles: Institut Lumière/ Editions Actes Sud, 1993), pp. 43–51; Micciché, *Cinema italiano: Gli anni '60 e oltre*, pp. 364–65; Tassone, *Parla il cinema italiano*, vol. 2, pp. 335–37, 350–51, 357–58, 360, 361, 370; and Bruno Torri, ed., *Il cinema dei Taviani* (Rome: Ministero degli Affari Esteri, Direzione Generale Relazioni Culturali, 1989), pp. 29–31 (with a—not very good—English version on pp. 79–82).

36. The original of Roman's, the young man's, objection to Mezhenetskii's political line (end of Tolstoy's chapter 11) is worded as follows: "We are not really enjoying our life. . . . If we are here, we must thank the reaction, and the reaction is a product of [your faction having killed Czar Alexander II on] March 1st [1881]." Ne ochen'-to naslazh-daemsia zhizn'iu . . . A esli sidim zdes' obiazany ètim reaktsii, a reaktsiia—proizvedenie imenno pervogo marta. (Tolstoi, *Polnoe sobranie sochinenii*, vol. 42, p. 222).

37. Friedrich Dürrenmatt's *The Car Breakdown: A Story That Could Still Happen (Die Panne: Eine noch mögliche Geschichte*, 1955) comes in three variants: as short story (in vol. 5 of *Gesammelte Werke in sieben Bänden* [Zürich: Diogenes Verlag, 1988], pp. 267–326); as a radio show or *Hörspiel* (in vol. 16 of *Werkausgabe in dreißig Bänden* [Zürich: Diogenes Verlag, 1980], pp. 9–56); and as a "comedy" (*Werkausgabe*, vol, 16, pp. 57–173).

38. On Scola's *The Most Exciting Evening*, see Ettore Scola, *Il cinema e io*, ed. Antonio Bertini (Rome: Officina Edizioni, 1996), pp. 108–13; Pier Marco De Santi and Rossano Vittori, *I film di Ettore Scola* (Rome: Gremese, 1987), pp. 107–10; and Roberto Ellero, *Ettore Scola* (Florence: La Nuova Italia, 1996), pp. 42–46.

4

Global Trends, Local Crises (1973–82)

One may have been excused for believing, in 1973, that the malaise running through Italian society could scarcely become worse. The future, however, would prove that prediction substantially wrong.

Not that the following years were entirely unable to offer reasons to hope for an evolution of the Italian polity toward a more open society, characterized by a "normal" Western-style democracy. In 1974, the feminist movement staged its first mass demonstrations, and Italians proved to have espoused unexpectedly undogmatic mores by voting, almost exactly 60 percent to 40 percent, to retain legislation allowing divorce. In 1975–76, the last two prewar Fascist dictatorships in Europe—Spain and Portugal—died; the Portuguese colonies in Africa obtained independence; the Vietnam War ended; and the Italian left made substantial gains at the ballot box, staking a credible claim not only to the local governance of a "red belt" in the central part of the peninsula, but also to a stab at running the country at the national level. In 1976, the election of Jimmy Carter as president of the United States seemed to promise a less direct foreign intervention in Italian political equilibria; and a handful of deputies from the Radical Party (supporting civil liberties) were first elected to Parliament. In 1977, the secret services were reorganized on a basis intended to improve their accountability to Parliament; Sandro Pertini, a Socialist who had been jailed with Gramsci under Mussolini, was elected president of the Republic; and, fifteen years after being forced out of a variety show at RAI 1 for political reasons, Dario Fo and Franca Rame were invited back by RAI 2 (the "Socialist" channel) to present a retrospective of their satirical plays.

In 1978, a bill was passed that allowed women, under certain circumstances, to request an abortion in public hospitals, rather than face prison and the life-threatening environment of clandestine surgery. In 1979, the European Monetary System again linked Western European currencies in a two-tiered mechanism, with an eye to reducing their fluctuations with respect to each other. In 1981, a number of referendums failed at the ballot box, including, most prominently, one intended to confine abortion again to an unlawful status; a modicum of democratic alternation was attempted with the appointment—within the usual center-left coalition—of the first non-Christian Democrat premier since 1947, Giovanni Spadolini; and the illegal activities of the Masonic lodge P2, enlisting plot-prone and Mafia-tainted bankers, industrialists, monarchists, military men, politicians, and journalists, were unmasked (the lodge was eventually disbanded). Enrico Berlinguer, the secretary of the Communist Party, explicitly announced—thereby paving the way for unlocking the peculiar Italian political system of democracy without alternation—that for Italian Communists "the lack of democratic life in Eastern Europe" proved that "the forward thrust for renovation" created in 1917 by the October Revolution was "now exhausted." Only a minority in the party criticized this important political step as a break (*uno strappo*) with Communist tradition. Finally, smoother times loomed ahead for the Italian economy, with a European recovery in sight and a weakening of disruptive strikes in the factories.

The general picture, however, remained a sorry one: most of Italy's hopes for progress were crushed during the years 1973–82, with the bleak moments far outweighing the heartening flickers. Inflation rose to unprecedented heights, and by the end of the 1970s reached 20 percent per year, the highest in any industrialized country. The *strategia della tensione* continued unabated, with terror bombings carried out both at random and with a discernible political motive (eight dead in 1974 at the Piazza della Loggia in Brescia during a labor union rally; twelve in the same year on the *Italicus* train between Florence and Bologna; eighty-five dead and many more wounded in 1980 at the Bologna train station). Ultra-left terrorism spread: it culminated in 1978, in the abduction and murder of Aldo Moro, at the time secretary of the Christian Democratic Party; only after the kidnapping, and the subsequent release, of the NATO General James Lee Dozier in 1981–82, did the phenomenon ebb significantly.

Assassinations continued apace: countless hapless citizens, along with politicians, journalists, judges, policemen, and terrorists themselves, were among the victims. The escalation of violence did not spare intellectuals (Pier Paolo Pasolini, bludgeoned to death in 1975), the Catholic hierarchy (Pope John Paul II, shot and wounded in 1981—the conspiracy had been hatched in Turkey and, probably, Bulgaria), diligent civil servants (Giorgio Ambrosoli, murdered in 1979 after steering through receivership an American-based bank owned by the financier Michele Sindona), or, for that matter, bankrupt bankers with one connection too many. (Roberto Calvi, member of the P2 lodge, was found hanged under a London bridge in 1982; Sindona, also a banker with dangerous friends, drank an espresso laced with strychnine in 1986.) In the ongoing frontline struggle against the Mafia, prosecutors, judges, and civil servants were killed for investigating the collusion between organized crime, politics, and the increasingly lucrative narcotics trade. Among the victims were Emanuele Basile and Gaetano Costa in 1980, and Pio La Torre and General Carlo Alberto Dalla Chiesa two years later. A new, more incisive anti-Mafia law did not go into effect until later in 1982.

Meanwhile, political corruption began to be uncovered on a grand scale: the Lockheed scandal in 1976–77, involving the bribing of politicians in exchange for the purchase of aircraft, led to the resignation of President Giovanni Leone (1978). Disasters continued to afflict the peninsula, whether natural (earthquakes in Friuli in 1976 and Campania in 1980), man-made (release into the atmosphere of dioxin, a deadly chemical, at Seveso near Milan in 1976), or unattributed (explosion of a civilian airliner over the island of Ustica in 1980, probably having been caught in cross fire between NATO and Libyan jets). Hopes for a definitive overcoming of a Cold War situation were disappointed, with a veto by the U.S. State Department against bringing "non-democratic" parties (i.e., Communists) into the government (1978), as well as a resurgence of the arms race with the deployment of medium-range nuclear warheads at Comiso (1981). To top it all off, a second global oil crisis came in 1979 as the final blow to the already fatigued structure of a society long out of kilter.

All things considered, the period 1973–82 must count among the darkest times of Italian democracy, not only—and perhaps not even primarily—because great physical danger affected every citizen and resident of the peninsula, but because the pervasive escalation of violence of those times brought in its wake a series of wide-ranging historical complications. To be sure, it was logical and desirable that all democratic parties rally together, as they did, to the defense of the founding values of the imperfect but democratic republic born of the Resistance; but the fact that the left, and the Communists in particular, thereby de facto rushed to prop up a thirty-year-old establishment run by Christian Democrat bigwigs could only add to the disaffection felt by precisely those who were, in the first place, manifesting their rejection of an increasingly necrotic system. Thus, the "national solidarity" against terrorist acts—in the short term, anyway—far from removing the causes of conflict paradoxically made them more acute.

On the one hand, given the experience of the Chilean bloodbath in 1973, as well as the contrary and more uplifting one of the recently successful German *große Koalition* after 1968, a "historical compromise" such as the one proposed by Berlinguer did in fact make the most sense politically. On the other hand, Berlinguer's strategy was predicated upon favorable circumstances including, at a minimum, the availability of Christian Democrats for a genuine democratization of ossified national structures (the army, the police, the press, public banks and enterprises, public TV, cultural institutions), as well as the willingness on the part of NATO allies—in essence, the United States—to accept that Italian Communists (the vast majority anyway) no longer were pro-Soviet. However, neither of these conditions obtained. Since it takes at least two for a political dance, the Italian Communist Party remained suspended, neither left nor center, still spurned by the centrist bourgeoisie but now also abhorred for its reformism by some of the ultra-left "extraparliamentarians." This is not to mention the Socialists, who, under Bettino Craxi's new leadership, saw the Communists as their natural rivals in the contest to seduce the Christian Democrat bride. Even when, switching their strategy from "historical compromise" to "democratic alternative," the Communists withdrew their offer of collaboration with the center-left government (1980), nothing of significance changed on the political scene, because none of the underlying fundamentals had.

Hence the oppressive feeling lingering over the peninsula at the end of the 1970s and in the early 1980s: with stasis dominating politics, hopelessness pervaded cultural life. As one can easily intuit, the polarization of positions around the theme of terrorism led, for all practical purposes, to excluding from debate all issues not susceptible to being oversimplified into a yes-or-no attitude toward police repression (with a "yes" to negotiation with terrorists being construed as a "yes" to terrorism). This quickly stifled the astonishing, and perhaps never since repeated, diversity of cultural and political grassroots initiatives (communities, newspapers, pedagogical and artistic experimentation, alternative lifestyles, and the like) that, following 1968, had until then fermented in the country. That Italian *auteur* cinema, in particular, had to be among the most egregious victims of this state of affairs is a sad statement of the obvious.

Only apparently bucking a trend of political and cultural paralysis, there were two societal phenomena that can be said with certainty to have had a growing impact on Italians in the period after the end of the conflictual 1970s. I am referring, first, to the spread of private TV stations (Silvio Berlusconi, a real-estate developer, turned to the airwaves in 1977; he launched Canale 5 in 1980, purchased Edilio Rusconi's Italia 1 in 1982, and acquired Mondadori's Rete-quattro in 1984); and second, to the fast increasing dependence of Italian youths on addictive illegal drugs (communities for the treatment of addicts began to spring up in the early 1980s; among these the best known was Vincenzo Muccioli's at San Patrignano near Forlì).

On the basis of what, at the beginning of the 1980s, were the fastest-growing segments of the consumer market, it is not difficult to identify the two items that, in replacement of some obsolete Fiat models, in the course of the decade to come would rise to new symbolic status among Italians as a consequence of the leaden years of terrorism: the needle and the remote control.

Despite themes and situations that are often somber or sometimes outright sinister, the 1970s and early 1980s witnessed an enduring vitality of Italian cinema: Italians continued to go to the movies and to expect to be stimulated by the expression of, among others, major societal or moral concerns. Because of this demand, directors able and willing to address their public on this terrain continued to flourish.

Among the most important films of this period are Antonioni's *The Passenger* (*Professione: reporter*, 1974), *The Mystery of Oberwald* (*Il mistero di Oberwald*, 1980), and *Identification of a Woman* (*Identificazione di una donna*, 1982); Bellocchio's *Triumphal March* (*Marcia trionfale*, 1976), *The Seagull* (*Il gabbiano*, 1977), *A Leap into the Void* (*Salto nel vuoto*, 1980), and *The Eyes, the Mouth* (*Gli occhi, la bocca*, 1982); Bernardo Bertolucci's *1900* (*Novecento*, 1976), *The Moon* (*La luna*, 1979), and *The Tragedy of a Ridiculous Man* (*La tragedia di un uomo ridicolo*, 1981); Giuseppe Bertolucci and Roberto Benigni's *Berlinguer, I Love You* (*Berlinguer, ti voglio bene*, 1977); Bolognini's *La grande bourgeoise* (*Fatti di gente perbene*, 1974) and *The Ferramonti Inheritance* (*L'eredità Ferramonti*, 1976); Brusati's *Bread and Chocolate* (*Pane e cioccolata*, 1974); Cavani's *Milarepa* (1974), *The Night Porter* (*Il portiere di notte*, 1974), *Beyond Good and Evil* (*Al di là del bene e del male*, 1977), and *The Skin* (*La pelle*, 1981); Sergio Citti's *Life Is a Beach* (*Casotto*, 1977) and *The Soup* (*Il minestrone*, 1981); Comencini's *Those Strange Occasions* (*Quelle strane occasioni*, 1976), *Ladies and Gentlemen, Goodnight* (*Signore e signori, buonanotte*, 1976), and *The Traffic Jam* (*L'ingorgo*, 1979); Faenza's *Go for It, Italy* (*Forza Italia*, 1978); Fellini's *Amarcord* (1974), *Casanova* (1976), *Orchestra Rehearsal* (*Prova d'orchestra*, 1978), and *City of Women* (*La città delle donne*, 1980); Giorgio Ferrara's *A Simple Heart* (*Un cuore semplice*, 1977); Ferreri's *The Last Woman* (*L'ultima donna*, 1976), *Goodbye Macho* (*Ciao maschio*, 1978), and *Tales of Ordinary Madness* (*Storie di ordinaria follia*, 1981); Giordana's *Curse You, I'll Love You* (*Maledetti vi amerò*, 1980) and *The Fall of the Rebel Angels* (*La caduta degli angeli ribelli*, 1981); Lattuada's *I'll Act as Her Father* (*Le farò da padre*, 1974), *Heart of a Dog* (*Cuore di cane*, 1976), *Stay as You Are* (*Così come sei*, 1978), and *Cicada* (*La cicala*, 1980); Leto's *The Vacation* (*La villeggiatura*, 1973); Lizzani's *Fontamara* (1980); and Monicelli's *We Want the Colonels* (*Vogliamo i colonnelli*, 1973), *My Friends* (*Amici miei*, 1975), *A Very, Very Petty Bourgeois* (*Un borghese piccolo piccolo*, 1977), and *The New Monsters* (*I nuovi mostri*, 1977).

Also important are Montaldo's *Agnese Is Going to Die* (*L'Agnese va a morire*, 1976); Moretti's *Ecce Bombo* (1978); Nichetti's *I Went Splash* (*Ho fatto splash*, 1980); Olmi's *The Tree of Wooden Clogs* (*L'albero degli zoccoli*, 1978); Pasolini's *Arabian Nights* (*Il fiore delle mille e una notte*, 1974) and *Salò* (1975); Petri's *By Hook or by Crook* (*Todo modo*, 1976); Piscicelli's *Immacolata e Concetta* (1980); Dino Risi's *The New Monsters* (*I nuovi mostri*, 1977) and *Dear Dad* (*Caro papà*, 1979); Rosi's *Illustrious Corpses* (*Cadaveri eccellenti*, 1975), *Christ Stopped at Eboli* (*Cristo si è fermato a Eboli*, 1979), and *Three Brothers* (*Tre fratelli*, 1981); Rossellini's *Year One* (*Anno uno*, 1974) and *The Messiah* (*Il Messia*, 1975); Salce's *Fantozzi* (1975); Scandurra's *I Am Mine* (*Io sono mia*, 1977); Scola's *We All Loved Each Other So Much* (*C'eravamo tanto amati*, 1974), *Down and Dirty* (*Brutti, sporchi e cattivi*, 1976), *A Special Day* (*Una giornata particolare*, 1977), *The Terrace* (*La terrazza*, 1980), and *The New World* (*Il mondo nuovo*), a.k.a. *The Night of Varennes* (*La nuit de Var-*

ennes, 1982); Paolo and Vittorio Taviani's *Allons enfants (Allonsanfán)*, 1974), *Padre padrone* (1977), *The Meadow (Il prato*, 1978), and *The Night of the Shooting Stars (La notte di S. Lorenzo*, 1982); Visconti's *Conversation Piece (Gruppo di famiglia in un interno*, 1974) and *The Innocent (L'innocente*, 1976); and Wertmüller's *All Screwed Up (Tutto a posto e niente in ordine*, 1974), *Swept Away (Travolti da un insolito destino*, 1974), and *Seven Beauties (Pasqualino Settebellezze*, 1975).

Having devoted a central chapter of *Masters of Two Arts* to Pasolini's *Salò or the 120 Days of Sodom (Salò o le 120 giornate di Sodoma*, 1975), I will here limit myself to contextualizing the film within the historical coordinates of a time that was of deep distress both for the director personally and for his country as a whole.

Italy was then in a phase of great conflict in the labor market; the specter of a bloody military coup in the style of Chile's recent one paralyzed the political scene; the impact of the first oil crisis had thrown the country into recession; the Red Brigades had begun, as they put it, to "strike at the heart" of the bourgeois state. Pasolini further saw that youths from the traditionally poor working classes, enticed (Pasolini argued "brainwashed") by schooling and television, gave up (Pasolini argued "reneged") on their class identity and began to imitate (Pasolini argued "to ape") the easy, consumerist (Pasolini argued "vacuous, decadent, fascistic") lifestyle previously exclusive to the bourgeoisie. *Salò* thus shows us Italian youths of both sexes who, enslaved by, well, sadistic manipulators, are caused to lose the perceived beautiful innocence of their past. Shorn of eyes, tongues, and other sundry organs, they are forced to gobble up the excrements dished out for them by an industrial society that prides itself on "modernity" (and on largesse toward the arts: a piano player is paid to entertain torturers and captives alike during the appetizing sessions). The parable could not be clearer: in re-creating Sade for his own purposes, Pasolini strenuously objects to the onslaught of a consumerism that, to him, is turning fifty million diverse individuals into a single mass made up of fifty million passive playthings. *Keep the customer stultified* is the commanding principle behind *Salò*'s coprophagy—a principle whose exasperated visualization in the film cries out for the director's point to be understood in all its urgency. Understood it is; but if, and only if, viewers have sufficient familiarity with Pasolini to decipher his allegorical ways for what they are.

A different, yet altogether comparable, kind of exploitative behavior on the part of the powers-that-be is thematized in Lattuada's neo-Bulgakovian *Heart of a Dog (Cuore di cane*, 1976). Suppose the Revolution were to succeed. Even then, Lattuada feels, hardly anything of substance would change, and the world would keep functioning much as it had under the previous oligarchy—as twentieth-century Russians, among others, sadly came to realize.

The twentieth century was anything but stingy in offering Russian writers the circumstances in which to cultivate a grotesque perception of reality. Among such authors, Bulgakov was (with Zoshchenko) perhaps the greatest: a privilege which guaranteed him the ostracism of officialdom during his lifetime, and thus ensured that his fame would become global only about thirty years after his death. *Heart of a Dog* (*Sobach'e serdtse*, 1925) was among many of Bulgakov's works that did not pass muster with Soviet censorship and could long be published only in the West.[1]

The novella describes the clash of two largely parallel neopositivistic delusions: on the one side, that of bourgeois science, which believes itself able to better human life by strictly material improvements; on the other, that of political utopianism, which claims that a successful revolution could change the nature of human beings and lead them from their historically abject state to one of enlightenment.

Professor Preobrazhensky—approximately translated "Transfiguration"—a supercilious aristocratic surgeon from Moscow, attempts to uphold his old-time lifestyle in the first years of Bolshevik rule. A specialist in eugenics, in order to finance his beloved studies he successfully carries out surgical implants aimed at rejuvenating his patients' bodies. (Hardly any ingenuity is needed to guess the rejuvenation of just which organs is most in demand among his decrepit clientele.)

One day, Preobrazhensky picks up a stray dog, Sharik—in Russian, "Little Ball" or "Little Globe"—and replaces one of the dog's glands, the pituitary, in the attempt to turn him into a human. The operation succeeds, in a way: Sharik develops an anthropoid resemblance. Alas, he retains most of his wild instincts. To add insult to injury, he joins the Communist mob, which occupies ever-growing areas of the building previously owned by the professor in its entirety, signing up for the Communist Party and obtaining from it a human identity in exchange—under the name Poligraph Poligraphovich Sharikov.[2]

The being now allegedly metamorphosed into comrade Sharikov misses no chance to prove that, though looking (almost) human, he has retained his original canine heart: he chases cats through the professor's apartment, floods the building for fun, and bites another resident when he runs into her on the stairs. Even worse, from Preobrazhensky's viewpoint, his creature begins to float to the top of the hierarchy among the rabble-rousers, and is instrumental in their occupying parts of the professor's apartment. Theft now becomes routine in the professor's home. To exonerate himself and the friends with whom he displays such an innate affinity, Sharikov callously puts forward the name of Preobrazhensky's young maid, Zina.

"At their wits' end, the professor and his assistant, Bormental, go through a night of dramatic scientific repentance: What was all their effort for? So that one fine day a nice little dog could be transformed into a specimen of so-called humanity so revolting that he makes one's hair stand on end. . . . Will you kindly tell me why one has to [attempt to] manufacture artificial Spinozas when some peasant woman may produce a real one any day of the week? Every year evolution ruthlessly casts aside the mass of dross and creates a few dozen men of genius who become an ornament to the world. . . ."[3]

The assistant suggests dispatching comrade P. P. Sharikov with arsenic, but Preobrazhensky is inclined to see the (however repulsive) human side of the newly acquired Soviet citizen more than the premoral animal one, and accordingly vetoes the criminal idea of getting rid of him chemically. Zina is not consulted—despite suffering an attempted nighttime rape that is averted only by robust intervention by Daria Petrovna, the cook. Poligraph Poligraphovich thus stays on in the apartment, absenting himself only for alcoholic revelry with buddies or for his long, job-related raids with the "Moscow City Sanitation Department responsible for eliminating vagrant quadrupeds (cats, etc.)."[4]

When, in rapid sequence, Preobrazhensky discovers he has been reported to the police for alleged counterrevolutionary activities, and then witnesses Sharikov threaten his assistant with a gun, the professor is finally jolted into corrective action. The two scientists grab the culprit, perform reverse surgery on him, and return him to the untainted innocence of a univocally canine status.

The epilogue of the novella celebrates the apotheosis of logic in a peculiarly absurdist variant: when, accompanied by Sharikov's Bolshevik friends, the criminal police show up at Preobrazhensky's with a search warrant—What happened to the dog you had turned into our comrade?—the professor disconsolately exhibits a Sharik fast regressing to his original state. Atavism, Preobrazhensky explains; science is not omnipotent, he admits ruefully . . . and altogether sincerely. Deprived of all recollection of his brief quasi-human existence, and quite comfortable in his new status as a home darling, Sharik remains as a permanent guest in the apartment.

In Lattuada's *Cuore di cane*, the hungry stray dog Bobi is picked up during a cold Muscovite winter night by Professor Preobrazhensky. Bobi is operated on by the professor and his assistant. Slowly, he loses his animal features and acquires a few semi-human ones—notably, a liking for good food and an inclination for Zina, the professor's maid. The true nature of the conflict between the professor and the Bolsheviks who are gradually occupying the building escapes Bobi, and is downplayed by Lattuada, who instead stresses the professor's cold-bloodedness in his pursuit of scientific investigation.

Now a biped, Bobi keeps dressing in a vulgar style and behaving like an animal around the apartment. He assaults Zina and then jumps onto the Bolshevik bandwagon, registering himself as as Comrade Bobikov. (He espouses, on the occasion, the most rabidly destructive interpretation of Communism.) He obtains a job at the City Sanitation Department as deputy director of the section in charge of catching stray cats. However, even Bolshevik women turn him down as too coarse, and this plunges Bobikov into deep depression.

The disasters caused by Bobikov continue unabated and eventually climax in his planned marriage to Zoia, a young fellow worker to whom he has lied about his true lineage. The professor reveals the truth to a not unreasonably shocked Zoia; then, with Bormental's help, he immobilizes Bobikov and proceeds to reverse the original operation. The Bolshevik prosecutor eventually shows up for an investigation, but Bobi is proudly displayed by Preobrazhensky: "Science is not yet able to transform animals into human beings. I tried, but unsuccessfully, as you can see."

The first Sharik-like protagonist who had crossed Lattuada's path was, almost exactly a quarter of a century before Bulgakov's unruly pet, Gogol's Akaki Akakievich in *Il cappotto*: not a dog but an underdog, not the drafter of denunciatory petitions but the mechanical reproducer of administrative ones. One understands, in these circumstances, why Lattuada could become so involved with Bulgakov's *Sobach'e serdtse*. The film *Cuore di cane* offered a golden opportunity for the director to score a maximum number of narrative points by, on the one hand, exposing callousness (the proletarian dictators' violence, the professor's hubris) and, on the other, sympathizing with innocence—an innocence embodied not only in the dog but also, quite attractively, in the professor's young maid.[5]

Lattuada stated explicitly the fact that he intended to give a "humanitarian" twist to his filmic re-creation of Bulgakov.[6] To mention only one example, he stressed that in the film he turned the scene of Poligraph's lecherous assault upon Zina into something almost gentle, a request for tenderness and protection on Bobi's part. He also pointed out that he introduced a new line for his protagonist to justify his (rebuffed) amorous approaches at a cocktail party: "No one loves me, so why did you create me?" Without a doubt, *Cuore di cane* is part of Lattuada's ongoing crusade for the dignity of the individual against what he calls the "dead end" taken by the technology of contemporaneous mass society.[7]

Yet it is precisely this approach that, however well meant, constitutes a problem. Lattuada is, of course, under no obligation to photocopy Bulgakov's intentions; and I am not about to object to him that Bulgakov's *Sobach'e serdtse* is a grotesque tale about power in which science and politics are united in the joint failure of a project that blows up in the faces of those who concocted it, while *Cuore di cane* amounts to a tear-wrenching apology for the eternal "poor dog." I am not about to, because I believe that recasting literature as deemed appropriate is the very essence of what filmic re-creation is all about. My doubts are of a different nature; they are related to the extent to which Lattuada achieves the goal he has set for himself.

In his comments, Lattuada does not mention the counterpart to the professor, the revolutionary party. Yet in the novella it is clear that, unlike Lattuada's Bobi, Sharik is saddled with a double failure: that of the scientists *and* that of the politicians. In other words, in Bulgakov's plot Sharik is not only the victim of mindless scientific ambition, but also a zealous accomplice in the collapse of the pseudoscientific revolutionary myth about human perfectibility. While, as Lattuada correctly sees, the *Homo scientificus* hits here a dead end, the *Homo sovieticus* fails no less resoundingly; and this, for the obvious (to Bulgakov) reason that no amount of whining about the exploited status of the masses will ever uplift them, *so long as they conceive themselves as mass and behave accordingly*. For Lattuada, the dog is a victim; for Bulgakov, "he" is a conniving and obtuse opportunist. Lattuada argues: "Like all little creatures, the little creature must be loved." Bulgakov retorts: "And be put in charge, for example, of running the anti-cat police?"

Because Lattuada tries to weave elements that are purely Bulgakovian (grotesque) into his own (humanitarian) story, his Bobi inevitably zigzags between repulsiveness and humanity in a way that is ultimately self-contradictory and can leave the spectator rather dry-eyed over the animal's predicament. With the admittedly facile wisdom of hindsight, it seems to me that the undistinguished reception enjoyed by *Cuore di cane* in 1976, which so wounded Lattuada, could largely be explained by the jarring impression conveyed by the juxtaposition of two narratives that simply do not function in the same way. That is indeed a pity, because *Cuore di cane* remains an important film—a film betraying a deep pessimism about hopes for social regeneration of any kind and, to that extent, an incursion into theriomorphic behavior eerily parallel to Pasolini's *Salò*.[8]

A no less painful sort of mourning pervades the next three items I am about to examine: Bellocchio's *The Seagull* (*Il gabbiano*, 1977), Ferrara's *A Simple Heart*, and the Taviani brothers' *The Meadow*.

Il gabbiano re-creates Chekhov's play by the same title, *The Seagull* (*Chaika*, 1896).[9]

Russian countryside, late nineteenth century. Konstantin and Nina are two young intellectuals, attracted by the glamor of cultural life in the capital: the melancholy Konstantin hopes to attain glory as a playwright, the meek Nina dreams of becoming a famous actress. Konstantin, who loves Nina, puts on a play, heavy with mystic-telluric effusions, in which Nina has the lead role. Falling on deaf provincial ears, however, the show flops.

The estate is visited by Irina, an egotistical theater star from the city who, very much on the side, is also Konstantin's mother. She is accompanied, among others in her entourage, by her former lover Trigorin, an aging fashionable writer sporting his self-importance and self-serving cynicism. Overnight, and without warning, Nina runs off to Moscow with Trigorin, who seduces and then abandons her.

Times goes by; drenched in postdelusionary dejection, Nina returns to her provincial abode. There, despite her painful experience of life—or precisely because of it—she once more rejects Konstantin's advances. Konstantin commits suicide.

Chekhov's drama lives on in Bellocchio's film with a minimum of adjustments: despite undergoing extensive microsurgery, the dialogue remains functionally identical to that of the original; the costumes and setting are typical of the late nineteenth century; the natural backdrop changes from the Russian countryside with a lake to the Italian countryside with a river (near Treviso); settings are moved by a few meters at most (from indoors to outdoors). What more do we need to dismiss the entire enterprise with that often-heard derogatory epithet, "filmed theater"?

Such reasoning, however, would be short-sighted. Let us look more closely. *Chaika* revolves around a generational conflict between up-and-coming, rebellious intellectuals, such as Konstantin, and their older, comfortably established predecessors, the likes of Trigorin. The banner of the former is intellectual inquisitiveness—indeed, restlessness; that of the latter, a smug relativism in all matters, moral no less than artistic. Konstantin and Trigorin joust for success both in the professional field and in the amorous one; they compete for Nina's love. Or do they really? There is such a disproportion between the obscurity of the young provincial and the fame, if not necessarily the talent, of the great man that the outcome of the conflict is, from the beginning, a foregone conclusion.

And therein lies the interest of this Chekhov film, *insofar as it is precisely Bellocchio who makes it*. Who of the two, the insecure Young Rebel or the satiated Famous Jerk, will Bellocchio identify with? That same Bellocchio who, in the span of little more than ten years, had given Italian cinema perhaps the longest list of politically subversive masterpieces created by one director—*Fists in the Pocket, China Is Nearby, In the Name of the Father, All or None—Fit to Untie (Nessuno o tutti—Matti da slegare*, 1975), and, just one year before *Il gabbiano, Triumphal March*? Whether he liked it or not, by 1977 Bellocchio was an established master in his own right. Can one logically profess oneself an authoritative "teacher of rebelliousness"?

Hence the ambivalence of Bellocchio's feelings:

I found in this text an autobiographic resonance. Konstantin is the young man who hopes to change reality by means of his poetry, and kills himself when he realizes that this is an impossible operation. Trigorin, on the other hand, is a successful writer who resolves by compromise the contradictions of his existential choices. These are the two sides of each one of us; and they coexist today in a dramatic manner in the intellectual who was shaped by the experience of 1968. On the basis of things I did, both successful and unsuccessful, I can recognize myself in either character. I instinctively sympathize with Konstantin, but I disagree with his final choice [to commit suicide]. Even though the reality in which we live is repulsive, we must carry on fighting and attempt to influence it.[10]

Bellocchio's re-creation of Chekhov is a balancing act, a challenge engrossing to today's viewers not only for how it is taken up but also for the very fact that it is taken up at all.

At the same time, we can, in retrospect, see clearly what the public of the 1970s could not yet discern: that *Il gabbiano* represented an irrevocable turning point in Bellocchio's filmography. All his preceding films were sharply political works, critical of the irrational societal anarchy that goes under the name of established order; in one guise or another, all those subsequent to it instead focus on exploring the labile border area between individual sanity and individual folly—similar, in this, to *All or None—Fit to Untie* but, crucially, without the emphasis on social denunciation which molded that film. *Il gabbiano* turns out, in historical perspective, to have been a pivotal point between the two groups.

Am I implying that, by 1977, Bellocchio had retreated into a position of "internal exile" in the face of the political reflux then affecting Italian society as a whole? I am not implying that; I am arguing so openly—not as a form of personal criticism, but in wistfulness at the thought of the many roads that could not be taken by Italian intellectuals and artists during the years of armed conflict between the First Republic and political terrorists. Over twenty years later, Italian cinema is, in almost every way, still the poorer for it.[11]

The same year as Bellocchio's *The Seagull*, a very similar mood of disillusionment pervaded an Italian film re-created from a work of literature also spiritually similar to Chekhov's drama: Giorgio Ferrara's *A Simple Heart* (*Un cuore semplice*, 1977), molded on Flaubert's novella of the same title (*Un coeur simple*, 1877).[12] *Un coeur simple* was part of *Three Tales* (*Trois contes*, 1877), the last work published by Flaubert during his lifetime, and was certainly the one most thoroughly steeped in the melancholy atmosphere that in those years lingered on the writer in his self-imposed solitude at Croisset, his financially troubled family around him, and on France as a whole after the tragedies of the Franco-Prussian War and the Parisian Commune in 1870–71.

It is the early 1800s. Felicita is a young peasant whose father, a mason, has died in an accident on the job. To support herself, the orphan goes to a large farm and works there as a maid. There she has a love affair—a *simple* one, that is—with a lad from the same social class as she. Things do, however, take an unexpectedly complicated turn for Felicita when, to dodge the draft, the young man marries a wealthy old woman and vanishes from sight. Felicita experiences immense grief but must, once more, move on.

Having been hired by a rich widow, Mme. Obin, Felicita becomes attached to her employer's two children, Paolo and Virginia. However, the former leaves for the city, and the latter dies of an illness; Felicita is deeply affected. Later, the only relative she loves, a young nephew who has enlisted as a sailor, dies in Cuba.

Uneventful years then roll by, marked only by small incidents in the village or religious festivals, which the pious Felicita scrupulously attends.

In Mme. Obin's empty house, Felicita finds her only soul mate in Lulu, a parrot given to her as a gift. Eventually, though, the parrot dies. To lessen her sadness, Felicita has it stuffed. When Mme. Obin passes away, Paolo, married to a woman who has no taste for the lifestyle of the countryside, comes back to the village to put the estate up for sale. Since there are no takers, Felicita can continue to occupy her small room on the premises. From then on, she lives in and of her recollections—until she dies in late springtime, on the day of the feast of Corpus Christi, during the religious procession.

Ferrara follows Flaubert's plot closely, and in the end produces a diligent visualization of the writer's discourse—a complex discourse that includes ironic detachment (Félicité is a naïve peasant woman almost literally able to mistake her parrot for an incarnation of the Holy Ghost) as well as sympathy, admiration, and possibly even a touch of envy. (Félicité is endowed with an unequaled ability to endure the trials of life courageously and peacefully.) Of course, given that the whole point of this film of reflux *is* to depict anew the loss of illusions and ambitions, one could certainly argue for the cogency of an artistic logic that specifically gives up on any attempt to re-create a Flaubert redivivus as great as the nineteenth-century one. Resignation is admittedly one of the virtues that seem more persuasive when practiced humbly, rather than flamboyantly.

Two statistical curiosities. First, the film was Ferrara's first work and received important awards in Italy when it appeared, although later on, the director hardly followed through. Second, at the opposite spectrum of both historical impact and age, the script was one of the latest contributions to cinema made by Cesare Zavattini, seventy-five years old at the time.[13]

As for the Tavianis' *The Meadow* (*Il prato*, 1978), the film consists of an intriguing mix of contemporaneous and archaic subject matter. The essential narrative structure of the story is a ménage à trois as old as that of Tristan, Iseult, and King Mark, or, if one will, that of Werther, Lotte, and Albert—in the Tavianis, respectively Giovanni, Eugenia, and Enzo. Goethe is in fact the tightest fit for the film, not least because in *The Meadow* the denouement of the story is brought about, just as in *The Sorrows of Young Werther* (*Die Leiden des jungen Werthers*, 1774), by the suicide of the younger of the two men.

Giovanni, who holds a law degree but whose dream is to be a film director, has just been appointed junior judge in Milan. Which of the two paths to choose? His father suggests that he take the time to think about his options and meanwhile go to San Gimignano, near Siena, where the family needs legal advice for a land sale. In San Gimignano, Giovanni falls in love with Eugenia. The young woman works at the Internal Revenue office in nearby Florence but spends most of her time in San Gimignano, where she organizes grassroots theater shows and utopian-style pastimes for children. Giovanni's next problem is that in San Gimignano he also meets Enzo, Eugenia's boyfriend. Enzo hopes to be able to work as an agronomist in a rural commune he and friends are planning to establish in the area by occupying fallow land.

For a short while, the platonic ménage à trois holds, but it eventually becomes too painful to endure. Giovanni returns to Milan—and thus will serve the bourgeois state—so as to remove himself from the source of his sorrows.

Time goes by. Eugenia and Enzo have had an inevitable brush with the law, which disapproves of squatting on someone else's property, and have decided to remove themselves to a nonextraditing country in Africa while they wait for the dust to settle. Advised at the last moment, Giovanni can only see the train on which his friends are traveling flash through the Tuscan countryside as they leave.

On the occasion, Eugenia's dog, which the young woman has left behind, accidentally bites Giovanni. The dog has rabies. Giovanni, who becomes infected, allows himself to die of it. Giovanni's father, deeply grieved by his son's death, cries out in distress that he refuses to accept his fate.

As we can see, the distribution of the three cinematic co-protagonists' roles is one of an absolute, almost archetypal simplicity; also, as is often the case with the Tavianis, Tuscans to a fault, *The Meadow* is set against a suprahistorical rural backdrop from their region. In San Gimignano, Giovanni's religious sense of Nature has a labile correlation with the actual time frame in which he lives.

And yet in the film there is plenty of topical material. *The Meadow* materializes myth by linking the story of Giovanni, Eugenia, and Enzo to a series of burning issues from the 1970s: Giovanni's uneasy rapport with an almost excessively antidogmatic father; the impact of the women's liberation movement; an open approach to couple relationships, with a view to the ultimate abolition thereof; the quest for alternative professions (for example, in education or theater); the faith in an agrarian, indeed bucolic, Utopia; the occupation of abandoned lands as a demonstrative political act; the perception of employment in the magistrature as a sellout to an unredeemably pro-establishment mechanism (in 1978, the Clean Hands investigations of the mid-1990s were still some fifteen light-years away); and, to top it all off, the portrayal of an invasive police state that quashes as criminal any manifestation, however qualified, of receptivity to anti-capitalistic arguments.

The result of the interaction between the different components of *The Meadow* is a rich and original hybridization of the political and the mythical, successful as perhaps no other work of Italian cinema or literature had been since Pavese's *The Moon and the Bonfires* (*La luna e i falò*, 1950). The manner of Giovanni's suicide is, to mention but one important element in the film, a splendid emblem of just such hybridization: in lieu of the modern pistols chosen by Werther, Giovanni is allowed to opt for a bite by Eugenia's dog, itself infected by one of the foxes haunting the three friends' favorite meadow.

Goethe's presence in the spiritual background of the film is made perceptible by the directors in the film's diegetic structure, the fundamental characterization of its protagonists, and a diffuse sense of awe toward a comforting, but also lethal, Nature. On at least one occasion, however, a crucial Wertherian locus literally tears through the fabric of the Tavianis' text and shows the ultimate source for the directors' meditation on their time and country in full light.

In Eugenia's apartment in central San Gimignano, the three friends (as Werther and Albert do in Goethe) casually examine some firearms. Shortly thereafter, they are sitting at a café in the Piazza della Cisterna, where they— Eugenia in the middle, directly facing us, with Enzo and Giovanni on either side of her—vigorously debate the subject of suicide. Eugenia says, "I am against suicide; I know that I would never kill myself . . . if nothing else, to avoid the gossip against which Maiakovskii warned." (Pavese would have been another possible reference in this connection.) Enzo states, "Today, suicide seems to me more a sign of folly than one of cowardice." Giovanni retorts, "How can you say that suicide is folly? It would be the same as saying of an agonizing man: Look, that madman is letting himself die of fever! In my opinion, human nature has its boundaries [*i suoi confini*]; it can withstand joy and suffering only to a finite degree, but not beyond that."

A comparison of the dialogue among the young people of 1978 can be made with the content and, indeed, the wording of that among their peers of 1774 (Part One, letter of August 12):

"For shame!" said Albert, pulling the pistol down, "what are you doing? . . . I can't imagine how a person can be so silly as to shoot himself; the mere thought of it repels me."

"O that you people," [Werther] burst out, "when you mention something, have to say: that is silly, that is wise, that is good, that is bad! And what does it all mean? Has it made you explore the conditions underlying an action? Are you able to unfold with precision the reasons why it happened, why it had to happen? If you had, you wouldn't be so ready with your judgments."

[Albert]. "Suicide . . . can certainly not be regarded as anything but a weakness. For it is admittedly easier to die than to endure with steadfastness a life of torment." . . .

"*Human nature* [Werther replied] *has its bounds; it can endure joy, sorrow, pain, up to a certain degree, and it perishes as soon as that degree is exceeded.* In this case it is then not a question of whether a man is weak or strong, but whether he can outlast the measure of his suffering—be it spiritual or physical; and *I find it just as strange to say that the man who takes his life is a coward, as it would be improper to call a man cowardly who dies of a malignant fever.*"[14]

While these few words may well be a dead giveaway for those who happen to have the text of *Werther* at their fingertips, for all other viewers it remains an example of the Tavianis' unobtrusive, almost shy, recourse to their great predecessor.

The Meadow did not have a good press when it was released.[15] It seems unlikely that the critics took offense at the—fairly obvious—symbolic equivalence in the film between Italy and the "sick" meadow where the three friends like to congregate. Rather, the most probable hypothesis is that the artists surprised everyone by producing something new and unexpected. After the engagé filmmaking of the preceding decade, culminating in the Cannes Golden Palm for *Padre padrone* (1977), *The Meadow* struck commentators as a retreat into sentimental inwardness; and the *Werther* connection was thus mentioned by them, if at all, only as an embarrassment.

One can certainly regret one's country involution into political apathy; but that historical development occurred through no fault of the Tavianis. It is thus absurd to deprecate their attendant shift from politically committed cinema to one with a more internal narrative focus. In 1978, Goethe's *Werther* was not a liability from which to hide, but a relevant cultural-historical point of reference to be faced squarely. In *The Meadow*, the Tavianis took up this challenge with great poetic power, and a lucidity that went undeservedly unnoticed at the time.[16]

The late 1970s echoed with thoroughly justified cries: What will happen if the world runs out of oil? If it runs out of wood, water, fish, breathable air? What if, creaking under the weight of untold billions of humans, it runs out of food? What if we run out of space for ourselves? In the wake of the second oil shock of 1979, these were issues so empirically present in Italy that it didn't take an MIT researcher to be aware of them—though two justly famous reports published by MIT at the time—*I limiti dello sviluppo* (*The Limits of Develop-ment*) and *I limiti dello sviluppo: Verso un equilibrio globale* (*The Limits of Development: Toward a Global Equilibrium*)—did quantitatively bear out the anecdotal impression.[17] For a car-frenzied country such as Italy, the most mo-mentous way of putting the question was one that had both a symbolic and an entirely realistic component to it: What if we run out of roads to drive on?

The dramatic turnaround experienced by Italian society in less than two decades can nowhere better be measured than in the polar opposition that sep-arates Comencini's *The Traffic Jam* (*L'ingorgo*, 1979) from Dino Risi's *Over-taking* (1962). In the first place, *Overtaking* depicts movement and exuberance in the physical enthusiasm with which Bruno, a good-looking good-for-nothing at the wheel of a shiny convertible Lancia sports car, and his hapless acolyte, the student Roberto, flash along the Aurelia highway, heading north to Civita-vecchia and the beaches. Second, it doubles that excitement by a no less real sense of liberation from the economic, physical, and moral shackles of a past that is so recent one can still catch glimpses of it along the road (where the local bumpkins, the *villici*, goofily attempt to dance the "twist"). Predictably, Bruno's long string of hair-raising *sorpassi* (overtakings, passings), intercut with almost as many picaresque tricks played by him on people on either side of the one-time imperial road, ends in tragedy—but only for the timid Roberto. The shy one of the two dies; the brazen one survives unscathed, ready to head for the nearest Lancia dealer in town. *Overtaking* belongs to a cultural moment in which life can always bounce back; death is no more than an unfortunate in-cident likely to hit *i fessi* (those who aren't smart enough to duck), and can thus be resorbed as but one of the many causes for sorrow within a tentacular, trans-personal will to live.[18]

Nothing of the sort in *The Traffic Jam*, which is also set in the immediate present: a present in which Italians have immoderately gorged themselves on cars for at least twenty years. (It is truly a pity that the English language does not allow the translation to preserve the "gorging" etymological overtones of the original title). Comencini's protagonist appropriately changes from a single, greater-than-life captivating scoundrel—the hero blessed by the rascal's charm (*le charme de la canaille*, as the French so perceptively put it)—to a mosaic of many moral dwarfs or monsters. The ideological dimension of Italian self-portrayal—of Italian characters as represented by Italian filmmakers for the Ital-ian public—here takes a twist perfectly corresponding to the gut-racking motions experienced at this time by the nation's polity.

For miles on end, cars are paralyzed on an *autostrada* outside Rome; the scene breaks up into a myriad flash points (between vehicles, within each vehicle). A cascade of gags develops: a nasty industrialist tries to push people around; husband and wife start bick-ering over misplaced keys; a flurry of easily satisfied young soccer fans celebrate Italy's victory in a game; a famous actor finds shelter from the crush and the heat in a shabby house by the freeway—one, it turns out, illegally built by a squatter. Thus, at first, the viewers laugh. But laughter quickly turns cold in *The Traffic Jam*: this is a demonic laughter, one that only Gogol's pen would be able to re-create adequately.

As, in a downward spiral, the film depicts verbal aggression, rape and other kinds of physical violence, sordid motivations, hypocritical self-complacency, and plain theft (a delivery truck loaded with food is looted), it becomes clear that what we are witnessing is an explicit portrayal of the unraveling of a society in which all ties have broken. And no one can go anywhere, locked forever in an unbearable cohabitation.

Human nature? Perhaps. But one need not look that far, when Italy and the late 1970s are so much closer at hand. To be sure, terrorism and other equivalent features are not portrayed by Comencini in a directly representational way; but in the director's time and place it would have been virtually unthinkable to do so. It is a figurative portrayal of the Italian 1970s, not a mimetic one, that we find in *The Traffic Jam*. Ideas, too, can go clandestine.

In this respect, it strikes as brilliant that the packages ransacked from the delivery truck by heretofore dignified car owners turn out, when opened, to contain homogenized baby food—on which the entire mob feeds without the shadow of a moral scruple. In 1975, symbolic consumers were forced to eat feces in Pasolini's *Salò*; in 1979, their consuming stolen baby food in *The Traffic Jam* seems a no less effective rephrasing of an equivalent concept. Insofar as it is *baby* food they eat, they are figuratively transformed into children, and thus reveal the infantile aspect of their social behavior; insofar as that food is *homogenized*, they show they have lost the real-life individuality they had in pre-motorized times; and insofar as they eat *stolen* food they lay bare the dramatic plunge in moral standards that has come with the spread of a consumerist society in which everything has a price, but nothing has a value. "Superfluous goods make life superfluous," Pasolini had poignantly written shortly before being murdered.

What is the solution? There is no solution. Despite recurrent rumors that the *ingorgo* will soon be removed, nothing happens: jammed the would-be drivers are, and jammed they remain. A sign from heaven seems, in the end, to bring the long-awaited release when a voice announces from a helicopter: "Start up your engines . . . you're going." Engines are thereupon started and revved up. But in fact, no release comes, and no one goes anywhere.[19]

And thus, with an ever-desired progress that never occurs, the film ends—just as does Beckett's famous *Waiting for Godot*:

Vladimir: "Well? Shall we go?"

Estragon: "Yes, let's go."

They do not move.

Curtain[20]

I have just alluded to the difficulty of undertaking a representational depiction of terrorism in the cinema—and, by extension, in the literature—of the 1970s and 1980s in Italy. Indeed, to this day the subterranean world of Italian political terrorism has not found its Dostoyevsky. Many causes have been put forward for this failure, and I will now attempt to elaborate further on it under the following five headings, which are of unequal weight but all of which have effectively conspired to produce a noticeable gap in late twentieth-century Italian cinema.

First, unlike the abrupt end of a war, the exhaustion of the phenomenon of political terrorism in Italy occurred over a long time, the early years of the 1980s. The fact that there was a slow, rather than a clear-cut, exit from a period of national anguish prevented a sudden outburst of artistic reelaboration even remotely comparable to that of post–World War II films.

Second—again reaching back to 1945 for a contrastive evaluation—celebrating the defeat of an obvious and seemingly all-powerful enemy was an eminently "narratable" event, whereas exploring the implications of a hidden scourge presents problems in the comprehension of many basic data about the very phenomenon to be probed.

Third, in the 1980s the victors in the struggle, the forces of democracy, were no longer culturally allied with an intellectual thrust toward the memory, cultivation, and continuation of an upright past, but stood for a democracy thoroughly infiltrated by the postindustrial, market-oriented ideals best exemplified by the TV commercial. Hard-won victories will, by definition, be celebrated only by those who attach great value to lessons to be learned, not by those who are uninterested in any learning process whatever. Thus it was that the celebrative process practiced by the media after the defeat of terrorism took a path that dispensed with a realistic representation of the struggle undergone. Why bother showing the blood, sweat, and tears of the past, when the whole point of fighting was to cater to the opium-munching consumers of the present?

Fourth, the sheer complexity of the phenomenon was daunting; no one could hope to make a serious film about terrorism without devoting very substantial attention to its root causes in society—and also, at the opposite end, to its far-reaching real consequences on the everyday life of millions of Italians. Accordingly, two opposite dangers would loom large for the truly thorough film director: on the one hand, that of shooting a historical documentary; on the other hand, that of producing little more than a modified thriller with weird cops (what are the roadblocks for?) chasing nutsy robbers (where is the money they are supposed to be after?). Convincingly hitting the middle ground—the psychological terrain of individual motivation, which dialectically mediates between the necessity of the historical context and the chance occurrences of daily existence—was by any standard a tall order.

Fifth, and finally, Italian producers seem to have shared a prejudice widely held in the Italian society of the time. Implicitly accepting the well-known adage that "to understand all is to forgive all," they acted as though undertaking a serious analysis of the causes behind terrorism would have meant taking up its defense. Any objective discussion of Italian political terrorism was demonized to the point of making it incomprehensible—and that is where the cinematic issue has, by and large, remained to this day.[21]

Rosi's *Three Brothers* (*Tre fratelli*, 1981) constitutes an early attempt to do all that is possible to elucidate the main aspects of the problem. The film displays a courage and a psychological depth that confirm the talent of the author of landmark works in the cinema of civic engagement such as *Salvatore Giuliano, Hands over the City, Just Another War, The Mattei Affair, Lucky Luciano,* and *Illustrious Corpses.*

None of Rosi's title brothers is a terrorist: Raffaele, the eldest, is a judge in Rome; Nicola, the middle one, works for Fiat in Turin; Rocco, the youngest, is a social worker in drug-racked Naples. Yet, when they join their father in their native village in Apulia on the sad occasion of their mother's death, each of them brings with him a sufficiently large splinter of Italy's societal mirror for the viewer to be able to reconstruct and contextualize what not they, but someone else rooted in the same polity, has chosen to do: reject a career in the judiciary, turn down a job at Fiat's assembly line, say no to drugs on a matter of principle—and take to violence instead.

At the same time, the beauty of the Apulian village, the warmth of the feelings nourished by the four men for one another despite their differences, the touching aura of nostalgia induced by the ongoing funerary wake, and the uplifting succession between older and younger generations (the grandfather, Donato, has a particularly close relationship to Marta, Nicola's daughter) ensure that the film is not just the illustration, however meritorious, of a painful juncture in Italian history, but also a model poetic performance in its own right.

Millicent Marcus has highlighted the interdependence between Rosi's film and its source of inspiration, Andrei Platonov's novella *The Third Son* (*Tretii syn,* 1936), in a detailed critical contribution to which I refer readers for a full appreciation of the degree to which Rosi and Tonino Guerra drew upon the Soviet writer.[22] Suffice it to add that as the six brothers of Platonov's original are halved in number, they become proportionally more individualized, acquiring a level of articulation that was denied to their counterparts from the newly born Soviet state. As a consequence, an all-important shift in emphasis occurs in the transition from literature to cinema. In the Russian original, the $5+1$ structure (five vociferous, jolly, world-shaking brothers, one quiet and sensitive one) reproduces a pattern typical of the folktale, and thus tends to encode on an epic-mythical level the passing away of the old Russia and the coming of age of a younger, modern one. By contrast, in the Italian cinematic re-creation of the story, the focus shifts to a rational consideration of fully developed persons, also symbolically involved in the transition from an archaic society to a new one, but certainly very far from partaking in any mystical tellurism.

Almost fifty years after Platonov's early collections of stories, in Rosi's *Three Brothers* the earth is no longer crisscrossed by giants, but by drug dealers and terrorists. It is no longer the time for superhuman material efforts, but for intrahuman analysis. As is his wont, in *Three Brothers* Rosi offers us not a self-celebratory appeal to enthusiasm, but a poetic stimulus to thought.[23]

As a film partially parallel to *Three Brothers*, at least as far as terrorism is concerned, one should also mention Amelio's *Strike at the Heart (Colpire al cuore*, 1982). In *Cahiers du cinéma*, Olivier Assayas renders the plot of the film (a plot "of extreme simplicity") as follows:

Almost by chance, an adolescent discovers that his father may have contacts with terrorists from the Red Brigades. The man is a university professor. Two of his students, husband and wife, participate in a bombing; he is killed, while she manages to escape. The professor remains in touch with the young woman, who is forced to take up a life of clandestineness. Eventually, the son reports the two quasi accomplices, who are arrested.

Having stated in the most unambiguous terms that in his opinion the true subject of *Strike at the Heart* is "the encounter of a son with his father," Assayas concludes by praising the film's "great force . . . and daring" for "taking up a theme—the political one—that made the fortunes of Italian cinema, and then casting it aside with contempt as a banal fact, as a secondary fact with respect to an intimate theme, which by contrast it posits as fundamental."[24]

Strike at the Heart qualifies for inclusion in the present book because in the film the father, a university professor of French literature, quotes lines from the romantic poet Gérard de Nerval. These lines can with little effort be identified as the first stanza of "Byron's Thought" ("La pensée de Byron") in *Little Bohemian Castles (Petits châteaux de Bohême [sic]*, 1852–53). Their content could be rendered in English as follows:

> By my love and my constancy
> I had hoped to sway your severity,
> And the breath of Hope
> Had penetrated my heart;
> But Time, which I prolong in vain,
> Revealed the truth to me.
> Hope has vanished like a dream,
> And I am left alone with my love![25]

One cannot but agree with the professor when, during his lecture, he states that Gérard was "a madman of genius" ("un pazzo geniale"); however, with all due respect for both the poet's greatness and his folly, one would be hard put to perceive him as either on the basis of the evidence supplied by Amelio's scholar. There is incomparably more madness, and the attendant amount of genius, in any of Gérard's *Chimères* poems (which prefigured and, some could argue, even outdid the best poetry by the Symbolists), or in the visionary prose of *Sylvie* and *Aurélia*, than in the flat lines just quoted. What is in "Byron's Thought" that any melancholy Béranger couldn't have written? Fine choice of a poet on

Amelio's part; yet anyone who knows the slightest bit about Nerval cannot help being puzzled by the insignificance of the actual poetic specimen chosen to show us Gérard in action. Unless, of course, mediocrity *is* the point here—and all the film is trying to show in action is *the father's* mediocrity in his choices as a professor. There would be some logic to this: the scholar's malpractice could be argued to be but one more example of fathers (if at all existent) cutting a sorry figure in Amelio's films.[26]

A subchapter in its own right could well now, in closing chapter 4, be devoted to the relationship between French culture and Scola, perhaps the most Francophile of Italian filmmakers. His pertinent films in the decade under scrutiny are *The Terrace* (1980), *The Night of Varennes* (1982), and *The Voyage of Captain Fracassa* (1990). For reasons that will become obvious in the course of my discussion, I will here position *Fracassa* between the other two.

If one were to compress into one paragraph the traits that lend continuity and homogeneity to Scola's diverse inspiration throughout a long career, one could perhaps articulate a micro-profile somewhat like the following. Scola is a Southerner and a Marxist who, since his youth, harbored a passionate love for France. Particularly beginning in the 1970s, as a mature *auteur*—his films most frequently seen in North America are perhaps *We All Loved Each Other So Much, A Special Day, Le bal* (1983), and *The Family* (1987)—Scola can be said to have consistently shown an interest in stories that could cinematically capture the particular rumblings running through Italian society at each given moment and in each given phase of its historical development. Throughout these years, France has ever acted as a cultural lighthouse for Scola, who time and again worked with important French actors in lead roles, drew inspiration from French subject matter for his films, and made films in France.[27]

Scola's *The Terrace (La terrazza,* 1980) and *The Voyage of Captain Fracassa* both re-create Gautier's well-known novel, of which the director was fond since his youth. Accordingly, I will begin with Gautier.

In 1863, when *Captain Fracassa (Le Capitaine Fracasse)* appeared in print, the author—a longtime journalist, writer, and poet of *l'art pour l'art*, hailed as "master" *(maître)* in no lesser a work than Baudelaire's *Fleurs du mal*—prefaced his cloak-and-dagger adventure novel by a few pages that, as though written on an Ash Wednesday, look back nostalgically to the days of the Romantic carnival of 1830, when all revolutions, aesthetic and political, seemed possible (and, indeed, proved to be). The book he was releasing that day, Gautier wrote, was really thirty years overdue; he was finally prompted to write it out of the shame he felt in having betrayed for so long the visions and memories from his youth. He continues:

During this long labor, I have to the extent of my ability divorced myself from today's milieu, and I have lived retrospectively, transporting myself back to the time around 1830, the beautiful days of Romanticism. Despite the date it bears and its recent execution, this book does not really belong to our time. Just as architects do when, in completing an old plan, they conform to a pre-established style, I, too, have written *Captain Fracassa* in the taste that prevailed at the moment when it should have been published.

One will find no political, moral or religious thesis in it. . . . It is a purely picturesque work. . . . Although the action takes place under Louis XIII, the only historical trait of *Captain Fracassa* is the color of its style.[28]

Not only is nostalgia the defining trait of the book in Gautier's eyes; it is also the implicit force that propels the most interesting character in its plot, the bone-thin Matamore—the knight fearless and pure in heart, but faithfully accompanied by hunger, who on stage and off yearns for the reestablishment of the golden age when glorious chivalric ideals unfailingly triumphed in the end. To be sure, Gautier's lengthy book carries on for hundreds of pages even after, one third into the events, Matamore meets his fate out of sheer physical exhaustion. Matamore's mission is passed on to the younger and plumper Sigognac, who is destined to hold high the torch of spiritual nobility in fulfillment of his own unfolding novel of education.

Appearances notwithstanding, it is only partially true that *Captain Fracassa* articulates "no political, moral or religious thesis," and that it is "a purely picturesque work"; it strikes one as entirely political that Matamore's *l'art pour l'art* should take on a half visionary, half puritanical streak precisely in the years of the Second Empire. That was just the time when François Guizot's old slogan from the 1830s, "Make yourselves rich!" (*Enrichissez-vous!*), was hastily transformed by the entrepreneurial class into a more specific call to make itself rich by connections with the railway lobbies, the banking capital, and the militarist circles that surrounded political power at Napoleon III's court.

Eight years after *The Most Exciting Evening in My Life* and six after *We All Loved Each Other So Much*, Scola again undertook an ambitious critical portrait of Italian postwar society. *The Terrace* centers on the political reflux of the late 1970s and the connected psychological (as well as biographically real) aging of the Italian intelligentsiia.

A group of well-heeled middle-aged acquaintances meet for a dinner party on the terrace of a luxurious penthouse in Rome; the film intercuts their life stories, and their present woes, with scenes of only apparent merriment at the soirée.

Amedeo is a vulgar, money-minded film producer; Enrico is a famous scriptwriter who can no longer get the public to laugh at his quips; Luigi is the director of an important political daily who tries to take up again with his unexpectedly successful former fiancée; Mario is a Communist politician who, involved in a relationship with a woman much younger than himself, lacks the courage to steer the course of passion; and Sergio (Dr. Sergio Stiller), a promising literary author in his youth, is now a depression-prone, middle-level administrator in the offices of the publicly owned RAI.

Despite their material affluence and the external trappings of success, all these men live under the pall of a deep-seated sense of fatigue and failure.

The vast majority of them left-leaning, the characters in *The Terrace* occupy positions of responsibility in politics and the cultural industry; but both in their private lives and in their capacity as opinion makers they prove increasingly unable to cope with the challenges of the time. These intellectuals must, on the one hand, deal with a conservative political regime that clings on to power despite a full decade of widespread questioning from below (*contestazione generale*) and, on the other hand, feel threatened in their own positions by what could be described as "new subjects"—specifically, in the film, professionally assertive or explicitly feminist spouses.

How does *The Terrace* relate to *Captain Fracassa*? Intimately. It so happens that the central (third) episode of the film consists of a splendid cameo revolving around Gautier's novel.

Dr. Stiller has for years secretly nurtured the literary component in his personality. He is especially fond of Gautier's *Captain Fracassa*, but has never been able to see it produced by RAI. One day, he receives a script based on *Captain Fracassa* from a highly politicized and—crucially—extremely well-connected young director. Having read the script and found fault with it (on which more below), Stiller interviews the author, but must face an unexpected barrage of trendy gibberish from the self-important young man:

"As a novel of ironic and poetic adventures, Captain Fracassa's voyage does not interest me, and, I assure you, does not interest young people either. I intend to explore the *modern* myth embodied in Fracassa and his theatrical company. What they seek is *a new rooting in the reality of theater, which itself is precisely the moment of a far-reaching reflection on the new role of actors in their community.*"[29]

To achieve this highly opaque goal it has been necessary for the young arriviste to increase the number of characters from the original seven to fifty-three, the additional forty-six representing—he pontificates—an indispensable chorus for the political enlightenment of the public. Aghast at the idea, Stiller asks what happened, to mention but one thing, to the touching scene of Matamore's death from cold and starvation in the snow. That didn't quite fit the new critical trend, explains the intellectual with contacts, so it had to be dropped.

Not content with this, the disheveled creator announces to Stiller that he has in fact already discussed the project with the local organization of the political party to which he belongs; the latter has, in turn, endorsed it and passed it on directly to the president of RAI. The president has found the idea excellent and has decided to fund it. (Top positions at RAI were, and are, routinely political appointments, distributed so as to apportion power depending on the relative punch of their respective holders' parties in government.)[30]

When the young man leaves his office, Dr. Stiller wipes his hands and takes his lunch break. Neither of these activities is undertaken by him in a neutral manner. To begin with, Dr. Stiller is maniacally obsessed with hygiene; the gesture of cleaning his hands is automatic, not related to his meager meal. Here is someone who feels dirty inside a building where dirty deals are the order of the day: not, one would think, an altogether inadequate metaphor to portray the situation that a dozen years later, under the Clean Hands judicial investigations, would lead to the collapse of the entire system of *partitocrazia* as Italy had known it for about half a century.[31]

Second, Stiller feeds himself as though on a starvation diet. It is not difficult to see why: the other purist, Matamore, had done the same before him. As Gautier writes, "he had less than two ounces of flesh on his bones. . . . For the sake of the scenic effects to be obtained once they would arrive in Paris, he had been curtailing his rations more with each day."[32]

When the president calls him into his office to discuss the upcoming *Captain Fracassa* project, Stiller tries to avoid endorsing its dogmatic reading of Gautier, which he finds no less incompatible with the author's spirit than with his own. Not that the president really cares about RAI's products. After pressuring Stiller into expressing a frank opinion about the—fictitious—American TV series *Honey Life* ("useless and, in fact, culturally harmful," is the frank answer), the president tells him that the rights to air the serial have already been purchased.

The arrival of the president's private chiropodist spices the conversation between the two civil servants. While the shape of very important toenails is being perfected, Stiller attempts to engage the president in a cultural argument. The way in which this tête-à-tête is shot by Scola is charged with symbolism. When our gaze is aligned with Stiller's, we see the president against the backdrop of the wall behind his desk, which displays in a prominent position the icons of the duopolists of political power in the country: the crucifix (for the Christian Democrat party) and the portrait of Sandro Pertini, the president of the Republic (for the Socialists). In the corresponding reverse shot, an antique bronze on the president's desk—a bearded head wearing a helmet and sporting what appears to be a cheerful mien—is positioned in such a way as to obstruct eye contact between the two interlocutors and to make fun of Stiller. Soon enough we, and Stiller, realize that the time has come for the subordinate to leave the president's office and return to his own. There, however, Stiller finds out that his office is being hastily remodeled to half of its original size for the benefit of a neighboring manager more in tune with the times.

With fatalistic resignation, Stiller dejectedly restores the missing item in the ambitious young director's "adaptation" of Gautier: having taken the elevator down to the basement, he walks into one of the TV studios at the precise moment when the murderous snowstorm in chapter 6 of *Captain Fracassa* ("A Snow Effect"/"Effet de neige") is being rehearsed. He staggers into the fictional forest and collapses in the deep and densely falling artificial snow, slowly becoming suffocated by it. Meanwhile, an unattributed off voice reads Gautier's justly famous elegiac lines:

This was, in fact, poor Matamoro. His back was leaning against the tree; his long legs, stretched out on the ground, were half-covered under a pile of snow. . . .

Poor Matamoro, here you are now, forever beyond the reach of the pinpricks, the snubs, the kicks and the blows you have had to endure because of your roles! No one will laugh in your face anymore.[33]

It is surprising that very little critical attention was devoted to a filmic episode which, well beyond its European literary context, speaks volumes about the circumstances of intellectual life in Italy in the late 1970s and early 1980s.[34]

By one of the ironies that Italian cinema seems to have been able to strew profusely into its history, about a decade after *The Terrace* Scola could finally make *The Voyage of Captain Fracassa (Il viaggio di Capitan Fracassa*, 1990), a full Fracassa story—without ideological meddling and without being forced into despair or suicide. Scola writes:

A stagecoach loaded with the vagabonds of Art crisscrosses France from the Pyrenees to Paris, the city of triumphs, the goal of all travel. . . .
The last, starving scion of the Sigognac family leaves his ancestors' castle and follows a group of comedians out of love for the experienced Serafina and the naive Isabella. The reason seems solid enough—the two young women are, after all, beautiful—and everyone takes it at face value, including young Sigognac himself. In fact, though, what has really captured him is Theater. If the two women weren't actresses, the baron would have let them go their way and remained behind, fighting hunger in his ruined castle rather than in a comedians' diligence. . . .
And when Isabella is taken away from him by the first blusterer who comes along, the lover feels true chagrin—but a chagrin accompanied by secret satisfaction as an author and as a performer: the theatrical plot has become richer, the actor's display of suffering more sincere. Theater lives on, and tomorrow there will be another show.[35]

In Scola's *Fracassa*, unsurprisingly, philological accuracy is reinstated and Matamore dies true to form. Dr. Stiller may rest in peace.[36]

Not in each and every respect, though. There is a slight degree of modification in the transition from Gautier to Scola as to the proximate cause of Matamore's death: it is sorrow, rather than inclement weather, that finishes him off. In the forest it is snowing all right; but it is Matamore who (like Stiller!) decides to walk out into the elements. This occurs when, an argument having developed between him and his beloved niece and daughter-figure Isabella, he must hear her not only reject his mystical standards of artistic perfection but, more damningly still, tax him for an outdated acting style that no longer makes anyone laugh. Wounded quasi-paternal love is only half of Matamore's pain; the other half is an intuition that, professionally speaking, his niece could be right after all.

Scola's new version of Gautier's *Fracassa* is as revealing of its times as the episode in *The Terrace* had been of its own. The story is no longer told from Matamore's (or Stiller's) perspective; it is now Pulcinella, introduced by Scola and elevated by him to the rank of narrator of the events, who holds a privileged position. A new breed is on stage, ready to take on the burden previously borne by the all-star cast, fictional and real, spinning aimlessly around *The Terrace*. Accordingly, *The Voyage of Captain Fracassa* is conceived by Scola and his scriptwriters as a full-blown Bildungsroman, showing the progress in education and the growth to full maturity of the young members of the theatrical company. It is significant, in this perspective, that Pulcinella's double role as both character and narrator is played to the fullness of its possibilities by Massimo Troisi, one of the top younger Italian actors. (Despite his reputation in Italy, Troisi became well-known in North America only after *The Postman/Il postino*, 1994.)[37]

Clearly, the sociohistorical background for *The Voyage of Captain Fracassa* was the ripening of a new generation of intellectuals at the time of the gradual retirement from the scene of many of the prominent cultural figures that had led Italy through its provincial fifties, roaring sixties, conflictual seventies, and teledoped eighties. One can only hope that the symbolic analogy with a new Italy coming of age will not extend too literally from the world of fiction to the real one, in which the delivery of all of Troisi's Bildungsromane to come was prematurely interrupted by a massive failure of the actor's heart.

While *Fracassa* plays entirely in the realm of the imaginary, Scola's *The New World* (*Il mondo nuovo*), a.k.a. *The Night of Varennes* (*La nuit de Varennes*, 1982) represents a perhaps exemplary case of the films made by the director with a commitment to France as a historical and cultural reality. The film takes its point of departure from a factual event, the flight of the French royal family toward the border with the Austrian Netherlands (today Belgium) in June 1791, and their subsequent capture at Varennes by revolutionary forces.

21 June 1791. Secretly, Louis XVI and his family have just fled Paris, where they found their forced cohabitation with the revolutionary Convention increasingly intolerable. If they can cross the northeastern border, they will join the émigrés and the loyalist troops ready to rally around them.

Tipped off by events he has witnessed in the city, the writer and chronicler Restif de la Bretonne—an actual historical character—takes a stagecoach heading in the same direction. He is joined in the vehicle by the American revolutionist Thomas Paine, a hysterical Italian opera singer, the *cavaliere* Giacomo Casanova (all of them unsuspecting passengers), as well as an aristocratic lady from the queen's retinue.

At staging point after staging point, the whereabouts of the king's carriage elude the assembled passengers. The denouement occurs when they reach Varennes: there, the king has been recognized and taken into custody by the National Guard. The lady-in-waiting's long pursuit has been in vain; her king will never be able to use the splendid uniform she was bringing him for his hoped-for triumphal return to the capital.

So *The New World/The Night of Varennes* is a historical film. Or is it? That is an issue the film long courts and dodges, finally giving viewers thirsting for royalty the scant satisfaction of contemplating little more than the king's uniform, meant for him to wear during a glorious return trip that will never take place. All we discern of Louis XVI's person in the film are feet and shoes, intuited by the camera from floor level in the impossibly crowded upstairs room of a shopkeeper's home with a glance that quite literally coincides with that of people surging from the stairwell. The film is not really about the revolution, either; messengers, to be sure, gallop from the capital to the border and then back again, but Scola gives us little material with which to satisfy the established notion of what a filmed revolution ought to be like—an event full of sound and fury, flag-waving, pillage, barricades, lofty proclamations, blood—and then more of the same, in a slightly different order.

What, then, *is* Scola's film about? It really is all of the above, but filtered through the consciousness of, and the interaction among, the characters assembled inside the stagecoach bound for Varennes. Where is the fleeing royal carriage with respect to our characters' vehicle: ahead? behind? in some mysterious parallel dimension nearby? One can smell that presence in a manner as impalpable and yet as real as the trail left behind by aristocratic perfume in a miserable hamlet would be. The ultimate interpretive consequences are clear. Power, Scola's film argues, is a thoroughly conventional construct; a king is but a uniform, plus a generalized willingness to call that uniform a king. When that willingness collapses, only the uniform remains.

Much of the work done by Scola and his scriptwriters is historical in nature; yet, literature is brought into the film with a brilliant sleight of hand by planting in the fictional stagecoach the slightly eccentric literary figure of Restif de la Bretonne (and a living myth to play his role: Jean-Louis Barrault). The next step is to team up Restif with Paine and Casanova (the latter being impersonated by the aging Mastroianni). The idea sounds improbable—and, historically speaking, it is. From the artistic point of view, however, the mix is unquestionably a winner.

Though all characters enjoy their own narrative spaces, Restif, a keen observer of French society, masterfully organizes the plot around him. There is a clear reason for the film to position Restif at the center of the narrative web: among the tomes of his real namesake's complete works, which run into the hundreds, a certain number are devoted to the Parisian nights before, during, and after the revolution. A passionate stroller and an enormously curious man, the historical Restif reveled in nocturnal explorations of the streets of Paris, and thus learned firsthand a wealth of details about events in French society, high and low, which by way of the printing press he eventually passed on to his contemporaries and thence to future generations. There is a great deal about everyday life or political intrigue in the France of his times whose knowledge we owe to him.

Restif's work in fact provided *The New World/The Night of Varennes* with at least the generative nucleus from which the idea of the stagecoach eventually germinated. This is found in the "Revolutionary Night" of 20/21 June 1791— the 393rd of his *Parisian Nights*. What we read in Restif's *Les nuits de Paris*, minus some violent details and plus some peaceable ones, is just what we witness him do and observe in the film.[38]

This is not to say that the film is stylistically simple or naive; among much else, it opens and closes with complex metacinematic statements.

The frame narration takes place in 1792, and the occurrences surrounding the royal family's flight are sandwiched in between various camera obscura–type reproductions of salient revolutionary events offered by Italian entertainers on a barge moored along the Seine. (This type of early predecessors of cinema was called "The New World"—hence the Italian title).

The film ends with Restif walking up the steps from the *quai* to the street level. Here the camera, zooming out, gradually takes in an ever-expanding vision of today's Parisian crowd and traffic, merging Restif into them as an off voice reads a passage from his works that gloomily predicts little or no improvement in human nature even at such a remote point in the future as, say, 1992.

The overall effect of these devices is impressive: it *is* Restif's character that controls the narration and, in the end, makes sense of it.[39]

Given that both Marxism and France have had such a strong impact on Scola's lifework, is it possible to identify a terrain in which the two come together, or at least imply one another at more than an episodic level? Certainly, and it is not difficult to see why: to the Italian Marxist, and particularly to the southern one, France must ever remain the country that was able to carry out that radical process of bourgeois modernization historically denied to the Mediterranean regions of the peninsula. In the South of Italy, the land reforms successfully implemented by revolutionary France remained an eternal mirage, and their very impossibility caused rebelliousness and lawlessness throughout the centuries. To the Italian Marxist from the South, France was—and still is—the image of the Other country: the country otherwise similar in language, history, and culture that succeeded in doing what Italy was unable to accomplish.

While historical awareness may not empower us (not in the short term, anyway) to eradicate the many variants of organized crime that to this day impoverish large parts of southern Italy, it will at least give us a better understanding of the deep-seated reasons for Scola's predilection for a historical approach to the individual and cultural events presented in his films.

The same trends observed in the earlier part of the 1970s continued to affect Europhile recreations in Italian cinema during the years of the terrorist crisis, coinciding with the period 1973–82.

Once more, French literature had the greatest impact on Italian cinema, with seven films: Pasolini's *Salò or the 120 Days of Sodom* (1975), from Sade; Ferrara's *A Simple Heart* (1977), from Flaubert; Comencini's *The Traffic Jam* (1979), from Beckett; Scola's *The Terrace* (1980) and the related *The Voyage of Captain Fracassa* (1990), from Gautier; Amelio's *Strike at the Heart* (1982), from Nerval; and Scola's *The New World/The Night of Varennes* (1982), from Restif de la Bretonne.

Russian has the second greatest representation, with three: Lattuada's *Heart of a Dog* (1976), from Bulgakov; Bellocchio's *The Seagull* (1977), from Chekhov; and Rosi's *Three Brothers* (1981), from Platonov.

German is once more in third position, with one: Paolo and Vittorio Taviani's *The Meadow* (1978), from Goethe.

In another sense, however, change maintains its momentum. Homological re-creations continue to recur: it is in the strongest sense of the word that Goethe's *Werther* is re-created in *The Meadow* for our day and age. Epigraphic re-creations are still on the upswing: *The Traffic Jam* incorporates Beckett; *Strike at the Heart*, Nerval; *Three Brothers*, Platonov. As for partially coextensive re-creations, these attest to the sophistication that can be displayed by Italian directors at this time via the inclusion of the Gautier-inspired death of Matamoro in Scola's *The Terrace*—not in the guise of a mechanical interpolation, but as part and parcel of its own plot.

This deprives totally coextensive re-creations of a majority (*A Simple Heart, Captain Fracassa, The New World/The Night of Varennes, Heart of a Dog, The Seagull*). Some of these are anyway unique specimens: Scola's re-creation of Restif is a sweeping reconstruction equal to Rossellini's best didactic works; Bellocchio's Chekhov was originally an RAI production for television.

I am leaving Pasolini's *Salò* to one side, on account of the difficulty of attributing a univocal status to the film (as, of course, to its prototype, *Les 120 journées*). Needless to say, that very difficulty reinforces, rather than undermines, the trend toward diversification already clear in the rest of the cinematographic production of this period.

If we then turn to considerations of narrative contents, we are immediately struck by the seemingly counterintuitive fact that, during the years of terrorism, revolution evaporates as a subject matter in Italian cinema, leaving many a ruin in its wake. Pessimism and melancholia (*Heart of a Dog, A Simple Heart*), paralysis (*The Traffic Jam*), torture or worse (*Salò*), and assassination (*Three Brothers, Strike at the Heart*) haunt these films, which at one level are certainly inspired by works of European literatures but evidently direct themselves in a selective manner to one or the other of those according to the concerns of their own historical context. Perhaps despair would be the best term to associate with the most somber of such films; there is suicide in *Salò*, there is suicide in *Fracassa*, there is suicide in *The Seagull*, and there is suicide in *The Meadow*—possibly the highest such concentration in any period of Italian cinematography.

Suicide is indeed a telling symbol of the sharp cultural reflux experienced in Italy during 1973–1982. The fortunate circumstance that in these years the wrong Italian revolution failed to happen could offer filmmakers only potential comfort vis-à-vis the indubitable fact that other desirable characteristics of Italian society—above all, the liveliness of its cultural and political debate—were extinguished by the extreme polarization of the epoch. Italian cinema suffered greatly from this: not only because societal interest in its products shrank, but also because its products shrank in the scope of the questions they were able to ask and in the answers they were able to give to society.

NOTES

1. The novella is available in English as Mikhail Bulgakov, *The Heart of a Dog*, trans. Michael Glenny (New York: Harcourt, Brace and World, 1968). The best edition of the Russian text is Mikhail Afanas'evich Bulgakov, *Sobach'e serdtse*, in *Povesti*, vol. 3 of his *Sobranie sochinenii*, ed. Ellendea Proffer (Ann Arbor, Mich.: Ardis, 1983).

The following is an introductory bibliography to *Sobach'e serdtse*: Volker Levin, *Das Groteske in Michail Bulgakovs Prosa* (Munich: Otto Sagner, 1975), pp. 32–56; Lesley Milne, *Mikhail Bulgakov: A Critical Biography* (Cambridge: Cambridge University Press, 1990); Nadine Natov, *Mikhail Bulgakov* (Boston: G. K. Hall, 1985), pp. 44–45; Ellendea Proffer, "Predislovie" (Preface) to Bulgakov's *Povesti*, pp. xix–xxx; Ellendea Proffer, *Bulgakov: Life and Work* (Ann Arbor, Mich.: Ardis, 1984), pp. 123–34; Vsevolod Sacharov, *L'addio e il volo: Biografia letteraria di Michail Bulgakov* (Venice: Il Cardo, 1995), pp. 74–80; Anthony Colin Wright, *Mikhail Bulgakov: Life and Interpretations* (Toronto: University of Toronto Press, 1978), pp. 59–63.

2. Names play an important role in the novella. The ambiguity between the two meanings in the original Russian of the word *sharik* ("Little Ball" or "Little Globe") unequivocally suggests a demiurgic intention in Preobrazhensky, thus symbolically confirming his role as parallel to that of the Bolshevik would-be world reformers. As for Sharikov's newly given names, "*Po*[ligraph] *Po*[ligraphovich]," what immediately strikes one about them is the extent to which their *po-po* parallels the *ka-ka* sound characterizing Sharik's great Gogolian ancestor, Akaki Akakievich. Second, the "much writing" etymologically adumbrated in Poligraph's name also refers us back to Gogol's scribe—*and* includes a further stab at the revolutionists' rhetorical dia-/logorrhea.

3. Bulgakov, *The Heart of a Dog*, pp. 122–23; *Sobach'e serdtse*, pp. 194–95.

4. Bulgakov, *The Heart of a Dog*, p. 130; *Sobach'e serdtse*, p. 199.

5. In this respect one can point out in particular Lattuada's short story "La burocrazia," in his *L'occhio di Dioniso: Racconti, ricordi, lettere d'amore* (Florence: La Casa Usher, 1990), pp. 110–14; repr. in Lattuada, *Il mio set*, ed. Vito Zagarrio (Ragusa: Libroitaliano, 1995), pp. 51–57.

6. I am here deliberately using the term that was traditionally argued over by different schools of research in the context of Gogol's *Shinel'*. For more details, see Carlo Testa, *Masters of Two Arts: Re-creation of European Literatures in Italian Cinema* (Toronto: University of Toronto Press, 2002).

7. Lattuada's statements on *Cuore di cane* can be found in Franca Faldini and Goffredo Fofi, eds., *Il cinema italiano d'oggi 1970–1984 raccontato dai suoi protagonisti* (Milan: Mondadori, 1984), p. 191; Lattuada, *Il mio set*, pp. 114–17; and Aldo Tassone, *Parla il cinema italiano* (Milan: Il Formichiere, 1980), vol. 1, pp. 162–63, 172. See also the relevant critical comments in Callisto Cosulich, *I film di Alberto Lattuada* (Rome: Gremese, 1985), pp. 109–14.

8. The screenplay of *Cuore di cane* was published—with a critical appendix on the film by Lucio Lombardo Radice with which, in accordance with my interpretation above, I would take substantial issue—as Bulgakov, *Cuore di cane: Il romanzo e la scenggiatura di Alberto Lattuada* (Bari: De Donato, 1975).

9. For an English translation of the play, see Anton Pavlovich Chekhov, *The Seagull*, in vol. 2 of *The Oxford Chekhov* (Oxford: Oxford University Press, 1967), pp. 229–81. The standard original *Chaika* is in Chekhov's *Sochineniia. P'esy 1895–1904*, vol. 13 of his *Polnoe sobranie sochinenii . . .* (Moscow: Nauka, 1978), pp. 3–60. For a general pre-

sentation of what the author interestingly calls a "comedy," see David Magarshack, *The Real Chekhov; An Introduction to Chekhov's Last Plays* (London: George Allen and Unwin, 1972), pp. 19–75.

10. Quoted from Lino Micciché, *Cinema italiano degli anni '70* (Venice: Marsilio, 1984 [1980]), p. 284. A number of further comments on *Il gabbiano* by Bellocchio and his cooperators can be gleaned from Faldini and Fofi, eds., *1970–1984*, pp. 136–40; and Tassone, *Parla il cinema italiano*, vol. 2, pp. 43–44.

11. Essential material on the film is also in Sandro Bernardi, *Marco Bellocchio* (Milan: Il Castoro, 1998 [1978]), pp. 91–97 (pp. 121–27 in the 1978 ed.); Paola Malanga, ed., *Marco Bellocchio* (Milan: Edizioni Olivares, 1998), pp. 96–97, 168–71, 230; Micciché, *Cinema italiano degli anni '70*, pp. 284–86; and Anita Nicastro, ed., *Marco Bellocchio* (Florence: Ferdinando Brancato Editore, 1992), pp. 134, 155–56, 259–69, 319, 352–54, 388–89.

12. In English, the choice of a good version of *A Simple Heart* is limited. In recent years, all we have is essentially Gustave Flaubert, *Three Tales*, trans. A. J. Krailsheimer (Oxford: Oxford University Press, 1991), pp. 3–40. In French, the story can be found in any good edition of Flaubert's complete works, for example, *Un coeur simple*, in vol. 2 of *Oeuvres complètes*, ed. Jean Bruneau and Bernard Masson (Paris: Seuil Intégrale, 1964), pp. 166–77.

13. Prizes notwithstanding, there is virtually no secondary literature on Giorgio Ferrara's *Un cuore semplice*—at most, a few entries in historical dictionaries of Italian cinema.

There is another, and indeed better-known, Ferrara in Italian cinema: Giuseppe, mentioned in this book in the introductions to chapters 5 and 6.

14. Goethe, *The Sufferings of Young Werther* and *Elective Affinities*, ed. Victor Lange (New York: Continuum, 1990), pp. 48–50. Emphasis added.

A more recent English translation of the passage in question is in Goethe, *The Sorrows of Young Werther. Elective Affinities. Novella*, ed. David E. Wellbery, trans. Victor Lange and Judith Ryan, vol. 11 of Goethe's *Collected Works*, ed. Victor Lange et al. (Princeton, N.J.: Princeton University Press, 1995), pp. 32–34. This translation, however, strikes me as slightly too colloquial, and I have therefore preferred the older one.

Pfui sagte Albert, indem er mir die Pistole herabzog, was soll das! . . . Ich kann mir nicht vorstellen, wie ein Mensch so törigt sein kann, sich zu erschießen; der bloße Gedanke erregt mir Widerwillen.

Daß ihr Menschen, rief [Werther] aus, um von einer Sache zu reden, gleich sprechen müßt: Das ist töricht [*sic*], das ist klug, das ist gut, das ist bös! Und was will all das heißen? Habt ihr deswegen die innern Verhältnisse einer Handlung erforscht? Wißt ihr mit Bestimmtheit die Ursachen zu entwickeln, warum sie geschah, warum sie geschehen mußte? Hättet ihr das, ihr würdet nicht so eilfertig mit euren Urteilen sein. . . .

[*Albert*]. Den Selbstmord [kann] man doch für nichts anders als eine Schwäche halten, denn freilich ist es leichter zu sterben, als ein qualvolles Leben standhaft zu ertragen. . . .

Die menschliche Natur [fuhr Werther fort] *hat ihre Grenzen, sie kann Freude, Leid, Schmerzen, bis auf einen gewissen Grad ertragen, und geht zu Grunde, sobald der überstiegen ist.* Hier ist also nicht die Frage, ob einer schwach oder stark ist, sondern ob er das Maß seines Leidens ausdauern kann; es mag nun moralisch oder physikalisch sein, und *ich finde es eben so wunderbar zu sagen der Mensch ist feig, der sich das Leben nimmt, als es ungehörig wäre, den einen Feigen zu nennen, der an einem bösartigen Fieber stirbt.* (Goethe, *Die Leiden des jungen Werthers*, in *Der junge Goethe. 1757–1775*, ed. Gerhard Sauder et al., vol. 1, pt. 2, of *Sämtliche Werke nach Epochen seines Schaffens*, ed. Karl Richter et al. [Munich: Carl Hanser, 1987], pp. 233–35; emphasis added.)

15. See Pier Marco De Santi, *I film di Paolo e Vittorio Taviani* (Rome: Gremese, 1988), pp. 108–13; Faldini and Fofi, eds., *1970–1984*, pp. 540–42; Riccardo Ferrucci and Patrizia Turini, *Paolo e Vittorio Taviani: La poesia del paesaggio* (Rome: Gremese, 1995), pp. 55–63; Goffredo Fofi, *Dieci anni difficili: Capire con il cinema parte seconda, 1975–1985* (Florence: La Casa Usher, 1985), pp. 32–34; Jean Gili, ed., *Paolo et Vittorio Taviani* (Arles: Institut Lumière/Editions Actes Sud, 1993), pp. 85–97; Micciché, *Cinema italiano degli anni '70*, pp. 323–26; Piero Spila, "La fine delle 'utopie' nel cinema dei Taviani," in Lino Micciché, ed., *Il cinema del riflusso: Film e cineasti italiani degli anni '70* (Venice: Marsilio, 1997), pp. 154–62, esp. 162; Tassone, *Parla il cinema italiano*, vol. 2, pp. 377–79; and Bruno Torri, ed., *Il cinema dei Taviani* (Rome: Ministero degli Affari Esteri, 1989), pp. 16–17.

16. Tassone is the critic who feels most explicitly uncomfortable with Werther's ascendancy (*Parla il cinema italiano*, vol. 2, p. 341). By contrast, in his rage to tear apart *The Meadow* at any cost, Fofi misses out on Goethe altogether—which is not to say that the connection would not have infuriated him even more, had he discerned it.

17. The translations of the two extremely alarming MIT reports were published in Italy by Mondadori in 1972 and 1973, respectively. Their echo was made enormous throughout the decade by the oil shocks of 1973 and 1979.

18. The fact that the noun *sorpasso* has no exact equivalent in English and had to be rendered, when Risi's film was distributed in North America, by the paraphrase *The Easy Life*, is, to my mind, in and of itself a road sign pointing to a peculiarly rough turn in intercultural communications.

19. Regrettably, scant critical attention has been devoted to *The Traffic Jam*. Among the few exceptions are Ezio Alberione et al., eds., *Stefania Sandrelli* (Palermo: Edizioni Papageno, 1998), p. 69; Peter Bondanella, *Italian Cinema from Neorealism to the Present* (New York: Continuum, 1991 [1983]), p. 328; Giorgio Gosetti, *Luigi Comencini* (Florence: La Nuova Italia, 1988), pp. 61–62; and Micciché, *Cinema italiano degli anni '70*, pp. 313–14.

Comencini explains that he did hear of a short story by Julio Cortázar about a gigantic traffic jam outside Paris (i.e., *La autopista del sur*), but "he swears that he has ever been unable to read it" (Faldini and Fofi, eds., *1970–1984*, p. 302). One can also read comments by Comencini on *The Traffic Jam* in Luigi Comencini, *Infanzia, vocazione, esperienze di un regista* (Milan: Baldini e Castoldi, 1999), pp. 141–42, as well as Tassone, *Parla il cinema italiano*, vol. 1, p. 111.

20. Samuel Beckett, *Waiting for Godot: Tragicomedy in Two Acts* (New York: Grove Press, 1954), p. 61.

Vladimir. "Alors, on y va?"

Estragon. "Allons-y."

   Ils ne bougent pas.

Rideau

Samuel Beckett, *En attendant Godot* (Paris: Les Editions de Minuit, 1990 [1952]), p. 134.

21. A useful synoptic source on terrorism in Italian cinema is Paolo D'Agostini's "Il cinema ritorna agli anni di piombo," *la Repubblica*, 4 July 1992, p. 29. On Rosi's position vis-à-vis history, see in particular Tassone, *Parla il cinema italiano*, vol. 1, pp. 276, 291.

22. Millicent Marcus, "Beyond *cinema politico*: Family as Political Allegory in *Three*

Brothers," in Carlo Testa, ed., *Poet of Civic Courage: The Films of Francesco Rosi* (Trowbridge, U.K.: Flicks Books, 1996), pp. 116–37.

23. Further essential titles on Rosi are the following: Francesco Bolzoni, *I film di Francesco Rosi* (Rome: Gremese, 1986); Michel Ciment, *Le dossier Rosi* (Paris: Ramsay, 1987 [1976]); Sebastiano Gesù, ed., *Francesco Rosi* (Acicatena: Incontri con il Cinema, 1991); Vittorio Giacci, ed., *Francesco Rosi* (Rome: Cinecittà International, 1994); and Anton Giulio Mancino and Sandro Zambetti, *Francesco Rosi* (Milan: Il Castoro, 1998 [1977]). To sections on *Three Brothers* contained in these works one must add Fofi, *Dieci anni difficili*, pp. 28–30, for an unusually positive evaluation of the film by perhaps the harshest among Italian critics.

The screenplay was published as Tonino Guerra and Francesco Rosi, *Tre fratelli: Sceneggiatura* (Mantua: Circolo del Cinema, 1999).

24. I am quoting Olivier Assayas's article, originally published in *Cahiers du cinéma* 340 (1982), from Mario Sesti and Stefanella Ughi, eds., *Gianni Amelio* (Rome: Dino Audino Editore, n.d. [1995?]), pp. 34–35, where it is excerpted in Italian.

25. The original lines of "Pensée de Byron" are "Par mon amour et ma constance, / J'avais cru fléchir ta rigueur; / Et le souffle de l'espérance / Avait pénétré dans mon coeur; / Mais le temps, qu'en vain je prolonge, / M'a découvert la vérité, / L'espérance a fui comme un songe, / Et mon amour seul m'est resté!" For full text and critical apparatus, see Gérard de Nerval, *Oeuvres*, ed. Henri Lemaitre (Paris: Garnier, 1966), pp. 23, 878–79.

A slightly fuller version of Nerval's poem than that recited in the film is included (with a number of typos) in the published screenplay: Gianni Amelio and Vincenzo Cerami, *Colpire al cuore: Trattamento e sceneggiatura* (Mantua: Circolo del Cinema, 1996), pp. 129–30.

26. Though the secondary literature on Gérard has grown to virtually unmeasurable proportions (Carlo Testa, *Desire and the Devil* [New York: Peter Lang, 1991] being among the culprits, albeit only in the appendix, pp. 161–79), that on Gianni Amelio is still contained within manageable bounds. On *Strike at the Heart* the following are recommended: David Bruni, "*Colpire al cuore* di G. Amelio: Lo sguardo discreto," in Lino Micciché, ed., *Schermi opachi: Il cinema italiano degli anni '80* (Venice: Marsilio, 1998), pp. 237–47; Alberto Cattini, "Edipo a Milano," in his *Le storie e lo sguardo: Il cinema di Gianni Amelio* (Venice: Marsilio, 2000), pp. 62–75; Alberto Crespi, "Di chi sono queste?," in Emanuela Martini, ed., *Gianni Amelio: Le regole e il gioco* (Turin: Lindau, 1999), pp. 43–48; Faldini and Fofi, eds., *1970–1984*, pp. 620–23; Goffredo Fofi, ed., *Amelio secondo il cinema: Conversazione con G. F.* (Rome: Donzelli, 1994); Goffredo Fofi, "Gianni Amelio," in his *Come in uno specchio: I grandi registi della storia del cinema* (Rome: Donzelli, 1995), pp. 260–62; Emanuela Martini, "Memorie degli anni dispari," in Vito Zagarrio, ed., *Il cinema della transizione: Scenari italiani degli anni novanta* (Venice: Marsilio, 2000), pp. 357–60; Giulio Martini and Guglielmina Morelli, eds., *Patchwork due: Geografia del nuovo cinema italiano* (Milan: Il Castoro, 1997), pp. 117–24; Mario Sesti, *Nuovo cinema italiano* (Rome: Theoria, 1994), pp. 37–43, 113–15; Sesti and Ughi, eds., *Gianni Amelio*, pp. 32–35; and Gianni Volpi, ed., *Gianni Amelio*, (Turin: Edizioni Scriptorium, 1995), pp. 112–20.

27. Copious English-language material on Scola in general is in Manuela Gieri, *Contemporary Italian Filmmaking: Strategies of Subversion* (Toronto: University of Toronto Press, 1995), pp. 157–97.

28. Théophile Gautier, *Le Capitaine Fracasse*, in his *Oeuvres complètes*, vol. 6 (Geneva: Slatkine Reprints, 1978 [Paris: Charpentier, 1889]), pp. iii–iv.

29. Emphasis added.

30. For the record, the privately owned counterparts to RAI are subject to no similarly embarrassing rules of representativeness.

31. Everyone knew about the dirty deals; but knowing about them was one thing, and being able to stop them was quite another. At a later time, however, this—temporarily—ceased to be the case. See the introduction to chapter 6.

32. Gautier, *Le Capitaine Fracasse*, p. 223.

33. Gautier, *Le Capitaine Fracasse*, pp. 221–223.

34. Comments by Scola on *La terrazza* are reported in Ettore Scola, *Il cinema e io*, ed. Antonio Bertini (Rome: Officina Edizioni, 1996), pp. 13, 150–56; Faldini and Fofi, eds., *1970–1984*, pp. 296, 300–02; and Tassone, *Parla il cinema italiano*, vol. 2, pp. 319–23. See also Alberione et al., eds., *Stefania Sandrelli*, pp. 73–74; Callisto Cosulich, "Ettore Scola tra l'eterno ritorno e la tentazione della fine," in Micciché, ed., *Schermi opachi*, pp. 172–75; Pier Marco De Santi and Rossano Vittori, *I film di Ettore Scola* (Rome: Gremese, 1987), pp. 137–42; and Roberto Ellero, *Ettore Scola* (Florence: La Nuova Italia, 1996), pp. 69–72.

35. Ettore Scola, quoted from Furio Scarpelli and Scola, *Il viaggio di Capitan Fracassa: Trattamento e sceneggiatura originali* (Mantua: Circolo del Cinema, 1992), p. 8.

36. In the film *Fracassa*, the second and third Gautier quotes given in this chapter are conflated and reattributed to Leandro, who utters them upon Matamoro's death. Scarpelli and Scola, *Il viaggio di Capitan Fracassa*, p. 68.

37. On *Fracassa*, see Vito Attolini, *Storia del cinema letterario* (Recco: Le Mani, 1998), pp. 260–62; Ellero, *Ettore Scola*, pp. 99–102; and Scola, *Il cinema e io*, ed. Bertini, pp. 23, 192–96.

38. Restif not being exactly the most frequently read French author (or, for that matter, the most generally available one in print), the following may represent a useful essential guide to his works: Nicolas-Edmé Restif de la Bretonne, *Les nuits de Paris: Or, The Nocturnal Spectator*, trans. Linda Asher and Ellen Fertig (New York: Random House, 1964), pp. 280–84; *Les nuits de Paris*, ed. Henri Bachelin (Paris: Editions du Trianon, 1930), vol. 1, pp. 248–52; *Les nuits de Paris* (Paris: Hachette, 1960), pp. 236–40 (a slightly different, shorter selection).

Some autobiographical guidance in the maze of Restif's works can be found in the section "Mes ouvrages" in Rétif [*sic*] de la Bretonne, *Monsieur Nicolas*, ed. Pierre Testud (Paris: Gallimard, 1989), vol. 2.

Useful scholarship on Restif is the following: Maurice Blanchot, *Sade et Restif de la Bretonne* (Paris: Editions Complexe, 1986); David Coward, *The Philosophy of Restif de La* [*sic*] *Bretonne* (Oxford: Voltaire Foundation, 1991); and Jean-Marie Graitson, ed., *Sade, Retif* [*sic*] *de la Bretonne et les formes du roman pendant la Révolution française: Actes du 3e colloque international des paralittératures de Chaudfontaine* (Liège: C.L.P.C.F., 1992) (contains in particular Pierre Testud's "*Monsieur Nicolas* et les problèmes de l'autobiographie," pp. 41–52, and "La révolution des *Nuits de Paris*," pp. 61–70).

39. For Scola's remarks on *The New World/The Night of Varennes*, see Faldini and Fofi, eds., *1970–1984*, pp. 301–02; and Scola, *Il cinema e io*, ed. Bertini, pp. 23, 165–68.

Among the critical comments, see Bondanella, *Italian Cinema from Neorealism to the*

Present, pp. 406–07; Cosulich, "Ettore Scola . . . ," in Micciché, ed., *Schermi opachi,* pp. 177–78; De Santi and Vittori, *I film di Ettore Scola,* pp. 147–52; Ellero, *Ettore Scola,* pp. 75–78; and Patricia Reynaud, "De la nuit de Varennes à la terreur: Le voyage de la mystification," *Canadian/American Journal of Italian Studies* 20, no. 55–56 (1997): 221–34. Two works comment positively on Scola's handling of historical reconstruction in this film: Sergio Bertelli, *I corsari del tempo: Gli errori e gli orrori dei film storici* (Florence: Ponte alle Grazie, 1995), pp. 128–29, 259–60; and Aldo Viganò, *Storia del cinema storico in cento film* (Recco: Le Mani, 1997), pp. 123–27.

The published screenplay is Sergio Amidei and Ettore Scola, *Il mondo nuovo: Sceneggiatura* (Mantua: Circolo del Cinema, 1989).

Some scholars' concerns notwithstanding, the video version of *Il mondo nuovo* which normally circulates in Italy—and which I have verified for this purpose—shows an ending corresponding to that of the French-language one distributed in North America.

5

Socialism Privatized: Just Fill Up the Cart (1982–89)

The essential events in Italian public life of the 1980s revolved around the Socialists' increased clout in the central government, which led to a disproportionate growth in the political appointments they were able to secure. Connected to this nucleus were the dramatic rise of Silvio Berlusconi's empire; the relative crisis and eventual metamorphosis of the Communist Party, paralleled by a drop in the impact of labor unions; and a perceptible waning in the bloodshed wrought by both far-left and far-right terrorism—though not yet its complete cessation (one more bomb on a train between Florence and Bologna in 1984: fifteen dead, ten times as many wounded). Further important trends during this period were a renewal in the killing of judges and prosecutors by the Mafia, proof enough that the first revelations by *pentiti* (turncoats, but literally "repentants") had begun to allow for inroads substantially threatening organized crime; and an unprecedented spate of industrial disasters, thankfully medium-sized compared to Chernobyl's tragedy in 1986.

On the international scene, political events in the 1980s that had direct bearing on Italy ranged from the entirely peaceful, such as the signing, in 1984, of a new concordat with the Vatican to replace the Fascist one of 1929 (henceforward, the Catholic religion was no longer the official religion of the Italian state), to the explosive, with the situation of near-war reached in 1986 between the United States and Libya, as well as a number of Palestinian attacks (1985, hijacking of the S.S. *Achille Lauro*; in the same year, thirteen dead during a suicide bombing at Rome's Fiumicino airport).

In the economy, a far-reaching technological evolution—driven, not least, by two oil shocks in quick succession—opened the path for more high-tech, capital-intensive industrial processes that drastically reduced the workforce employed in factories. A historical age thus neared its end: facing competition from East Asia, certain industries were phased out altogether (the steel mill at Bagnoli, first opened in 1906, was wound down in 1989). As labor-intensive production began, worldwide, to emigrate from industrialized countries to the Third World, exoduses of a more conventional type suffered considerable setbacks: the net outflow of Italian workers to other countries virtually ceased. A further circumstance obviously contributed in a decisive way to determine the fact just mentioned: following a global trend, Italy's attaining material well-being brought with it first a stabilization, then a contraction (and thus, on average, an aging) of the population.

The uncertain health of the Italian employment rate did not stop the period under consideration from developing something like economic euphoria for many. The price of oil steadied and, after 1986, contracted markedly, ceasing to put upward pressure on production costs; the same effect ensued from the weakened bargaining position of the labor unions. Propelled by a devalued lira (-8 percent in 1985 alone) and by the giant sucking effect of an overvalued U.S. dollar, the export-led Italian economy sailed along and repeated feats already performed during its "economic miracle"—not surprisingly, since most of the same conditions obtained again. To add fuel to the flames, the Socialist-led (or -supported) Italian governments embarked on a borrow-and-spend frenzy which enormously increased the public deficit. While the high-interest bonds issued for this purpose added a great burden to the national treasury, they also enriched a great many risk-averse small investors. The economic results were not slow in coming: soon enough, the Italian economy roared past that of Great Britain, to occupy—as measured by physical output—the fifth position among industrialized countries.

Bettino Craxi's long march to the top had begun in 1976, when, upon being appointed secretary of a lethargic Italian Socialist Party (PSI), he had undertaken a vigorous policy of rejuvenation (read: deideologization) of his party. In an attempt to capture voters fluctuating between a neoconservative Christian Democratic Party and an as yet not fully reformist Communist Party, in the 1980s Craxi determined to present himself as the ultimate alternative to both. Armed with a new symbol for his party—the carnation, originally adopted by the Portuguese anti-Fascists in 1974—in 1983 he succeeded in his strategy: in the wake of national elections in which the Christian Democrats lost six percentage points and the Socialists and Republicans between them gained four, he obtained the premiership.

Just as Ronald Reagan and Margaret Thatcher had done before him, in 1984 Craxi took on the labor unions: his government issued a decree-law that substantially cut the *scala mobile* (escalator), the automatic cost-of-living salary increases granted in any given year on the basis of the previous one's measured rate of inflation. The labor unions split in their reaction, with some of them accepting the fait accompli, and the Communist-led CGIL filing for a referendum to repeal the government's measure. Meanwhile, the Socialist Party began to pull out of the left-leaning coalitions that had controlled many of the local governments in Italy for the previous decade. The new alternative was, generally, a five-party coalition (*pentapartito*) that brought on board local counterparts of the Socialists' partners in Rome. The triumvirate established between Craxi, Glulio Andreotti, and Arnaldo Forlani (the latter two being, respectively, the gray eminence and the secretary of the Christian Democrats), the so-called CAF, became the cornerstone of Italian political equilibria.

True to his policy of muscle-flexing (*decisionismo*), Craxi stood up to the United States: when the U.S. Air Force intercepted a plane transporting the four Palestinian hijackers of the S.S. *Achille Lauro* and forced it to land in Sicily, the Italian government took the suspects into custody on the ground, then promptly arranged for them to be removed to Yugoslavia. The influential daily *la Repubblica* began in its political cartoons to portray the Socialist leader as donning the military uniform and black boots typical of his quasi lookalike and quasi homonym Benito (Mussolini). In 1986, no one was much surprised when, the PSI mayor of Milan having had to step down over a real-estate scandal, his appointed successor was Paolo Pillitteri, another Socialist. Pillitteri was Craxi's son-in-law.

However, the elections of 1987 disappointed Craxi; they halted the Socialists' advance, and were instead remarkable for a separate set of reasons. In the new Parliament, the Communists shrank to an historical low (about 27 percent of the electorate); for the first time, the new Greens overtook the old Liberal Party; the Radicals included the porno actress Cicciolina among their appointees; and the medieval-sounding Lega Lombarda made its first-ever appearance in the Roman Parliament, with one representative.

Someone else, too, was growing. In October 1984, Berlusconi's three TV stations, having been found by several district judges to be in breach of existing laws on state monopoly over information, were ordered off the airwaves. Supporting an important media player who could become a precious ally, the Socialist-led government thereupon issued two decree-laws (end of 1984, early 1985) that allowed the tycoon's stations to resume broadcasting; the decrees thus enshrined the de facto situation of general anarchy that had evolved over a decade. Berlusconi meanwhile retained an important minority stake in Mondadori, the largest Italian press conglomerate (magazines and publishing house).

In 1988, the "Mammì decree-law," from the name of Oscar Mammì, the minister who presented it, marked an even more important watershed for Berlusconi's fortunes: while the new law established an antimonopolistic ceiling on the concentration of TV stations and newspapers, thus setting an at least notional limit to the ambitions of Berlusconi's conglomerate, Fininvest, to expand in the area of dailies, it also stipulated that Fininvest's three channels did not represent a breach of antitrust principles—and allowed each of them to launch news programs on a national scale. Emboldened, Berlusconi had his financial giant, despite its debts, purchase the Standa store and supermarket chain (1988), then attempted a full takeover of the Mondadori group, which in the meantime had acquired control over the weekly *L'Espresso* and the daily *la Repubblica* (1989). Largely thanks to the decisive support of Socialist circles, a new empire was clearly in the making.

In the 1984 elections for the European parliament, the Italian Communists secured their best performance ever, partly on account of the death, just a few days earlier, of their high-profile secretary, Enrico Berlinguer. However, in the regional elections of the following year the party lost ground, and it again saw its influence curtailed when (9–10 June 1985) Italians voted 54 percent to 46 percent *not* to abolish the Socialist-inspired decree-law enacted the previous year to cut the *scala mobile*. With Communists and labor unions thus weakened, the associations of Italian industrialists proceeded to tear up the long-standing negotiated agreement on inflation-indexing of salaries.

In 1988, the Communists experienced another setback in local elections; regionalist lists, for their part, made the strongest showing to date—the Lombard League obtained up to 10 percent of votes in certain northern areas. In 1989, the unthinkable happened: the Soviet bloc began to crumble, and young Germans took to dancing atop the Berlin Wall. Facing the choice between boldness and further decline, Achille Occhetto, the Communist Party secretary, called for an extraordinary congress to establish a new identity for the largest organization of the Italian left. The soul-searching debate lasted many months.

As for the political scandals of 1982–89—did they tick along at the same "normal" rate as those to which the previous decades had accustomed Italians, or did they mark an intensification in lawlessness, and thus signal the excesses of a capitalist class that had become too rich too fast for its own good (to say nothing of that of the nation)? One would be curious to put the question directly to a number of those who resigned, were investigated, or were convicted, among whom stand out the entire Turin City Council (1983); Aldo Moro's former secretary, Sereno Freato (1983); the Socialist politician Alberto Teardo (1983); the banker Fausto Calabria (1984); the public manager Ettore Bernabei (1984); the head of the Guardia di Finanza—the militarized police body of the Internal Revenue Service—General Raffaele Giudice (1984); the mayor of Milan, Carlo Tognoli (1986); the banker Michele Sindona, who, while serving a life term for the murder of the lawyer Giorgio Ambrosoli in 1979, bizarrely decided to commit suicide by poisoning his own coffee (1986); Rocco Trane, secretary to the Socialist former Minister for Public Transportation Claudio Signorile (1987); the puppet master of the P2 Masonic lodge, Licio Gelli (arrested in Switzerland in 1982, escaped in 1983); and the president of the Italian State Railways, Ludovico Ligato, forced to resign over the "golden bedsheets" scam (1988) and gunned down in Reggio Calabria, presumably for knowing too much, a year later.

Meanwhile, at the opposite end of the economic spectrum, immigrants, particularly from Africa (the *extracomunitari*) were working in the fields or peddling trinkets in the streets, demanding a consistent and fair immigration law.

In sum, a comprehensive snapshot of Italy at the end of the 1980s would have to include at least the following subjects: private TVs disgorging ads with shopping carts that overflow with goods; images of the Eastern bloc collapsing; a newly multiracial Italian audience in front of the screens; and Socialist comrades' faces beaming to all and sundry with told-you-so, self-important smiles. This may well have been Craxi's finest hour.

The 1980s were certainly among the most difficult years in the history of Italian cinema, and they have been characterized by more than one observer as the most forgettable of them all. This was because, as moneymaking rose to become the top item on the ideal agenda to be pursued by the population, the interest in a public, cinema-led debate on social and moral themes correspondingly plummeted. Of course the 1960s were hardly inferior in this respect (except, perhaps, for the scale of the growth in apparent wealth), but nonetheless were capable of producing a substantial number of great films, self-ironic ones first and foremost. However, the sad fact is likely to be that by the early 1980s the painful experience of political terrorism had spoiled Italians' taste for "debate" of any kind for a long time to come. Or, more simply, lucre without any time wasted on a sense of humor was the path most of the world was taking then: from Hollywood to Beijing, the rustling of banknotes quickly established itself as the most sophisticated trend in existential argumentation.

As important, in Italy there was the stark fact of unfair competition: during the years in question TV stations, public and private, offered a daily deluge of the best films available in the history of Western cinema. Less and less money was thus left for the risky funding of *new* cinema related to the lives of the people of the times. With financing becoming scarcer than ever before, far fewer projects came to be realized; and, of those that did, most were conceived on a minimalist scale. Such were the circumstances that gave rise to the "chamber cinema" of the 1980s: small budgets, small expectations, and almost inevitably small issues too.

Among the films that, despite all this, did honor to themselves and to their decade, one ought to mention at least the following: Archibugi's *Mignon Has Left (Mignon è partita*, 1988); Bellocchio's *Henry IV (Enrico IV*, 1984), *Devil in the Flesh (Diavolo in corpo*, 1986), and *The Vision of the Sabbath (La visione del sabba*, 1988); Benigni's *You Perturb Me (Tu mi turbi*, 1983), *All There's Left to Do Now Is Cry (Non ci resta che piangere*, 1984), and *The Little Devil (Il piccolo diavolo*, 1988); Betti's *Kafka: The Penal Colony (Kafka, La colonia penale*, 1988); Cavani's *Behind the Door (Oltre la porta*, 1982), *The Berlin Affair (Interno berlinese*, 1985), and *Francesco* (1989); Fellini's *And the Ship Sails On (E la nave va*, 1983), *Ginger and Fred* (1986), and *Interview (Intervista*, 1987); Giuseppe Ferrara's *One Hundred Days in Palermo (Cento giorni a Palermo*, 1984) and *The Moro Affair (Il caso Moro*, 1986); Ferreri's *The Story of Piera (Storia di Piera*, 1983) and *I Love You* (1986); Loy's *Where's Picone? (Mi manda Picone*, 1984); Luchetti's *It Will Happen Tomorrow (Domani ac-*

cadrà, 1988); Mazzacurati's *Italian Night (Notte italiana*, 1987); Montaldo's
The Golden Spectacles (Gli occhiali d'oro, 1987); Moretti's *Bianca* (1984),
Mass Is Over (La messa è finita, 1985), and *Palombella rossa* (1989); Nichetti's
Icicle Thieves (Ladri di saponette, 1989); Olmi's *Long Live the Lady! (Lunga
vita alla signora!*, 1987) and *The Legend of the Holy Drinker (La leggenda del
santo bevitore*, 1988); Piavoli's *The Blue Planet (Il pianeta azzurro*, 1982);
Marco Risi's *Forever Mary (Mery per sempre*, 1989); Rosi's *Carmen* (1984)
and *Chronicle of a Death Foretold (Cronaca di una morte annunciata*, 1987);
Scola's *Macaroni (Maccheroni*, 1985), *The Family (La famiglia*, 1987), *What
Time Is It (Che ora è*, 1989), and *Cinema Splendor (Splendor*, 1989); Paolo and
Vittorio Taviani's *Kaos* (1984) and *Good Morning, Babylon (Good Morning,
Babilonia*, 1987); Tornatore's *Cinema Paradiso (Nuovo cinema Paradiso*,
1988); and Wertmüller's *A Joke of Destiny (Scherzo del destino*, 1983).

The first three entries in this chapter examine Europhile Italian films that, in
different ways, revolve around love stories: Moretti's *Bianca*, Rosi's *Carmen*,
and Bellocchio's *Devil in the Flesh*. Love is, of course, *the* insuperably escapist
topic in which eras of intellectual and political reflux like to take refuge. Fortunately, however, upon closer scrutiny it turns out that our three stories are but
a part of a more complex picture—and are very special love stories indeed.

Moretti's *Bianca* (1984) is cast from the "underground" viewpoint of a revolutionist in hiding. Michele, the protagonist with a secret criminal life who is
eventually arrested and confesses to some unusually motivated murders, could
be, and in my opinion should be, understood as a potential ciphered personification of those "erring comrades" who, in the first half of the 1970s, began to
devise entirely untheoretical ways of pulling the centrist and reformist souls of
the Italian Communist Party into an increasingly tight bond with its insurrectional one.[1]

Michele Apicella, a high-school teacher in Rome, moves to a new apartment building
and there meets a young couple, Massimiliano and Aurora, his neighbors across the
courtyard. The next day, Michele shows up at his *liceo* only because another neighbor
wakes him up and reminds him to do so. The institution itself is hardly more conventional
than this: it is named after Marilyn Monroe, and it has a bar, an ultramodern gym, and
a game room at the center of the building. The curriculum and the colleagues are similarly
untraditional, and in most respects perfectly attuned to new times. (For example, there
is a full-time resident psychiatrist on the premises—for the faculty.)

At home, Michele, who spies on Massimiliano and Aurora, discovers that Aurora is
unfaithful to her husband. He steals a photo of the two and files it in a maniacally detailed
data library he keeps on all his acquaintances. At school, Michele meets his colleague
Bianca, the teacher of French, and is charmed by her.

One day Aurora is found murdered. Michele brushes off the police inspector's questioning and focuses his emotions on Bianca instead. He harasses Bianca's boyfriend.
When the two break up, he invites Bianca for a dinner that soon takes—sexually speak-

ing—a distinctly blank turn, but in compensation leads to Michele's orgiastic downing of Nutella chocolate spread.

(This scene, in which Michele sits at the kitchen table, taking Nutella from a surreal, three-foot-tall jar, has attained cult status among filmgoers of kindred tastes.)

Michele can be happy only when he sees happy couples around him. He keeps tabs on Matteo and Martina, two pupils in one of his classes, and Ignazio and Maria, who are friends of his. One day Ignazio and Maria declare that they want to try out an "open couple" relationship. Shortly afterward, they are found dead.

Bianca loves Michele and now lives with him. She reaps scant rewards for her devotion: Michele is uncontrollably jealous and indulges in much unbalanced behavior. He begins to think of committing suicide. When the marriage of Matteo and Martina is announced, this seems to push him over. Michele goes to the neighborhood police station, located in a basement, and asks to see the inspector who had previously questioned him.

It was he, Michele acknowledges as he turns himself in, who committed the crimes presently under investigation. Why? Because people around him made his life intolerably difficult by the diversity of their preferences. They simply refused to make their behavior conform to the homogeneous pattern which he found so reassuring and expected them to adopt.

Dostoyevsky substantially influences the film by way of *Notes from Underground*.[2] That Michele is a committed neurotic presumably needs no further elucidation or comment. Furthermore—and, I believe, decisively—his long, final autobiographical confession occurs in a police station located in a basement whose small windows open onto the sidewalk. It is against the background of these windows that Michele articulates his thoughts on the Italian polity by making reference to a great number of legs of all ages and shapes, "shot" by the camera from the knee down. His implied status as a terrorist reinforces his symbolic role as the embodiment of a camouflaged existence played out in depth, below the superficial conventions of automatized social life. Whether watching and controlling styles of shoes or uncovering and undermining other people's often wishy-washy, self-deceiving approach to interpersonal relations, Nanni Moretti's and Dostoyevsky's men from underground share a radical skepticism toward easygoing, happy-go-lucky common sense.

They share other important features as well. Both texts purport to be autobiographical confessions; both are fictional autobiographical confessions made by *unreliable* narrators—by narrators, that is, whose aim is to manipulate, rather than inform, their interlocutors (respectively, Liza, a young prostitute from the countryside, and Bianca, along with the police inspector). It is revealing that in *Bianca*, a film devoted to the symbolic projection of an Italy mired in the issue of political terrorism, the math teacher Michele Apicella cannot address—or, rather, can address only in a repressive manner—the fact that issues of identity may require equations of a higher order than those known to him.[3]

While Moretti's thematization of certain disquieting issues in Italian society is, despite the director's symbolic ways, explicit, the Franco-Spanish heritage that imbues Rosi's *Carmen* (1984) conveys things Italian without being articulated in the film's actual diegetic content. To avoid duplicating what I write on the subject in the corresponding chapter of *Masters of Two Arts*, I will here simply point out that the crux of the matter lies in the specific way in which Rosi rediscovers a South already colonized in the past by an imperialistic northern glance (Mérimée's novella, Bizet's opera).

By having systematic recourse to naturalistic effects, references to his earlier films (*The Challenge, Salvatore Giuliano, Hands over the City, The Moment of Truth, Just Another War, Christ Stopped at Eboli, Three Brothers*), and complex semiotic strategies, in *Carmen* Rosi proudly reappropriates the Italian cultural heritage at the precise historical moment when Italy is elbowing her way back to self-assertiveness on the European scene. This is also the time when Italy, traditionally a nation of emigrants, for the first time in modern history becomes a desirable destination for the impoverished masses of disadvantaged regions of the globe. The cultural colonization suffered in the past is thus resorbed, though not necessarily in order to give way to a less traumatic cohabitation with geographical neighbors.

The third item in our love trilogy, Bellocchio's *Devil in the Flesh* (*Diavolo in corpo*, 1986), is the most directly and representationally topical of the three. A re-creation of Raymond Radiguet's novel *The Devil in the Flesh* (*Le diable au corps*, 1923), the film deals as a matter of course with the everyday presence of political terrorism in Italian society.

That said, the most pressing clarification needed about Bellocchio's *Diavolo in corpo* and Radiguet's *Le diable au corps* is that, titles notwithstanding, there is no devil in either; in both cases, it is the flesh that carries the day. To be sure, the novel, written and published shortly after the mass slaughter of World War I, could lay an at least partially valid claim to demonism by virtue (if that is the word) of the casual treatment to which it exposed the supreme moral values of the bourgeois society of the time. Its main character is a young man who speaks and says "I"—and tells the story of the love affair that, beginning at the tender age of about fifteen, he had with Marthe, a woman barely older than he. Since Marthe was married to a soldier who was defending the motherland against the enemy, the two young lovers had all the leisure in the world to enjoy each other.

In the course of the retrospective account, not a word is expended by the narrator on the misery, deprivations, and death which were being suffered throughout his country—and many others—at the time of the events. All he is concerned with is the passion that he and Marthe nourished: "Love anesthetized in me everything that did not pertain to Marthe."[4]

The protagonist is young, but not so young that one can exonerate him on account of his innocence. Besides, it would not seem unreasonable to argue that the beginning of sexual experience in and of itself ought to mark the transition to a psychic age in which the distinction between good and evil can no longer be ignored. Of such discernment, however, there is no trace in Radiguet's young lovers. Cruelly oblivious to any sympathy for the mourning all around them, they beaver away at their sex while the bourgeois in their town (with the exception of the narrator's father) look at them in reprehension and disgust.

Toward the end of the war, Marthe becomes pregnant; early in 1919, she gives birth to the narrator's child. Shortly thereafter she dies, apparently of poorly treated pneumonia. The soldier-husband, now discharged, stays home to raise "his" son. The last few lines in the novel offer a perfect example of Radiguet's trenchant laconism, which can honorably compete with that of the most outstanding seventeenth-century *moralistes*:

I wanted to see the man to whom Marthe had given her hand.

Holding my breath, I tip-toed over to the half-open door. I arrived in time to hear him say:

"My wife called out his name just before she died. Poor child! He is the only [reason] I have to live."

Seeing this [dignified] widower striving to master his despair, I realized that in the end order reasserts itself [around] everything. Had I not just learnt that Marthe had died calling my name, and that my son would have a reasonable life?[5]

It is clear that in *Le diable au corps* sex acts as a robust slap in the face of nationalistic rhetoric, bourgeois decorum, and religious conventions—and that it can do so all the more effectively because in writing about it the author rigorously eschews any clumsy sentimentalism of his own.

Let us now transport ourselves to the Italy of the mid-1980s, a country at this juncture cognizant of the existence of round-the-clock, hard core TV channels.

Subjecting the original context to a thorough restructuring, *Diavolo in corpo*—which Bellocchio made under the close supervision of his (enthusiastically anti-Freudian) psychiatrist Massimo Fagioli—proposes the following situation to the Italian public.

Giulia is a middle-class young woman from Rome who harbors a deep malaise toward her environment: she rejects the petty materialism that surrounds and, she feels, drowns her. Not least because she has no intellectual or artistic interests to pursue, she is deeply destabilized by her moral claustrophobia, and develops psychotic traits (principally, for our purposes, a compulsive interest in sex) that do nothing to offer her permanent relief. Her mood swings suddenly from dejection to hysteric hilarity; her social behavior is unpredictable, and certainly incomprehensible to the conformists around her. It does not help Giulia that she is an orphan, the daughter of a policeman recently killed by terrorists in a street clash in Rome. Western science further complicates her position: Giulia's glib-talking psychiatrist reads Freud as a herald and mentor of normalcy and, accordingly, attempts to bring his patients back to the fold as uncritically and insensitively as one ever could. Little wonder, then that after a while Giulia breaks off the treatment.

Giulia is betrothed to a man who is in jail awaiting trial, the terrorist Giacomo Pulcini.

This is not just any young terrorist; he happens to be one of the group that killed Giulia's father.

The film never explains how the liaison came about; in particular—while on the subject of psychoanalysis—we have no way to know whether it preexisted or was engineered by Giulia as a way to "reward" Pulcini for his symbolic parricide.

Having, alone in his group, disowned his comrades and collaborated with the prosecutors, Giacomo is about to be set free; thus, her fiancé's detention is not exactly Giulia's most painful concern. The point is, rather, that in jail Giacomo has developed an obsessive yearning for the mainstream, as attested by the nursery rhymes he composes, *inter alia*, about the bliss of "calling children by their grandparents' first names"—hardly a matter to set Giulia's senses aflame. Nor can she find a better interlocutor in her future mother-in-law (no future father-in-law in the film). Giacomo's mother is smothering, bigoted, reactionary, and, to top it all off, demonstrative about her wealth: everything, in other words, that explains Giacomo's having become a terrorist to begin with. The marriage is to take place as soon as Giacomo is released.

Andrea is a calm and mature young man of about eighteen, who is in his last year of high school in Rome. Although he is a good pupil, he studies only enough to perform reasonably well; in other words, he is not a fanatic of speculative knowledge, just as he declines identification with any other "fanatical" label among those which professors try to slap on him (fundamentalist Christian, Marxist, Green . . .). Next to his high school is a mental hospital, but an enormous chasm separates Andrea's balanced world from that hidden under the roof which his *liceo*'s windows overlook. If Andrea has any troubles at all, they stem from his relation with his father, a middle-aged professional who is jealous of his son's girlfriend and feels haunted by a sense of inadequacy on the job.

Giulia and Andrea become acquainted when, at the very beginning of the film, a deranged young woman escapes from the hospital building to its roof and disrupts the classes being held in the *liceo*. Giulia, who lives in a small attic across the courtyard, is attracted to her terrace by the commotion. There the two young people's eyes meet; and from then on, their asymmetrical, yet doubtlessly enthusiastic, affair develops.

Youth apart, where do Giulia's and Andrea's worlds overlap? In a very significant area, it turns out.

Andrea's father, so staunchly opposed to his son's relationship, happens to be the psychiatrist whom Giulia has rejected. Thus the plot's circle closes, with the lovers doubly harassed by the adults' antics: the tricks put in place by Giulia's future mother-in-law, and the threats brandished by Andrea's father. Under such pressures Giulia, never very self-assured, risks—as she correctly sees—sinking into permanent insanity. Andrea, on the other hand, does not lose his composure. He passes his graduation exam with flying colors, among other things judiciously illustrating to the examination committee (with a self-referential hint at the terrorism of the 1970s and early 1980s) the clash between the laws of the state and the dictates of human compassion which shape Sophocles' *Antigone*.

As Andrea does this, Giulia drops in on his oral, joining a group of other friends and relatives of students being examined . . . and thereby skips her marriage ceremony, at which her whole entourage is anxiously awaiting her. Will she eventually appear, or will she choose open rebellion? The latter seems more likely, but the film does not tell us.

Diavolo in corpo has at its core Bellocchio's attempt to turn an external tragedy such as Radiguet's World War I into an internal one. Giulia's psychic disequilibrium is meant to take the place of the material disruptions that loom large around the lovers of *Le diable au corps*.

Though the film is particularly lucid and cogent in pursuing its goal, there is one respect in which it may appear problematic. Who are the targets of *Diavolo in corpo*? Its chief villains are clearly the pompous psychiatrist and the dull mother; yet the two seem to be, by many indices, unworthy of such honor. They are powerless, worthless nonentities who allow the allegedly "subversive" love affair to go on peacefully under their noses. As for the eternal husband, Pulcini, he is so briefly sketched in the film that it remains unclear if he gets his cuckold's badge (to say nothing of an even crueler fate, the "Chick" of his last name) because he "chickens out" of society and into the pseudo answer of terrorism, or because he then "chickens out" of terrorism and opts instead for what he believes will be a solid bourgeois marriage.[6]

Whether or not in making the film Bellocchio was indeed brainwashed by his anti-Freudian psychiatrist (there was a heated discussion on this in Italy at the time of the film's release) is irrelevant for our purposes. Fagioli's ideas may be exciting stuff, or not; the point is that in *Diavolo in corpo* there does not seem to be an equivalent able to make up for the inevitable loss of one characteristic of Radiguet's masterpiece—its diamond-like clarity and precision, its keen observation of the invariant features of the human soul. Giulia and Andrea are, to be sure, interesting characters; but when all is said and done, they are also fairly average young people who get impatient with nondescript adults and try to get over their frustrations by engaging in athletic, but far from deeply passionate, sex.

On the other hand, for the sake of fairness one must certainly add that it is through no fault of Bellocchio's (or, for that matter, of Fagioli's) if in a cultural sense the 1980s proved to be among the most passionless and mediocre decades on record for a very long time with respect to the issues available for public discussion in Italian society.[7]

By some unusual—though likely significant—wink of destiny, the next three films, too, have a strong bond. In this case, what they share is that they are all re-created from works of German literature which in various guises focus on the difficulty of establishing one's place in society. (Finding a meaningful social role for oneself can be problematic at all times and in all places, but in the last two centuries it is the tradition of the German Bildungsroman that seems to have taken up the issue most systematically.) That three important works in this category should have crystallized, in rapid sequence, in the second half of the 1980s confirms the presence of a definite malaise in the Italian polity of the time.

I will dwell only briefly on the first two of these films, Fellini's *Intervista* and Archibugi's *Mignon Has Left* because they are the object of two chapters in my *Masters of Two Arts*.

Fellini's *Intervista* (1987) shows us around a peculiarly inflected universe, on a visit to directorial reminiscences of Kafka's fragment *The Lost One* or *America* (*Der Verschollene* or *Amerika*, 1912–13 [posthumously] published 1927), interpolated with highly personal Fellinian memories of just about everything else: Cinecittà in the 1930s, the Rome of the *dolce vita* in the 1960s, and of course the lost paradise of dreams—whether cinematically or erotically inspired—from the director's youth.

The structure of *Intervista* is made up of three different strands, of which the first, the interview, represents the frame narration. The person to be interviewed is a Famous Italian Director, impersonated on stage by the actor Federico Fellini; the interviewers are a group of Japanese film fans eager to see the Famous Italian Director at work and to ask him questions about his art. The second narrative strand arises out of the fact that the Famous Italian Director, ever creatively committed, is now hard at work on a rendition of Kafka's American novel. He is engaged in the selection of the cast, the shooting of screen tests, and the coordination of other sundry organizational aspects of the project. The third fictional strand is the one centering around the Famous Italian Director's recollections of his first trip to Cinecittà many years in the past, as well as of a number of episodes surrounding that visit. We thus have a triple source of narrative impulses that interact with one another, further enriched by a wealth of cinema-within-the-cinema intuitions that make for a cornucopian audiovisual experience.

In this hide-and-seek film we encounter Kafka in the rehearsed scene of the bath to be taken by Brunelda, the fat singer, when she begins to sigh: "Such a heat, such a heat, Delamarche. . . ." However, in true Fellinian fashion, the film about America is never presented to us: the slot to be allotted to Kafka's narrative, allegedly the generative pretext for the whole project, remains an ironically empty one (a "lost one"?).

As Fellini, with an autobiographical veracity we would be well advised not to take at face value, intercuts Kafka's story with his own, we realize that there is no ultimate core to his filmic sequence of Russian dolls one inside the other; or, rather, the multilayered doll *was* the core we stepwise put aside in our expectation of a climax. Fellini's para-autobiographical "striptease" is interminable: indeed, it is always already contained in each of its increments.

Are we certain we are living in the 1980s? Very much so: the "indiani" (first-nation Americans) on horseback that attack the stagecoach (in the instance, a suburban Rome streetcar) wield not sharp lances, but hardly less deadly—to the mind, anyway—TV antennas.[8]

Archibugi's *Mignon Has Left* (*Mignon è partita*, 1988) is more a reversal than a reproduction of Goethe's *Wilhelm Meister's Years of Apprenticeship* (*Wilhelm Meisters Lehrjahre*, 1795–96). Goethe's young protagonist, Wilhelm, briefly encounters the ethereal Italian artist and singer Mignon as he sets out to explore and comprehend his Nordic world, only to discover at the end of his journey that a mysterious Tower Society has been watching over him and guiding his every step toward success. Mignon, in contrast, vanishes from the horizon of Goethe's novel (dead from hypothermia, presumably) as soon as she has outlived her usefulness. To Goethe it is obvious that art is only one ingredient of our experience, while life itself is the supreme final product; to live happily ever after we must *also* be artists but, clearly, never artists alone.

In Archibugi, the male protagonist, Giorgio, is at best coequal with his young French cousin Mignon; in fact, he is much the more naive of the two. Mignon, a Parisian, is sent south to Italy against her will; she dislikes the cacophony of the utterly unartistic Roman environment in which she is trapped; she detests the lack of authenticity and sincerity of the locals; and, taking a leaf from her hosts' book, manages to arm-twist her family into recalling her to the North— she feigns a pregnancy that, postmodern mores notwithstanding, at her age still smacks of a scandal.

This is not to say that Archibugi's Mignon duplicates the almost archetypal virginity of her Goethean counterpart: although the film does not tell us unequivocally, it seems safe to infer that in mingling with her Roman friends, she has steered herself to a successful attainment of adulthood. In contrast, Giorgio is far from achieving a Wilhelm-like mastery over his own environment as a consequence of such events: desperate over Mignon's cruelty toward him, he attempts suicide by swallowing mothballs—but he swallows too few, and thus shamefully fails in his plan.

As for the presence in Archibugi's Italy of a counterpart to Goethe's Tower Society, no such thing even remotely exists there. The Tower of Babel, perhaps?

The third film in the German triad of the later 1980s is Olmi's *The Legend of the Holy Drinker* (*La leggenda del santo bevitore*, 1988). Sympathy for the innocent and simple at heart has been the hallmark of Ermanno Olmi's art since his earliest films: from the watchman in the alpine hut of *Time Stood Still*, Domenico in *The Job*, and the young boy Angelo Roncalli (later Pope John XXIII) in *A Man Named John*, all the way to the patient and God-fearing nineteenth-century peasants from the province of Bergamo in *The Tree of Wooden Clogs*, they are recurrently his protagonists. Having recovered from a life-threatening illness, ten years after *The Tree of Wooden Clogs* Olmi delves into the plight of yet another simple heart: the homeless man who is the peculiar hero of *The Legend of the Holy Drinker*.

The ways in which Olmi's film re-creates Joseph Roth's last and partially autobiographical work, *Die Legende vom heiligen Trinker* (1939),[9] can be briefly summarized as follows.

The protagonist of both novella and film is Andreas, an ex-miner with a criminal record who is now a *clochard* living in Paris under the bridges of the Seine. A mysterious, well-dressed stranger appears to him one day and, out of Christian compassion, gives him two hundred francs. This the gentleman explains by making a claim that is plausible-sounding only if understood symbolically:

"I too have no address . . . and I too may be found under a different bridge every day."[10]

Should Andreas ever be in a position to return the sum, the stranger tells him, he may do so in care of little Saint Theresa in the church of Ste. Marie des Batignolles.

The two hundred francs do not last very long. Generous (and gullible, and bibulous) to a fault, the honest Andreas repeatedly tumbles back into destitution after appearing to have obtained almost enough wealth to acquit himself. In three weeks he is again sleeping under the bridge where the stranger found him.

The wealthy stranger shows up again. Once more, Andreas shamefacedly accepts two hundred francs from him. Despite his sincere intention at least to pay off the first loan by means of the second one, intervening complications prevent him from being able to do so.

Finally, fortune smiles on Andreas.

On the fourth Sunday after the beginning of our story, he sits in a bistro in front of the church of Ste. Marie, drinking and waiting until the end of Mass in order to return the money owed. A blue-clad young girl named Theresa walks in. Andreas believes that she is the saint, and has come to see him. As, delirious and triumphant, he is about to reach for the money and hand it to her, he collapses onto the ground. He is carried across the street to the sacristy, where, in vain attempting to deliver the small treasure, he dies a painless death. With a prayer-like wish expressed by the narrator—"May God grant us all, all of us drinkers, such a good and easy death!"[11]—both the book and the film then expire.

The original text is not shy about offering an interpretive key to the story. At one point the novella says: " 'I will try to show you the way,' said *the gentleman /the Lord.*"[12] In this, it takes advantage of the perfect ambiguity of *der Herr* in German.

To my mind the novella is, in fact, constructed as a sustained allegory of Christianity. In the figurative reading I am suggesting, Andreas (whose name is characterized by the same A-A alliterative sound as Adam's) could, first, be said to represent the human soul in the fallen, post-Edenic state. Second, the dignified old man who finances him acts in the same way as does Christ, the Redemptor, who at his own cost "buys him back" (such being precisely the etymological implication of the word "re-demptor") from the claws of Hell. Third, the generous gesture, an utterly *grat*-uituous one, is quite simply a stand-in for *Grace*—which by definition is not obtained, earned, or deserved, but bestowed. Fourth, Andreas's sincere but weak resolve to settle his debt represents human fragility in the face of temptations of all kinds. Fifth, the Redemptor's willingness to bail out yet again a simple human being, no questions asked, transcodes the doctrinal concept that there can be no arithmetic correlation between guilt as measured by human parameters and the infinity of divine pardon. Sixth, the girl who happens to be called Theresa is a young Mother of God figure (she is dressed in blue, and "her" chapel is located in the church of Ste. Marie). Seventh, when the unappealable hour finally strikes, the good-natured Andreas only seems to own the money necessary to pay back his debt, and he only apparently deserves salvation by arithmetic standards. In fact, he is *twice* in debt, and so is in a very real sense only making good on half of his shortfall. For the other (first) half of it—translation: the original sin—he remains entirely at the mercy of *der Herr*.

One need not seek far afield in order to explain why Olmi felt attracted to this touching Christian "legend." As he had done in his works throughout the 1960s and 1970s, the director reiterated here, in the vein of a certain magic realism, the need for humankind to reach back to the authenticity of a perhaps faulty, but essentially honest, life.

This was not despite but, I would argue, precisely *because* of the affluence of the Italian 1980s. Indeed, the fact that Roth's and Olmi's plot is, ostensibly anyway, "about money" makes it all the more topical in an age of particularly nasty venality. To the extent that the film allows for a reading related not to its theological implications but to the civic circumstances of its time, it is not Andreas's condition as a homeless man that Olmi addresses, but his very special type of uprightness, to enshrine which the former is but a means.[13]

On the other hand, purity of heart is not the only possible representational clue to the film. The 1980s were precisely the time in Italy when undocumented, non-European "extracommunitarians" began to roam the peninsula in precarious conditions, dwelling under bridges, in public areas, inside flimsy cardboard boxes; the phenomenon soon reached such a level that no one could claim ignorance of it. By what looks like an entirely deliberate coincidence, Andreas, the ex-miner, also happens to be an "extracommunitarian" in France: he is an undocumented Pole who fears being deported. Certainly, after Adam's fall we are all exiled souls in the world, but some happen to be more exiled than others. And Roth, a converted Galician Jew fleeing the Nazis in Paris, was eminently among those.[14]

Both Roth's and Olmi's versions of the *Legend* revolve around the question of what it means for human beings to abide by laws, civic or moral. They ultimately come down in favor of a lenient interpretation of legality, in which the individuals' heartfelt intentions matter more than disembodied literal conformity. By implication, both also entail estrangement from the behavior of many people who are in only formal compliance with codes (and thus never even come close to having to sleep under bridges) because they act, to put it in Balzac's superbly expressive words, "legally, but not legitimately."[15] Yet, all of the above is really applicable only in the case of laws that appear just or, at least, reasonably useful to society; an entirely separate argument is needed to tackle laws which happen to be neither. That argument is cogently developed in the film I will discuss next, Betti's *Kafka: The Penal Colony (Kafka, La colonia penale*, 1988), an apt hyperbolic addendum to the trilogy of social ill-being just broached.

Kafka is, of course, the one European author who most intensely portrayed—indeed, suffered through—the anguish caused by laws seemingly not made by humans and for humans. His *In the Penal Colony* (*In der Strafkolonie*, written in 1914, published in 1919) represents an extreme occurrence of an arcane and, whatever the colony's military may say, cruel world order.

At an unspecified time, in an unspecified overseas settlement of an unspecified colonial nation, an unnamed traveler patiently witnesses the elaborate ritual deployed, and the copious energy expended, by the army's hierarchy in order to punish an unnamed prisoner who has committed an unspecified transgression. An unnamed officer illustrates and explains the process to the traveler as it unfolds. The novella's killing machine is, quite literally, the centerpiece of the narration. Its defining trait, imagined and described by Kafka in unendurably fine detail, is its ability to "write" (in the etymological sense: carve) into the convict's flesh the very law—a law not spelled out to readers—in whose name he is about to be executed.

As it turns out, however, the colony's superior statutes are no longer as solid as they used to be. The new commander barely tolerates the punishment now being administered by the officer; in fact, he begrudges him the means to keep the machine operational. Would the traveler mind stepping in, the officer asks, and arguing with the new commander for the honorability, indeed the deep morality, of the procedure he is observing?

When the traveler politely declines, the dejected officer concludes that it is time for him to act. He releases the man presently being victimized, and he stretches himself out in his stead. In the end, the officer meets a doom that (presumably against his expectations) is unredeemed by any last-minute transfiguration. Meanwhile, the prisoner goes free, and the traveler slips away to the boat that is awaiting him. What will happen next in the colony? Is a new, tolerant regime in the making? Conversely, could the Old Commander one day be resurrected, as a local prophecy asserts? Or is there any teleology at all to the events just told? No one knows, readers least of all.[16]

Betti subjects Kafka's inscrutable atmosphere to a radical reworking: in the film, metaphysical riddle gives way to a thoroughly historical recontextualization.

The flags, the uniforms, the civilians' clothes, the social mores—all the images we see indicate that we are in a French colony in Africa, run by the Foreign Legion, about one generation after the belle époque (approximately in the 1930s). The officer is specifically a captain; the traveler is identified as a liberal journalist committed—and vocally so—to the principle of humane treatment of prisoners, whatever their alleged crimes. While all these are white colonizers, the sentenced man is, most visibly, one of the colonized; and most visibly he is black.

As in Kafka, the story ends with the prisoner's liberation and the officer's death, which the horrified journalist narrates in flashback to the captain of the boat ready to take him back to mainland France.

Kafka brackets out anything but the most symbolic reference to empirical reality; Betti, in contrast, removes those brackets and makes empirically verifiable historical situations the focus of his attention. Hence the importance allotted in the film, with a few slight but unequivocal touches, to the captain's personal history. "I can appreciate the uprightness of your intentions," the journalist at one point shrieks at him, "but they are nonetheless mistaken, and your logic is delirious!" To explain how the wrong turn could occur in a potentially well-meaning man's life, the film introduces a retrospective short subplot. The new commander's daughter, the progressive-minded Silvia, tells the journalist that she used to be in love with the captain many years ago. A corny directorial faux pas? No—a logical way to introduce a direct testimony. The captain was humane, Silvia recounts, when he arrived at the colony; it was the colonial system that warped him into what he became.

The thrust of the film's re-creative process is thus unambiguous. Kafka's *In der Strafkolonie* is an enigma about the indecipherability of Power (or, if one will, Being) which might modulate different institutional variants but does so only within consistently opaque dynamics—and thus remains ever monolithic, monological, and monolingual. Betti's *Kafka, La colonia penale*, on the other hand, zeroes in on the identification, present but unspoken in Kafka, between *penal colony* and *colony* in a political sense; it is a parable about the historical phenomenon of decolonization and the liberating release of cultural diversity which this can bring in its wake.[17]

Once again, it is time to examine a film by Scola—and, once again, the director is true to his Francophile inspiration. In Scola's *What Time Is It (Che ora è, 1989)*, we encounter both Stendhal in Italy (as French consul in the Papal States) and Italians in Stendhal (in *The Charterhouse of Parma*).[18]

The film's two protagonists are a middle-aged father, Marcello, who is a wealthy and successful professional from Rome, and his twenty-year-old son, Michele, drafted into the Italian army for the national year of service. On a rainy winter Sunday, Marcello goes to the garrison in Civitavecchia—a small port on the Tyrrhenian coast—to visit Michele while he is off duty.

Never far from open embarrassment, father and son wander perfunctorily around the provincial town, exchanging banalities that make obvious just how wide is the gap that separates them. The day crawls along as they wander from restaurant to café to pub, until in the evening Michele accompanies Marcello back to the station to board a train bound for the city. They have arrived early, and there is ample time before the train leaves; Michele, too, boards the empty train car. In the compartment, the two men sit facing one another, and await the moment of departure without quite knowing how to talk around the silence. "What time is it" the father eventually sighs, without a question mark and in the same tone of voice as that in which one would say "Oh, well." Freeze-frame, and end of the film.

At first glance, Stendhal may seem to have little to do with Scola's Civitavecchia; but in the film the director quickly proceeds to prove the contrary when he takes the two strollers to the entrance of the town's public library. Feeling excited for once, the introvert Michele describes to his father his favorite pastime, which he has devised with a local friend, a retired schoolteacher:

"We've come up with a game . . . a game of memory about famous phrases by literary characters. For example, suppose I come out here to the library to meet him and ask him point-blank: 'Have you eaten anything?—who says that?' He'll say: 'Clelia Conti to Fabrizio Del Dongo, imprisoned in the Farnese tower. *The Charterhouse of Parma*, Stendhal, 1839.' Tough, hein?"[19]

Slightly taken aback, the father politely nods—and is immediately dragged into the contest by his son: "Here's another one for you: 'Brother, I am as pure as if I had just left my mother's womb.' " Though provoked into participation in a game to which he cannot, as a whole, relate, Marcello does like this particular question, and he triumphantly bursts into the correct answer: "Cepparello from Prato, a.k.a. Ser Ciappelletto . . . 'an evil man and a sinner if ever there was one'—*Decameron*, Boccaccio, A.D. 1350 . . . or thereabouts!"[20] This is Marcello's best performance in the day, and thus also the day's best performance in intergenerational communication.

Or is it? In the very way it is successful, the exchange shows that the moment of consonance between father and son is more apparent than real. The two classics of literature mentioned by Scola prove, upon closer inspection, to have been extracted from the body of European literature, if not by means of a Ciappelletto-like fraud, at least with something not unlike a certain authorial mischievousness. It is painfully obvious that Marcello proves well-versed only in the picaresque tradition of literature: a tradition perfectly in tune with the preferences and cultural needs of the ragged "empire builders" of the Italian state after 1945. Michele is instead inclined to cultivate a different type of literary heritage: one of interiority indebted to the Romantic and Symbolist tradition of *raccoglimento* (*recueillement* [meditation] for Baudelaire).[21] This can easily be evinced from the *Charterhouse*, where the relationship between Fabrizio and Clelia is deeply marked by the physical layout of the tower, with its upward thrust and its symbolism related to the vertical axis. The very fact of imprisonment (a condition to which Michele can no doubt relate all the more readily from his bunk in the army barracks) opens up infinite internal spaces for Fabrizio's imagination beyond the material obstacle of four walls: a concept that readers of Novalis or Leopardi—or, for that matter, fans of Gino Paoli's *Il cielo in una stanza*—will no doubt find as familiar as Stendhalophiles do.[22]

The film stresses that the young man's favorite spot for his long evenings in town is a pub frequented by a tightly knit community of locals and seafarers who relish telling and hearing marvelous sea stories. This is Scola's way of driving home the point that Michele's interior quest is really an attempt at (to put it in Baudelaire's unsurpassably effective expression) "cradling our infinite spaces on the finite space of the seas."[23]

It hardly comes as a surprise that Michele proves less than enthusiastic about his father's offer to finance his studies (studies in "something useful," it goes without saying) in the United States. Knowledge-minded young Italians of the late 1980s are shown in *What Time Is It* as far more inward-looking than the Italians who preceded them, and, to that precise extent, altogether incompatible with them. Having missed out on a protagonistic role in the economic takeoff of the 1960s, the political adrenalin of the 1970s, and the money-spinning of the 1980s, such youths seem to be unsure whether they should join the social fray at all. Who knows, maybe in their minds neither gadgets, appliances and consumer items, nor revolution, nor even plentiful money in a bank account holds the adequate answer to the eternal question on the clock of history: what time is it.

This is the serious moral of Scola's story. But the situation presented in the film also has aspects of a paradoxical strangeness—a strangeness due to the cultural reversals that occurred during the century and a half between Stendhal's times and our own. Whenever he has time off, Michele, definitely not of a generation that will rush to Rome on furlough for a weekend in the hustle-bustle, will stay in Civitavecchia to muse on Stendhal, his adoptive spiritual father. But where, exactly, was Stendhal French consul to the Papal States? In Civitavecchia. Whither did he travel, at all respectable times as well as at a fair number of unrespectable ones, for psychic and physical relief? To the balls and merriment of Rome, where Michele's father lives . . . and does "useful" things.[24]

Toward the end of the decade, immediately before the fall of the Berlin Wall, Moretti made *Red Lob*—generally referred to by its original title, *Palombella rossa* (1989). While this film receives chapter-length treatment in my *Masters of Two Arts*, it deserves at least a cursory mention here for its importance in thematizing the diverse problems of an age of transition: a transition that, far from occurring overnight in November 1989, had been building up over the entire 1980s.

In spinning its complex web on the theme of history, memory, and the heritage we receive from our past, *Palombella rossa*—among other things—explicitly incorporates footage from David Lean's film *Doctor Zhivago* (1965), in turn remotely descended from Pasternak's novel (1957) with which it shares the title.

The protagonist of *Palombella rossa*, Michele Apicella (whom Moretti portrays), is a Communist, but hardly a run-of-the-mill one. On the one hand, he is a member of Parliament, eagerly and seriously attempting to help his party find a new identity in the rapidly changing times that will soon lead to the vertical collapse, economic and political, of the Italian Communists' traditional Soviet lighthouse. On the other hand, he plays water polo with fanatic enthusiasm and participates in the national water polo championship with his team—a team which thus, by implication, becomes symbolic of the Italian Communist Party (PCI) and its varying political fortunes.

The bar next to the swimming pool where Michele's latest water polo match is being fought out has a TV screen for the entertainment of its customers. Viewers of *Palombella rossa* are shown five excerpts from Lean when Moretti's camera pauses on *Zhivago* as it follows athletes and public wandering to and fro. Is that problematic? Very much so, in a political sense at any rate. It is problematic because Michele Apicella's Communist comrades clearly show that they take David Lean's film, for all intents and purposes a mockery of Pasternak's tragic *Zhivago*, for a truthful representation of the Russian Revolution. They thereby display a political naïveté that is bound to undermine even Apicella's best efforts. The PCI's identity crisis at the end of the 1980s, which *Palombella rossa* both expresses and attempts to exorcize, is a predictable consequence of the Italian Communists' failure to draw explicit lessons from an ominously circular past. If, theoretically speaking, the lesson of Pasternak's *Zhivago* had been absorbed, and the logical consequences drawn, by Italian comrades—and, for example, the transformations undergone under duress in 1989–90 had been undertaken squarely at an earlier time, perhaps in the wake of the Afghan war that started in late 1979—their party would have been perceived as having intuited and dominated the events. And, because in politics perception is everything, it might well have been rewarded beyond its political merits, thus forestalling the occurrence of the crisis around which *Palombella rossa* revolves. That, however, was not the case; hence Apicella's anguish and final defeat.

The fifth phase covered in *Italian Cinema and Modern European Literatures*, spanning the years from the demise of political terrorism to the collapse of the Eastern bloc (1982–89), was in Italy a period that hurt cinema more and more deeply. During this time, fewer and fewer films were being made; it is a comforting surprise to realize that we have anything at all in the group of items involved with European cultures.

France has three occurrences: Rosi's *Carmen* (1984), from Mérimée by way of Bizet; Bellocchio's *Devil in the Flesh* (1986), from Radiguet; and Scola's *What Time Is It* (1989), from Stendhal.

German literature appears four times, with Fellini's *Intervista* (1987), from Kafka; Archibugi's *Mignon Has Left* (1988), from Goethe; Olmi's *The Legend of the Holy Drinker* (1988), from Roth; and Betti's self-explanatory *Kafka:The Penal Colony* (1988).

Russia—at a time when revolutions were decidedly out of fashion—had an impact below average, with only two films: Moretti's *Bianca* (1984), from Dostoyevsky, and, by the same director, *Palombella rossa* (1989), from Pasternak via David Lean.

Most striking is the diversification of approaches in this cluster of years: no one type predominates. Among the films just mentioned, two are *homological re-creations* (*Bianca* absorbs concepts from Dostoyevsky and *Mignon Has Left* from Goethe); two are *epigraphic re-creations* (*Intervista* incorporates Kafka, *What Time Is It*, Stendhal); one is a *partially coextensive re-creation* (*Devil in the Flesh* includes narrative blocks from Radiguet); two are *totally coextensive re-creations (The Legend of the Holy Drinker* from Roth, and *Kafka: The Penal Colony*); finally two are *mediated re-creations (Carmen* and *Palombella rossa).*

To rephrase the above statistics diachronically: by the 1980s, the days were gone when the majority of Italian films re-created from European literatures were generated by the mere imitation of easily recognizable famous plots. A much more nuanced critical confrontation with an original text had become common; in fact, in some sense it had become the norm. This process of valorization of authorial choice fed back, in turn, even to items that were totally coextensive re-creations. As Olmi's and Betti's films show, when these become but a small group among the many, undertaking one becomes a willed act, no less deliberate, and requiring no less ingenuity and creativity, than any of the other "minority" practices in earlier contexts. Losing mainstream status does, after all, sharpen one's motivation, artistic or otherwise.

And so does becoming poor. It just might be that the few Italian films of the 1980s which did materialize could be ever more diverse in their approaches precisely because, unlike most of their earlier counterparts, they were relatively free from the mandate to consider box-office receipts as their primary goal.

On a more somber note, interiorization and a retreat from public activity on the part of the protagonists—often young protagonists—are generally the characteristic traits of the films of these years; individual conflicts, in particular with parents, frequently come to the fore. (Religious piety, of sorts, features in *The Legend.*) Kafka's Karl could easily be elected as their representative, if he had any confidence in the democratic process—which, as *The Lost One/America* tells us only too clearly, Karl has not. A widespread civic abstention may be sadly inevitable during years when the din of great cultural campaigns has all but vanished, both in Italian society and in Italian film.

NOTES

1. Most immediately relevant to the political side of the subject are the following: Massimo D'Alema, *Un paese normale: La sinistra e il futuro dell'Italia* (Milan: Mondadori, 1995); Stephen Gundle, *I comunisti italiani tra Hollywood e Mosca: La sfida della cultura di massa (1943–1991)* (Florence: Giunti, 1995); Stephen Gundle and Simon Parker, eds., *The New Italian Republic: From the Fall of the Berlin Wall to Berlusconi* (London: Routledge, 1996); Piero Ignazi, *Dal PCI al PDS* (Bologna: Il Mulino, 1992); Robert Lumley, *States of Emergency: Cultures of Revolt in Italy from 1968 to 1978* (London: Verso, 1990); Frederic Spotts and Theodor Wieser, *Italy, a Difficult Democracy: A Survey of Italian Politics* (Cambridge: Cambridge University Press, 1986); Joan Barth Urban, *Moscow and the Italian Communist Party: From Togliatti to Berlinguer* (London: I. B. Taurus, 1983); Philip Willan, *Puppetmasters: The Political Use of Terrorism in Italy* (London: Constable, 1991). Specifically on terrorism in Italian cinema, see the section devoted to Rosi's *Three Brothers* in chapter 4 of this volume.

2. *Notes from Underground* can be found with *The Double,* trans. Jessie Coulson (Harmondsworth: Penguin, 1972); or as Fyodor Dostoyevsky, *Notes from Underground,* ed. and trans. Michael R. Katz (New York: Norton, 1989); Fëdor Dostoievskii, *Zapiski*

iz podpol'ia, in *Povesti i rasskazy 1862–1866*, vol. 5 of his *Polnoe sobranie sochinenii* (Leningrad: Nauka, 1972).

3. This text condenses parts of Carlo Testa, "From the Lives of Underground Men: Dostoevsky, Moretti's *Bianca*, and the Italian Revolution," *Romance Languages Annual* 8 (1996): 328–34, to which I refer readers for fuller details.

The most significant recent contributions to the literature on *Bianca* are the following: Flavio De Bernardinis, *Nanni Moretti* (Milan: Il Castoro, 1998), pp. 62–76; Fernaldo Di Giammatteo, "*La notte di San Lorenzo* e *Bianca*, l'ossessione del vuoto," in his *Lo sguardo inquieto* (Florence: La Nuova Italia, 1994), pp. 379–96; Marco Pistoia, "Le scarpe di Nanni: *Bianca* e il paradigma morettiano," in Sandro Bernardi et al., *Nanni Moretti* (Turin: Paravia Scriptorium, 1999), pp. 102–09; Georgette Ranucci and Stefanella Ughi, eds., *Nanni Moretti* (Rome: Dino Audino Editore, n.d. [1995?]), pp. 38–43; and Federica Villa, "*Bianca*," in Bernardi et al., *Nanni Moretti*, pp. 57–60.

4. Raymond Radiguet, *The Devil in the Flesh: A Novel*, trans. A. M. Sheridan Smith (London: Calder and Boyars, 1968), p. 110. "L'amour anesthésiait en moi tout ce qui n'était pas Marthe" (Raymond Radiguet, *Le diable au corps*, in his *Oeuvres complètes*, ed. Chloé Radiguet and Julien Cendres [Paris: Stock, 1993], p. 626).

5. Radiguet, *The Devil in the Flesh*, p. 127.

Je voulus voir l'homme auquel Marthe avait accordé sa main.

Retenant mon souffle et marchant sur la pointe des pieds, je me dirigeais [*sic*] vers la porte entrouverte. J'arrivais [*sic*] juste pour entendre:

"Ma femme est morte en l'appelant. Pauvre petit! N'est-ce pas ma seule raison de vivre."

En voyant ce veuf si digne et dominant son désespoir, je compris que l'ordre, à la longue, se met de lui-même autour des choses. Ne venais-je pas d'apprendre que Marthe était morte en m'appelant, et que mon fils aurait une existence raisonnable? (Radiguet, *Le diable au corps*, p. 639)

6. Incredible but true, a Pulcini (Carlo, not Giacomo) did appear among the terrorists of the 1980s—*after* Bellocchio's film. Subsequent to his death a *colonna* of the Red Brigades was named after him; it became involved in attacks against NATO targets and local sections of the DS (*Democratici di Sinistra*) party as late as 1996.

7. In books that cover the subject, there is rarely much secondary literature on *Diavolo in corpo*. See, however, Sandro Bernardi, *Marco Bellocchio* (Milan: Il Castoro-1998 [1978]), pp. 127–34; Laura Bertuzzi, *Il cinema di Marco Bellocchio* (Castelsangiovanni: Pontegobbo, 1996), pp. 101–114: Paola Malanga, ed., *Marco Bellocchio* (Milan: Edizioni Olivares, 1998), pp. 45–47, 106–09, 194–97, 236–37; and Vito Zagarrio, "Conversazione con Marco Bellocchio. Gli occhi, la bocca, il corpo," in Lino Micciché, ed., *Schermi opachi* (Venice: Marsilio, 1998), pp. 393–99.

One would like to know more about the exact nature of the conflict between director and producer on the subject of the final cut—a circumstance which *Diavolo in corpo* shares with an illustrious predecessor, Rossellini's *Vanina Vanini*. Reviews from periodicals and interviews with the director can be reaped from Anita Nicastro, ed., *Marco Bellocchio* (Florence: Ferdinando Brancato Editore, 1992), pp. 288–95, 326–30, 371–72, 389–91, 425–27. My personal preference goes to Giovanni Bottiroli's comments, reproduced from *Segnocinema*, pp. 425–26.

8. Two more of Fellini's projects were devoted to the TV-induced stultification of Italians: the film *Ginger and Fred* and the posthumously discovered screenplay *Venice (Venezia)*.

9. Joseph Roth, *The Legend of the Holy Drinker*, trans. Michael Hofmann (London:

Chatto and Windus, 1989); *Die Legende vom heiligen Trinker*, in *Romane und Erzähl-ungen*, vol. 6 of Roth's *Werke*, ed. Fritz Hackert (Cologne: Kiepenheuer und Witsch, 1991), pp. 515–43.

10. Roth, *The Legend of the Holy Drinker*, p. 3. " 'Auch ich habe keine Adresse,' antwortete der Herr gesetzten Alters, 'auch ich wohne jeden Tag unter einer anderen Brücke.' " (Roth, *Die Legende vom heiligen Trinker*, p. 516).

11. Roth, *The Legend of the Holy Drinker*, p. 49. "Gebe Gott uns allen, uns Trinkern, einen so leichten und so schönen Tod!" (Roth, *Die Legende vom heiligen Trinker*, p. 543).

12. Roth, *The Legend of the Holy Drinker*, p. 2. Emphasis added. "Ich werde ver-suchen, Ihnen den Weg zu zeigen, sagte *der Herr*" (Roth, *Die Legende vom heiligen Trinker*, p. 515; emphasis added).

13. Having given here a historico-cultural context for Olmi's money-averse picture of the world, I long wished I could do the same economically for Roth, too—until I dis-covered the task already masterfully accomplished in Claudio Magris's "Il tempo non è denaro. Note sull'anticapitalismo nella letteratura austriaca," *Nuova Antologia* 2205 (Jan-uary–March 1998): 32–42.

14. On Olmi's film, see Alessandro Cappabianca, *Il cinema e il sacro* (Recco: Le Mani, 1998), pp. 117–18; Tullio Kezich and Piero Maccarinelli, eds., *Da Roth a Olmi: La leggenda del santo bevitore* (Siena: Nuova Immagine Cinema, 1988), which includes the screenplay and an interview with Olmi; Lino Micciché, ed., *Cinema italiano: Gli anni '60 e oltre* (Venice: Marsilio, 1995 [1975]), pp. 225–31, 383–85; Flavia Rossi, *La leggenda del santo bevitore: Roth e Olmi* (Rome: Edav, 1993); and Aldo Viganò, ed., *Il cinema delle parabole*, vol. 1 (Cantalupa: Effatà Editrice, 1999), pp. 91–111. Jeanne Dillon, *Ermanno Olmi* (Florence: La Nuova Italia, 1985), predates the release of the film.

15. The expression "légalement, sinon légitimement" is used by Balzac to characterize old Grandet's rise to extraordinary wealth (second paragraph of *Eugénie Grandet*).

16. Good editions of the story are the following: Franz Kafka, *The Penal Colony, Stories and Short Pieces*, trans. Willa Muir and Edwin Muir (New York: Schocken, 1995 [1961]); *In der Strafkolonie*, in *Ein Landarzt und andere Drucke zu Lebzeiten*, vol. 1 of Kafka's *Gesammelte Werke in zwölf Bänden*, ed. Hans-Gerd Koch (Frankfurt am Main: Fischer, 1994).

Among the countless ones available, the methodologically most satisfactory (quite aside from bibliographically comprehensive) critical work I have been able to consult on the subject is Walter Müller-Seidel, *Die Deportation des Menschen: Kafkas Erzählung In der Strafkolonie im europäischen Kontext* (Frankfurt am Main: Fischer, 1989 [1986]).

17. The film's linguistic diversity is sure to attract the viewer's attention: the colonized blacks speak Spanish (i.e., Spanish in the sound track), not the presumed "French" (in fact, Italian) of the white colonizers.

The most curious thing about *Kafka, La colonia penale* may well be its critical fate: practically no one has written about it. Yet Betti's film has both merit and profile—the latter being provided by Franco Citti, an actor among the best known to the Italian public since the time of his lead role in Pasolini's *Accattone*.

18. *The Charterhouse of Parma* has already been touched upon in this book in the section on Bertolucci's *Before the Revolution*.

19. Although it does accurately condense the essence of Clelia Conti's concerns, the actual wording of the question attributed to her in *What Time Is It* is a bit of a mysti-fication on Scola's part; the "conversation" between the two lovers is in fact fairly diffuse, taking up a number of pages in book 2 of the novel. See Stendhal, *The Charterhouse of*

Parma, trans. C. K. Scott Moncrieff (London: Zodiac, 1980), pp. 280–84. The original can be found in Stendhal, *La Chartreuse de Parme*, vol. 25, ed. Ernest Abravanel, vols. 24–25 of Stendhal's *Oeuvres complètes* (Geneva: Cercle du Bibliophile, 1969), pp. 128–35.

20. Readers interested in finding out more about the novella of Ser Ciappelletto can also view Pasolini's *Decameron*, one of whose episodes centers on him.

21. Baudelaire's "Recueillement" is a poem added to the 1868 edition of *Les fleurs du mal*. See more on the Baudelairean connection in note 23.

22. On the impossibility of expressing infinity in language—a theme familiar by way of Leopardi's poetry—see Antonio Prete, *Finitudine e infinito: Su Leopardi* (Milan: Feltrinelli, 1998).

Paoli's early 1960s song ("The Sky Inside a Room") did indeed attain canonical status at least once in Italian cinema—in the curriculum adopted, some twenty years after its original release, by the Marilyn Monroe High School portrayed in Moretti's *Bianca*.

23. "Berçant notre infini sur le fini des mers" (Charles Baudelaire, "Le voyage," in *Les fleurs du mal*, poem CXXVI [126], line 8.)

The idea of infinity being able to take a tangible shape only in and through finitude is articulated by Baudelaire in his private diaries as well. See entry 55 of *Journaux intimes: Mon coeur mis à nu*, in vol. 1 of his *Oeuvres complètes*, ed. Claude Pichois (Paris: Gallimard Pléiade, 1975), p. 696. (This volume also contains *Les fleurs du mal*.)

24. Useful sections on *What Time Is It* are in Ettore Scola, *Il cinema e io*, ed. Antonio Bertini (Rome: Officina Edizioni, 1996), pp. 190–91, as well as Roberto Ellero, *Ettore Scola* (Florence: La Nuova Italia, 1996), pp. 97–99. The published screenplay is Ettore Scola, Beatrice Ravaglioli, and Silvia Scola, *Che ora è: Sceneggiatura* (Mantua: Circolo del Cinema, 1989).

6

Italy in Europe: Opportunities Found and Lost (1989–2000)

In the international arena, the year 1990 brought "the mother of all wars": Kuwait's invasion by Saddam Hussein's troops, reversed in the end only by the force of arms. Italy, in the meantime, experienced smaller-scale upheavals: under Achille Occhetto, the Communist Party completed and formalized a drift away from its Leninist identity, renaming itself Democratic Party of the Left (Partito Democratico della Sinistra or PDS, later DS). While one more split in the history of the Italian left occurred (hard-liners launched a new party, Rifondazione Comunista or RC), the northern bourgeoisie, which once had solidly supported the Christian Democrats, had already experienced a first schism: running on a simple but perfectly intelligible anti-theft, anti-Roman platform ("Roma ladrona"), Umberto Bossi's League scored as high as 20 percent in regional elections, sending shockwaves through the political system.

Also in 1990, a bitter judicial confrontation ended with Silvio Berlusconi being ordered to relinquish control of the recently raided L'Espresso-la Repubblica publishing group, which he was holding in contravention of the existing antitrust law on media ownership. The same law, however, allowed him to retain his three national TV channels. The tycoon shortly thereafter acquired the Milanese daily *Il Giornale nuovo*, forcing out its director and founder, the aging "law and order" opinion maker Indro Montanelli. (True to form, *Il Giornale nuovo* came to be nominally owned not by Silvio Berlusconi but by his brother Paolo, already in charge of running the real estate part of the Fininvest empire.)

In 1990 and 1991, two crises that had been building up suddenly came to a head. The first was entirely homegrown: near the end of his mandate the president of the Republic, the right-wing Christian Democrat Francesco Cossiga, made a series of public statements that were promptly described by the neologism *esternazioni* (i.e., comments made outside the president's official purview as a guarantor of the Constitution). One such *esternazione* caused particular uproar throughout the peninsula: Cossiga revealed that during the Cold War there had indeed existed a secret counterinsurgency military body, called Gladio, in charge of putting down any destabilizing left-wing rebellion. Cossiga's revelations not only unearthed the deep implications of a specific subversive incident, but also retroactively confirmed suspicions that there had long been more than met the eye in the never-ending string of political mysteries haunting the Republic. The second crisis, a variation on the collapse-of-Communism theme, was an imported one related to the problem of immigration at a time of slow domestic growth and high unemployment. Located a mere fifty miles east of Italy's heel across the Adriatic, the small nation of Albania—long oppressed by one of the most extreme Communist regimes in the world, and for almost as long enticed by the deceptively joyous image of capitalism beamed across the sea by Italian TV—in 1989 finally believed it had seen the dawn of an age of instant plenty. Endowed with the same enthusiasm as generations of their Italian counterparts before them, but without encountering, on the Italian shore, the economic expansion that alone makes immigrants welcome, Albanians began to take to the sea and head west in doubtfully seaworthy vessels. A steady trickle turned into a flood in 1991, when the tens of thousands of a flotilla that included ships landed on the Apulian coast.

Meanwhile, in the North, a sharp intensification occurred in the prosecution of what quickly become known as Clean Hands (*Mani pulite*) cases against corrupt politicians and their cronies both in private businesses and the public administration. Italians had, of course, long been aware of the vicious circle by which politically appointed public managers, whether behind the desks of nationally owned banks and conglomerates or those of local governments, used to siphon copious amounts of money from inflated contracts into the coffers of the parties to which they owed their positions. The judiciary seemed to intuit this; but in the past, investigations had run aground with dispiriting predictability. In 1992, however, a turning point was reached when Mario Chiesa, the Socialist director of a Milanese home for needy senior citizens, was caught red-handed with stacks of banknotes in his office. Having in vain tried to flush the evidence down the toilet, Chiesa was cajoled by Antonio Di Pietro, a dynamic young magistrate from the office of the head prosecutor in Milan, Francesco Saverio Borrelli, to spill the beans and disclose the mechanisms of his frauds as well as the names of their beneficiaries. Repeating, only with more hubris, a pattern well rehearsed by a generation of politicians during the previous decades, Bettino Craxi attempted to shrug off the charge with a bon mot: "Every party has its little crook" ("*Ogni partito ha il suo Mariuolo*"—a pun on the diminutive form of Chiesa's first name).

Craxi's line soon proved untenable, as scandals started surfacing left and right and could no longer be dismissed as regrettable irrelevancies. In fact, an entire parallel, parasitical economy of corruption was gradually uncovered—a subterranean world of such widespread ramifications that, on the basis of an Italian word for "kickback" (*tangente*), it quickly came to be metaphorized spatially as *Tangentopoli*. At that point an already weakened system imploded, as notifications of an ever-growing number of investigations for a broad range of offenses were showered by the judiciary on the top names, political and administrative, among the Socialists, the Christian Democrats, and their lesser allies in power. (A few splashes of mud also hit the PCI-PDS; one even reached Bossi's young Northern League.)

What made the *Mani pulite* cases of the early 1990s so much more disruptive than similar scandals of the 1960s, 1970s, and 1980s was not their magnitude (though even by Italian standards, the scale of the scams engineered by Craxi and his accomplices was indeed staggering) but the fact that, for complex reasons, at this juncture the Italian political system proved suddenly unable to sustain the conditions necessary to hush them up.

Soon the magistrates' inquiries could no longer be labeled by politicians and corrupt entrepreneurs as obscure conspiracies masterminded by prosecutors hungry for fame; and Bettino Craxi, Giulio Andreotti, and Arnaldo Forlani—among many others—lined up before the judges to account for their actions. In the process, computerization became a new national ideal, with Di Pietro as its prophet: in the Milan courthouse, the southern-born prosecutor nailed groggy, driveling former potentates to their responsibilities as, in live televised hearings, he used computer screens to map out to the nation the countless pilgrimages—and the sadly foreseeable final destinations—of the missing money. Illegal transfers made by Enimont, the state-owned chemical giant, into the Socialists' and other government parties' foreign bank accounts ran into such unheard-of amounts (hundreds of millions of dollars) that the sorry episode ended deserving the bitter, parodistic name "the mother of all kickbacks" ("*la madre di tutte le tangenti*").

In 1992–93, the larger traditional parties went the way of all things human. The Christian Democrats, who after the end of the Soviet threat no longer needed to hold their rightist soul together with their populist one, split into three major segments: one left-leaning (the Popolari), one right-leaning (the Christian Democrat Union or CDU), one akin to the CDU but more locally based in the South (the Christian Democrat Center or CCD). The traditional "lay" (i.e., non-confessional) middle-class parties—Socialists, Republicans, Social-Democrats, Liberals)—vanished from the electoral map, meeting a fate which, compared to that of the ex-Communists—abandoned by their *Rifondazione Comunista* hard-liners—seemed a mild one. A true leap forward was made by Bossi's Northern League: in 1992, the League member Marco Formentini, previously an accountant with no public profile, swept to mayoral dignity in Milan, Craxi's hometown and a Socialist stronghold since the time of the center-left coalitions in the early 1960s.

Despite the ferment, many middling politicians, busybodies, footmen, and kickback runners (for whom the Italian word *portaborse*, "briefcase carrier," offers an unsurpassably graphic general term) got off lightly in court; and none of those who controlled the goings-on in their respective parties received a prison term. (Just in case, however, Craxi removed himself to his summer home in Tunisia, a country that conveniently had no extradition agreement with Italy, and had received many benefits from the Ministry of Foreign Affairs' development agency at the time of Craxi's premiereship.) It was public managers who appeared to find their predicament most intolerable: faced with the unheard-of prospect of jail while awaiting trial, Raul Gardini (the president of publicly owned Montedison, one half of Enimont) and Gabriele Cagliari (the president of ENI, its equally public other half) committed suicide in 1993. From beginning to end, the defendants claimed to be innocents unjustly persecuted; it was the system that was corrupt, they pleaded, not they who had thrived off it.

Deprived of political cover by the collapse of his traditional Socialist allies, and wishing to avoid the implementation of a less notional antitrust law by a potentially hostile new Parliament-to-be, Berlusconi at this juncture took the fate of his TV stations in his own hands and decided to join the political fray. For the 1994 elections, he switched on the media machine of Fininvest and instantly spun off from it a party called Forza Italia (Go for it, Italy). (The politically noncommittal name was a duplication of the tried and tested Forza Milan slogan familiar to soccer fans—Berlusconi being the proud owner of the Milan Football Club.) Fininvest/Forza Italia was awe-inspiring in logistics, but lightweight in political experience; the reverse was true of the Northern League and the right-wing Movimento Sociale, not long previously rebaptized Avanguardia Nazionale and nostalgic for the times and ideals of the Duce. Even a less skillful entrepreneur than Berlusconi would have sensed that those were ideal conditions for a strategic business alliance. With an utter lack of interest in the anti-Fascist principles underpinning the history of the Republic, an electoral pact was quickly struck among the three: on the right sat a fiercely nationalist (and in some cases openly neo-Fascist) team led by Gianfranco Fini; on the relative left was perched the no less fiercely independence-bound Northern League; and Berlusconi's corporate team occupied the middle ground between the two allies, not least to keep them away from one another's throats. For good measure, the divorced and remarried Berlusconi also took a couple of insurance policies in matters religious by including two conservative neo-Catholic parties in the alliance.

Overwhelming media coverage provided the means to paper over the fissures within the newly created "Pole of Liberties" (Polo delle Libertà), and in March 1994 the alliance outgunned a loose coalition of center-left parties not accurately represented by the choice of the veteran Occhetto as their leader. (Bossi's Northern League contributed to the Polo votes from the North; the nationalists, mostly from the South.) The success of the operation led to what a business-inspired metaphor of Berlusconi's described as the "release from customs" (*sdo-*

ganamento) of extreme right-wing votes: for the first time since 1945, politicians whose ideas were descended from Fascism took up government posts, beginning to shape policy not by occasional backroom deals but with the full pomp of officialdom.

Most Italians had indeed voted for change, change of any sort over the discredited "partitocracy" of old. As the Forza Italia argument ran, how could Berlusconi, the can-do businessman who had been able to do so much for himself in such a short time, fail to pursue the same magical policy on behalf of the entire country's interests? Well, perhaps by continuing—exactly as before—to defend *his own*. Some such realization flashed through Bossi's mind before the year was out. At the end of 1994, with not one step taken in the anti-monopolist, federalist direction it had bargained into the electoral platform of the Polo, the Northern League walked out of the coalition, amid shrill but unheeded cries of foul play from Berlusconi and his bloc in the press and on TV. The first avowedly right-wing Republican government thus collapsed after only a few months in office.

All Berlusconi could obtain was to anoint his own successor, the centrist banker Lamberto Dini, whose cabinet in many ways continued the earlier and nonpolitical, technical one of Carlo Azeglio Ciampi. There was, after all, urgent business to conduct: the deadlines of the Maastricht Treaty loomed closer and closer, and a recovering economy (the 1992 devaluation of the lira had helped competitiveness) could not alone be counted on to work the necessary wonders. In particular, for both economic and demographic reasons public spending on pensions was skyrocketing and needed to be brought under control.

Unfortunately, much of the political energy expended in Italy during Dini's premiership was lost in friction and heat over the anomaly, unique in developed countries, of the *padre padrone* of a major political party also owning the three largest private TV channels in the country (to say nothing of the public ones, which, during his tenure as premier, he was also able to influence politically). The matter of this obvious conflict of interest came under the scrutiny of the Constitutional Court, which found Berlusconi's media holdings (grouped under the label Mediaset) indeed illegitimate, and, for a solution, sent the entire dossier back to Parliament—where the tycoon's party controlled the largest block of votes. Eventually, in response to Berlusconi's persistent complaints, Dini resigned his mandate at the end of 1995. Predictably, political and constitutional stalemate ensued, and new elections became necessary to break it.

In 1996, Berlusconi's gamble coincided with the fiftieth anniversary of the foundation of the Italian Republic—and it backfired on him. All-important among the reasons for his failure to duplicate the 1994 winning streak was perhaps a growing disenchantment in the country with his habit of lining the inside of suave talk with ruthless, winner-take-all political action. Further perplexity was nourished by his repeated pledges of allegiance to an extreme form of economic Thatcherism, his past links to the Socialist establishment, and by persisting doubts about his behavior as a corporate taxpayer. The winner was a new center-left coalition endowed with a solid symbol (an olive tree, whence its name, l'Ulivo) and a solid leader—Romano Prodi, one of the few important public managers of Christian Democrat extraction untainted by the scandals of the past. Antonio Di Pietro accepted to run on the Ulivo slate as a candidate for the post of minister of public works. Italians acknowledged the strategic improvements carried out by the center-left between 1994 and 1996, and gave the Ulivo a clear electoral mandate to run the country.

Just how clear, though? The victory of the Ulivo on the fiftieth anniversary of the Republic did not exactly mean that more than 50 percent of Italians had suddenly swung behind a "normal" social-democratic national ideal of, say, the Scandinavian type. The Northern League made a strong showing; in a large number of districts, it was only because of its refusal to ally itself again with the Polo that the Ulivo attained a relative majority. The Northern League's voters remained as disaffected as ever with the way their part of the country was run from south of the Po River; and their mistrust of Berlusconi's autocratic ways in no way implied a tender heart for any of the state-sponsored social provisions dear to many on the center-left. A further factor of instability was represented by the Refounded Communists, who rejected any tampering with the status quo in the matter of (defined benefit) state-funded pensions, and thus objectively represented a hurdle on the path to sustainable future budgets. And there obviously could be nothing politically "normal" in a country whose single largest party was a direct emanation of the owner of half of that country's airwaves—to say nothing of newspapers, publishing houses, and distribution networks.

The fragility of Italy's polical system was made worse by changes in 1998–99, when the Refounded Communists pulled out of the Ulivo coalition and caused the collapse of Prodi's government. Massimo d'Alema, of the DS, replaced Prodi as premier—but, crucially, the coalition itself was lost in the process, and with it any reasonable prospect of countering the fragmentation that has haunted Italy's governments most of the time since the failure of Mussolini's autocracy.

Further political developments have occurred in 2001. At the helm of the ruling center-left coalition, D'Alema's job has been taken over by the politically more adroit Giuliano Amato, perhaps the least indecorous among the Socialists left from Craxi's times; and the right-wing triad Bossi-Berlusconi-Fini, with their conservative Catholic partners, have regrouped behind a single banner, renaming themselves Casa (as opposed to Polo) delle Libertà. Whether either change makes any sense, except from a cosmetic perspective, remains open to question: on the center-left, Amato cannot but remind of a past that Di Pietro loathes, and on the center-right, the Northern League is eager to implement constitutional changes which the centralizing nationalists of Alleanza Nazionale abhor.

In general, far from cashing in on Italy's acceptance among the members of the Euro currency area, which it was instrumental in bringing about, the brittle center-left alliance stands to lose the most from the probable, sobering post-accession anticlimax. If the various components of the former Ulivo coalition cannot sustain the momentum of 1996—that is, if they fail to lighten the burden of a state still characterized by centralization, intrusiveness, and heavy taxation; to provide infrastructures that meet the needs of today's society; to develop a new and up-to-date idea of social compassion, while responsibly and responsively accepting the challenge of criminality, petty and otherwise; and, last but not least, if they prove unable to unite solidly behind the profile of Francesco Rutelli, their young new leader—Italians will inevitably turn to the competition and again follow the free-for-all (i.e., free-for-few, free-for-the-powerful) brand of capitalism preached by Berlusconi and his associates. Such a sorry outcome might, of course, be viewed in the future as a self-inflicted retribution for the inadequacies of the Italian center-left; but Europe—most of Europe, at any rate—would definitely not deserve it.

On the constitutional front, things look hardly more reassuring. In 1998, the two-chamber, multipartisan commission in charge of constitutional revisions disbanded without being able to settle not only some comparatively less vital matters (for example, the direct election of the president of the Republic—not surprisingly, an issue dear to the hearts of media emperors and their allies), but a number of very serious ones as well. Among such basic issues were how to adapt Italian institutions to an increasingly integrated Europe; how to streamline the workings of a famously inefficient Parliament; how to respond properly to regional diversity; and, perhaps most important, how to protect public prosecutors from recurrent attacks by the politico-economic groups whose interests they threaten by their investigations. Today, Italian democracy is strong, but not nearly as strong as it should, and could, be.

The economic arena, too, offers a mixed outlook. On the one hand, the economy is doing nicely: Italian exports are in strong demand around the world; the reduction of tax evasion is making progress; and a shrinking budget deficit has allowed Italy to be among the founding members of the Euro currency system. On the other hand, unemployment is still very high, especially in the South; those squeezed by increased "Euro" taxes are, as ever, not the usual evaders but the usual law-abiding citizens on fixed incomes; and the long-term issue of state-funded pensions, despite years of nibbling at the problem, has not yet been satisfactorily resolved. How to ensure, in the face of an aging population, a decent survival level for the truly needy and the truly deserving, without lavishing on the nonneedy or undeserving the resources that a newly lean government and a demographically changed society can no longer afford? This seems to be the defining issue of the Italian economy at the turn of the new century, as Italy prepares to join the ever tighter embrace of the European Union. Finally, when all of this is dealt with successfully, there still remains the minor issue of integrating into the productive fabric of Italian society millions of new immigrants from the four corners of the world.

Will all the right answers come from Europe? Most Italians seem to think so.

Today, Italians top the charts of Europhilia—though, apparently, because of a widespread belief among them that European effectiveness will cause their future governments finally to implement those measures which they would not have the determination to adopt on their own. Besides, the impending closer membership in a stable, affluent federal entity brings the perception that, far from contradicting demands from local autonomists, Europe can in fact contribute to resorbing their complaints.

However, even this is not certain to mean that a new European age will be dawning on Italians at the beginning of the twenty-first century. As the long-standing post-unification plight of the former East Germany clearly shows, discarding a historically weak currency and adopting a strong neighbor's one can be a very mixed blessing. Optimism is good, but competitiveness is better. Italian enthusiasm for the Euro could be based on a mass delusion: a delusion nourished by the misguided hope to have life both ways—with Germany's rigor and low interest rates, but also with the profligacy of Italian governments' traditional spending habits. Which of the two will have to give? With closer and closer integration looming, Italy will indeed get the Euro it covets, but a large cloud looms over the future horizon: For how long will Italy like it?

Thankfully, the 1990s showed that news of the death of the Italian cinema had been exaggerated. On the other hand, merely being alive can seem either a grand accomplishment or a pretty mediocre one, depending on what one is accustomed to; and the latter of the two views is frequently taken by critics who are inclined to look pessimistically at what is often referred to as the *nuovo cinema italiano*.

Whether such a position is fair may be questionable, however. In an age of radical technological and social realignment of historically established media it is, after all, far from certain that cinema (and not only the Italian one) will ever be the same again from the point of view of its "socio-artistic" significance. Blaming a vast number of players for no longer producing masterpieces with the impact of *Bicycle Thieves, La dolce vita*, or *The Leopard* makes sense only if equivalent artifacts can be shown to pour forth with ease from other national film industries—a proposition that seems difficult to subscribe to at this moment.

In the long term, of course, only time can tell whether Italian cinema is bound for renewed fame or heading toward provincial irrelevance. My personal predictions lean toward guarded optimism: after all, for many centuries Italians have had to learn to cope and live with the apparently crushing weight of their historical and cultural heritage. Sometimes they have done better, sometimes they have done worse at this task; but often enough they have done a perfectly good job of it. Since the fall of the Roman Republic, Italy has witnessed many a revival, political and otherwise, and one more would hardly be surprising news.

Surely, though, the ultimate, dramatic question seems to be not whether Italian directors of the future will make films worth seeing, but whether their country's

Hollywood-dominated distribution system will allow those films to be seen by a meaningful number of viewers—or will grant them no more than a shadow existence as a niche product. Very few Italians, after all, own a video store or have time to fly weekly to Rome or can afford a detective's services to find out where and for how many days an Italian film will be coming to a very small theater acceptably near them.

Among the films of the period 1989–2000 that most deserve being remembered—and, in fact, global media giants willing, deserve being seen—are Amelio's *Open Doors* (*Porte aperte*, 1990), *Stealing Children* (*Il ladro di bambini*, 1992), *Lamerica* (1994), and *The Way We Laughed* (*Così ridevano*, 1998); Antonioni's *Beyond the Clouds* (*Al di là delle nuvole*, 1995); Archibugi's *Toward Evening* (*Verso sera*, 1990), *The Great Pumpkin* (*Il grande cocomero* [*sic*], 1993), *With Closed Eyes* (*Con gli occhi chiusi*, 1994), and *Shooting Up* (*L'albero delle pere*, 1998); Bellocchio's *The Conviction* (*La condanna*, 1991), *The Butterfly's Dream* (*Il sogno della farfalla*, 1994), *The Prince of Homburg* (*Il principe di Homburg*, 1997), and *The Wet Nurse* (*La balia*, 1999); Benigni's *Johnny Stecchino* (1991), *The Monster* (*Il mostro*, 1994), and *Life Is Beautiful* (*La vita è bella*, 1998); Calopresti's *The Second Time* (*La seconda volta*, 1995), *The Word Love Exists* (*La parola amore esiste*, 1998), and *I Prefer the Sound of the Sea* (*Preferisco il rumore del mare*, 2000); Capuano's *Vito and the Others* (*Vito e gli altri*, 1991) and *Pianese Nunzio Will Be 14 Next May* (*Pianese Nunzio 14 anni a maggio*, 1996); Sergio Citti's *The Three Homeless Kings* (*I magi randagi*, 1996) and *The Dogs Are Watching Us Too* (*Anche i cani ci guardano*) in Francesco Laudadio's *Exercises of Style* (*Esercizi di stile*, 1996); Faenza's *My Dear Dr. Gräsler* (*Mio caro Dr. Gräsler*, 1991), *Jonah Who Lived Inside the Whale* (*Jona che visse nella balena*, 1993), and *Pereira Declares* (*Sostiene Pereira*, 1995); Fellini's *The Voice of the Moon* (*La voce della luna*, 1990); Giuseppe Ferrara's *Giovanni Falcone* (1993); Ferreri's *Silver Nitrate* (*Nitrato d'argento*, 1996); Giordana's *Pasolini: An Italian Crime* (*Pasolini, un delitto italiano*, 1995); and *One Hundred Steps* (*I cento passi*, 2000); Labate's *My Generation* (*La mia generazione*, 1996); Lizzani's *Celluloid* (*Celluloide*, 1996); and Luchetti's *The Footman* (*Il portaborse*, 1991).

Also in the group are Maiorca's *Viol@* (1998); Martone's *Death of a Neapolitan Mathematician* (*Morte di un matematico napoletano*, 1992), *Harassment and Love* (*L'amore molesto*, 1995), and *Theater of War* (*Teatro di guerra*, 1998); Mazzacurati's *Another Life* (*Un'altra vita*, 1992), *Vesna in the Fast Lane* (*Vesna va veloce*, 1996), and *Holy Tongue* (*La lingua del santo*, 2000); Monicelli's *Very Close Relatives* (*Parenti serpenti*, 1991), *A Construction Idyll* (*Idillio edile*) in Laudadio's *Exercises of Style* (1996), and *Dirty Laundry* (*Panni sporchi*, 1999); Moretti's *Dear Diary* (*Caro diario*, 1993) and *April* (*Aprile*, 1998); Nichetti's *Volere volare* (1991), *Stefano So-Many-Stories* (*Stefano Quantestorie*, 1993), and *Luna and Her Other* (*Luna e l'altra*, 1996); Piccioni's *Ask for the Moon* (*Chiedi la luna*, 1991), *Broke Hearts* (*Cuori al verde*, 1996), and *Not of This World* (*Fuori dal mondo*, 1999); Piscicelli's *The Body of the Soul*

(*Il corpo dell'anima*, 1999); Placido's *Pummarò* (1990), *A Bourgeois Hero* (*Un eroe borghese*, 1995), and *On Love Lost* (*Del perduto amore*, 1998); Pozzessere's *Southbound* (*Verso sud*, 1992), *Father and Son* (*Padre e figlio*, 1994), and *High-Risk Witness* (*Testimone a rischio*, 1997); Marco Risi's *The Rubber Wall* (*Il muro di gomma*, 1991); Rosi's *The Palermo Connection* (*Dimenticare Palermo*, 1990) and *The Truce* (*La tregua*, 1997); and Rubini's *The Station* (*La stazione*, 1991), *Extraordinary Performance* (*Prestazione straordinaria*, 1994), and *All the Love There Is* (*Tutto l'amore che c'è*, 2000).

Further films in this group are Salvatores's *Marrakech Express* (1989), *The Tour* (*Turné*, 1990), *Mediterraneo* (1991), *Puerto Escondido* (1992), and *South* (*Sud*, 1993); Scola's *The Voyage of Captain Fracassa* (*Il viaggio di Capitan Fracassa*, 1990), *The Novel of a Young Man in Poverty* (*Romanzo di un giovane povero*, 1995), and *The Dinner* (*La cena*, 1998); Soldini's *The Clear Skies of the West* (*L'aria serena dell'ovest*, 1990), *A Soul Split in Two* (*Un'anima divisa in due*, 1993), *The Acrobats* (*Le acrobate*, 1997), and *Bread and Tulips* (*Pane e tulipani*, 2000); Squitieri's *And They Called Them Brigands* (*E li chiamarono briganti*, 1999); Paolo and Vittorio Taviani's *The Night Sun* (*Il sole anche di notte*, 1990), *Floréal* (*Fiorile*, 1993), *Elective Affinities* (*Le affinità elettive*, 1996), and *You Laugh* (*Tu ridi*, 1998); Ricky Tognazzi's *Hooligans* (*Ultrà*, 1991), *The Escort* (*La scorta*, 1993), and *Choked Lives* (*Vite strozzate*, 1996); Tornatore's *Everybody's Fine* (*Stanno tutti bene*, 1990), *A Mere Formality* (*Una pura formalità*, 1994), *The Star-Maker* (*L'uomo delle stelle*, 1995), and *The Legend of the Ocean-Borne Pianist* (*La leggenda del pianista sull'oceano*, 1999); Torre's *Tano unto Death* (*Tano da morire*, 1997); Virzì's *The Good Life* (*La bella vita*, 1994), *Summer Vacations* (*Ferie d'agosto*, 1996), *Ovosodo* (1997), and *Hugs and Kisses* (*Baci e abbracci*, 1999); Wertmüller's *Ciao Professore!* (*Io speriamo che me la cavo*, 1992) and *Ferdinando e Carolina* (1999); and Zaccaro's *The Stone Valley* (*La valle di pietra*, 1992), *The Article 2* (*L'articolo 2*, 1993), *The Gamebag* (*Il carniere*, 1997), and *A Decent Man* (*Un uomo perbene*, 1999).

Given the present, exponentially growing ease of travel and cultural exchange, it seems only logical that the Italian cinema of the last decade of the twentieth century should have produced a peak number of films that re-create French, German, and Russian literary texts. Moretti's *Palombella rossa* was dealt with in chapter 5; I will now refer synthetically to another work linked to Russian culture, Paolo and Vittorio Taviani's *The Night Sun* (*Il sole anche di notte*, 1990), which receives in-depth treatment in my *Masters of Two Arts*.

The Tavianis' *The Night Sun* is a re-creation of Tolstoy's novella *Father Sergius* (posthumously published in 1911, written in 1890–98). One can easily recognize the relevance of Tolstoy's hero to the Italy of the last few years of the so-called First Republic, if one considers that he is a visionary young man who attempts to cultivate his calling in seclusion and at a remove from the corruption of all churches of the world. When Sergius thinks that, as a hermit, he may have finally triumphed over the most sophisticated temptations and achieved a calm contemplation of the Absolute, the devil pulls him back to his century: spiritually undermined by the flattery of a growing public and by the stimulus of an excessively rich diet, Sergius caves in to the comparatively banal charms of a tycoon's mad daughter, and eventually sinks into utter despair about himself and his vocation.

Clearly, there is much in the Tavianis' film that amounts to a reflection on the difficult status of the recluse—the auteur, by any chance?—during years when faith in absolute values is ever harder to sustain in the face of the ubiquitousness, in fact the irresistible invasiveness, of the forces of "evil." Whither to abscond, if even in a hermitage atop a mountain one cannot pull the plug on the cackle emitted by the demented child of a well-connected millionnaire? A society imbued with the quick, abundant, and vulgar money of private TV empires clearly acts here as the Tavianis' cultural subtext. What in ideological times used to go by the name of "Mammon" might as well now be called "the market" with little appreciable difference.

Soldini's *The Clear Skies of the West* (*L'aria serena dell'ovest*, 1990), too, zeroes in—altogether coincidentally, be it understood—on easy money, taking viewers on a guided tour of the highs and lows of contemporary Milanese yuppie life. The protagonists of successive episodes in the film's long narrative chain are linked by a not altogether unexpected rationale: carnal-sentimental involvement.

The chain starts with Cesare, a former student of anthropology who abandons his unremunerative vocation to make a much easier living by doing market surveys. Through a telephone interview he becomes acquainted with Olga, with whom he soon ends up in bed. Early the next morning, Olga leaves Cesare's place and vanishes from his life— but, crucially, forgets her pocket phone book in the bedroom. In the attempt to locate Olga, Cesare starts calling her women friends. Though he has little success, he does find consolation in one of his respondents. This is Irene, a Sienese newcomer to Milan who, in addition to professional maladjustment, experiences a troubled relationship with her husband, a university professor. Irene is on the point of breaking up her marriage and attaching herself to Cesare; but her husband. . . .

Meanwhile, Olga's half of the narrative *ronde* pushes forward in an opposite and symmetrical direction. Olga is not, in fact, the young woman's real name; she is really Veronica, and works as a nurse in a hospital. One day Tobia, a technician for a pharmaceutical company, is stabbed by a thug and hospitalized; Veronica tends him. Tobia and Veronica are attracted to one another and plan to elope to Paris for a physical-romantic vacation, leaving behind Tobia's career-crazed wife—who in turn. . . .

Eventually, the revelry affects Veronica's career. She is forced to give up her job in Milan and, in the film's epilogue, goes to work in a private clinic in Switzerland.[1]

The *ronde* goes on and on, in potentially infinite turns. How, then, does Soldini choose the particular moments that are to act as chronological terminus a quo and terminus ad quem for his story? He does so somewhat arbitrarily, and yet altogether meaningfully. To begin and to end his longitudinal slice of Milanese life he selects two high points of global history: the Tienanmen Square massacre in Beijing of June 1989, and the collapse of the Berlin Wall just a few months thereafter—two dramatic events between which the frivolous machinations of the hedonistic, inane characters unfold. At the opening and at the close of the film, we see real footage of just those epoch-making events pour from TV screens into the philistine living rooms of Italy's alleged "moral capital," implicitly (though no less eloquently for that) contrasting the concerns of people in the real world with the private ghosts of careerists safe inside their cocoons. Hence the sarcasm compressed into the film's title: Welcome, post-Communist Easterners of the world, to the clear skies under which the West thrives!

Di Giammatteo suggests[2]—rightly, I feel—that the structure of *The Clear Skies of the West* re-creates the one in the drama *La Ronde* (*Reigen*, 1900) by the Viennese Arthur Schnitzler.[3] This is a "circular" play which holds together not by virtue of any internal psychological development in its characters, but mechanically, insofar as each of these introduces the next one: A has sex with B, then B with C, then C with D . . . and so on, until, getting back to the beginning, X has sex with A.[4]

While I am persuaded that the structural homology does hold, I would add for enhanced precision that in a very real sense *La Ronde* is not a play at all; in fact, it can probably best be understood as the modern incarnation of a medieval *danse macabre*. (A metaphorical link with the spread of syphilis is discernible not too far below the surface of the *Totentanz* composed by Arthur Schnitzler, M.D.) If the comparison is correct, then the main message of *La Ronde* comes down to a perennial memento mori—a memento mori conveyed less by the actual lines its characters utter than by what could be called the metasignification lent to those lines by the peculiar literary genre into which they can be inscribed. Narrative irony is the substance filling the gap thus created between the apparent, literal meaning and the substantial, hidden one.

Although it would be excessive to claim that *The Clear Skies of the West* carries out an equally protracted foray into medieval literary typology, I am inclined to think that it shares with Schnitzler's *La Ronde* more than the mere "narrative mechanism" to which Di Giammatteo calls attention. Specifically, I would argue that the film also sees fully eye to eye with Schnitzler's text in its other, "ideological" component (as Di Giammatteo calls it), the view that "the rising young bourgeois of industrialized society are cynics and conformists, deprived of morals and insensitive to feelings."[5] Di Giammatteo appears to believe that Schnitzler would not have recognized the Vienna of his own times in such a portrait; and this position most Schnitzlerians would probably find too timid. In a different sense, of course, Di Giammatteo may well be right: the dancers in the sexual chain of the original *La Ronde* are in fact unlike Soldini's, to the extent that they cover the entire spectrum of human age and belong to all walks of death.[6]

The next film I am going to turn to, Faenza's *My Dear Doctor Gräsler (Mio caro Dottor Gräsler*, 1991), will cause some of my readers to exclaim: What— nothing on Schnitzler so far, and now two items in a row? Clearly, it makes sense to pause briefly and take stock of Italian Schnitzleriana in the early 1990s.

In Italy, mentioning the name of Schnitzler to anyone not affiliated with academic departments of German literature could—depending on when the survey was conducted—elicit one of two responses: "Ah, Schnitzler!" or "Arthur who?" The former answer is more typical after the end of the 1970s; the latter would have been the norm before then. Why?

The cultural-historical context of post-World War II Europe offers compelling arguments to rationalize Schnitzler's homecoming to fame as part of something very closely resembling a tidal shift. Until the late 1970s, a politically riven Europe, with still vivid recollections of its latest war, understandably favored political authors, or at least authors who lent themselves to a tragic reading. Foremost among the Germanic ones were Thomas Mann (*Doctor Faustus*), Karl Kraus (*The Last Days of Humanity*), and Bertolt Brecht (whose programmatically "epic" theater remained altogether tragic, at least in the nontechnical sense of the word). Brecht's dictum that "literature will be scrutinized" might well have been chosen as the intimidating-sounding principle of those years: according to that maxim, literature would one day be scrutinized for signs that people of the past attached high value to the supreme themes of human existence, and the frivolous would be disapprovingly left to one side.[7] Within this frame of expectations, what self-respecting Italian intellectual would have had recourse for inspiration to the cultural heritage of the belle epoque: decadence, hedonism, operetta, or suchlike? Perhaps only Visconti—who had sufficient further familiarity with the unfrivolous traditions of European cultures to be able to distill from apparently contradictory discourses stern, if not even somber, works of art.

The 1980s offered a wholly different picture. With the rise to power of the Italian Socialists and the first echoes of Bettino Craxi's resounding goose steps on the world stage, operetta became (in Italy, at any rate) a concept whose time had at long last come back. The decade was the peak time of a reassuring, homey empire cultivating interiority under the powerful protection of NATO's nuclear umbrella and of high-yield treasury bonds; a mini-empire having an obvious, irrepressible spiritual affinity with the cheerful Vienna of the time before 1918. After us the deluge ... please step forward, Doctor Schnitzler![8]

Schnitzler is, of course, not just a very trendy minor classic; he is a very complex and rich classic. His novels and dramas excel above all in depicting and unmasking pettiness and provincialism. Some of them, particularly those of his last, post–World War I years, are masterpieces of psychological introspection, technical virtuosity, and—*pace* Schnitzler's detractors—even pathos (for example, *Miss Else/Fräulein Else*, 1924). *Dr. Gräsler, Health-Resort Physician (Dr. Gräsler, Badearzt*, 1917), published when Schnitzler had been famous for over two decades, coincides with a sharpening war-induced crisis in Austria and reflects a state of mind in which a still sizable but perceptibly decreasing amount of life-affirming satire is being overtaken by an even more rapidly growing amount of dark pessimism, if not outright dysphoria.

It is not easy to do justice to *Dr. Gräsler* economically. The most convenient approach to the novel might be to treat it as an uncanny double to Thomas Mann's slightly earlier *Death in Venice (Der Tod in Venedig,* 1912)—a double that shows many narrative elements corresponding to those in Mann's novella, but inverts their signs to give them opposite values. The following is a brief characterization aimed at bringing out some of the traits in Schnitzler's hero by way of contrast with his more famous alter ego.

Both protagonists are educated male bourgeois; but while Mann's Aschenbach is an intellectual great-bourgeois, Gräsler is a business-conscious petty-bourgeois who at most reads, when read he does, his deceased sister's love letters. While the name "Aschenbach" evokes a brook (*Bach*) lined with ash trees (*Eschen*), "Gräsler" strays far beyond the serenely pastoral and into the never-never realm of bovine rumination. Aschenbach has a motto, "Endure!"; Gräsler does not have one, but if he did, his would be very different—perhaps "When in doubt, shrink back." Aschenbach cultivates a classical love for the Beautiful and the Good that leads him to court pedophilia; Gräsler is a heterosexual less out of choice than out of laziness, and simply grazes along with whatever willing woman might happen to come within his reach.

Early in their respective texts, both Mann's and Schnitzler's heroes go to the sunny South on vacation: Aschenbach to Venice, and Gräsler to Lanzarote in the Canary Islands. Hotel life is flat and stuffy in both places; however, while the slick Italian hotel manager at least wears a French-styled frock coat, his uncouth counterpart off the African coast is a mix of German and American vulgarity. While, in Thomas Mann, Venice grandly delivers on what her fame promises, in morbidity if nothing else, Schnitzler's Lanzarote shows a pitiful gap between its chivalrous, courtly aura (as "Lancelot's island," no less) and its utterly commercial reality.

In Mann, Aschenbach dies at the end of the novella; in Schnitzler, death takes place at the beginning—and, crucially, it is *someone else's* death: not mediocre Emil's, but his sister Friederike's, who commits suicide in belated acknowledgment that she has too long led a life as dull as her brother's.

Aschenbach succumbs; Gräsler returns peacefully home after his sister's death. There, he takes up wishy-washy relationships with three women in succession. He loses the pragmatic, strong-willed Sabine to his own undecisiveness; the simple-minded, good-natured, life-loving Katharina, to measles; as for the third one, the short and plump widow Sommer, she marries him. One year after Friederike's suicide, Gräsler shows up at the usual Canarian hotel for his usual routine. Death in Lanzarote—and then life creeps on.

Throughout Schnitzler's long novella/short novel, Gräsler shows himself aware of his own mediocrity; he often debates within himself whether he is "too much" or "not enough" of a philistine to attain success in life. (Of course, this is in itself a philistine's dilemma.) Even his eros is unpoetic in the extreme: the volume he and Katharina slam closed on his bed on the first occasion they engage in mutual anatomical explorations—the equivalent of Lancelot's and Guenevere's romance that acted as a go-between for Dante's Paolo and Francesca—is Dr. Gräsler's atlas of human anatomy.

Only jealousy manages, and then just one time, to extract some fire from Gräsler's loins. This occurs when Gräsler thinks Katharina is playing games with him (he, rather than she, has in fact been playing games during their relationship):

"I'm going to Berlin first, then perhaps to Paris to have a thoroughly good time such as I've never had in my life." In imagination he saw himself in certain places of ill repute, dancing with half-naked women; he planned monstrous orgies as a sort of demoniacal revenge on the wretched sex that treated him so trickishly—revenge on Katharina, Sabine, Friederike.[9]

This is a striking, small-scale remake of Thomas Mann's climactic evocation of Aschenbach's Eleusinian mystery:

In the fragmented light [one] could see people, animals, a swarm, a roaring mob, all rolling and plunging and whirling down from the forested heights, past tree-trunks and great moss-covered fragments of rock, overflowing the slope with their bodies, flames, tumult, and reeling circular dance. Women, stumbling over the fur skirts that hung too long from their belts, moaned, threw their heads back, shook their tambourines on high, brandished naked daggers and torches that threw off sparks, held serpents with flickering tongues by the middle of their bodies, or cried out, lifting their breasts in both hands. . . .

[Aschenbach's] heart pounded with the rhythm of the drum beats, his mind whirled, rage took hold of him and blinded him, he was overcome by a numbing lust, and his soul longed to join in the reeling dance of the god.[10]

We can find here condensed the essence of the dialogism that runs through the two texts: what occurs as grand in *Der Tod in Venedig* recurs as suffocatingly petty in *Dr. Gräsler, Health-Resort Physician*. Schnitzler's conclusion is consistent in studiously avoiding any cathartic relief: by bringing us back to the beginning, the tongue-in-check denouement of his novel induces a sense of stifling claustrophobia.

Roberto Faenza came to *My Dear Dr. Gräsler* with a background, in the 1960s and 1970s, as director of thrillers and science fiction films aspiring to cultural status and political sophistication. In the difficult political atmosphere of the late 1970s, Faenza made *Go for It Italy (Forza Italia*, 1978)—a film with a sarcastic title that, in quasi-documentary cold blood, lined up evidence of a long string of misdeeds tolerated, fomented, or directly instigated by the long-ruling Christian Democrats. (Berlusconi, who some fifteen years later would pick the very same soccer-style slogan, "Forza Italia," as the label for the political wing of his economic empire, seems not to have been aware that he was echoing the bitter burlesque in the film's title.) Aside from university teaching (sociology of mass media at Pisa) and participation in an important cooperative production house, Faenza's curriculum includes further re-creations from literature: *Jonah Who Lived Inside the Whale*, from Jona Oberski's *Childhood* (1978) and *Pereira Declares*, from Antonio Tabucchi's novel by the same title (*Sostiene Pereira*, 1994).

My Dear Dr. Gräsler reproduces Schnitzler's story, costumes and decors with great accuracy—too much accuracy, perhaps. The transition from Schnitzler's words to Faenza's images and dialogue retains almost every twist and turn in the plot, but it neglects the protagonist's psychological dimension, his internal polyphony. What particularly suffers in the film is the portrayal of Gräsler's insignificance: his constant fear of, and flight from, anything out of the flattest ordinary, and his perennial reckoning with his own philistinism.

By the end of the film, the spectators are able to draw their own unequivocal conclusions about Gräsler; but Schnitzler's very point is Gräsler's passive acceptance of a mediocrity he is aware of—not just any old mediocrity, but, so to speak, a second-degree one.

A sense of deliberate incongruity permeates Schnitzler's novel, beginning with the title's reference to a "health-resort physician"—a physician, that is, for affluent patients whose bodies hardly needed a physician. The film largely blanks out this and other similar narrative ironies. Perhaps because of its accelerated rhythm, made necessary by the choice to cover in two hours' running time all the piquant details of the multiple gyrations in the doctor's ninety-plus pages of gallantry, *My Dear Dr. Gräsler* does not dwell adequately on the inanity of the world around Gräsler, the irrelevance of his oxymoronic profession, and the full extent of his moral cowardice. The film does come across as an entertaining comedy; but precisely for that reason it ultimately misses a more important target, the broadly understood "political" one at which Schnitzler had aimed. Further poorly served by an aseptic, homogenized dubbing in the style of TV serials, *My Dear Dr. Gräsler* looks and feels like a Hollywood sitcom in costume.[11] Faenza has, on other occasions, proved able to do much better than that.[12]

Easy money, with a particularly nasty link to politics, again recurs as the societal terrain from which sprang the item I next turn to, Luchetti's *The Footman* (*Il portaborse*, 1991).

What if, in order to articulate a discourse on contemporary Italian polity, modern European literatures were broached in a film not by way of a direct citation or re-creation, but in the metatextual guise of an open public discussion? It seems as though it would take a professor of literature to do that—with the attendant danger of slipping into utter cinematic boredom. However, Luchetti's *The Footman* brilliantly proves such fears wrong, not despite the professor (here actually a high school teacher, though the latitude of the term covers him in Italian for that purpose), but thanks to the way it casts him, the fictional character

Luciano Sandulli: an archetypal reincarnation of the poet-in-the-garret in an age of consumeristic—indeed, truly cornucopian—corruption.

Luciano cultivates poetry most fervently. His bedside book is a collection by an (imaginary) twentieth-century Italian author, Carlo Sperati, whose inspiration, we learn from fragments of the teacher's lectures, descends from Francis of Assisi by way of Folgore da San Gimignano and Lorenzo de' Medici. However (as Pasternak's Zhivago, a fictitious poet invented by a real one, so aptly puts it), art is a way of being, not a profession;[13] and this well explains why, in the attempt to feed himself and prop up his historical, beautifully located, but crumbling family home on the Salerno coast, Luciano must scramble to find sources of income. He can obtain a minimum of security from his official profession at school; teaching is an activity he undertakes with zeal both because he loves poetry and a proper use of language in general, and because he enjoys dealing with young adults not yet committed to duplicating the narrowly materialistic ambitions of their parents. For the needed complementary revenue, however, he must resort to moonlighting as a ghost writer for a famous (also imaginary) Italian novelist, essayist, and journalist, Sartorio, who is going through a patch of ill health. For Sartorio, Luciano has already written three novels.

Since the foundations of his home urgently need to be reinforced, Luciano offers Sartorio to write copiously for him. No such luck, alas: now Sartorio feels better. Luciano panics; he is left alone to face his edificatory debts—and the costly routine of a commuter relationship with his fiancée, Irene.

The philosophical—but also highly realistic—apologue contained in *The Footman* then unfolds, as the quintessentially pure soul meets the quintessentially corrupt one.

Luciano is approached by the private secretary of the politician Cesare Botero, Minister for state-owned enterprises (*Ministro delle partecipazioni statali*), the youngest and most ambitious minister in the country. Italian audiences do not need much extra detail to respond to these cultural allusions: once fed these scant pieces of information, they can infer the rest and construe Botero as an unprincipled power broker whose political allegiance depends, at any given time, not on any moral scruples but solely on pragmatic considerations.

The Footman precedes the time of the Clean Hands judicial investigations, and we are here still within the horizon of the "first" Italian Republic. The film stops short of identifying Botero as a card-carrying member of the Italian Socialist Party, but the Socialists who attacked the film as offensive (to them) certainly proved that it was unnecessary to.

Why has Botero—presumably tipped off by Sartorio—sought out our teacher? Not because Luciano cultivates poetry; that, if anything, would be an excellent reason to disqualify him. But, true to his own postideological personality, Botero does not stop at such feeble-minded considerations. He can recognize talent when he sees it, and Luciano has just what the minister needs in a speechwriter . . . if only that speechwriter could divorce *how* he writes from *what* he is to write. Hence the proposal, which meets with Luciano's initial hesitation. Then need takes the upper hand; under economic duress, the poet accepts the demonic contract.

There is little reason, for our purpose, to dwell on the many scandals and episodes of corruption that in *The Footman* dot Italian history, past and in the making. Suffice it to say that in the end justice, or at least the poetic variant of it, is restored when Luciano, having grown disenchanted with the mechanism into which he has been sucked, jumps out of it to moral safety.

Two passages in the film call our attention to the subject of modern European literatures. The first of these features a brief excerpt from a video viewed by Luciano's students. Feeling guilty for having left his pupils behind and taken up a life of hectic commuting to and from the capital, the teacher supplies them with the minimum help necessary to pass their final, standardized *esame di maturità*. In introducing a poem by Emily Dickinson, Luciano mixes a fanatical Europhilia with ludicrous self-justification:

. . . these are the initial verses of one of the great lyrics by Emily Dickinson. Remember? We devoted three hours of class time to that. And in the logbook I wrote instead that we had talked about Vittorio Alfieri, whom I had spared you. . . . I would have liked to carry on in the same way . . . to talk to you about the Brontë sisters, not about Giacomo Zanella; about *Moby Dick*, not about [Carducci's] "Through the Tuscan Maremma" . . . about Rimbaud, not bombastic D'Annunzio. . . . This, too, is my fault; and for this, too, I beg you to excuse me. But my house is collapsing! . . . I am not asking you to forgive me, but at least to understand me![14]

His second spiritual outpouring, an impromptu lecture he gives during a review session at his home, is even more abrasive against the inflexible backwardness of centrally mandated Italian education:

The Italian literature of the nineteenth century, I told you thousands of times already, is pitiful, it should be skipped in one leap. . . . What do we care about a Silvio Pellico, a Berchet, a Zanella, a Carducci? And even Manzoni! Let us tell the truth, for once: while Manzoni takes fifty years to write and rewrite *The Betrothed* [*I promessi sposi*, 1827 and 1840], Balzac completes a string of ten masterpieces, Melville writes the immensely great *Moby Dick*, and Dostoyevsky . . . well, Dostoyevsky writes *The Idiot, Crime and Punishment*, and *The Brothers Karamazov*! The only thing one could, perhaps, salvage from the Italian nineteenth century is painting! But . . . for some reason your fine arts teacher has left it out of the program altogether![15]

Luchetti's imaginary update to contemporary Italy of Luciano's quasi-Faustian fable of a pact with evil thus found an entirely realistic dimension not only in its portrayal of current political (mal)practices, but also in the precise depiction of an intellectually ebullient teacher's frustration with Italy's outdated educational system—a system essentially unchanged since the time of Fascism, and one in which students of the 1990s were, by and large, instructed to ignore the vital trends of modern world literature and focus instead on obscure provincial pedants.

The uproar caused by *The Footman* at the time of its release was predominantly political in nature, and its other features, both artistic and cultural, were left comparatively undiscussed. It may be an appropriate time now to reverse that neglect, and to observe how frequent it is in Italy for a trend toward cultural rejuvenation to take the form of a renewed interest in foreign literatures—the most egregious example of such a behavior having been, in the twentieth century, the anti-Fascist Pavese's and Vittorini's "subversive" cultivation of the great classics in the history of the American novel.[16]

Not that, to Luciano, Italy is necessarily bad and Europe necessarily good; his answer as a teacher is to develop a flexible approach, resorting to interdisciplinarity wherever useful, and meanwhile putting the greatest in a league of their own—from Saint Francis to Balzac and Dostoyevsky. If the great Italian poet Carlo Sperati existed, it seems safe to assume, he could only have nodded in approval.[17]

The next two entries focus on the unusual personalities of strange, almost misanthropic anticonformists: the first, the historical figure of a contemporary Italian Marxist; the second, a fictional nineteenth-century Christian from Central Europe. The biography of the former is the subject matter of Martone's *Death of a Neapolitan Mathematician* (*Morte di un matematico napoletano*, 1992)— a film that made a deep impression on Italian audiences in the early 1990s, not least because of its almost antiquarian courage in resurrecting images and themes from a time when Italians felt there was no shame in not being young, rich, and brash.

A widespread cultural stereotype holds that a few privileged professional categories—poets, philosophers, nuclear physicists, oracles, mathematicians—work elbow to elbow with God in the accomplishment of their routine tasks. Whether or not that is indeed the case, it is certain that the life of the mathematician Renato Caccioppoli (1904–1959) lends solid anecdotal support to that view.

Conforming to available biographical reports, Martone's film portrays Caccioppoli as an eccentric and genial but depression-prone denizen of a world of his own, who habitually wanders without aim about his labyrinthine native city. Introverted and self-absorbed, during his perambulations Caccioppoli mixes excitement about the indubitable truths of mathematics with utter dejection over the highly dubitable ones of human existence and international politics.

A grandchild of the Russian anarchist Mikhail Aleksandrovich Bakunin and a convinced Communist sympathizer, Caccioppoli was devastated by the Hungarian uprising of 1956 and the subsequent Soviet invasion. Clearly, such soul-searching immediately after the crisis of 1956 could only appear highly topical to pro-Soviet Italians in the wake of the Eastern bloc's collapse in 1989. Shunning all facile sensationalism, Martone—again in conformity with biographical evidence—explores the hidden paths that can link global tragedies to individual crises. He presents the motivation and dynamics of Caccioppoli's suicide as being logical, yet somehow mysterious, and probably destined to remain such.

In the film, as in real life, literature is a favorite pastime of Caccioppoli's. Martone shows us his Neapolitan mathematician as, typically for him, he reads aloud for some of his friends the first few lines from Beckett's appropriately existential *Waiting for Godot*:

Vladimir. I'm beginning to come round to that opinion. All my life I've tried to put it from me, saying, Vladimir, be reasonable, you haven't yet tried everything. And I resumed the struggle. (*He broods, musing on the struggle. Turning to Estragon.*) So there you are again.

Estragon. Am I?

Vladimir. I'm glad to see you back. I thought you were gone for ever.[18]

Caccioppoli can empathize with these lines via a very slight amount of hermeneutic arm-twisting. For him, "All my life I've tried to put it from me" and "I resumed the struggle" obviously subsume the same two polar opposites that have long been vying for hegemony inside his own mind: on the one hand, depression; on the other, commitment to a suprapersonal level of concerns where individual anguish should cease to matter. The film's goal is precisely to probe with us by what process which of the two inclinations ultimately turns out to be the stronger in Caccioppoli's case.

Suppose, though, we felt that a Beckett quote was a touch passé? Well, we would be guilty of anachronism in doing so. While that opinion might possibly be common in the cultural atmosphere of the early twenty-first century, in 1959 it would have been anything but. Beckett became well-known in Italy only in the 1960s (he won the Nobel Prize in 1969); Caccioppoli is years ahead of fashion in cultivating him. A few exceptional individuals seem to read not only more inspired books, and with greater inspiration, than the average public does; they evidently also read them sooner—too soon, in some respect, for their own good.[19]

The second loner I alluded to above is the protagonist of the *opus primum* by a young director, Maurizio Zaccaro, today better known for some socially critical films he made later in the 1990s, particularly *Article 2*.

Perhaps Olmi's keenest pupil, Zaccaro re-created *The Stone Valley* (*La valle di pietra*, 1992) from the mid-nineteenth-century *Limestone* (*Kalkstein*, first published 1847), a novella included in the collection *Colored Stones* (*Bunte Steine*, 1853) by the Austrian Adalbert Stifter.[20] Olmi wrote the script with Zaccaro.

Why Olmi and Zaccaro would be attracted to Stifter's *Limestone* is not difficult to see.

Like the novella, the film tells the story of an aging parish priest from an unspecified but remote past who leads an extremely frugal existence. While he shuns social life, he generously helps the people—particularly the children—in his mountain community. He has only one characteristic that is perceived as inappropriate by the educated and better off in his area: whenever he is not fulfilling his duties, our otherwise selfless minister seems to cultivate penny-pinching as one of his greatest concerns. His appreciation for fine linen also causes a number of eyebrows to be raised, at least among those not privy to an innocent episode from his youth.

When, after the old man's death, his will is unsealed and its contents are made public, the mystery is finally explained: he had secretly pledged to himself to save enough to be able to fund the rebuilding of a school for the children in the valley, and an endowment to pay the salary of a teacher to staff it.[21] In the film, the bishop and other local potentates, having heard the news, traverse the rugged, inhospitable landscape to the abode of the deceased churchman, and they attend his funeral there. Praise for the misunderstood and misjudged clergyman posthumously spreads, to the edification—but, frequently, also the perplexity—of the more world-oriented brethren he has left behind.

The portrait of the laconic mountain pastor in *The Stone Valley* fits seamlessly into Olmi's curriculum, which includes a number of God-fearing individuals involved in their communities, bent on hard work and little talk, and disinclined to share their secrets with anyone other than their omniscient divinity. The film's setting, too, is Olmian through and through: the backdrop for the hardly eventful human events consists of a natural scenery of a rough, almost intractable majesty—beautifully rendered by Zaccaro—where time seems to have all but stopped. As, most notably, in Olmi's *Time Stood Still* and *The Tree of Wooden Clogs*, in *The Stone Valley*, too, the time of Christian salvation lies outside the human horizon—yet must be prepared for, well in advance, in this life.[22]

Amelio's *America*—usually quoted by the deliberately misspelled original title *Lamerica* (1994)—suddenly removes us to a contemporary environment and to a number of very special places. First, the film's conceptual core takes us to "America": today's ragged Albanians sail off to Italy in the same way the ragged Italians of yore sailed off to the United States. Second, its setting takes us to Albania, just across the Adriatic Sea; there, at the time of the events, locals were busy undoing a monolithic Communist society.[23] Third, its plot takes us to Russia—the Russia of Gogol's *Dead Souls*. I shall now, in reverse order, examine each of these components, and then show how they interact to produce a powerful film.

Chichikov, the protagonist of *Dead Souls (Mërtvye dushi*, 1842), roams Russia on an obscenely inverted pilgrimage. His get-rich-quick scheme aims at absconding to a remote province with the comfortable viaticum of a large loan—a large, fraudulent loan obtained by registering as collateral the possession of dead serfs (i.e., serfs showing on the latest census rolls, but since deceased) whom he intends to buy on the cheap from unsuspecting landowners. As we advance in Gogol's novel, we realize more and more fully the extent to which the dead souls alluded to in the title are less those being bargained over during the scoundrel's negotiations than the very ones who do the bargaining, Chichikov's own most egregiously. The ending of the novel leaves the protagonist's future in suspense as he flashes through the countryside at the reins of his troika, with the narrator musing about the inscrutability of his fate—as well as wondering loudly and solemnly about a more important destiny which Chichikov's can easily be made to symbolize: that of Russia, a country itself seeking to secure an established place in the world.

The *Dead Souls* we have today is, or at least was considered by Gogol to be, the first part of a trilogy oriented toward a spiritual goal located in the volumes-to-be. After publication, the author was dumbfounded to see that his book obtained great success with both public and critics on the basis of what seemed to him an incorrectly realistic interpretation of it. It was wrong, Gogol argued after the fact, to construe the novel as saying something—and, still more, something cutting to the quick—about the sorry state of provincial Russia; *Dead Souls* was really a prolonged allegory about the human soul imprisoned in earthly existence, and its true aim was to describe that soul's errancy before it can attain otherworldly reconciliation. (Gogol thrust an identically allegorical retrospective interpretation upon the other work that had made him famous, the comedy *Revizor/The Inspector General*, 1836.) He equated *Dead Souls* with a latter-day *Inferno*, to be matched by two uplifting sequels: one to correspond to Dante's *Purgatorio*, and the final and most glorious one to echo *Paradiso*. We have, however, next to nothing left about volume 3, and only early drafts of volume 2.

Gogol turned to volume 2 intermittently, in feverish bouts alternating with work on essays on moral edification. In the latter, his constant concern was to preach the need for the world to put—and keep—all persons in the exact societal positions assigned to them by divine providence: the serfs in the fields; the nobility in their respective administrative regions, to act as the serfs' landlords; the czar in the capital, to act as the landlord of the entire country; and finally God in heaven, to act as the landlord for humanity, and to ensure that all respect their contractual obligations to each other. However, sketching hopeful visions of collective salvation seems to have been for Gogol more an attempted hyper-correction of unresolved internal conflicts than the expression of a peace already attained. Racked by guilt feelings and self-doubt, both as a Christian and as an artist, in 1852 Gogol burned the latest manuscript of *Dead Souls*, volume 2, and within a matter of days died from the consequences of what today would probably be diagnosed as compulsive (and mystically cultivated) anorexia.

In the Italian cinema of the mid-1990s, Chichikov's old troika is no longer an ideal vehicle by which to reach Tirana, the capital of post-Communist Albania. Rather, the most convenient means of transportation for present-day corruption is a shiny, brand-new four-wheel-drive alighting on the Albanian shore from an Italian ferry. Gogol's original scam, too, is reengineered in *Lamerica* to reflect new technologies and a changed historical context.

Two Italian crooks, one older (Fiore), the other an apprentice (Gino), plan to use the capitalistically inexperienced Albanians to their own advantage by setting up a phantom factory in Albania and then using that "factory" as collateral to obtain very real financing from a governmental development agency in Rome.

The idea is less fictional than it may seem at first glance: during the 1980s and early 1990s, the Italian government's soft money fund aimed at supporting regimes in friendly Third World countries selflessly disbursed billions of lire, much of which inexplicably became unaccounted for between departure and landing.

The number of Albanian dead souls required to set up the scheme is small; for the time being, one will suffice. What Fiore and Gino need is a puppet "president" for their company to fulfill a bureaucratic local residency requirement; all he will ever have to do is put his signature on a few documents daily. Thus, the only qualification necessary for the job is total obedience to the Italian racketeers. Combing, with the help of their contacts, recently stormed but not yet physically dismantled Albanian political prisons, Fiore and Gino quickly retrieve an ideal subject from that limbo: it is Spiro Tozaj, a skeletal, unkempt, illiterate, deranged old man who communicates more by gestures than by language—and firmly believes he is twenty years old.

From this point on, the novel's and the film's plots part ways. Instead of embarking upon sequential variations on the dead-soul theme and scouring other geographical areas for more of the same, Gino remains in Albania, where a radical change in lifestyle is forced upon him by subsequent events.

Having returned to Rome to continue wheeling and dealing in the Italian ministries, Fiore finds out that the shady affair has collapsed at the source, and thereupon decides to abandon Gino to his destiny. During a precarious telephone connection with Italy from a remote Albanian hamlet, Gino is shocked to learn that he is out of a job—and of a presumed friend as well.

A true product of the Italian 1980s, Gino has no idea of hunger or physical deprivation, and is therefore unable to imagine that Albanians may experience any stimuli other than those resolvable by Italian banknotes.

Unwittingly given a chance to reach for the moral metamorphosis that had so stubbornly eluded Gogol's Chichikov, Gino undergoes a long string of ordeals in a post-Communist no-man's-land. These impose on him, if not outright repentance, at least a sobering firsthand experience of the absurdity of his earlier, consumeristic approach to life.

Spiro, for his part, gradually reacquires the use of language, and emerges from semibestiality to a moral leadership of sorts. Part of his memory is restored, though not his sanity, and so is his Italo-Sicilian elocution. He finally recollects having deserted "not long ago" (in fact, exactly half a century in the past) from the Fascist army then occupying Albania. Now that the war is apparently over, he feels it is high time to go back to Sicily, to his wife and his newborn baby. Gino is quite welcome to go with him, if he has been let down by his well-heeled buddy; Talarico Michele—his real name before he made his own armistice with the enemy—will not stand up a friend in need.

Yet, standing up a "friend" in need is precisely what Gino is hell-bent on doing: he intends to dump the useless old crank in Albania, in the fallacious persuasion that his own Italian passport will help him get back home quickly and easily once he has gotten rid of the unexpected nuisance.

Gino's plan, however, fails; many are the pitfalls of doing business in countries where greasing palms is still an unrefined, unpredictable art. When the police nab him for the collapsed scam and threaten him with the death penalty for bribing officers, Gino resorts for self-justification to a type of casuistry that speaks volumes about the capitalistic culture from which he comes:

"Bribery, execution . . . what is the point of such words? The trouble is that you Albanians are not yet competent in Western methods. In Italy we always do things this way, to speed up the bureaucracy. It helps files and applications be looked at faster [*Si aiutano le pratiche ad andare avanti*]. . . . There's more efficiency. . . . It's better."[24]

When in Durazzo a desperate mob storms a ship bound for Italy, the crowd includes Gino, who has managed to talk himself free from both the police and his embarrassing father figure. But, on the impossibly crowded decks of the vessel that is taking him to freedom, destiny again brings the ex-yuppie face to face with Talarico Michele—who, despite being on his last leg, has not forgotten his young friend, and treats him as warmly as ever.

Michele's last breath, uttering the delirious persuasion that on the next day they will all land in New York, America, definitively formulates the historical analogy that Italians with a memory of their own past have gradually been developing as the film's plot unfolded: the Italy of today is to Albania what the America of World War II was to Italy.

The core stance of Amelio's *Lamerica* is thereby made clear with utmost lucidity: at one point or another in our history, we have all been "Albanians"; and that is the condition we return to, as soon as our technological comforts and economic privileges are taken away from us. Humanity's natural state of existence is a struggle for survival, and only exceptionally that of civilized well-being; our affluence is therefore more akin to a strange quirk in world history than to something of which we should naturally be proud.

It seems possible that a realization of this kind, if attained, would have waved Chichikov through to the end of his Purgatory, and, once on the far side of the ocean, could even have readied him for the challenges of Paradise. If this had been the case, the later versions of volume 2 might never have been burned by Gogol, and the souls dead at the beginning of the scoundrel's trip might have been resurrected in volume 3.

Evidence of an explicit parallel with Gogol's *Dead Souls* having been pursued in *Lamerica* is elusive, though such an impression is ever-present. The scriptwriters Andrea Porporati and Alessandro Sermoneta write that "Since the first draft, Amelio was prodding us on toward a quest for a Gogolian inspiration . . . Spiro is a *dead soul* resurrected by the rapacity of Italian speculators."[25] On the other hand, there is no mention of Gogol by Amelio in the book *Lamerica: The Film and the Story of the Film,* which documents that as the film was being shot, it underwent such radical adaptations to the Albanian reality that little of the original scenario can be recognized in the final screenplay.[26] On balance, I would argue, the case for the Gogolian ancestry of *Lamerica* rests less on empirically verifiable biographical sources than it does on the homology in the relation between the two narratives and their respective historical situations: those, in Russia and in Italy, where endemic corruption caused the drawing of a line between "speeding up the bureaucracy" and devising an elaborate fraud to seem a matter of pedantic fastidiousness.[27]

Bettino Craxi was not the first to contend, as substantial charges of corruption started hitting him in 1993, that in a system where "everyone" is tainted, no one is; and that where "everyone" steals, no one is really stealing.[28] Almost a century and a half before the soon-to-be-dethroned secretary of the Italian Socialist Party high-mindedly flaunted it, an identical argument had been presented in court to plead for Chichikov's speedy release from the cruel and unusual punishment of sitting in jail for his crookedness.[29]

Brass will occupy us next, by virtue of the sole example of intellectually ambitious X-rated movie in this book: *The Voyeur (L'uomo che guarda,* 1994).

After assisting Rossellini on *India* (1957) and being praised in the 1960s as a promising young director of socially critical *commedie all'italiana,* Tinto Brass turned to developing a slightly different line of products: erotic films. In Brass's view, these are set apart from their direct competitors, soft porn, by a greater and specific artistry ("Tinto" being, after all, an homage to the painter Tintoretto)—and, the viewer might add, by certain cultural pretensions. *The Key (La chiave,* 1983) re-created Junichirô Tanizaki's novel of the same title, transposing it to Brass's native Venice against the backdrop of Italy's Fascist epoch. *The Voyeur* is based on the homonymous novel by Moravia (*L'uomo che guarda,* 1985).

Dodo, a young professor of French literature, is depressed: his wife, Silvia, has left him—temporarily, she reassures him—for a more experienced man whose identity she will not disclose. So should they go ahead with their original plan to move into an apartment owned by Dodo's father, or would it be better to call off the deal? After much back-and-forth panning from one scantily clad character to the next (including Dodo's ailing, though exuberant, father and his maid-cum-nurse), the film winds down with Dodo meekly accepting Silvia's decision to proceed with the move after all—and to welcome at any time visits by the consummately experienced relative and property owner.

The Voyeur did not duplicate the success of *The Key,* but it is a no less interesting film from the point of view of its indebtedness to world literature.

Suffice it to say that the young professor, who is also the eponymous voyeur, boldly tackles in class—and comments in some detail—Mallarmé's erotic poem "Possessed by the Demon, a Negress" ("Une négresse par le démon secouée," 1866 and 1887). Since, to the best of my knowledge, the poem has not been translated into English other than in the specific context of Moravia's novel, it seems useful to include it here for the record:

> Possessed by the demon, a Negress
> readies a ragged and sad girl to taste
> with new and guilty fruits under her dress.
> And the glutton for crafty labors makes haste.
>
> To her belly she applies two fortunate tits,
> And she thrusts, high beyond measure,
> of her button-boots the obscure wits,
> as one would tongues not designed for pleasure.
>
> Rubbing against the naked gazelle
> that trembles, an elephant wild,
> on her back she waits; and coquettish, the belle
> laughs with her innocent teeth at the child.
>
> With the victim between her legs, the nanny
> lifts her black skin, and the palate propels,
> from below her fleece, of a mouth uncanny—
> pale and rose as are the seashells.[30]

This text is, of course, both obscene and racist, and that is precisely why the Italian author relishes quoting it as he practices 360-degree subversiveness: Moravia has the fictional first-person narrator of his novel elaborate in his mind on "Une négresse" as he . . . takes Polaroid pictures of Saint Peter's in Rome. Brass, though, redeploys the poem from academic exegesis to altogether unpolitical physical education: in the film, Dodo and a callipygian female student of his discuss Mallarmé as a warm-up to an inquisitive photographic session.

The Voyeur also includes an allusion to Louis-Ferdinand Céline's work: a copy of his semiautobiographical novel *The North* (*Le nord*, 1960) flashes altogether recognizably across the screen as, one beautiful day, the professor cleans up his bookshelves. However, this quickie with an eminently stern author does not seem to leave any particular trace in the film. Most likely it represents a red herring, included by the ever-playful Brass to lead his public astray; or, just possibly, it is an homage by the director to an author long ostracized by the literary establishment for his objectionable ideas.[31] Either way, the incident strikes the unsuspecting viewer—viewer, but not necessarily voyeur—as a bit of nonphysical exhibitionism on the director's part; one senses there the menace of a possible authorial self-denudation. Luckily for us, in *The Voyeur* the less than statuesque Brass keeps that threat reasonably metaphorical.[32]

How does Brass's *The Voyeur* speak to Italian society? In about the same way as the Moravia novel from which it was re-created. On the one hand, news that Moravia had published a novel about sex elicited, in 1985, more yawning than salivation; such had recurrently been the case for some twenty years, and to that extent the repetition owed little or naught to events marked on any Italian's calendar other than Moravia himself. On the other hand there are, it seems to me, unambiguous signs that the novel's sex *is* topical for its times— that it is, in other words, in some significant way representative of the ever awaited and never accomplished transition to a rejuvenated second Italian Republic.

I shall be more explicit. On a symbolic level, it seems to be perfectly in tune with the gerontocratic, top-heavy Italy of the years between the mid-1980s and the mid-1990s that the old father in our two parallel texts should take all: money, power, and the son's girl. On a symbolic level, it seems to be perfectly in tune with the have-it-all tastelessness of those years that in our two parallel texts the girl should be attracted by the money and power of the pot-bellied autumn chicken. And, again on a symbolic level, it seems to be perfectly in tune with the mores—and the economy—of those times that in our two parallel texts the son should accept, as a matter of course, living with his wife in his father's apartment. (Actual Italian statistics massively confirm trends of this nature until at least the end of the century.)[33] All this information is present in Brass— admittedly in an oblique manner, as an inadvertent slip of the tongue; but it is all the more precious for that. There definitely is, in this particular sample of X-rated filmmaking, more than meets an innocent voyeur's eye.[34]

From extreme carnal fervor we now move to extreme frigidity, and from landbound issues to the clouds—in fact, to some ethereal space above them. I am alluding to Antonioni's algid (though not necessarily chaste) *Beyond the Clouds* (*Al di là delle nuvole*, 1995).

Along with Visconti, Antonioni is perhaps the Italian film director who has been most open to intellectual stimuli from abroad and most thorough in keeping abreast of them, irrespective of the artistic realm in which they were expressed. But whereas Visconti permitted at least his literary sources of inspiration to come out into the open by explicitly acknowledging their impact on his cinematic re-creations, Antonioni has carefully, indeed almost systematically, resisted allowing his own artistic activity to arise out of direct interaction with any one work by a literary predecessor.[35] And even in the matter of cultural affinities, Antonioni is loath to venture beyond the admission of a circumstantial similarity with the French *école du regard* of the likes of Alain Robbe-Grillet and Michel Butor; he read their *nouveaux romans*, he assures us, not before but after making his most famous films.[36] In sum, it seems fair to state that if Antonioni shares with fellow intellectuals a concern for the "thusness" of the objects that surround us (a fact perhaps best captured and summarized in the subtitle of Chatman's monograph, *Antonioni: Or, the Surface of the World*), this is not due to direct influence by them but arguably to the fact that both the *école du regard* itself and Antonioni's cinema, in homologous forms though in different media, express a Zeitgeist that permeates Western Europe during the present historical age of mass consumerism.

Still, the fact remains that the synergy between works of modern European literatures and Antonioni's filmmaking appears impalpable. Not only is this critical predicament tantalizing, it is in some respect an unfair one: a comparable destiny is, by a lucky twist of fate, spared to scholars specializing in Argentine literature—Cortázar's short story "Las babas del diablo" having transmuted itself into Antonioni's *Blow-Up*, and thereby offered them ample opportunity to comment on an ideal match between great literature and great cinema.[37] By contrast, a Europe-focused researcher would in principle have to make do with the glorified TV stage production *The Mystery of Oberwald* (*Il mistero di Oberwald*, 1980), which re-creates for the small screen Cocteau's play *The Two-Headed Eagle*—and, alas, was made by Antonioni for reasons almost entirely unrelated to his artistic priorities. Given the circumstances (including the critics' position, as well as Antonioni's own),[38] *The Mystery of Oberwald* seems hardly a practicable path to capture even a fraction of our director's mastery. Royal *The Mystery* is, but only in technical virtuosity.

With respect to Antonioni's European connections, what alternative is there to critical silence? Perhaps none;[39] but it might be of interest to point out that there exists a strong homology between an episode in Antonioni's (and Wender's) *Beyond the Clouds* and an early play by Ionesco, *The New Tenant* (*Le nouveau locataire*, written in 1953).

The third episode in Antonioni and Wenders, "Do Not Look for Me" ("Non mi cercare"), occurs in Paris, where a middle-aged couple—Patrizia, a Parisian, and Roberto, a New Yorker—is falling apart: for three years Roberto has been involved in a liaison, which he is unable to end, with a temperamental young Italian named Olga. Eventually, enough is enough for Patrizia, and she decides to move out of the upper-class, elegantly furnished home she shares with her husband. Answering an ad in a paper, she goes to see an apartment advertised for rent in an entirely glass-walled high-rise overlooking the Seine.

When Patrizia, Antonioni's "new tenant," rings the doorbell and the door opens, what she sees strikes her as an icon of her own spiritual condition: the premises are drearily empty, and the floor-to-ceiling glass walls make the individuals inside them feel utterly exposed and at the mercy of the world. The previous occupant, whom Patrizia meets there, has scant comfort to offer her; he has just come home from one of his many business trips, only to find his residence in the conditions in which she sees it. It was his wife's decision, not his, to clear out and move on; as he tells Patrizia, he does not yet know whether he agrees with what he calls his wife's "personal initiative." The apartment, in other words, is not really available. So where is Patrizia going to put her belongings, which she is expecting to be delivered any moment? The film does not tell us.

Ionesco's *The New Tenant* also focuses on furniture's uneasy relationship to apartments as a metaphor to address existential failure in humans. In the play, the new tenant's plight derives not from any difficulty in the installation of possessions in the comfortable security of a home, but from the explosive proliferation of those objects. As, inside the apartment, Ionesco's generically named *Monsieur* attempts to control the moving-in process, he is gradually drowned by accoutrements of all imaginable kinds and shapes that literally bury him alive.

"Is there much left?," *Monsieur* finally asks the movers outside. "It's full on the stairs, people can't circulate anymore." "It's full in the courtyard, too. And in the street." "Cars can't drive around town anymore. Full of furniture." The metro, too, is paralyzed. The Seine stops flowing: "It, too, is obstructed. No more water." The two movers have to open the apartment's ceiling to fit in more objects. Eventually, they slam it closed and throw the now invisible *Monsieur* a bunch of flowers. Is there anything else he may need before they leave? Nothing, the entombed man answers—just turn off the light.[40]

As we can see, the analogy between play and film is not in the details of the story but in its theme; that is, in the metaphysical anxiety that permeates both Ionesco's and Antonioni's characters. Clearly, the issue is less one of plot than one of cultural atmosphere. But, it will be observed, Ionesco's play dates from the first half of the 1950s, whereas *Beyond the Clouds* was made over forty years later. Can the spirit of such two vastly different moments in European history truly be called the same?

The answer is, largely, yes—an answer for which there are both external reasons and intrinsic ones. The external reason for an affirmative answer is that the master text underlying *Beyond the Clouds* was Antonioni's book of literary sketches *That Bowling Alley by the Tiber* (*Quel bowling sul Tevere*, 1983), published over a decade before the film was made, and itself the product of many years of work.[41] The real chronological gap between *The New Tenant* and "Do Not Look for Me" is thus about half the apparent one, a matter of two decades rather than four.

Yet surely—to shift to the substantial aspect of the question—two decades can make a world of difference in treating certain themes. Indeed, they may. However, it so happens that the triangle (or rectangle, or pentagon) of solitude which the director examines in Paris is not, to my mind at least, among those narrative subjects. Rather, the Patrizia-Roberto-et al. episode in *Beyond the Clouds* focuses exclusively on relationships seized (nowhere does the term seem more appropriate) in vitro and without any historical or cultural feature that would make them recognizably, unequivocally French rather than American or Italian, or uniquely linked to the year 1995 rather than 1983 or 1953. It is Antonioni's aloofness from specific events within Western societies, and his demonstrative holding fast to their existential fundamentals, that allows for the enduring comparability of some of his work to some of Ionesco's. In a few decades' time, so Antonioni's views could be rendered, the West has gone from electric to electronic; but the change undergone in the transition has amounted to little more than the irrelevance of one word's phonetic variation.

Antonioni argues that despite technological progress, despite increased affluence (or because of technological progress, because of increased affluence), in the past century we have neglected to correct the essential traits of our Western societies. Not only is evil still—as his quote of Lucretius reminds us in the epigraph to *That Bowling Alley by the Tiber*—the all-pervasive driving force behind phenomena in the universe, but we seem to be as unwilling today as we were in the past to focus on an effective quest for an antidote to its ubiquitousness. The apologue which Olga had told Roberto at the dawn of their relationship in "Do Not Look for Me" offers a dazzling illustration of this:

Olga.   There once were scientists in Mexico who had hired some porters. They wanted to reach an Inca city lost on the top of a mountain. At a certain point, the porters stop dead where they are and refuse to walk on. The scientists are upset; they don't know what to do, because they can't understand the reason for the standstill.

After a few hours, the porters start up again. Finally, their leader agrees to give an explanation.

Roberto. And what *was* the reason?

Olga.   He says they had walked too fast, and they had to wait for their souls.

Roberto. Their . . . souls?

Olga.   Isn't that amazing? . . . We, too, chase after all our things and leave our soul behind. Instead, we ought to wait for it to catch up. . . .

Roberto. To do what with it?

Olga.   All the things that seem useless to us.[42]

We, the explorers, will never be able to find an answer to the riddle of evil, so long as we behave like scientists who rush ahead on a merely material level, leaving the spirit behind; that is, so long as (figuratively speaking) we look for the Incas in Mexico, where no Inca has ever been.[43]

Another sensitive portrayal of difficult interpersonal relationships in a thoroughly consumeristic age is offered—from a viewpoint that combines the psychological with the sociological—by Scola's *The Novel of a Young Man in Poverty (Romanzo di un giovane povero*, 1995). Before analyzing the film, however, a few words are necessary to contextualize it and, in particular, its title.

The following is what in 1859 Flaubert, not exactly a literary apprentice, had to report to Gautier, another reasonably qualified practitioner of the trade, on the matter of the enormous success that was being reaped at the time by a tear-wrenching product of the *république des lettres*:

People swoon in reading and listening to *The Novel of a Young Man in Poverty* by that wet noodle of Octave Feuillet. The aforementioned thing is swallowed, according to one's taste, in pills or as a decoction, in the guise of a volume or that of a play! What a wretched drug!—That's all I know on the subject of that immense latrine called the World of the Arts.[44]

Scola had already performed virtuoso feats, in the 1980s, re-creating for the screen Iginio Ugo Tarchetti's novel *Fosca* (1869) as *Passion of Love (Passione d'amore*, 1981); the story, set in 1863, featured the turmoil caused by an extraordinarily ugly young woman among a group of army officers of the newly unified country. This time Feuillet's work, another narrative loaded gun (for the reasons so tactfully articulated by Flaubert), was chosen by Scola as part of an entirely different strategy. In implicit agreement with the aesthetic judgment expressed a century and a half earlier by a man who changed literature about the products of someone who merely milked it, Scola wisely gutted the actual content of Feuillet's novel and—"with a lot of irony," as he stressed in an interview—kept the only part of it apparently susceptible to survive the test of time: the title.[45]

What did Scola use in lieu of Feuillet's storyline? Though not an economist, Scola broached a theme that economists eye with great interest: the expansion without growth in employment characteristic of most of Europe during the 1990s. (At the time, unemployment in Italy involved over 12 percent of the workforce, and was disproportionately higher among young first job seekers in the South.)[46] Against this backdrop, Scola and his scriptwriters replaced Feuillet's story by constructing a deceptively simple alternative that at first sight seems to duplicate the pattern of a film noir.

The protagonist, Vincenzo, lives in Rome and holds a degree in literature. Frustrated by his failure to find a regular job, he spirals ever more deeply into self-rejection and into a bellicose relationship with his widowed mother.

One of the neighbors in the large, Fascist-style building where Vincenzo lives, *commendatore* Bartoloni, in private conversations with our anti-hero repeatedly claims to be oppressed by his alcoholic, obese, despotic wife. He will have no peace, he avers to Vincenzo, until he can be rid of her. Given Vincenzo's difficult economic circumstances, the *commendatore* goes on to ask, would he perhaps be interested in picking up on the side a small job of this kind? Bartoloni knows how to be generous to his friends.

At first, Vincenzo turns down the offer. (Or does he really? He answers Bartoloni: "I'll kill your wife if you kill my mother.") He also tries to get a job with a friend of his late father, the owner of a printing shop. However, it quickly becomes clear that in the 1990s there is neither bread nor butter to be earned in typography, and Vincenzo must give up. In dejection, he breaks up with his girlfriend and withdraws to a life of mutism and self-isolation.

Then, suddenly, deadlock turns to frenzy: one dark and stormy night, the isostatically challenged Mrs. Bartoloni plunges headlong into her high-rise's courtyard, and there surrenders her soul.

A few days later, a substantial amount of cash previously in Bartoloni's apartment is discovered by the police at Vincenzo's place. (It is, of course, the *commendatore* who has reported the young man to the police.) Whodunnit?

The feature by means of which *The Novel of a Young Man in Poverty* decisively veers away from the conventions of the film noir, opting to chart deep social waters instead, is that the film never does tell us who really "did it." What we do find out is that Vincenzo, incriminated with Bartoloni, is jailed while awaiting trial. In prison, he almost feels relieved; he is certainly relieved from the stress and the excessive expectations inflicted on him while he was out, only notionally enjoying "freedom." ("To do what with it?" he comments when questioned on the subject.) He whiles away his time teaching Italian to recent immigrants who are fellow inmates.

Establishing the identity of the murderer (Or was it an accident? That, too, is presented by Scola as a possibility) is beside the point. What matters to the director is the hopelessness of Vincenzo's position at a time when not partaking in the trends that dominate society amounts to being wiped off the social map.

Scola sketches a thoughtful portrait of the many years of Italian history to which his filmmaking testifies when he says about *The Novel of a Young Man in Poverty*:

Despite the merits it may have had, my generation has exerted vis-à-vis young people a form of subtle corruption. As opposed to [what we see portrayed in *The Novel of a Young Man in Poverty*], it did so by instigating them not to crime, but to affluence; proposing, that is, a take-it-or-leave-it existential model, according to which you forfeit your rights unless you live in a particular way. Unless you have privileges, unless you attain affluence, unless you consume, you are not a first-class citizen. Unless you accept mainstream attitudes and apply the prevailing logic in order to elbow your way to success in life, your path will be blocked.[47]

After suggesting a parallel with *What Time Is It*, where also "the father hands down to his son negative teachings, against which the young man tries to rebel," Scola goes on to argue that in *The Novel of a Young Man in Poverty*

[Bartoloni] embodies, to extreme consequences, the corruptor and instigator: the instigator of a lifestyle foreign to our culture, amplified and celebrated by the media. Study, merit, knowledge, reflective and critical abilities are today obsolete values, they are passé; the winners are those who, by their wiles, obtain money, success and recognition. Ignorance is now a thriving plant, daily watered by lotteries, quizzes, games, variety shows, bare-skinned young women [on TV screens]. Children spend four hours a day of their time in school, and four, on average, in front of a TV set; that's a volunteer school in each home, in color, with no grades or homework to do.
    Just as in *A Special Day*, where the voice of the [Fascist] regime was ubiquitously broadcast on radio, in [*The Novel of a Young Man in Poverty*] the story of the young man who loses his identity and his hopes has as its constant backdrop the voice of the TV regime.[48]

With a lucidity that makes all further commentary superfluous, Scola's words remind us of the easily forgotten dark side of success after many decades of ever-increasing economic affluence in Italy.

It is not an insignificant technical coincidence, I surmise, that the only building available in the capital with the prerequisites necessary to shoot *The Novel of a Young Man in Poverty* turned out to be the same one where, almost twenty years earlier, Scola had made *A Special Day* (1977). Featuring Hitler's visit to Mussolini's Rome in 1938, *A Special Day* was another great film about solitude, about the madding crowd, about the perverse link between conformism and a totalitarian regime's propaganda through the mass media.[49]

And now for something completely different: Francesco Laudadio's *Exercises in Style (Esercizi di stile*, 1996). Laudadio, who was the project's editor (and also contributed one episode to it), points out that the film was freely inspired by Raymond Queneau's *Exercises in Style (Exercices de style*, 1947).[50]

Queneau's is a work that could today be called an early masterpiece in postmodern textuality. The book is based on a loose narrative content, a ride in a crowded Parisian bus by a young fellow who appears to sport a hat, have a long neck, and wear a coat with a button sewn in an imperfect position. If I say that the content of the narration is loose and that the central character only appears to show certain features, this is because we do not, in fact, ever get to know with certainty: *Exercices de style* approaches one and the same nucleus ninety-nine times from ninety-nine different stylistic "angles"—the operatic, the philosophical, the declamatory, the understated, the pig Latin, the abusive, and so on. The focus is thereby put not on what is said but on how it is said.

The empirical information released to us each time varies slightly with the wording of the particular report through which it is refracted; the reports are, in turn, controlled by the special needs imposed by their respective discourses. Thus, while there are a few things we can say with a fair degree of certainty about the targeted bus trip—though little more than the extremely rudimentary ones indicated above—most of the circumstantial information we receive happens to be highly slanted (or "stylized"), of no practical use in attempting to reconstruct a consistent sequence of events. Most important, what *Exercices de style* refrains from producing is a cohesive interpretation of the facts so many times rehearsed: Who observes? Who is the young man being observed? What is the point of his going? In an extreme anti-Platonic gesture, in which one can measure Queneau's debt to the Surrealist tradition, the book denies us the (onto)logical core of the story: many narratives are possible, but there is none available to us that can function as a metanarrative and account for all of the hypotexts at one time. Not that the ninety-nine in any way contradict each other; even this would imply too direct an interconnection among them, that of mutual exclusion. Quite simply, the reports in *Exercices de style* are all copresent and contemporaneously possible.

The film *Esercizi di stile* consists of fourteen shorts, each of which modulates a different variation on one and the same basic episode: a declaration of love. *Fourteen ways of (not) telling each other "I love you"* is the film's subtitle. Not unreasonably, style is here strongly linked to the concept of genre. The film could well, in fact, be titled *Exercises in cinematic genres*: we get our declaration of (non)love in variants such as the costume film, the thriller, the silent comic, the *commedia all'italiana*, the horror film, the science fiction film, the spaghetti western, and so on.

Yet, because of the film's very conception, something unexpected happens in it. None of the fourteen episodes (with only one exception, to which I shall presently return) is sufficiently long to articulate a particular rhythm within well-defined narrative conventions, and thus could be said to embody the essence of a specific cinematic style. The shorts in *Esercizi di stile* obey what must perforce have been the editor's mandate to compress into an average duration of little over six minutes the full parabola of a story: beginning, middle, and end. The paradoxical, though probably inevitable, consequence of this enormous narrative foreshortening is that while the episodes in the film indeed belong to a wide array of genres, upon closer inspection they all turn out to practice one style only: the cramped one. Thus, for better or worse, they come across as variably willing samples of parody.

Of course, the idea was there in Queneau to begin with, and the very point of the film is to re-create the French author's jocularity in a self-aware post-modern context. However, it is probably no coincidence if the short in the collection that can be said to convey the greatest sense of artistic accomplishment seems to be the one whose generic prerequisites match a priori the film's Procrustean specifications. I am referring to Mario Monicelli's silent comic "A Construction Idyll," inspired by Chaplin.

For a different reason, we should also take note of Sergio Citti's "The Dogs Are Watching Us Too," an episode which explores with verve one of the residual islands of material destitution in Italy dear to Citti's cinema.

Here, as elsewhere in Citti's shantytowns, the people presented to us may be ugly, dirty, and on occasion nasty, but at least they sport solidly authentic and unique selves. The dogs in the title, and in the plot, almost completely turn on their heads the assumptions and stylistic features that underlie De Sica's proto-neorealist masterpiece, *The Children Are Watching Us* (*I bambini ci guardano*, 1943). Implied is, of course, a parodic mini treatise on the loss of humanity suffered by what could be called "mainstream Italians" in the half-century between the two films. Citti's cinema picks up where Pasolini's had left off: in a marginalized universe located far from the culturally homogenized cities of disembodied affluence.

After Scola's social concerns and Laudadio's playfulness, the three final items in this book take us back to the sphere of literature in its most complex relation to society—a relation best exemplified in this chapter by the Tavianis', Antonioni's, and Amelio's works already discussed. The recurring question of where to locate the connection with contemporary society ought to be answered, here perhaps more than ever, not in an episodic manner but with an approach aimed at uncovering broad historical homologies. To understand these films—and their likes—most effectively, we can align ourselves with the view expressed with unequaled concision by Vittorio Taviani:

In our films, a given historical moment is . . . but a coagulant for certain ideas, for certain queries we entertain about today. . . . It is not exact reconstruction that we are interested in. We address the past as a way of addressing the present.[51]

There are, in fact, substantial amounts of the past requiring assimilation in the Tavianis' own *Elective Affinities (Le affinità elettive,* 1996), as there were in Goethe's novel of the same title *(Die Wahlverwandtschaften,* 1809), that inspired the film.

"Nature! Nature!" cried the twenty-two-year-old Goethe in his essay "On Shakespeare's Day" ("Zum Schäkespears [*sic*] Tag," 1771). What the enthusiastic adept of the Sturm und Drang movement saw and extolled in the great master he had newly discovered was the ability to depict in his dramas Promethean figures that swept away ossified conventions of human personality, as portrayed in—or, rather, deformed by—successive centuries of antinatural cultural representation. To the young *Stürmer,* the rule-obsessed neoclassical aesthetic dominant in his time had produced characters and "passions" that were only perfunctorily different, all resembling each other as a shoe resembles its symmetrical companion.[52]

Thirty-five years later, catastrophic political and cultural convulsions had changed the face of Europe. In France, *le peuple* and its feminine personification, *la nation,* had replaced divine right as the ultimate source to which to appeal for the justification of political power. In Germany, by a politically less dramatic but culturally just as far-reaching development, a parallel transformation had turned *das Volk* into the final guarantor of poetic truthfulness and moral authenticity.

Despite the fact that, or perhaps because of it, political upheaval had been so deep in France, the artistic forms of neoclassicism could live on there: the very vigor with which a neoclassical aesthetic was fostered by the Napoleonic empire acted as what retrospectively seems an obvious overcompensatory pursuit by a regime well aware of its own parvenu nature. (However adroit, this ideological maneuver could be only partially successful; for French loyalists, Napoleon generally remained the impostor to the bitter end.) By contrast, Germany's constitutional turmoil at the turn from the eighteenth to the nineteenth century was limited to giving the coup de grâce to the thousand-year-old Holy Roman Empire, which, having descended almost directly from Charlemagne's, was dissolved in 1806 under French hegemony.[53] In the Germany of the early 1800s, political concerns thus did not discourage a radical spiritual rejuvenation; indeed, an entirely new cultural cement became desirable as an ideological counter to foreign military supremacy—which explains why a nationalistic romanticism could increasingly carry forth with it the fantasy and artistic allegiance of the German ruling classes. To be sure, this passion was never shared by Goethe, who, considering himself a citizen of the world, remained ever opposed to the vibrant nationalism of most of his romantic peers.[54]

A full generation after Goethe's early Shakespeare essay we thus encounter in Germany a fundamentally changed politic-cultural context, in which the young Goethe's eruptively laudatory perception of Nature's qualities has spent itself—not to vanish into nothingness, to be sure, but to work its way into the poet's worldview and to feed through to a successive stage of it. For the mature Goethe the theme of Nature's regenerative role retained little usefulness as such: not because it had been discarded, but because it had been dialectically absorbed.[55]

When, in the new century, Goethe again turned his attention to the subject of precultural modes of being, he broached it in the substantially larger frame of what he no longer perceived as the dichotomy, but rather as the dialectics, between nature and culture, between individual desires or proclivities and societal harmony. It was with this aim in mind that he originally planned his text on "elective affinities," *Die Wahlverwandtschaften*, as a novella embedded in the sequel to the first *Wilhelm Meister* of 1795–96. Just like the original *Wilhelm Meister*, the subunit of the new one was meant to explore the ways in which subjective inclinations conflict or harmonize, and in general interact with the social context in which they are inscribed. However, these notions required more sustained attention than they could find within the limits of a short excursus. More characters were added, the story grew in complexity, and *Die Wahlverwandtschaften* was finally published as a novel in two parts.[56]

At no time more than when attempting to render the conceptual core of *Die Wahlverwandtschaften* does one perceive a danger parallel to that of describing, say, Stonehenge as a group of puzzlingly arranged rocks. However, bowing to a necessity inherent in any metadiscourse, I will venture to condense here part of the source text, mentioning that of such strange rocks *Die Wahlverwandtschaften* has four.[57]

Eduard and Charlotte, deeply in love during their youth, are now a middle-aged married couple, more wise and sedate than passionate, who live on their estate in the country. Otto, who goes to visit them, is an army captain and a friend of Eduard's; Ottilie, the last member of the group, is Charlotte's young niece and foster child. Eduard is impulsive; Charlotte is patient; Otto is diligent; and Ottilie is mystical. Of course, all of them invariably conduct themselves within the bounds of utter composure, as befits people so civilized that they have chosen to flee the hustle-bustle of the court and stay aloof from the irrational, petty concerns which poison daily life there.

Eduard is linked to Charlotte; Otto and Ottilie are free. How are they going to react to being exposed to one another? The short answer to that question is that dealing with what proves to be a sui generis chain reaction takes Goethe as close as he will ever get to a "romantic" position.

The scientific imagery underlying the novel is a deliberate, indeed provocative, authorial choice; *Die Wahlverwandtschaften* is not about marital squabbling, but about subrational drives. And so it is that the interaction unfolding among the four is seized by Goethe in its deep "natural"-vs.-"cultural" ambi-

valence (chemical metaphor, here as elsewhere, intended—if only to reinforce Goethe's point about how close, in fact inextricable, experience and figurative discourse always are). Eduard is attracted to Ottilie, who is attracted to him in return; Otto loves Charlotte, while Charlotte's bond to Eduard begins to weaken to the point that it seems possible for the two to break free from one another.

One night, the married couple's lovemaking becomes exceptionally passionate, as the two partners commit mental adultery: they imagine they are holding in their arms the respective objects of their unconfessed desires. Chemistry now strikes back at the two with a vengeance: a little boy is conceived and, in the due course of time, born. On the one hand, he shows an impressive resemblance to Otto—and, on the other, a no less striking one to Ottilie. Predictably, the odd, embarrassing mishap speeds the breakup of the marriage. Eduard volunteers to fight in a European war; Otto, meanwhile, accepts employment as a civilian in a distant city. The two women, now linked by the baby, remain alone on Eduard and Charlotte's estate and tend him together.

When Eduard returns from war, his passion for Ottilie is stronger than ever; and, in Ottilie's own spiritual way, so is hers for him. Eduard, who is aware of Otto's feelings for Charlotte, wins Ottilie's consent to marry him, on the condition, put forward by Ottilie, that Charlotte not remain alone; she must agree, once her own marriage is dissolved, to bind herself to Otto. Though reluctant at first, Charlotte eventually accepts.

Just as the old links seem about to resolve themselves definitively into new ones, the irreparable happens.

While taking the small child for an outing in a rowboat, Ottilie loses her balance and causes him to plunge and drown in the pond. Eduard (doubtfully responsible father that he is) views the event as a favorable sign of destiny, one that removes the last obstacle between him and the full accomplishment of his desires; at the opposite extreme, Charlotte understands it as a punishment by fate for her past attempts at obstructing the breakup with her husband.

Yet the expected recombination of elements fails after all. Ottilie, who now feels that she is under the influence of an especially unfortunate star, believes that she is destined to spread unhappiness around her. Fleeing Eduard, she embarks upon an extreme form of asceticism that soon leads to her death. Eduard dies shortly thereafter; and the two are buried together, in a chapel from whose vault angels guard the would-be lovers' communal peace while they await resurrection.

Many nineteenth-century readers who did not follow Goethe's figurative intentions to the end accused the novel of being immoral and "siding" with adultery. However, Goethe displays no favoritism for any of the four protagonists of *Die Wahlverwandtschaften* (except, as Bettina Brentano rightly saw, for a soft spot for Ottilie);[58] had he been a twentieth-century psychiatrist, he might, in fact, have formulated his argument in terms of suprapersonal concepts such as the reality principle and the pleasure principle. While Goethe did not use a terminology comparable to Freud's, which is derived from biology, he did express in literary form ideas linked to chemistry, the cutting-edge science of his own time. Beyond the historical issue of which specific field of metaphorical discourse to choose, *Die Wahlverwandtschaften* is certainly congruent with the questions raised by Freud almost exactly a century later.

The adjustments applied by the Tavianis to Goethe's novel in their cinematic re-creation are limited to a few light, felicitous touches.

The action is transposed from Germany to the familiar landscape of Italy; by a very small anachronism, its time is made to coincide with that of the book's publication, 1809; and the characters are cast—or at any rate impress the viewer—as slightly younger than their literary counterparts. Finally, a number of careful excisions eliminate from the story some Goethean episodes that would have distracted us from concentrating fully on the amorous rectangle before our eyes.

Ambrosini and Occhipinti are right to conclude that, on the whole, the Tavianis' interventions succeed in deemphasizing possible contingencies of the plot (for example, a sociologically mimetic portrayal of the landed gentry in the nineteenth century; the implications of a relationship between a middle-aged married man and a very young woman) and in concentrating instead on its metahistorical potential. As a result, the Tavianis' *Le affinità elettive* is, if possible, even more symbolic than Goethe's.

It is, in fact, the film's symbolic emphasis that justifies the Tavianis' only injection of new narrative material into their prototype: in a cinematic prologue, they have divers (nineteenth-century divers, be it understood) plunge to the bottom of a light-filled blue sea to retrieve an ancient classical statue overgrown with weeds. This is clearly a pressing preemptive exhortation to the viewer: beware, the film you are about to see aims at extracting timeless truths from depths of the soul that lie beneath the surface-level agitation of the story line. The Tavianis' prologue, in sum, presents itself as an eloquent entreaty to reach below the face value of the plot and actively seek a deeper meaning to it. Goethe had done as much for the book by telling anyone willing to listen—and even by specifying in the advertisement circulated at the time of publication—that a symbolic reading was essential to a proper understanding of the novel.[59] From a conversation with Goethe, Riemer reported that "his idea in the new novel *Die Wahlverwandtschaften* is to represent social relationships and their conflicts, symbolically grasped."[60]

What we could call Goethe's—and the Tavianis'—peculiarly "postrevolutionary" thought might, then, be rendered as follows: while it seems chimerical to embark upon an antihistorical, Utopian hope to witness a successful power grab on the part of "the imagination" (i.e., desire, instinct, a presocial "subversive" nature), it would be no less unrealistic to expect a viable alternative from the exact opposite, namely, an unquestioned predominance of "reality" (i.e., self-control, rationalism, a "repressive" culture). Should an answer be sought, then, in a balanced coexistence of impulse and norm, of the egotistic and the social sides of the individual? In an ideal world, perhaps—which ours assuredly is not. In our world, that coexistence is ever precarious; it is somehow possible, though painful, in certain cases, yet all but out of reach in others. Socially conditioned restrictions can, at the most, inhibit certain reactions, but not indefinitely sustain different ones for which our individual psychophysical makeup may simply not allow. Such is (so the novel's and the film's argument concludes) the "chemical" condition of our Being-in-the-world; and it is a condition we cannot tame by hortatory, pedagogically minded attitudes, however much we wish we could do so in an attempt to allay our fears.

In arguing thus, Goethe's and the Tavianis' apparently neoclassical *Elective Affinities*, book and film, show that mere neoclassicism will not do—and certainly will not fit either of them as an interpretive key. *Elective Affinities*, book and film, explodes the illusion that instincts can be contained and governed by renunciation, and thereby be resolved without a residue. Drives can, of course, be so approached; but defeating them will also defeat the purpose of addressing them in just such a manner. In society, in other words, the triumph of rationalism might well be inevitable—but empty.[61]

Reasons that will immediately become obvious recommend assigning the slot closest to the Tavianis' *Le affinità elettive* to a film made by a much younger director: Donatella Maiorca's *Viol@* (1998).

A young woman, a self-assertive professional, briefly gets distracted from almost everything in her life by a strange relationship she develops with an unknown interlocutor over an electronic chat line. Before she can return to her usual, successful self, she endures the complete disruption of her emotional life brought about by her bizarre fascination with "Mittler," the virtual Other—an Other who, hiding behind the hieratic majesty of The Machine, proves able to manipulate her mind and body. This manipulation occurs, in particular, when "Viol@" (her real name is Marta) interacts with men: specific instructions by "Mittler," which she is unable to resist, dictate to her when and how she is to yield to their advances—or, indeed, provoke them.

Who is the mysterious "Mittler"? That is, by and large, the whole point of this captivating quasi thriller, which deeply probes the psychology—feminine and otherwise—of the age of the PC.

While the true identity of "Mittler" is best left unrevealed here, in a narrower sense the answer to the question "Who is Mittler?" is an altogether straightforward one: as the e-dialogue between the two chatters' screens makes clear to us early on, "Mittler is" (who didn't know?) "of course, the character from Goethe's *The Elective Affinities*."

Unexpected, but true. Mittler is, in fact, a minor player in *Die Wahlverwandtschaften* who revels in pacifying people at odds with one another and packing them off together to live happily ever after. He is an ever-optimistic character with whom Goethe does not appear to empathize too strongly—the novel, after all, supports a contrary position—and who, perhaps for this very reason, suffers from an embarrassingly clumsy last name (*Mittler* = middleman, mediator). Maiorca implicitly shares Goethe's skepticism by showing us that, when push comes to shove, some drives simply cannot be meaningfully mediated; in fact, in her film mediation itself ultimately includes, or even amounts to, a form of manipulation of others in one's own interest. Elective some of our affinities may be, but not necessarily pacifying, least of all when explored by fetishizing an electronic intermediary between ourselves and reality.

Viol@ takes the *Affinities* connection quite seriously, as one can tell from the considerable back-and-forth of actual copies of Goethe's novel which occurs between the two protagonists via an anonymous postal box. Could the Tavianis' film from Goethe have been instrumental in creating such responsiveness vis-à-vis the German classic? This is certainly possible. At the same time, Maiorca shows an insider's confidence with Goethe's text (Mittler belongs precisely to the part of the book the Tavianis excised from their own work) that may well be accounted for by a preexisting familiarity.[62]

Whereas the predominant worldview of Goethe's *Wahlverwandtschaften* is a stoically pessimistic one, we find one that is little short of tragic when we move into the sphere of influence of Kleist, as we do in following Bellocchio for his two Europhile films of the 1990s, *The Butterfly's Dream* (*Il sogno della farfalla*, 1994) and *The Prince of Homburg*.

In the wake of the political reflux that began in the late 1970s, Bellocchio turned his attention from themes of social conflict to those of interpersonal and individual maladjustment. Without necessarily excluding a social dimension from the causes of malaise among the characters that populate his narrative universe, in the 1980s and 1990s Bellocchio refocused his attention on the exploration of the contrast between mainstream rationality and what are considered "eccentric" variants of it, between folly and commonly accepted reality. More accurately, perhaps, the director has zeroed in on what can be perceived as the arbitrariness of any precise demarcation line between the two.

From the politically charged *All Or None—Fit to Untie*, shot in a psychiatric hospital and conceived as a powerful indictment of the very system which it portrayed, it was but one step to the exploration of the gray conceptual area where the distinctions essence/appearance and dream/reality collapse. In this pursuit, Bellocchio made *A Leap into the Void, The Eyes, the Mouth*, and *The Conviction*. Two of his re-creations from European literatures, *The Seagull* (from Chekhov) and *Devil in the Flesh* (from Radiguet), which also fit this pattern, have already been analyzed. Completing an ideal European trilogy is Bellocchio's homage to one of the paroxysmal works of German romanticism, Heinrich von Kleist's drama *Prinz Friedrich von Homburg* (1809–1811).

A first, single excerpt from the prince's tragedy occurs in *The Butterfly's Dream*.

The Butterfly's Dream features as its protagonist Massimo, a young actor so ill at ease in his bourgeois environment that he has lost the power of speech in everyday situations. He can speak "properly" only when he is on stage—or, very exceptionally, in daily life if he can retrieve from some tragic role he knows by heart the lines to match a given situation.

Despite his girlfriend's efforts to bring him back to a less extremist lifestyle, whenever he is not on stage Massimo is inclined to flee to remote Alpine villages and to their marginalized peasant culture. To her and to his own family, he remains a thorn in the flesh, disquieting by the permanent enigma of his silence.

The Kleistian scene we see Massimo act out in *The Butterfly's Dream* is an abbreviated version of act III, scene 5 of *Prinz Friedrich von Homburg*. At that time, the hero is imprisoned and faces court-martial—the reason for this being that, in battle, he dared launch a (victorious, decisive) cavalry attack before he received from his commander in chief, the Elector of Brandenburg, the signal to do so.

The film shows us the prince, shorn of all bellicose pride, imploring the Electress to intervene with her consort the Elector, so that forgiveness will be allowed to take precedence over justice strictly defined. Having played his scene to the end, Bellocchio's young protagonist walks away from the stage and becomes Massimo again—to face problems no Electress can hope to fix.[63]

To follow Bellocchio's full re-creation of Kleist, *The Prince of Homburg* (*Il Principe di Homburg*, 1997), we need to look farther into the sequence of the prince's trials. In the event, Kleist's drama forfeits its expected tragic ending. Electoral pardon—not due solely to feminine intercession—is exactly what Homburg is granted, though only after being subjected to the shattering experience of a mock execution. And his is not just any mock execution.

As he faces the firing squad, Homburg faints. Thereupon, all lights go on around him in the royal castle, cannons shoot, and a procession of torchbearers and courtiers materialize on the premises—his fiancée, Princess Natalia, foremost among them. The grand finale is so spasmodically Kleistian that no amount of periphrasis can adequately convey it:

Kottwitz.   Hail, hail
    To him, all hail the Prince of Homburg!

Officers.   Hail!
    All hail!

All.   All hail to whim who conquered gloriously
    At Fehrbellin!

                (Momentary silence.)

Homburg.   No, it's a dream! Do say—
    Is it a dream?

Kottwitz.   A dream, what else?

Officers.   To arms! To arms!

Truchss. To arms and into battle!

Field Marshal.   Victory!

All.   Down, enemies of Brandenburg, into the dust![64]

A dream, what else? Life and dream are here, in extremis, inverted and confused with one another. Chronologically and, more to the point, conceptually, we find ourselves positioned somewhere between Pirandello and Calderón; and it would not take a Mephisto to call *Prinz Friedrich von Homburg* another *La vida es sueño* in sauce *à la prussienne*.

Re-creation occurs in *Il principe di Homburg* (as it had in *Il gabbiano*) essentially as condensation. By comparing the director's dialogues against their originals we can precisely measure the extent of the compression undergone by Kleist's tragedy as it materializes on the screen: the film is Kleist, compacted to an almost intolerable textual intensity.

The taming of Homburg is visualized by Bellocchio with an almost obsessive insistence on nocturnal scenes. Night is, of course, the logical backdrop for Homburg's hallucinated, oneirically unanchored perception of existence—from the first scene when he inadvertently makes off with one of Princess Natalia's gloves, to the final apotheosis of the Elector of Brandenburg's belligerent power.[65]

In the film's published screenplay, Bellocchio gives us a wealth of details essential for a full comprehension of his approach to Kleist and, in general, his critically conscious brand of cinematic re-creation. First the director explains that what links *Homburg* to *The Butterfly's Dream* is "their common inquiry into the relationship between dream and the waking state." In their parallel quests for the subconscious, he says, the young man who does not speak and the prince meet with different destinies: the former wins out, while the latter is defeated. If only because in the nineteenth-century intergenerational conflicts operated differently than they do today, there was an important historical component to Homburg's failure. Standing up to the formalism of the law, Homburg

finally reconquers his dignity, but only by accepting the Law of the Father. The image he has of himself is not sufficiently autonomous from that of the Father; and it is precisely such an . . . identification with the Father—inevitable in Kleist's times—that leads him to collapse.[66]

One might have expected a director with Bellocchio's reputation to look altogether sympathetically at Homburg's plight. In fact, that is only partially the case. "My position," Bellocchio continues, "entails a [constructive] criticism of the prince's, whose attitude is understandable but deeply flawed by immaturity." Had he made the film earlier, he would have portrayed conflicts in such a way as to cast the Elector in a much more negative role, whereas the prince would have been entirely "right."

Today, in contrast, one cannot overlook Homburg's rashness. . . . The prince's impetuousness and . . . lack of self-control betray a component of blindness, of negative irresponsibility. If that were not the case . . . it would be impossible to explain why in the face of death the great hero is seized by an entirely unexpected panic . . . and begs for mercy. . . . It seems to me that it is not enough for the hero to be visionary and brave;

one must also possess prudence and calm. Gambling one's life away is tantamount to suicide; and suicide, in turn, is but a sign of despair. . . . What I mean is that Homburg's disobedience . . . contains within itself the subconscious kernel of a demented self-destructive drive.[67]

In conclusion, Bellocchio summarizes a long time span in his own (and Italy's) intellectual history when he argues that Homburg's story is the story of a defeat after all. The reason for this, he points out, is that the problem is not so much to kill fathers or replace them on their thrones or university chairs as it is to break away altogether from them, abolishing all identification with them and developing an autonomous identity. Hence his interest in Homburg.

To a certain extent, Kleist's text, too, proposes just such a conflict. The difference is that [Homburg] reconquers his dignity and his image of himself at the cost of accepting the Law of the Father. In other words, at the end of the drama the true winner is the prince elector, who represents the dictatorship of the rationality of the law. I am of the opinion, therefore, that the ending of *Prinz Friedrich von Homburg* is an only deceptively happy one. . . . Homburg remains alive, but at the cost of accepting the Law of the Father.[68]

In a nutshell: Bellocchio's approach does not amount to criticizing romanticism because classicism was better; rather, it entails criticizing romanticism because the romantic critique of classicism proved not to be sufficiently self-assured. And that is an entirely different story.[69]

What story next? The obvious "next" author on Bellocchio's path to an exploration of the mutual interdependence between subjectivity and objectivity was, quite logically, Pirandello, who had already captured the director's attention in 1984 in *Henry IV* (from the identically titled play of 1922). In 1999 Bellocchio made *The Wet Nurse* (from the homonymous novella of 1903).

There is, to be sure, a great historical irony about Bellocchio's choice of a literary model in a "classic" of German "romanticism" such as *Prinz Friedrich von Homburg*. Only by a thoroughly paradoxical development have two centuries of cultural normalization been able to absorb Kleist's poetically subversive position into the establishment's aesthetic pantheon, largely distorting it in doing so.[70] By an ever-repeated, uncanny ideological process, the mechanism of canonization ever again recuperates for mainstream discourse even the authors most doggedly critical of established institutions: political, literary, or otherwise. What next—scholarly books on Pasolini? the Nobel Prize to Dario Fo?

At the beginning of the twenty-first century, the momentous changes looming for most western European countries seem to foster in Italian cinema the mood for both a philosophically speculative glance and a reassessment of the historical development undergone in the past fifty years: a glance and a reassessment that appear to be at their most effective when operating under the aegis of classics of European literatures. Does that mean that a cross-border European cultural identity is now truly becoming the norm? In the period immediately preceding the imminent time when the currency controlled out of Frankfurt is scheduled to begin replacing its provincial forebears, it is tempting to think so.

This hypothesis should not be understood as predicting, naïvely, that the process of convergence now in motion will of necessity bring quick political, economic, and cultural glory in its wake. After all, the last time an *Imperium*, the Holy Roman Empire, stretched over Europe from the Baltic to the Tyrrhenian Sea, intra-European conflicts were all the more acute for it—so much so that, when ridiculing that empire with impunity in Auerbach's cellar, Goethe's Brander displayed more than the ring of a war-averse carnivalesque dissent in intoning his mocking song: "Thank God each morning therefore/That you have not the Roman realm to care for!"[71]

The decade of the 1990s, which is the object of this chapter, has brought to Italian cinema a welcome quantitative and qualitative revival in productions, both among those that were inspired by European literary texts and those that were not. The numbers' testimony is eloquent.

In the closing period of the twentieth century, six Italian films can be linked to French literature: Luchetti's *The Footman* (1991), paying homage to Balzac (but also to Dostoyevsky and other European authors); Martone's *Death of a Neapolitan Mathematician* (1992), quoting Beckett; Brass's *The Voyeur* (1994), glossing Mallarmé; Antonioni's *Beyond the Clouds* (1995), germane to Ionesco; Scola's *The Novel of a Young Man in Poverty* (1995), evoking Feuillet; and Laudadio's *Exercises in Style* (1996), re-creating Queneau.

Seven are located in the German orbit: Soldini's *The Clear Skies of the West* (1990), connected to Schnitzler; Faenza's *My Dear Dr. Gräsler* (1991), also from Schnitzler; Zaccaro's *The Stone Valley* (1992), from Stifter; the Tavianis' *Elective Affinities* (1996), from Goethe; Bellocchio's *The Butterfly's Dream* (1994) and *The Prince of Homburg* (1997), from Kleist; and Maiorca's *Viol@* (1998), echoing Goethe.

Finally, two are related to Russian culture: Paolo and Vittorio Taviani's *The Night Sun* (1990), from Tolstoy; and Amelio's *Lamerica* (1994), reminiscent of Gogol. We also have Luchetti's homage to Dostoyevsky in *The Footman*.

Although the nature of the phenomena we are studying precludes a mathematically exact manipulation of our data, it is noticeable that in the most recent past the impact of German literature on Italian filmmakers can be said to have surpassed not only that of the Russian one (this had already been the case in the period 1982–89), but even that of the usually predominant French, and this for the second decade in a row.[72]

The rise in importance of the German connection becomes even more perceptible if one divides our films according to their category of re-creation.

Homological re-creations (*Beyond the Clouds, Exercises in Style; The Clear Skies of the West; Lamerica*) are distributed reasonably evenly, and thus show no especially striking pattern. However, the picture changes considerably when we start looking for epigraphic re-creations. This group includes four items in the French group (*The Footman, Death of a Neapolitan Mathematician, The Voyeur*, and *Novel of a Young Man in Poverty*); one in German (*Viol@*); and none in Russian. In other words, four of the six items in French between 1989 and 2000 are epigraphic re-creations. This is unusual; traditionally, the French lineage had been strongest in coextensive re-creations, particularly of the total kind.

The verso of the same coin appears when we shift our focus to partially and totally coextensive re-creations. During the period under examination, for the first time not a single such item features in the Francophile slot. Russian culture's score, one (*The Night Sun*), is not very much below the average of an admittedly downward trend. In contrast, films from German literature include one partially coextensive re-creation (*The Butterfly's Dream*) and no less than four totally coextensive ones (*My Dear Dr. Gräsler, The Stone Valley, Elective Affinities*, and *The Prince of Homburg*), re-creating truly complex and important works. Again, this trend had begun in the 1980s.

With respect to the 1940s and 1950s, the relative positions of France and Germany are thus, in effect, reversed. Does this mean that in the immediate aftermath of World War II, Italians were consciously shunning German culture, preferring to flock to the perceived more democratic and popular one of France? Or does it mean that today's accelerating process of European integration, in which Germany is by far the most important player, is making it more natural for Italians to be familiar with the German tradition? Probably each of these two hypotheses contains one side of the truth.

If we then probe the films from the 1990s for their subject matter, we will find it reassuring to be able to note that within the target group—as outside it—this is the most diverse decade Italian cinema has known for a long time. *The Footman* exposes the inadequacies of Italy's high school system, to say nothing of the political one; *Death of a Neapolitan Mathematician* and *Beyond the Clouds* (and in its own, unwitting way even *The Voyeur*) reveal different variants of a lack of communication that material well-being seems to aggravate rather than resolve; *The Novel of a Young Man in Poverty* denounces the psychological ravages that unemployment can bring about; and *Exercises in Style* systematically tests the limits of postmodern approaches to cinematic writing. Furthermore, *The Clear Skies of the West* and *My Dear Dr. Gräsler* mock mediocrity and selfishness in young and less young professionals; *The Stone Valley* raises the issue of an individual's patient and constructive work for his own community; *Elective Affinities* and *The Prince of Homburg* question the degree to which individual truths or passions can be made compatible with compromises imposed by social interaction; and *Viol@* explores the shortcomings of a supposedly cure-all electronic age. Finally, *The Night Sun* portrays the painful isolation of those seeking to flee the fast life, and faster oblivion, to be endured in the world's arena; and *Lamerica* points to the pitfalls that lurk in the growing interaction between Italy's fragile capitalism and the unruly, indeed lawless, one of her Balkan neighbors. Life may not always be beautiful, but there certainly is a lot of it in the Italian cinema of our days.[73]

NOTES

1. There seems to be every reason to believe that the film's finale is a stab by Soldini at the proud self-assurance routinely paraded by the sanatorium industry, in Switzerland and elsewhere. In this, Soldini's *The Clear Skies* has illustrious ancestors in high culture—Schnitzler's *Gräsler* (on which see more below), Italo Svevo's *Confessions of Zeno* (*La coscienza di Zeno*, 1923), and, of course, Thomas Mann's *The Magic Mountain* (*Der Zauberberg*, 1924). That Soldini relishes literary intertexts for his films was recently confirmed by the influence exerted by Ariosto's *Orlando furioso* on his *Bread and Tulips*.

2. Fernaldo Di Giammatteo, *Nuovo dizionario universale del cinema: I film* (Rome: Editori Riuniti, 1994), vol. 1, pp. 79–80; repr. in his *Dizionario del cinema italiano* (Rome: Editori Riuniti, 1995), pp. 24–25. Di Giammatteo suggests that (other than in book form) Schnitzler's *La Ronde* may have reached Soldini by way of Max Ophuls' 1950 cinematic re-creation—which, by a culturally significant coincidence, became available again and was circulated in the 1980s. If that is in fact the case, I would argue that the lineage Schnitzler-Ophuls-Soldini would prove to have been remarkably parallel to the earlier one Radiguet-Autant Lara (*Le diable au corps*, 1947)-Bellocchio (*Diavolo in corpo*, 1986).

3. *La Ronde* can be found in English translation in Arthur Schnitzler, *Plays and Stories*, ed. Egon Schwarz, trans. Eric Bentley (New York: Continuum, 1982), pp. 53–116. The standard German edition is *Reigen*, in vol. 1 of Schnitzler's *Gesammelte Werke: Die dramatischen Werke* (Frankfurt am Main: S. Fischer, 1962), pp. 327–90. The work was written in 1896–97. A private edition (200 copies) was printed in 1900, and the first regular publication—with (partial) performance in a theater—occurred in 1903.

4. An inkling of the enormous scandal that for decades *Reigen*'s sex caused among right-thinking German speakers can be gained from two anthologies: Thomas Koebner, ed., *Arthur Schnitzler:* Reigen, *Erläuterungen und Dokumente* (Stuttgart: Reclam, 1997); and Gerd K. Schneider, *Die Rezeption von A. S.s* Reigen, *1897–1994* (Riverside, Calif.: Ariadne Press, 1995).

5. Di Giammatteo, *Nuovo dizionario universale . . .*, vol. 1, p. 80.

6. The best publication on Soldini available to date is Paola Malanga, ed., *Silvio Soldini: Nella città dell'anima* (Bologna: Alphabet, 1998). On *The Clear Skies*, see also Emilia Audino and Francesco Medosi, eds., *Silvio Soldini* (Rome: Dino Audino Editore, 2000), pp. 30–39; Gianni Canova, *L'occhio che ride* (Milan: Editoriale Modo, 1999), pp. 70–72; Gianni Canova, "Silvio Soldini: Il caso e l'occasione," in Lino Micciché, ed., *Schermi opachi* (Venice: Marsilio, 1998), pp. 190–200; Giulio Martini and Guglielmina Morelli, eds., *Patchwork due* (Milan: Il Castoro, 1997), pp. 208–11; Marlo Sesti, *Nuovo cinema italiano* (Rome: Theoria, 1994), pp. 100–02, 177–78; and Vito Zagarrio, *Cinema italiano anni novanta* (Venice: Marsilio, 1998), passim. The screenplay was published as Silvio Soldini and Roberto Tiraboschi, *L'aria serena dell'ovest: Sceneggiatura originale* (Mantua: Circolo del Cinema, 1995).

For the record, there is at least one other promiscuous young nurse named Veronica in the history of Western cinema: Veronika, one of the three protagonists of Jean Eustache's *The Mother and the Slut (La maman et la putain*, 1973)—a quasi-Surrealist classic of post-1968 *rive gauche* cinema that was undoubtedly known to Soldini.

7. The poem "Literature Will Be Scrutinized" ("Die Literatur wird durchforscht werden," 1939) can be found in Bertolt Brecht, *Poems 1913–1956*, ed. John Willett et al. (New York: Methuen, 1976), pp. 344–45; *Gedichte 4. Gedichte und Gedichtfragmente 1928–1939*, vol. 14 of Brecht's *Werke*, ed. Werner Hecht et al. (Berlin-Weimar: Aufbau; Frankfurt am Main: Suhrkamp, 1993), pp. 433–34. (However, the poem's definitive title dates only from 1951.)

8. The best technical term to define the sort of atmosphere I have been sketching is, not coincidentally, German—*machtgeschützte Innerlichkeit*. No fewer than fifty titles by Schnitzler are available in print to the Italian public at the latest count (*Catalogo dei libri in commercio 1998*)—a sure sign, however belated, of unequivocal appreciation.

Specialists of Stanley Kubrick will be able to assess the extent to which the Italian argument may or may not be applied to *Eyes Wide Shut* (1999), re-created by Kubrick from Schnitzler's *Dream Novella (Traumnovelle*, 1926).

9. Arthur Schnitzler, *Dr. Gräsler [Health-Resort Physician]*, trans. E. C. Slade (New York: Thomas Seltzer, 1923), p. 158.

Vorher werde ich nach Berlin, möglicherweise auch nach Paris fahren und mich einmal ordentlich amüsieren, so wie ich mich noch nie amüsiert habe. Und er träumte sich in übel-berüchtigte Lokale mit wilden Tänzen von halbnackten Weibern, plante ungeheuerliche Orgien als eine Art dämonischer Rache an dem erbärmlichen Geschlecht, das so tückisch und treulos an ihm gehandelt, Rache an Katharina, an Sabine und an Friederike. (Arthur Schnitzler, *Doktor Gräsler, Badearzt*, in vol. 2 of his *Gesammelte Werke. Die erzählenden Schriften* [Frankfurt am Main: S. Fischer, 1961], p. 194)

10. Thomas Mann, *Death in Venice*, ed. and trans. Clayton Koelb (New York: Norton, 1994), pp. 56–57.

In zerrissenem Licht, von bewaldeter Höhe, zwischen Stämmen und moosigen Felstrümmern wälzte es sich und stürzte wirbelnd herab: Menschen, Tiere, ein Schwarm, eine tobende Rotte,—und überschwemmte die Halde mit Leibern, Flammen, Tumult und taumelndem Rundtanz. Weiber, strauchelnd über zu lange Fellgewänder, die ihnen vom Gürtel hingen, schüttelten Schellentrommeln über ihren stöhnend zurückgeworfenen Häuptern, schwangen stiebende Fackelbrände und nackte Dolche, hielten züngelnde Schlangen in der Mitte des Leibes erfaßt oder trugen schreiend ihre Brüste in beiden Händen. . . . Mit den Paukenschlägen dröhnte sein Herz, sein Gehirn kreiste, Wut ergriff ihn, Verblendung, betäubende Wollust, und seine Seele begehrte, sich anzuschließen dem Reigen des Gottes. (Thomas Mann, *Der Tod in Venedig*, in *Erzählungen. Fiorenza. Dichtungen*, vol. 8 of his *Gesammelte Werke in dreizehn Bänden* [Frankfurt am Main: S. Fischer, 1974], pp. 516–17)

11. In such a highly "homogenized" film as *My Dear Dr. Gräsler*, one distinctly nonhomogeneous element is the systematic mispronunciation of "Gräsler" (correctly [grɛslɑ] as [graslɛr]—still bovine enough, to be sure, but nonetheless wrong.

12. For information on Faenza's life and works, see Gian Piero Brunetta, *Storia del cinema italiano* (Rome: Editori Riuniti, 1993), vol. 4, pp. 445–46; Fernaldo Di Giammatteo, *Nuovo dizionario universale del cinema: Gli autori* (Rome: Editori Riuniti, 1985), vol. 1, pp. 414–15; Martini and Morelli, eds., *Patchwork due*, pp. 157–63; and Zagarrio, *Anni novanta*, passim.

13. When Iurii Zhivago went to Moscow University, he opted for medicine over literature because

he thought that art was no more a vocation than innate cheerfulness or melancholy was a profession. ... He ... believed that a man should do something socially useful in his practical life. (Boris Pasternak, *Doctor Zhivago*, trans. Max Hayward and Manya Harari [New York: Ballantine Books, 1981], p. 64 [book 1, part III, sect. 2])

On schital, chto iskusstvo ne goditsia v prizvanie v tom zhe samom smysle, kak ne mozhet byt' professei prirozhdennaia veselost' ili sklonnost' k melankholii. ... On nakhodil, chto v prakticheskoi zhizni nado zanimat'sia chem-nibud' obshchepoleznym. (Boris Leonidovich Pasternak, *Doktor Zhivago* [Ann Arbor: University of Michigan Press, 1959 (1958)], p. 65; *Doktor Zhivago. Roman* [Paris: Société d'Edition et d'Impression Mondiale, 1959], p. 78; *Doktor Zhivago. Roman*, vol. 3 of Pasternak's *Sobranie sochinenii v piati tomakh* [Moscow: Khudozhestvennaia Literatura, 1990], p. 66 [book 1, part III, sec. 2]).

14. Daniele Luchetti, Sandro Petraglia, and Stefano Rulli, *Il portaborse* (Milan: Feltrinelli, 1993), pp. 43–44.

15. Luchetti et al., *Il portaborse*, p. 79.

16. A serious explanation of the puzzling fact that so many of the later twentieth-century Italian intelligentsiia, from hermetic poets to comic actors, have been politically left-leaning, should probably be prefaced by an equally serious analysis of the puzzling circumstance that during the same time frame, so many of the institutions of Italian culture—school first and foremost—were Fascist through and through (that is, molded, stamped, and shaped between 1922 and 1945). For a highly professional account of who was reading whom in Italy after 1945, see Umberto Eco's thorough article "L'egemonia fantasma nella scuola," *la Repubblica*, 15 November 2000, p. 1.

17. Information on Daniele Luchetti is in Sesti, *Nuovo cinema italiano*, pp. 68–72, 149–50 (with an interview); and Zagarrio, *Anni novanta*, passim. The film was soon popular enough to justify a paperback edition of the screenplay (quoted above). This book also contains a rich collection of reviews, as well as an interview with the producer, Nanni Moretti.

Significantly, references to *The Footman* have broken through the boundaries of scholarly specialization and become common fare in publications on Italian political history. For one significant example, see Sergio Turone, *Politica ladra: Storia della corruzione in Italia, 1861–1992* (Rome and Bari: Laterza, 1992), p. 358.

18. Samuel Beckett, *Waiting for Godot* (New York: Grove Press, 1954), p. 7.

Vladimir.	Je commence à le croire. (*Il s'immobilise*). J'ai longtemps résisté à cette pensée, en me disant, Vladimir, sois raisonnable, tu n'as pas encore tout essayé. Et je reprenais le combat. (*Il se recueille, songeant au combat. A Estragon*). Alors, te revoilà, toi.
Estragon.	Tu crois?
Vladimir.	Je suis content de te revoir. Je te croyais parti pour toujours. (Beckett, *En attendant Godot* [Paris: Les Editions de Minuit, 1990 (1952)], p. 9)

19. The script of the film, with substantial documentation, was published as Mario Martone and Fabrizia Ramondino, *Morte di un matematico napoletano* (Milan: Ubulibri, 1992). On the film see also Martini and Morelli, eds., *Patchwork due*, pp. 164–69; Georgette Ranucci and Stefanella Ughi, eds., *Mario Martone* (Rome: Dino Audino Editore, n.d. [1996?]), pp. 23–45; and Zagarrio, *Anni novanta*, passim.

20. Good editions of the novella can be found in Adalbert Stifter, *Brigitta. With Abdias, Limestone,* and *The Forest Path*, trans. Helen Watanabe-O'Kelly (London: Angel Books; Chester Springs, Pa.: Dufour Editions, 1990); and *Kalkstein*, in *Bunte Steine*, vol.

2, pt. 2 of Stifter's *Werke und Briefe: Historisch-kritische Gesamtausgabe*, ed. Alfred Doppler and Wolfgang Frühwald (Stuttgart: Kohlhammer, 1982).

21. The priest's relation to money is thus governed by the same, broadly speaking, "anti-capitalistic" traits typical of Austrian culture which Magris describes in "Il tempo non è denaro . . . ," *Nuova Antologia* 2205 (January–March 1998): 32–42.

22. On Zaccaro's film, see Vito Attolini, *Storia del cinema letterario* (Recco: Le Mani, 1995), pp. 269–71; Sesti, *Nuovo cinema italiano*, pp. 187–88; and Zagarrio, *Anni novanta*, passim.

23. For an eloquent testimony to the euphoria that spread over Albania—and the Italian region of Apulia facing it—after the 1991 crisis subsided, and before the collapse of bogus "pyramid" investment schemes triggered new chaos in 1997, see Giorgio Lonardi, "La nuova frontiera. Tirana, la Taiwan oltre l'Adriatico," *la Repubblica*, 30 December 1996, p. 20.

24. Gino's self-justification is quoted in translation from Gianni Amelio, *Lamerica: Film e storia del film*, ed. Piera Detassis (Turin: Einaudi, 1994), p. 156. The film's script also exists as Gianni Amelio, Andrea Porporati, and Alessandro Sermoneta, *Lamerica: Sceneggiatura originale* (Mantua: Circolo del Cinema, 1999).

25. The scriptwriters' Gogolian reference can be found in Andrea Porporati and Alessandro Sermoneta, "E' meglio diffidare di chi ti chiede troppo poco," in Mario Sesti and Stefanella Ughi, eds., *Gianni Amelio* (Rome: Dino Audino Editore, n.d. [1995?]), p. 61.

26. On Amelio's mixed feelings at having recourse to a direct literary source, see his interview with Mimmo Rafele, in Lucilla Albano, ed., *Il racconto tra letteratura e cinema* (Rome: Bulzoni, 1997), pp. 139–45.

27. Further secondary literature on the film includes Alberto Cattini, "Il viaggio anacronistico," in his *Le storie e lo sguardo* (Venice: Marsilio, 2000), pp. 131–51; Piera Detassis, "Il giaccone blu," in Emanuela Martini, ed., *Gianni Amelio* (Turin: Lindau, 1999), pp. 85–88; Emiliano Morreale, "Sud," in Mario Sesti, ed., *La "scuola" italiana . . . (1988–1996)* (Venice: Marsilio, 1996), pp. 415–21; Gianni Volpi, ed., *Gianni Amelio* (Turin: Edizioni Scriptorium, 1995), pp. 146–56; and Zagarrio, *Anni novanta*, passim.

28. Craxi's exercise in moral relativism for his own benefit was presented in a speech to the lower house of the Italian Parliament on 4 August 1993, and newspapers widely reported it on the following day. (The event was almost a parting shot; shortly thereafter, Craxi fled to Tunisia to escape prosecution.)

29. The case aimed at the moral laundering of Chichikov's soul was made, apparently in good faith, by the landowner Murazov in two of the older extant drafts of *Dead Souls*, vol. 2. Gogol', *Mërtvye dushi 2*, vol. 7 of his *Polnoe sobranie sochinenii* (Moscow and Leningrad: Izdatel'stvo Akademii Nauk SSSR, 1951), pp. 119, 262.

30. While my version takes some marginal liberties with the literal meaning of Mallarmé's original, these are far less considerable than the liberties taken by Mallarmé with respect to classical French syntax. A more literal-minded rendering of the poem can be found in what, to the best of my knowledge, is the only published English translation of the poem: Alberto Moravia, *The Voyeur: A Novel*, trans. Tim Parks (London: Secker and Warburg, 1986), p. 54.

Moravia's original Italian and Mallarmé's original-original French are hardly easier to come by, and I therefore include them here.

Una negra invasata dal demonio / Vuole assaggiare una bimba trista dai frutti acerbi / E anche criminali sotto la veste bucata. / Questa porca si appresta ad astuti travagli. // Al ventre, felice, strofina due piccole tette / E così alto da non arrivarci con la mano / Dardeggia l'urto oscuro degli stivaletti / Come una lingua inabile al piacere. // Contro l'impaurita nudità di gazzella / Che trema, simile ad un folle elefante, riversa / Sul dorso, aspetta e intanto si compiace con zelo / Ridendo con i suoi denti ingenui alla bimba. // E fra le cosce dove la vittima si stende, / Sollevando la pelle nera dischiusa sotto il pelo / Ecco avanza il palato di quella strana bocca / Pallida e rosa come una conchiglia marina. (Alberto Moravia, *L'uomo che guarda* [Milan: Fabbri, Bompiani, Sonzogno, Etas, 1985], p. 41)

The translation from the French—apparently Moravia's own—is reasonably accurate, except for the incorrect *porca* in 1.4 (*goinfre* actually means "glutton").

Une négresse par le démon secouée / Veut goûter une enfant triste de fruits nouveaux / Et criminels aussi sous leur robe trouée, / Cette goinfre s'apprête à de rusés travaux: // A son ventre compare heureuses deux tétines / Et, si haut que la main ne le saura saisir, / Elle darde le choc obscur de ses bottines // Ainsi que quelque langue inhabile au plaisir. // Contre la nudité peureuse de gazelle / Qui tremble, sur le dos tel un fol éléphant / Renversée elle attend et s'admire avec zèle, / En riant de ses dents naïves à l'enfant; // Et, dans ses jambes où la victime se couche, / Levant une peau noire ouverte sous le crin, / Avance le palais de cette étrange bouche / Pâle et rose comme un coquillage marin. (Stéphane Mallarmé, *Poésies*, vol. 1 of his *Oeuvres complètes*, ed. Carl Paul Barbier and Charles Gordon Millan [Paris: Flammarion, 1983], p. 350). This is the 1887 version of the poem, which is the one used by Moravia and Brass. Another good, more generalist edition is Stéphane Mallarmé, *Oeuvres complètes*, ed. Bertrand Marchal (Paris: Gallimard Pléiade, 1998), pp. 55–56.

31. Moravia's novel does not discuss Céline; it dwells instead on Dostoyevsky's *Crime and Punishment* and the Bible's Apocalypse.

32. The danger of a different outcome is a very real one: in *The Voyeur* Brass reserves for himself a cameo role in the epilogue.

33. For copious data on the subject, see those released by ISTAT and widely commented upon in the Italian press on 28 March 2000.

34. A pre-*Voyeur* introduction to Brass is Lorenzo Codelli, *Nerosubrass* (Rome: Dino Audino Editore, 1996). Information on the film is in Stefano Iori, *Tinto Brass* (Rome: Gremese Editore, 2000), p. 119; and Antonio Tentori, *Tinto Brass: Il senso dei sensi* (Alessandria: Edizioni Falsopiano, 1998), pp. 103–7. Three books on Brass in four years may seem more than strictly necessary from an intellectual point of view; this is certainly not the record of an underexposed filmmaker.

35. The exceptions are *The Girlfriends* (*Le amiche*, 1953), re-created from Cesare Pavese, on which see Gian Piero Brunetta, *Forma e parola nel cinema: Il film muto, Pasolini, Antonioni* (Padua: Liviana, 1970), pp. 123–58; and *Blow-Up* (1966), on which see below, note 37.

36. On Antonioni and the *nouveau roman*, see Aldo Tassone, *Parla il cinema italiano* (Milan: Il Formichiere, 1980), vol. 1, p. 46. There, Antonioni also discusses his *ars poetica* in general (pp. 29–49).

37. On *Blow-Up* and Cortázar, see at least Terry J. Peavler, "*Blow-Up*: A Reconsideration of Antonioni's Infidelity to Cortázar," *PMLA* 94, no. 5 (October 1979), 887–93.

38. Useful information on *The Mystery of Oberwald* is in Seymour Chatman, *Antonioni: Or, the Surface of the World* (Berkeley: University of California Press, 1985), pp. 202–12; Franca Faldini and Goffredo Fofi, eds., *1970–1984* (Milan: Mondadori, 1984), pp. 270–72; Nicola Ranieri, *Amor Vacui: Il cinema di Michelangelo Antonioni* (Chieti: Métis Editrice, 1990), pp. 142–79; Sam Rohdie, *Antonioni* (London: British Film Institute, 1990), pp. 45–46, 95, 137–39, 166–78; Aldo Tassone, *I film di Michelangelo Antonioni* (Rome: Gremese, 1990), pp. 169–71; and Giorgio Tinazzi, *Michelangelo Antonioni* (Florence: La Nuova Italia, 1994 [1989], pp. 128–30 (pp. 125–27 in the 1989 edition).

Antonioni's own comments on the subject can be gleaned from Michelangelo Antonioni, *The Architecture of Vision: Writings and Interviews on Cinema*, ed. Carlo di Carlo and Giorgio Tinazzi, trans. Marga Cottino-Jones (New York: Marsilio, 1996), pp. 127–29, 374; *Fare un film è per me vivere*, ed. Carlo di Carlo and Giorgio Tinazzi (Venice: Marsilio, 1994), pp. 115–17, 331.

39. Well, not really none at all. On the subject of Antonioni and European literatures, it is important to note that in *La notte* (1961) Valentina (Monica Vitti) eagerly cultivates Hermann Broch, and on a couple of occasions comes within a whisker of reading out aloud to us—in Italian—from her cherished copy of the German author's most famous work: *The Sleepwalkers*, trans. Willa Muir and Edwin Muir (London: Quartet, 1986); *Die Schlafwandler*, vol. 1 of Broch's *Kommentierte Werkausgabe*, ed. Paul Michael Lützeler (Frankfurt am Main: Suhrkamp, 1978 [1931–32]).

Clearly, the fact that Antonioni cited *The Sleepwalkers* in *La notte* acts as a meta-narrative comment on the exceedingly low level of self-awareness of which the film's characters are capable. *The Sleepwalkers* might have been, it seems to me, a fitting alternative title for *La notte*—and Broch's work a reasonable alternative path by which to access Antonioni's.

40. Dialogue translated from Eugène Ionesco, *Le nouveau locataire*, in vol. 2 of his *Théâtre* (Paris: Gallimard, 1967 [1958]), pp. 199–202.

41. The book—Michelangelo Antonioni, *Quel bowling sul Tevere* (Turin: Einaudi, 1983)—was republished in 1995, after the release of *Al di là delle nuvole*.

42. I am quoting (translating) directly from the Italian video. An important caveat: the prose texts from *Quel bowling sul Tevere* are not readily recognizable in the film as we have it. In particular, the content of the book's sketch titled "Do Not Look for Me" does not match that of its equivalent in the film—it does *not* contain the philosophical exchange between the two lovers on anthropological expeditions to Latin America. There is a reference to such an expedition to Peru (the correct abode of the Incas) on p. 154—in a different context and a different story.

43. Within the massive critical corpus on the director, the best general surveys available in English are probably Peter Brunette, *The Films of Michelangelo Antonioni* (Cambridge: Cambridge University Press, 1998); and Chatman's *Antonioni*, already cited. On the other hand, if I were to recommend the most readable and rewarding introductory pages on Antonioni's work that I have encountered, I would mention two short items by Pasolini: "Moravia e Antonioni" and "Difendo *Deserto rosso*," in his *I film degli altri*, ed. Tullio Kezich (Parma: Guanda, 1996), pp. 75–77 and 78–81, respectively.

Wenders published a richly illustrated diary of the circumstances surrounding his co-operation with Antonioni. Wenders buffs can choose among four equivalent options: the German original, Wim Wenders, *Die Zeit mit Antonioni: Chronik eines Films* (Frankfurt am Main: Verlag der Autoren, 1995); the French version, *Avec Michelangelo Antonioni: Chronique d'un film*, trans. Henri Christophe et al. (Paris: L'Arche Editeur, 1995); the Italian one, *Il tempo con Antonioni: Cronaca di un film*, trans. Silvia Bortoli (Rome: Edizioni Socrates, 1995); and most recently, an English one, *My Time with Antonioni*, trans. Michael Hofmann (London and New York: Faber and Faber, 2000).

44. The quality of Flaubert's prose deserves full quote in the original:

D'autre part on se pâme à lire et à écouter *Le roman d'un jeune homme pauvre* par cet escouillé d'Octave Feuillet. Ladite chose s'avale, suivant les goûts, en pilule ou en tisane, sous forme de volume ou de pièce! Triste drogue!—Voilà tout ce que je sais touchant cette immense latrine appelée le Monde des Arts. (Gustave Flaubert, letter to Théophile Gautier, 27 January 1859, in vol. 3 of Flaubert's *Correspondance*, ed. Jean Bruneau [Paris: Gallimard Pléiade, 1991], p. 11)

45. Scola's comment on the film ("I only kept the title. There is a lot of irony in this") appeared in the Parisian *Le dimanche*, 16 November 1996. (For the record, a cloak-and-dagger silent film conventionally re-created from Feuillet had been made in Italy in the 1920s.)

46. In Italy, unemployment was above 12 percent through 1996 (admittedly, an average not too different from those of Belgium, France, or Germany), and rose the following year. For more details, see Marco Esposito, "Disoccupazione salita al 12,5%," *la Repubblica*, 26 June 1997, p. 30. More data on the problem—as well as a refreshingly frank assessment of at least some of its causes—can be found in "European Unemployment: Fiddling," *The Economist*, 4 October 1997, pp. 54–57.

47. Ettore Scola, *Il cinema e io*, ed. Antonio Bertini (Rome: Officina Edizioni, 1996), p. 205. (The interview refers to the film's title as *Diary*, rather than *Novel*.)

48. Scola, *Il cinema e io*, p. 206. See also Roberto Ellero, *Ettore Scola* (Florence: La Nuova Italia, 1996), pp. 106–08.

49. For those interested in pursuing further the French connection in Scola, it seems thought-provoking to compare segments of narration in *The Novel of a Young Man in Poverty* with patterns prefigured in literary masterpieces from France. Regarding the proposed murder for the sake of money, with attendant devil pact overtones, see Balzac's *Old Goriot / Le père Goriot* (Vautrin proposes to Rastignac the murder of Taillefer); for the honest printer ruined by the way of today's cruel world, see Balzac's *Lost Illusions / Illusions perdues* (David Séchard); with respect to a young man's reluctance, or outright refusal, to defend himself "properly" against charges of murder, see Camus's *L'étranger* (Meursault), as well as, with a different slant, Stendhal's *Red and Black / Le rouge et le noir* (Julien Sorel).

The Novel of a Young Man in Poverty also shows a number of cinematic reminiscences, the most easily recognizable of which can be identified in the protagonist's conflictual relationship with his mother, akin to that in Bellocchio's *Fists in the Pockets*.

50. Raymond Queneau, *Exercises in Style*, trans. Barbara Wright (London: Gaberbocchus Press, 1958); *Exercices de style* (Paris: Gallimard, 1964 [1947]).

51. "Come sempre, nei nostri film il momento storico è . . . il coagulo di certe idee, di certi nostri interrogativi di oggi. . . . Non ci interessa la ricostruzione esatta. Si parla del passato per parlare del presente" (Aldo Tassone, *Parla il cinema italiano*, vol. 2, pp. 361–62).

52. Goethe's enthusiasm for Shakespeare's "natural" human beings, and his correspondingly negative comments on neoclassical French plays, are documented in his "Zum Schäkespears [sic] Tag," in *Der junge Goethe: 1757–1775*, ed. Gerhard Sauder et al., vol. 1, pt. 2 of *Sämtliche Werke*, ed. Karl Richter et al. (Munich: Carl Hanser, 1987), pp. 411–14. (The two quotes can be found on pp. 413 and 412.)

A somewhat more conventionally formulated, but little different assessment of the master can be found in the much later "Shakespeare and No End!" ("Shakespear [sic] und kein Ende!" written in 1813), in vol. 11, pt. 2 of the same edition (1994), pp. 173–81.

After more than two centuries' wait, the first was translated into English as "Shakespeare: A Tribute," in *Essays on Art and Literature*, ed. John Gearey, trans. Ellen and Ernest H. von Nardroff, vol. 3 of *Goethe's Collected Works*, ed. Victor Lange et al. (Princeton, N.J.: Princeton University Press, 1994), pp. 163–65 (quotes on pp. 165 and 164, respectively). The later of the two Shakespeare essays had already been translated into English as "Shakespeare *Ad Infinitum*," in *Goethe's Literary Essays*, ed. J. E. Spingarn (New York: Frederick Ungar, 1964 [1921]), pp. 174–89. A new version is included in the 1994 edition immediately after its companion (as "Shakespeare Once Again," pp. 166–74—but "Shakespeare *Ad Infinitum*" was a far more accurate title).

53. On the twilight of the first Reich, in particular from the angle of constitutional law, see James A. Vann and Steven W. Rowan, *The Old Reich: Essays on German Political Institutions, 1495–1806* (Brussels: Editions de la Librairie Encyclopédique, 1974).

For details on the genetic correlation between Charlemagne's empire and the later Holy Roman Empire of the German Nation (and much else besides), see Werner Goez, *Translatio Imperii: Ein Beitrag zur Geschichte des Geschichtdenkens und der politischen Theorien im Mittelalter und in der frühen Neuzeit* (Tübingen: J.C.B. Mohr [Paul Siebeck], 1958).

54. I am, of course, simplifying the cultural dynamics of the rise of romanticism in Germany. For one thing, protoromantic themes were already perceptible there before the French Revolution, most notably in the works of Hamann and Herder. Conversely, a nationalistic "undertow" of a definite romantic ilk was already present in the young Goethe's specifically anti-French aesthetic position of his first Shakespeare essay.

55. Later still, the difficult dialectics between nature and culture—or, more exactly, between innate instincts and the socially and culturally developed *art* of taming them— would be persuasively broached one last time by the aging Goethe in his symbolically dense *Novella* (*Novelle*, 1828).

56. For an English version of the novel, one can choose between the older *Elective Affinities*, trans. Elizabeth Mayer and Louise Bogan (Chicago: Henry Regnery, 1963); and the more recent and colloquial one in *The Sorrows of Young Werther. Elective Affinities. Novella*, ed. David Wellbery, trans. Victor Lange and Judith Ryan, vol. 11 of *Goethe's Collected Works* (1995).

For the original, I have used *Die Wahlverwandtschaften. Ein Roman*, ed. Erich Trunz and Benno von Wiese (Munich: Deutscher Taschenbuch Verlag, 1980 [1977]). This volume includes not only the text, corresponding to vol. 6 of the Hamburg critical edition, as well as to vol. 9 of *Sämtliche Werke*, ed. Christoph Siegrist et al. (Munich: Carl Hanser, 1987) but also a rich anthology of comments by Goethe and his contemporaries. These range from indispensable clues (e.g., Goethe admits "I understand that [Solger] cannot stand Eduard; neither can I; but I had to make him so, in order to bring about the facts," 21 January 1827, p. 264) to revealing coincidences (e.g., Jakob Grimm writes to his brother Wilhelm that had he been the author instead of Goethe, he would have dropped certain parts of the story, 11 November 1809, pp. 279–80—exactly those parts of the novel, it turns out, which were excised by the Tavianis).

57. The consistently, quasi-cabalistically quadratic structure of Goethe's novel certainly draws attention to itself: the book comprises thirty-six chapters divided into two parts of eighteen each—thus, its total can be expressed as either (6 × 6) or (2 × 2 × 3 × 3).

58. For Bettina Brentano's quip on Ottilie (9 November 1809), see Goethe, *Die Wahlverwandtschaften. Ein Roman*, p. 288.

59. For Goethe's advertisement to the first edition of *Die Wahlverwandtschaften* (4 September 1809), see *Die Wahlverwandtschaften. Ein Roman*, pp. 259–60.

60. For Riemer's report on Goethe's intentions ("seine Idee bei dem neuen Roman . . . sei: sociale Verhältnisse und die Conflicte derselben symbolisch gefaßt darzustellen," 28 August 1808), see *Die Wahlverwandtschaften. Ein Roman*, p. 259.

61. The Tavianis had been working for a long time on *Die Wahlverwandtschaften*, hesitating over how best to approach the "exacting master." Their account can be found in Jean A. Gili, ed., *Paolo et Vittorio Taviani* (Arles: Institut Lumière/Editions Actes Sud, 1993), pp. 85–86.

An analysis of the film's structure is in Maurizio Ambrosini and Ignazio Occhipinti, *Le affinità elettive di Paolo e Vittorio Taviani* (Milan: Sapiens, 1996), esp. pp. 44–56. For fuller information on details of the cinematic re-creation, see pp. 36–43. Also useful are Attolini, *Storia del cinema letterario*, pp. 278–81; and Riccardo Ferrucci and Patrizia Turini, *Paolo e Vittorio Taviani: La poesia del paesaggio* (Rome: Gremese, 1995), pp. 103–09.

62. For Goethe's novel, see the notes to the earlier section on the Tavianis' *Le affinità elettive*. Maiorca's *Viol@* has not yet reached the secondary literature in any grand way, but the film's merits are well assessed in Zagarrio, *Anni novanta*, passim and p. 166.

63. For *The Butterfly's Dream*, see Sandro Bernardi, *Marco Bellocchio* (Milan: Il Castoro, 1998 [1978]), pp. 144–48; Sandro Bernardi, "La politica dell'estetica," in Vito Zagarrio, ed., *Il cinema della transizione* (Venice: Marsilio, 2000), pp. 348–49; Paola Malanga, *Marco Bellocchio* (Milan: Edizioni Olivares, 1998), pp. 51–53, 110–14, 208–11; and Zagarrio, *Anni novanta*, passim.

64. Heinrich von Kleist, *Prince Frederick of Homburg*, in *Five Plays*, ed. and trans. Martin Greenberg (New Haven, Conn.: Yale University Press, 1988), p. 350.

Kottwitz:	Heil, heil dem Prinz von Homburg!
Die Offiziere:	Heil! Heil! Heil!
Alle:	Dem Sieger in der Schlacht bei Fehrbellin! *Augenblickliches Stillschweigen.*
Homburg:	Nein, sagt! Ist es ein Traum?
Kottwitz:	Ein Traum, was sonst?
Mehrere Offiziere:	Ins Feld! Ins Feld!
Graf Truchss:	Zur Schlacht!
Feldmarschall:	Zum Sieg! Zum Seig!
Alle:	In Staub mit allen Feinden Brandenburgs! (Heinrich von Kleist, *Prinz Friedrich von Homburg*, in vol. 2 of his *Werke und Briefe in vier Bänden*, ed. Siegfried Streller [Berlin: Aufbau, 1978], p. 441 [act V, scene 11])

65. For *The Prince of Homburg*, see Bernardi, *Marco Bellocchio*, pp. 150–55; Bernardi, "La politica dell'estetica," pp. 350–52; Malanga, *Marco Bellocchio*, pp. 114–16 and 214–19; and Zagarrio, *Anni novanta*, passim. See also Bellocchio's interview with Vito Zagarrio in Lino Micciché, ed., *Schermi opachi*, (Venice: Marsilio, 1998), p. 396.

66. Marco Bellocchio, *Il principe di Homburg di Heinrich von Kleist: Sceneggiatura*, ed. Giovanni Spagnoletti (Milan: Baldini e Castoldi, 1997), p. 145.

67. Bellocchio, *Il principe di Homburg di Heinrich von Kleist . . .*, pp. 147–49.

68. Bellocchio, *Il principe di Homburg di Heinrich von Kleist . . .*, pp. 150–51.

69. A third story perhaps waiting to be written is related to yet another Homburg on Italian soil. In 1982, the theater and film director Gabriele Lavia had made *The Prince of Homburg (Il principe di Homburg)*, a filmed version of Kleist's drama, in which he played the eponymous role. Bellocchio fleetingly alludes to Lavia's version (Bellocchio, *Il principe di Homburg di Heinrich von Kleist . . .*, p. 143), but remains remarkably

reticent on the subject. Aside from the little that Bellocchio tells us, what else could Lavia have given him?

70. In the nineteenth century, the German (Prussian) philologico-academic establishment canonized Kleist mainly on account of the poet's anti-French and in general anti-Latin nationalism, despite his appearing in most other respects to be a dangerous crackpot. The following is a summary bibliography on *Prinz Friedrich von Homburg*, presented here as a guide for interested readers to form their own opinion on the matter: Seán Allan, *The Plays of Heinrich von Kleist: Ideals and Illusions* (Cambridge: Cambridge University Press, 1996); Fritz Hackert, ed., *Heinrich von Kleist. Prinz Friedrich von Homburg: Erläuterungen und Dokumente* (Stuttgart: Reclam, 1979); Walter Hinderer, ed., *Kleists Dramen: Neue Interpretationen* (Stuttgart: Reclam, 1981); Georg Lukács, "Die Tragödie Heinrich von Kleists" [written 1937], in his *Deutsche Realisten des 19. Jahrhunderts* (Bern: Francke; Berlin: Aufbau, 1951), pp. 19–48; repr. in his *Deutsche Literatur in zwei Jahrhunderten* (Neuwied: Luchterhand, 1964), pp. 201–31; Walter Müller-Seidel, ed., *Kleists Aktualität: Neue Aufsätze und Essays 1966–1978* (Darmstadt: Wissenschaftliche Buchgesellschaft, 1981); Gerhard Neumann, ed., *Heinrich von Kleist: Kriegsfall—Rechtsfall—Sündenfall* (Freiburg im Breisgau: Rombach Verlag, 1994); Helmut Sembdner, *In Sachen Kleist: Beiträge zur Forschung* (Munich: Carl Hanser, 1974); Anthony Stephens, *Heinrich von Kleist: The Dramas and Stories* (Providence, R.I.: Berg, 1994); and Thomas Wichmann, *Heinrich von Kleist* (Stuttgart: Metzler, 1988).

71. Johann Wolfgang von Goethe, *Faust. A Tragedy*, trans. Bayard Taylor (New York: Modern Library, 1967 [1870]), p. 72. "Dankt Gott mit jedem Morgen, / Daß ihr nicht braucht fürs Röm'sche Reich zu sorgen!" Goethe, *Faust I*, in *Weimarer Klassik. 1798–1806*, ed. Victor Lange, vol. 6, part 1 of his *Sämtliche Werke*, ed. Karl Richter et al. (Munich: Carl Hanser, 1987), p. 592 (vv. 2,093–94).

72. Clearly, Russia's fortunes in this respect are not helped by the fact that, since Blok at the latest, establishing a dialogue with one of her authors has directly or indirectly entailed having to come to terms with the 1917 Revolution and its aftermath—something which need not top the list of all filmmakers' priorities.

73. The most thorough assessment to date of Italian filmography in toto during the 1990s is provided by Zagarrio, ed., *Il cinema della transizione*.

Conclusion

Good historians need thorough statistics. Having collected their data, they arrange them on charts with a view to identifying in them a trend, which they then proceed to verbalize and interpret. Eventually, they aim at producing a theory that accounts for the facts they have been observing. This is the time and place for us to do likewise—"with, to be sure, differences in the object and manner of [our] imitation of reality," as Lessing would have put it.[1] How can we meaningfully summarize our summaries, and thus elaborate on our results at a higher level of generalization?

Among the phenomena which the preceding six chapters charted in scrutinizing re-creations from major European literatures in the Italian cinema of the second half of the twentieth century, the major ones we detected are the following: (1) a gradual demise of the more conventional approaches to cinematic re-creation; (2) a corresponding growth in the number of films that take a complex textual approach to literature; (3) a strong French influence throughout the earlier part of the period under consideration, which later on levels out; (4) a later rise to prominence by the Germanic world; and (5) a peculiarly untypical performance by the classics of Russian literature. These do indeed follow an unexpected pattern. In the decades immediately following World War II, Russian culture makes a strong showing by riding on the coattails of the demand for an unproblematic commercial production; then, in a marked reversal, it bases its appeal on the strength of the Italian public's welcome of the treatment of revolutionary themes; finally, it wanes when, in the 1980s, both trends just mentioned give way.

As for the artistic originality and strength of the films involved, these are more difficult to assess. Within our target group, there are items that are true landmark works in the history of cinema—and others that are not. What one can say with certainty is that, on the basis of the evidence examined, Italian cinema re-created from European literatures can boast a higher-than-average performance in terms of intellectual relevance or long-term impact, if only because of the virtuous selection generally associated with the willingness to act upon one's open-mindedness toward relatively less well explored cultural traditions.

It is of course true that any outstanding film of the year 2001, however successful at the box office, will affect societal awareness less deeply and less enduringly than any of its counterparts could have in 1951; but that is simply related to the quantity and nature of the competing media that sprang up during the preceding half-century. A weaker resonance and shorter life span of what show business refers to as "evergreens" is characteristic of our times everywhere: today's gods are richer, but they die faster, and are forgotten faster, than those of old. This situation is not limited to European literatures, Italy, or even cinema. Among others, musicians, writers, and athletes, as well as philosophers and scientists, seem to complain of the same ill.

More could be added on each of the subjects just touched upon, but I will refrain from doing so for the sake of brevity. I would now rather use any residual patience in my readers to suggest that some further engrossing results can be distilled by an alternative final ranking of the information scanned in the course of this book. The question I am interested in raising at this juncture is the following: What conclusions can be arrived at by classifying our material at its European source, rather than at the receiving end of Italian cinema? What happens if, slicing our pie at a different angle and for a different purpose, we cross-reference the results so far obtained with an arrangement of our prototype texts by nation?

For this task, I will ignore the particular nature of each re-creative process and simply foreground the title of the literary texts involved. Let us see what the lists reveal, both synchronically and diachronically.[2]

FRENCH (Thirty films)

Balzac's *Eugenie Grandet* (Soldati's *Eugenia Grandet*, 1946)

Hugo's *Les miserables* (Freda's *I miserabili*, 1947)

Cocteau's *The Human Voice* (Rossellini's *A Human Voice*, 1947)

Claudel's *Joan of Arc Burned at the Stake* (Rossellini's *Giovanna d'Arco al rogo*, 1954)

Verne's *Michael Strogoff* (Gallone's *Michele Strogoff*, 1956)

Dumas's and Sartre's *Kean* (Gassman's *Kean*, 1956)

Stendhal's *Vanina Vanini* (Rossellini's *Vanina Vanini*, 1961)

Sartre's *The Condemned of Altona* (De Sica's *I sequestrati di Altona*, 1962)

Maupassant's "On the Edge of the Bed" (Visconti's "The Job" in *Boccaccio '70*, 1962)

Stendhal's *The Charterhouse of Parma* (Bertolucci's *Before the Revolution*, 1964)

Camus's *L'étranger* (Visconti's *Lo straniero*, 1967)

Artaud's *The Theatre and Its Double* (Bertolucci's *Partner*, 1968) (see also Dostoyevsky)

Rimbaud's *The Deserts of Love* (Pasolini's *Teorema*, 1968) (see also Tolstoy)

Sèchehaye's *Diary of a Schizophrenic Girl* (Nelo Risi's *Diario di una schizofrenica*, 1968)

Sade's *The 120 Days of Sodom* (Pasolini's *Salò or the 120 Days of Sodom*, 1975)

Flaubert's *A Simple Heart* (Giorgio Ferrara's *Un cuore semplice*, 1977)

Beckett's *Waiting for Godot* (Comencini's *The Traffic Jam*, 1979)

Gautier's *Captain Fracassa* (Scola's *The Terrace*, 1980, and *Il viaggio di Capitan Fracassa*, 1989)

Nerval's "Byron's Thought" (Amelio's *Strike at the Heart*, 1982)

Restif de la Bretonne's *Revolutionary Nights* (Scola's *The New World/The Night of Varennes*, 1982)

Mérimée and Bizet's *Carmen* (Rosi's *Carmen*, 1984)

Radiguet's *The Devil in the Flesh* (Bellocchio's *Diavolo in corpo*, 1986)

Stendhal's *The Charterhouse of Parma* (Scola's *What Time Is It*, 1988)

Balzac et al. (Luchetti's *The Footman*, 1991)

Beckett's *Waiting for Godot* (Martone's *Death of a Neapolitan Mathematician*, 1992)

Mallarmé's "Possessed by the demon, a Negress" (Brass's *The Voyeur*, 1994)

Ionesco's *The New Tenant* (Antonioni's *Beyond the Clouds*, 1995)

Feuillet's *The Novel of a Young Man in Poverty* (Scola's *Romanzo di un giovane povero*, 1995)

Queneau's *Exercises in Style* (Laudadio's *Esercizi di stile*, 1996)

GERMAN (Eighteen films)

Stefan Zweig's *Fear* (Rossellini's *La paura*, 1954–55)

Thomas Mann's *Joseph and His Brothers* (Visconti's *Rocco and His Brothers*, 1960)

Kafka's work in general (Olmi's *The Job/The Sound of Trumpets*, 1961)

Faustian legends (Bellocchio's *In the Name of the Father*, 1971)

Thomas Mann's *Death in Venice* (Visconti's *Morte a Venezia*, 1971)

Dürrenmatt's *The Car Breakdown* (Scola's *The Most Exciting Evening in My Life*, 1972)

Goethe's *The Sorrows of Young Werther* (the Tavianis' *The Meadow*, 1978)

Kafka's *The Lost One/America* (Fellini's *Intervista*, 1987)

Goethe's *Wilhelm Meister's Years of Apprenticeship* (Archibugi's *Mignon Has Left*, 1988)

Roth's *The Legend of the Holy Drinker* (Olmi's *La leggenda del santo bevitore*, 1988)

Kafka's *In the Penal Colony* (Betti's *Kafka: The Penal Colony*, 1988)

Schnitzler's *La ronde* (Soldini's *The Clear Skies of the West*, 1990)

Schnitzler's *Dr. Gräsler, Health-Resort Physician* (Faenza's *My Dear Dr. Gräsler*, 1991)

Stifter's *Limestone* (Zaccaro's *The Stone Valley*, 1992)

Goethe's *Elective Affinities* (the Tavianis' *Le affinità elettive*, 1996, and Maiorca's *Viol@*, 1998)

Kleist's *Prince Frederick of Homburg* (Bellocchio's *The Butterfly's Dream*, 1994, and *Il principe di Homburg*, 1997)

RUSSIAN (Fifteen films)

Pushkin's *The Captain's Daughter* (Camerini's *La figlia del capitano*, 1947)

Gogol's *The Overcoat* (Lattuada's *Il cappotto*, 1952)

Dostoyevsky's *White Nights* (Visconti's *Le notti bianche*, 1957)

Pushkin's *The Captain's Daughter* and *A History of Pugachëv's Rebellion* (Lattuada's *The Storm*, 1958)

Chekhov's *The Steppe* (Lattuada's *La steppa*, 1962)

Dostoyevsky's *The Double* (Bertolucci's *Partner*, 1968) (see also Artaud)

Tolstoy's *The Death of Ivan Il'ich* (Pasolini's *Teorema*, 1968) (see also Rimbaud)

Tolstoy's *The Divine and the Human* (the Tavianis' *Saint Michael Had a Rooster*, 1971)

Bulgakov's *Heart of a Dog* (Lattuada's *Cuore di cane*, 1976)

Chekhov's *The Seagull* (Bellocchio's *Il gabbiano*, 1977)

Platonov's *The Third Son* (Rosi's *Three Brothers*, 1980)

Dostoyevsky's *Notes from Underground* (Moretti's *Bianca*, 1984)

Pasternak's *Doctor Zhivago* (Moretti's *Palombella rossa*, 1989)

Tolstoy's *Father Sergius* (the Tavianis' *The Night Sun*, 1990)

Gogol's *Dead Souls* (Amelio's *Lamerica*, 1994)

By far the most important fact that seems to stand out when we arrange our material in this manner is the overwhelming predominance of canonic texts as prototypes for re-created cinema. The issue has noticeable theoretical import, and I would like to condense its most important aspects as follows.

First, when it comes to cinematic re-creation, the literary canon has a tradition of dominating the cinematic canon. In 1945, at the beginning of the period we are considering, novels (or novellas) made up the lion's share; they were re-created by directors—and producers—because they were read and known by the public, and were therefore likely to attract it. Other genres were squeezed into the margins.

However, this grip generally became less tight over time, as cinema developed its own artistic parameters and thus became less dependent on the need to conform to hierarchies created in different contexts and for different purposes. Thus, inspiration from outside the canon of the French, German, and Russian novel increasingly asserted itself in Italian filmmaking in the decades following World War II. In particular, perhaps the most evident trend shown by Italian cinema during the last half of the twentieth century is that, when it came to literary re-creations, the French novel turned out to be the primary victim of a transformation away from uniformity and toward heterogeneity.

Nevertheless, the process of diversification just described went only so far. That is, if we examine from a greater remove the above sampling of re-created texts, we cannot deny that as a whole it still duplicates with a high degree of accuracy traditions recognizably central to the French, German, and Russian literatures as they have been handed down by the cultural institutions of the relevant countries. The fact that, for example, Mittler should appear in *Viol@* is unexpected from a conventional Italian point of view; but from a German point of view, one more recurrence of Goethe's Mittler seems hardly anticanonic. How to account for the apparent contradiction?

The phenomenon, which typically shapes cross-border literary influences, has been studied by Franco Moretti, who summarized his findings as follows:

A limited availability of texts leads to "safe" choices [in translation and distribution]. More cynically: a limited availability of texts equals hegemonic forms, as if [in the host tradition] there were not enough critical mass to resist the gravity of the [original tradition's] cultural hegemony. . . .
If there is only one bookshelf, the canon will take it up.[3]

These circumstances explain well the two seemingly contradictory sides of the same issue: that innovation and variation are obviously detectable in today's Europhile Italian cinema, while at the same time the corpus of modern European literatures taken into account by Italian cinema for its re-creations remains, from the other countries' perspective, comparatively conservative. As Moretti persuasively explains, this has to do with the process of intercultural exchange, which is eagerly pursued by the markets, but only within well-defined bounds—bounds essentially dictated by cultural and socioeconomic factors.

Of course, the fact remains that from the point of view of Italian cinema, the last part of the twentieth century saw a great deal of diversification occur in the way directors read European literary texts and applied them to their own artistic quest. At the tail end, the final result *was* a culturally richer tradition. It is too soon to say whether this could be called a subversion of older canons, preluding to their eventual replacement, or their mere enlargement. Time will make evident trends we are not yet in a position to discern with certainty.

To return—on this subject—to Italian cinema, what does seem clear to me is that the revival it has experienced during the 1990s bodes favorably for its future. As Scola, certainly a qualified commentator, aptly points out, great cinema does indeed need great issues;[4] and for great issues to arise, one needs a society that is lively and rich in debate. Despite the clouds on the political, economic, and cultural horizon of Italy, it is not unreasonable to hope that, perhaps in concomitance with the deployment of some as yet unexplored technology, the fortunate times might return when cinema is able to act as a conduit for the artistic formulation of issues at the core of Italy's social history. If this situation should obtain again, it would be all the more welcome because it would prevail in a country, such as today's Italy, that is considerably more diverse and culturally open than it was fifty years ago.

Greater cultural openness in Italian society may mean, among other no less important things, an even greater flourishing of interest in cinema inspired by masterpieces of literature. This is almost bound to mean world literature: though getting smaller by the day, the world is, after all, still a lot bigger than the Italian boot, and there remains a lot more to be discovered out there by inquisitive Italian filmmakers. If all this comes to pass, then those filmmakers' course of action in seeking out literary partners for the intermedia dialogue between literature and cinema may well track closely the one outlined by Bellocchio in describing his own approach to Kleist's *Homburg:* "I am not in favor of disfiguring classical texts, but rather, of *personalizing them without making them unrecognizable.*"[5]

I would argue that, explicitly or implicitly, this is the methodology which has produced the greatest re-creations from European literatures in Italian cinema; if I may venture a prediction, it will likely reap ever greater acclaim during the next decades of Italian cultural history. Bellocchio's lucidity about the purpose of engaging in re-creative filmmaking offers us an ideal paradigm of the reasons that make it desirable, in Italy or anywhere else in the world, to re-read our historical ancestors and understand who they were—which is something indispensable to understanding who we are today.

NOTES

1. For the reference to Lessing, see Introduction, note 8.

2. These lists are not exhaustive; they only reflect the main items actually discussed in the book. More could be added by including all titles cited in the six chapters *supra*—though with results that, in my estimation, would only marginally modify the general picture.

3. Franco Moretti, *Atlante del romanzo europeo: 1800–1900* (Turin: Einaudi, 1997), p. 151.

4. This is the first epigraph to this volume.

5. "Io non sono dell'idea di stravolgere i classici, ma di *personalizzarli senza renderli irriconoscibili.*" Bellocchio, *Il principe di Homburg di Heinrich von Kleist. . . .* (Florence: Baldini e Castoldi, 1997), p. 151. Emphasis added.

Filmography

Gianni Amelio: *Strike at the Heart (Colpire al cuore*, 1982)

Scenario: Gianni Amelio

Screenplay: Gianni Amelio, Vincenzo Cerami

Photography: Tonino Nardi

Art Direction: Marco Dentici

Costumes: Lina Nerli Taviani

Music: Franco Piersanti

Editing: Anna Napoli

Main Cast: Vanni Corbellini (Sandro, the terrorist), Laura Morante (Giulia, the terrorist's companion), Fausto Rossi (Emilio, the professor's son), Jean-Louis Trintignant (Dario, the professor)

Producers: Enzo Porcelli and Enea Ferrario for Antea Cinematografica (Rome), RAI TV 1

Availability: Italy/video (Italian)

Gianni Amelio: *Lamerica* (1994)

Scenario and Screenplay: Gianni Amelio, Andrea Porporati, Alessandro Sermoneta

Assistant Director: Marco Turco

Photography: Luca Bigazzi

Art Direction: Giuseppe M. Gaudino

Costumes: Liliana Sotira, Claudia Tenaglia

Music: Franco Piersanti

Editing: Simona Paggi

Main Cast: Carmelo Di Mazzarelli (Spiro / Michele), Enrico Lo Verso (Gino), Michele Placido (Fiore)

Producers: Mario and Vittorio Cecchi Gori and Enzo Porcelli for Cecchi Gori Group, Tiger, Alia Film (Rome)

Availability: North America/video (Italian with English subtitles)

Michelangelo Antonioni: *Beyond the Clouds (Al di là delle nuvole, 1995)*

Direction: Michelangelo Antonioni, Wim Wenders (frame story)

Scenario: from Michelangelo Antonioni's *Quel bowling sul Tevere*

Screenplay: Michelangelo Antonioni, Tonino Guerra

Assistant Directors: Beatrice Banfi, Andrea Boni, Donata Wenders

Photography: Alfio Contini, Robby Müller

Art Direction: Thierry Flamand

Costumes: Esther Walz

Music: Lucio Dalla, Laurent Petitgand, Van Morrison, U2

Editing: Michelangelo Antonioni, Claudio Di Mauro, Peter Przygodda, Lucian Segura

Main Cast ("Do Not Look for Me" episode): Fanny Ardant, Jean Reno

Producers: Vittorio Cecchi Gori for C.G. Group Tiger, Cinematografica, Sunshine, Cine B, France 3 Cinéma, Road Movies, Zweite Produktionen GmbH et al.

Availability: North America/video (French with English subtitles)

Francesca Archibugi: *Mignon Has Left (Mignon è partita, 1988)*

Scenario: Francesca Archibugi

Screenplay: Francesca Archibugi, Gloria Malatesta, Claudia Sbarigia

Photography: Luigi Verga

Art Direction: Massimo Spano

Costumes: Paola Marchesin

Music: Roberto Gatto, Battista Lena

Editing: Alfredo Muschietti

Main Cast: Céline Beauvallet (Mignon), Massimo Dapporto (Aldo), Jean-Pierre Duriez (Federico), Leonardo Ruta (Giorgio), Stefania Sandrelli (the mother)

Producers: Leo Pescarolo and Guido De Laurentiis for Ellepi Film, RAI 3 (Rome) and Chrysalide Film (Paris)

Availability: Italy/video (Italian)

Marco Bellocchio: *In the Name of the Father (Nel nome del Padre, 1971)*

Scenario and Screenplay: Marco Bellocchio

Assistant Director: Ugo Novello

Photography: Franco Di Giacomo, Giuseppe Lanci

Art Direction: Amedeo Fago

Costumes: Enrico Job

Music: Nicola Piovani

Editing: Franco Arcalli, Silvano Agosti

Main Cast: Yves Beneyton (Angelo), Laura Betti (Franc's mother), Lou Castel (Salvatore), Aldo Sassi (Franc), Renato Scarpa (Vice Corazza)

Producer: Vides (Rome)

Availability: Italy/video (Italian)

Marco Bellocchio: *The Seagull (Il gabbiano,* 1977)

Scenario: from Anton Chekhov (trans. Angelo Maria Ripellino)

Screenplay: Marco Bellocchio, Lu Leone, Sandro Petraglia, Stefano Rulli

Assistant Director: Stefano Rulli

Photography: Tonino Nardi

Art Direction: Amedeo Fago

Costumes: Gabriella Pescucci

Music: Nicola Piovani

Editing: Silvano Agosti

Main Cast: Laura Betti (Arkadina), Giulio Brogi (Trigorin), Gisella Burinato (Masha), Remo Girone (Konstantin), Remo Remotti (Dorn), Pamela Villoresi (Nina)

Producers: Lu Leone, Roberto Levi, Enzo Porcelli for RAI 1

Availability: Italy/private or institutional collections only

Marco Bellocchio: *Devil in the Flesh (Diavolo in corpo,* 1986)

Scenario: Marco Bellocchio, Enrico Palandri

Screenplay: Marco Bellocchio, Ennio De Concini

Photography: Giuseppe Lanci

Art Direction: Andrea Crisanti

Costumes: Lina Nerli Taviani

Music: Carlo Crivelli

Editing: Mirco Garrone

Main Cast: Marushka Detmers (Giulia Dozza), Riccardo De Torrebruna (Giacomo Pulcini), Alberto Di Stasio (Professor Raimondi), Anita Laurenzi (Ms. Pulcini), Anna Orso (Ms. Dozza), Federico Pitzalis (Andrea Raimondi)

Producers: Leo Pescarolo for L.P. Film, Istituto Luce/Italnoleggio (Rome), Film Sextile (Paris)

Availability: North America/video (Italian with English subtitles)

Marco Bellocchio: *The Butterfly's Dream* (*Il sogno della farfalla*, **1994**)

Scenario and Screenplay: Massimo Fagioli

Photography: Yorgos Arvanitis

Art Direction: Amedeo Fago

Costumes: Lia Francesca Morandini

Music: Carlo Crivelli

Editing: Francesca Calvelli

Main Cast: Bibi Andersson (the mother), Henry Arnold (Carlo), Thierry Blanc (Massimo), Nathalie Boutefeu (Anna), Simona Cavallari (young girl), Roberto Herlitzka (the father), Anita Laurenzi (old woman)

Producers: Filmalbatros (Rome), RAI 2, Waka Films, Pierre Grise Productions (Paris), Televisione della Svizzera Italiana

Availability: Italy/video (Italian)

Marco Bellocchio: *The Prince of Homburg* (*Il principe di Homburg*, **1997**)

Scenario: from Heinrich von Kleist

Screenplay: Marco Bellocchio

Photography: Giuseppe Lanci

Art Direction: Giantito Burchiellaro

Costumes: Francesca Sartori

Music: Carlo Crivelli

Editing: Francesca Calvelli

Main Cast: Toni Bertorelli (the Elector), Barbara Bobulova (Princess Natalia), Fabio Camilli (Hohenzollern), Bruno Corazzari (Kottwitz), Andrea Di Stefano (Homburg), Anita Laurenzi (the Electress), Diego Ribon (Truchss)

Producer: Piergiorgio Bellocchio for Filmalbatros, Istituto Luce (Rome)

Availability: Italy/video (Italian)

Bernardo Bertolucci: *Before the Revolution (Prima della rivoluzione*, **1964**)

Scenario and Screenplay: Bernardo Bertolucci

Assistant Director: Gianni Amico

Photography: Camillo Bazzoni, Aldo Scavarda, Vittorio Storaro

Costumes: Federico Forquet

Music: Ennio Morricone, Gino Paoli

Editing: Roberto Perpignani

Main Cast: Domenico Alpi (Fabrizio's father), Adriana Asti (Gina), Cecrope Barilli (Puck), Francesco Barilli (Fabrizio), Emilia Borghi (Fabrizio's mother), Allen Midgette (Agostino), Morando Morandini (Cesare), Cristina Pariset (Clelia)

Producer: Mario Bernocchi for Iride Cinematografica, Cineriz (Rome)

Availability: North America/video (Italian with English subtitles)

Bernardo Bertolucci: *Partner* (1968)

Scenario: from Fyodor Dostoyevsky

Screenplay: Bernardo Bertolucci, Gianni Amico

Assistant Director: Gianluigi Calderone

Photography: Ugo Piccone

Art Direction: Francesco Tullio Altan

Costumes: Nicoletta Sivieri

Music: Ennio Morricone

Editing: Roberto Perpignani

Main Cast: Tina Aumont (peddler), Giulio Cesare Castello (Professor Mozzoni), Pierre Clémenti (Jacob I and II), Romano Costa (Clara's father), Stefania Sandrelli (Clara), Sergio Tofano (Petrushka)

Producer: Giovanni Bertolucci for Red Film (Rome)

Availability: North America/video (French with English subtitles)

Giuliano Betti: *Kafka: The Penal Colony (Kafka, La colonia penale*, 1988)

Scenario: from Franz Kafka

Screenplay: Giuliano Betti

Assistant Director: Enrico Grassi

Photography: Franco Villa

Art Direction: Antonio Marcon

Costumes: Lucia Portanova

Music: J. S. Bach

Editing: Alessandro Perrella

Main Cast: John Armstead (the captain), Turi Catanzaro, Franco Citti (the journalist), Louis Antonio Da Mendoza, Gianni Pulone, Henry Joseph Riley, Loredana Romito (Silvia), Dante Tabolacci

Producer: Remo Angioli for Cinematografica Romana Cineproduzioni (Rome)

Availability: Italy/video (Italian)

Tinto Brass: *The Voyeur (L'uomo che guarda*, 1994)

Scenario: from Alberto Moravia

Screenplay: Tinto Brass

Photography: Massimo Di Venanzo

Art Direction: Maria Luigia Battani

Costumes: Millina Deodato

Music: Riz Ortolani

Editing: Tinto Brass

Main Cast: Franco Branciaroli (Dodo's father), Martine Brochard, Francesco Casale (Dodo), Cristina Garavaglia, Raffaella Offidani, Katarina Vasilissa (Silvia)

Producers: Marco Poccioni for Rodeo Drive and Marco Valsania for Erre (Rizzoli) Cinematografica

Availability: Italy/video (Italian)

Mario Camerini: *The Captain's Daughter (La figlia del capitano*, 1947)

Scenario: from Aleksandr Pushkin

Screenplay: Mario Camerini, Mario Monicelli, Carlo Musso, Ivo Perilli, Steno (Stefano Vanzina)

Assistant Director: Ivo Perilli

Photography: Aldo Tonti

Art Direction: Piero Filippone

Costumes: Maria De Matteis

Music: Fernando Previtali

Editing: Mario Camerini

Main Cast: Cesare Danova (Pëtr), Irasema Dilian (Masha), Vittorio Gassman (Shvabrin), Amedeo Nazzari (Pugachëv)

Producer: Dino De Laurentiis for Lux, R. D. L. (Rome)

Availability: Italy/public media libraries

Luigi Comencini: *The Traffic Jam (L'ingorgo*, 1979)

Scenario: Luigi Comencini

Screenplay: Luigi Comencini, Ruggero Maccari, Bernardino Zapponi

Assistant Directors: Fabio Galimberti, Riccardo Tognazzi

Photography: Ennio Guarnieri

Art Direction: Mario Chiari, Enzo Eusepi

Costumes: Paola Comencini

Music: Fiorenzo Carpi

Editing: Nino Baragli

Main Cast: Gérard Depardieu (Franco), Annie Girardot (Irene), Ciccio Ingrassia (the wounded man), Marcello Mastroianni (Marco Montefoschi), Miou Miou (Angela), Angela Molina (Martina), Fernando Rey (Carlo), Stefania Sandrelli (Teresa), Alberto Sordi (De Benedetti), Ugo Tognazzi (the "Professor")

Producers: Silvio and Anna Clementelli for Clesi (Rome), Greenwich Film, Gaumont (Paris), José Frade P. C. (Madrid), Albatros Produktion (Munich)

Availability: Italy/video (Italian)

Vittorio De Sica: *The Condemned of Altona (I sequestrati di Altona*, **1962)**

Scenario: from Jean-Paul Sartre

Screenplay: Abby Mann (after Cesare Zavattini)

Assistant Director: Luisa Alessandri

Photography: Roberto Gerardi

Art Direction: Elvezio Frigerio, Carlo Tommasi

Drawings: Renato Guttuso (attributed to Franz)

Costumes: Pier Luigi Pizzi

Music: Dmitri Shostakovich

Editing: Manuel Del Campo, Adriana Novelli

Main Cast: Sofia Loren (Johanna, Werner's wife), Fredric March (Gerlach Senior, the industrialist), Françoise Prévost (Leni Gerlach), Maximilian Schell (Franz Gerlach), Robert Wagner (Werner Gerlach)

Producers: Carlo Ponti for Titanus (Rome), Société Générale de Cinématographie (Paris)

Availability: Italy/video (Italian)

Roberto Faenza: *My Dear Dr. Gräsler (Mio caro Dottor Gräsler*, **1991)**

Scenario: from Arthur Schnitzler

Screenplay: Roberto Faenza, Ennio De Concini

Photography: Giuseppe Rotunno

Art Direction: Giantito Burchiellaro

Costumes: Milena Canonero, Alberto Verso

Music: Ennio Morricone

Editing: Claudio Cutry

Main Cast: Keith Carradine (Gräsler), Sarah Jane Fenton (Katharina), Miranda Richardson (Friederike; the widow), Kristin Scott Thomas (Sabine), Max von Sydow (Schleheim)

Producer: Mario Orfini for Mediapark (Budapest), Eidoscope International (Rome), Rete Italia (Milan)

Availability: Italy/video (Italian)

Federico Fellini: *Intervista* **(1987)**

Scenario: Federico Fellini

Screenplay: Gianfranco Angelucci and Federico Fellini

Assistant Director: Maurizio Mein

Photography: Tonino Delli Colli

Art Direction and Costumes: Danilo Donati

Music: Nicola Piovani

Editing: Nino Baragli

Main Cast: Anita Ekberg (herself), Federico Fellini (himself), Paola Liguori (the star), Marcello Mastroianni (Mandrake/himself), Maurizio Mein (himself), Pietro Notarianni (the Fascist bigwig), Nadia Ottaviani (the vestal), Sergio Rubini (the young journalist), Lara Wendel (the bride)

Producer: Ibrahim Moussa for Aljosha Productions, Cinecittà, RAI 1 (Rome)

Availability: North America/video (Italian with English subtitles)

Giorgio Ferrara: *A Simple Heart* (*Un cuore semplice*, 1977)

Scenario: from Gustave Flaubert

Screenplay: Cesare Zavattini

Assistant Directors: Giampiero Ricci, Robert Kleyn

Photography: Arturo Zavattini

Art Direction: Gianni Silvestri

Costumes: Raimonda Gaetani

Music: Franco Mannino

Editing: Roberto Perpignani

Main Cast: Adriana Asti (Felicita), Alberto Asti (Paolo), Tina Aumont (Virginia), Ugo Bologna, Joe Dallesandro (Teodoro), Alida Valli (Mme. Obin)

Producer: Coopertiva Nashira/Filmcoop

Availability: Italy/public media libraries

Riccardo Freda: *Les Miserables* (*I miserabili*, 1947)

Scenario: from Victor Hugo

Screenplay: Riccardo Freda, Mario Monicelli, Nino Novarese, Steno (Stefano Vanzina)

Photography: Rodolfo Lombardi

Art Direction: Guido Fiorini

Costumes: Dario Cecchi

Music: Alessandro Cicognini

Editing: Otello Colangeli

Main Cast: Gino Cervi (Jean Valjean), Valentina Cortese (Cosetta), Gabriele Ferzetti, Giovanni Hinrich (Javert), Marcello Mastroianni, Rina Morelli, Aldo Nicodemi, Andreina Pagnani (the nun)

Producer: Carlo Ponti for Lux Film (Rome)

Availability: Italy/video (Italian)

Carmine Gallone: *Michael Strogoff* (*Michele Strogoff*, 1956)

Scenario: from Jules Verne

Screenplay: Marc-Gilbert Sauvajon

Photography: Robert Le Febvre

Art Direction: Léon Barsacq

Costumes: Marcel Escoffier

Music: Norbert Glanzberg

Editing: Nicolo Lazzari, Armand Ridel

Main Cast: Curt Jurgens (Strogoff), Sylva Koscina (the Gypsy), Geneviève Page (Miss Nadia)

Producer: Emile Natan for Les Films Modernes (Paris), Produzione Gallone (Rome), et al.

Availability: Italy/video (Italian)

Vittorio Gassman: *Kean* (1956)

Scenario: from Jean-Paul Sartre (and Alexandre Dumas *père*)

Screenplay: Suso Cecchi D'Amico, Vittorio Gassman, Francesco Rosi

Technical Supervision: Francesco Rosi

Photography: Gianni Di Venanzo

Art Direction: Gianni Polidori

Costumes: Giulio Coltellacci, Jacques Lecocq, Marilù Carteny

Music: Roman Vlad

Editing: Enzo Alfonsi

Main Cast: Cesco Baseggio (Salomon), Mario Carotenuto (Peter Patt), Helmut Dantine (Lord Mewill), Anna Maria Ferrero (Anna Damby), Vittorio Gassman (Edmund Kean), Gérard Landry (Prince of Wales), Eleonora Rossi Drago (Countess Elena Koefeld)

Producer: Franco Cristaldi for Vides Cinematografica, Lux Film (Rome)

Availability: Italy/video (Italian)

Alberto Lattuada: *The Overcoat* (*Il cappotto*, 1952)

Scenario: from Nikolai Vasilevich Gogol

Screenplay: Alberto Lattuada, Luigi Malerba, Cesare Zavattini et al.

Assistant Director: Aldo Buzzi

Photography: Mario Montuori

Art Direction: Gianni Polidori

Costumes: Dario Cecchi

Music: Felice Lattuada

Editing: Eraldo Da Roma

Main Cast: Silvio Bagolini (the driver of the hearse), Giulio Calì (the tailor), Anna Carena (the landlady), Antonella Lualdi (Vittoria), Ettore G. Mattia (the secretary), Renato Rascel (Carmine De Carmine), Yvonne Sanson (Caterina), Sandro Somarè (Vittoria's fiancé), Giulio Stival (the Mayor)

Producer: Faro Film (Rome)

Availability: Italy/video (Italian)

Alberto Lattuada: *The Storm (La tempesta*, **1958)**

Scenario: from Alexandr Pushkin

Screenplay: Alberto Lattuada, Ivo Perilli

Assistant Director: Aldo Buzzi

Photography: Aldo Tonti

Art Direction: Mario Chiari

Costumes: Maria De Matteis

Music: Piero Piccioni

Editing: Otello Colangeli

Main Cast: Helmut Dantine (Shvabrin), Vittorio Gassman (the prosecutor), Van Heflin (Pugachëv), Geoffrey Horne (Grinëv), Robert Keith (Captain Mironov), Viveca Lindfors (Catherine II), Silvana Mangano (Masha)

Producer: Dino De Laurentiis for Dino De Laurentiis Cinematografica (Rome), Bosna Film (Sarajevo), Gray Film (Paris)

Availability: Italy/video (Italian)

Alberto Lattuada: *The Steppe (La steppa*, **1962)**

Scenario: from Anton Chekhov

Screenplay: Enzo Curreli, Alberto Lattuada, Tullio Pinelli

Photography: Enzo Serafin

Art Direction: Luigi Scaccianoce

Costumes: Danilo Donati

Music: Guido Turchi

Editing: Leo Catozzo

Main Cast: Cristina Gajoni (the young woman in the river), Daniele Spallone (Iegorushka), Charles Vanel (Father Christopher), Marina Vlady (Countess Dranitsky), Pavle Vuisic (Uncle Kuzmichëv)

Producer: Moris Ergas for Zebra Film (Rome), Aera Films (Paris)

Availability: Italy/public media libraries

Alberto Lattuada: *Heart of a Dog (Cuore di cane*, **1976)**

Scenario: from Mikhail Bulgakov

Screenplay: Alberto Lattuada, Viveca Melander

Assistant Directors: Fabrizio Castellani and Maurizio Rotundi

Photography: Lamberto Caimi

Art Direction: Vincenzo Del Prato

Costumes: Marisa D'Andrea

Music: Piero Piccioni

Editing: Sergio Montanari

Main Cast: Mario Adorf (Bormental), Eleonora Giorgi (Zina), Vadim Glowna (Schwonder), Rena Niehaus (Zoia), Cochi Ponzoni (Bobikov), Gina Rovere (Daria Petrovna), Max von Sydow (Preobrazhensky)

Producers: Mario Gallo and Alberto Lattuada for Filmalpha (Rome), Corona Filmproduktion (Munich)

Availability: Italy/video (Italian)

Francesco Laudadio, ed.: *Exercises in Style (Esercizi di stile*, **1996)**

Scenario: from Raymond Quéneau

Participating directors (in the order in which they feature): Francesco Laudadio, Luigi Magni, Lorenzo Mieli, Pino Quartullo, Alessandro Piva, Faliero Rosati, Dino Risi, Maurizio Dell'Orso, Alex Infascelli, Sergio Citti, Volfango De Biasi, Cinzia Torrini, Claudio Fragasso, Mario Monicelli

Photography, Art Direction, Costumes, Music, Editing: all vary with each director

Cast: Elena Sofia Ricci, Massimo Wertmüller

Producers: Jacopo Capanna and Giuseppe Perugia for Produttori Associati, RAI, Cinecittà et al. (Rome)

Availability: Italy/video (Italian)

Daniele Luchetti: *The Footman (Il portaborse*, **1991)**

Scenario: Franco Bernini, Angelo Pasquini

Screenplay: Daniele Luchetti, Sandro Petraglia, Stefano Rulli

Assistant Director: Riccardo Milani

Photography: Alessandro Pesci

Art Direction: Giancarlo Basili, Leonardo Scarpa

Costumes: Maria Rita Barbera

Music: Dario Lucantoni

Editing: Mirco Garrone

Main Cast: Guido Alberti (Carlo Sperati), Giulio Brogi (Francesco Sanna), Renato Carpentieri (Sartorio), Angela Finocchiaro (Irene), Nanni Moretti (Cesare Botero), Silvio Orlando (Professor Luciano Sandulli)

Producers: Nanni Moretti and Angelo Barbagallo for Sacher Film (Rome)

Availability: Italy/video (Italian)

Donatella Maiorca: *Viol@* **(1998)**

Scenario: Claudio Antonini

Screenplay: Fabrizio Bettelli

Photography: Marcello Montarsi

Art Direction: Beatrice Scarpato

Costumes: Annmarie [*sic*] Heinreich

Music: RestArt (Cinzia Danti, Isabella Colliva)

Editing: Ugo De Rossi, Patrizio Marone

Main Cast: Maddalena Crippa, Ennio Fantastichini (Mittler's voice), Stefania Rocca (Marta/Viol@), Stefano Rota

Producers: Donatella Palermo and Loes Kamsteeg for A.S.P., Dania Film, VIP Media

Availability: Italy/video (Italian)

Mario Martone: *Death of a Neapolitan Mathematician (Morte di un matematico napoletano*, **1992)**

Scenario and Screenplay: Mario Martone, Fabrizia Ramondino

Assistant Director: Alessandro Dionisio

Photography: Luca Bigazzi

Art Direction: Giancarlo Muselli

Costumes: Metella Raboni

Music: Michele Campanella

Editing: Jacopo Quadri

Main Cast: Anna Bonaiuto (Renato's wife), Renato Carpentieri (Renato's brother Luigi), Carlo Cecchi (Renato Caccioppoli), Lucia Maglietta (Emilia, Luigi's wife), Antonio Neiwiller (assistant professor), Toni Servillo (Pietro, mathematician)

Producer: Angelo Curti for Teatri Uniti et al. (Naples, Rome)

Availability: Italy/video (Italian)

Nanni Moretti: *Bianca* **(1984)**

Scenario: Nanni Moretti

Screenplay: Nanni Moretti, Sandro Petraglia

Photography: Luciano Tovoli

Art Direction: Giorgio Luppi, Marco Luppi

Costumes: Lia Morandini

Music: Franco Piersanti

Editing: Mirco Garrone

Main Cast: Claudio Bigagli (Ignazio), Dario Cantarelli (the principal), Enrica Maria Modugno (Aurora), Laura Morante (Bianca), Luigi Moretti (psychiatrist), Nanni Moretti (Michele Apicella), Remo Remotti (Siro Siri), Vincenzo Salemme (Massimiliano), Margherita Sestito (Maria), Roberto Vezzosi (the police commissioner)

Producer: Achille Manzotti for Faso Film (Rome), Rete Italia (Milan)

Availability: Italy/video (Italian)

Nanni Moretti: *Palombella rossa* (1989)

Scenario and Screenplay: Nanni Moretti

Assistant Director: Donatella Botti

Photography: Giuseppe Lanci

Art Direction: Giancarlo Basili and Leonardo Scarpa

Costumes: Maria Rita Barbera

Music: Nicola Piovani

Editing: Mirco Garrone

Main Cast: Asia Argento (Valentina, Michele's daughter), Imre Budavari (himself), Eugenio Masciari (the referee), Luigi Moretti (the labor unionist), Nanni Moretti (Michele Apicella), Claudio Morganti (the character harassing Michele), Silvio Orlando (the coach), Mario Patanè (Simone), Alfonso Santagata (the second character harassing Michele), Fabio Traversa (the old-time friend), Mariella Valentini (the journalist)

Producers: Nanni Moretti and Angelo Barbagallo for Sacher Film, RAI 1 (Rome), Nella Banfi for Palmyre Film (Paris)

Availability: North America/video (Italian with English subtitles)

Ermanno Olmi: *The Job/The Sound of Trumpets (Il posto*, 1961)

Scenario and Screenplay: Ermanno Olmi

Photography: Lamberto Caimi

Art Direction: Ettore Lombardi

Music: Pier Emilio Bassi

Editing: Carla Colombo

Main Cast: Loredana Detto (Antonietta), Tullio Kezich (the psychologist testing candidates), Sandro Panseri (Domenico)

Producers: Titanus, The 24 Horses (Rome)

Availability: North America/video (Italian with English subtitles)

Ermanno Olmi: *The Legend of the Holy Drinker (La leggenda del santo bevitore*, 1988)

Scenario: from Joseph Roth

Screenplay: Tullio Kezich, Ermanno Olmi

Assistant Director: Mimmola Girosi

Photography: Dante Spinotti

Art Direction: Gianni Quaranta, Jean-Jacques Caziot

Costumes: Anne Marie Marchand

Music: Igor Stravinsky

Editing: Ermanno Olmi

Main Cast: Jean-Maurice Chanet (Kaniak), Sandrine Dumas (Gabby), Rutger Hauer (Andreas), Joseph De Medina (Tailor), Anthony Quayle (the gentleman/the Lord), Sophie Ségalen (Karoline)

Producers: Roberto Cicutto and Vincenzo De Leo for Aura Film, Cecchi Gori Group, Tiger Cinematografica (Rome)

Availability: Italy/video (Italian)

Pier Paolo Pasolini: *Teorema* (1968)

Scenario and Screenplay: Pier Paolo Pasolini

Assistant Director: Sergio Citti

Photography: Giuseppe Ruzzolini

Art Direction: Luciano Puccini

Costumes: Marcella De Marchis

Music: W. A. Mozart, Ennio Morricone

Editing: Nino Baragli

Main Cast: Laura Betti (Emilia), Andres José Cruz Soublette (Pietro), Ninetto Davoli (Angelino), Massimo Girotti (Paolo), Silvana Mangano (Lucia), Susanna Pasolini (old peasant woman), Terence Stamp (the Guest), Anne Wiazemsky (Odette)

Producers: Franco Rossellini and Manolo Bolognini for Aetos Film (Rome)

Availability: North America/video (Italian with English subtitles)

Pier Paolo Pasolini: *Salò or the 120 Days of Sodom (Salò o le 120 giornate di Sodoma*, 1975)

Scenario: from the Marquis de Sade

Screenplay: Sergio Citti and Pier Paolo Pasolini

Assistant Director: Umberto Angelucci

Photography: Tonino Delli Colli

Art Direction: Dante Ferretti

Costumes: Danilo Donati

Music: Ennio Morricone

Editing: Nino Baragli, Tatiana Casini Morigi

Main Cast: Paolo Bonaceli (the duke), Caterina Boratto) (Ms. Castelli), Giorgio Cataldi (the *monsignore*), Elsa De Giorgi (Ms. Maggi), Uberto Paolo Quintavalle (the excellency, Sonia Saviange (the pianist), Hélène Surgère (Ms. Vaccari), Aldo Valletti (the president)

Producer: Alberto Grimaldi for PEA (Rome), Les Productions Artistes Associés (Paris)

Availability: North America/video (Italian with English subtitles)

Nelo Risi: *Diary of a Schizophrenic Girl (Diario di una schizofrenica,* **1968)**

Scenario: from Marguerite-Andrée Sèchehaye

Screenplay: Fabio Carpi, Nelo Risi

Assistant Director: Renato Frascà

Photography: Giulio Albonico

Art Direction and Costumes: Renato Frascà

Music: Ivan Vandor

Editing: Otello Colangeli

Main Cast: Margarita Lozano (Mme. Blanche), Gabriella Mulachié (Mrs. Zeno, Anna's mother), Ghislaine d'Orsay (Anna Zeno), Umberto Raho (Mr. Zeno, Anna's father)

Producer: Gian Vittorio Baldi for Idi Cinematografica (Rome), RAI

Availability: Italy/video (Italian)

Francesco Rosi: *Three Brothers (Tre fratelli,* **1981)**

Scenario: from Andrei Platonov

Screenplay: Tonino Guerra, Francesco Rosi

Assistant Director: Gianni Arduini

Photography: Pasqualino De Santis

Art Direction: Andrea Crisanti

Costumes: Gabriella Pescucci

Music: Piero Piccioni

Editing: Ruggero Mastroianni

Main Cast: Maddalena Crippa (Giovanna, Nicola's wife), Vittorio Mezzogiorno (Rocco, the educator, and Donato as a young man), Philippe Noiret (Raffaele, the judge), Michele Placido (Nicola, the FIAT worker), Charles Vanel (Donato Giuranna, the father), Marta Zoffoli (Marta, Nicola's daughter)

Producers: Giorgio Nocella and Antonio Macri for Iter Film (Rome), Gaumont (Paris)

Availability: North America/video (Italian with English subtitles)

Francesco Rosi: *Carmen* **(1984)**

Scenario: from Prosper Mérimée by way of Bizet's opera

Librettists: Ludovic Halévy and Henri Meilhac

Script: Ariane Adriani

Assistant Director: Giovanni Arduini

Photography: Pasqualino De Santis

Choreography: Antonio Gadès

Set Design and Costumes: Enrico Job

Music: Georges Bizet

Editing: Ruggero Mastroianni, Colette Semprun

Main Cast: John Paul Bogart (Zuñiga), Maria Campano (Manuelita), Susan Daniel (Mercédès), Accursio Di Leo (guide), Placido Domingo (Don José), Faith Esham (Micaëla), Gérard Garino (Remendado), Julien Guiomar (Lillas Pastia), Jean-Philippe Lafont (Dancaïre), François Le Roux (Morales), Julia Migenes Johnson (Carmen), Ruggero Raimondi (Escamillo), Lilian Watson (Frasquita)

Producer: Patrice Ledoux for Gaumont, Marcel Dassault (Paris), Opera Film (Rome)

Availability: North America/video (French with English subtitles)

Roberto Rossellini: *A Human Voice (Una voce umana*, 1947), in *L'amore* or *Amore* (1948)

Scenario: from Jean Cocteau

Screenplay: Roberto Rossellini

Photography: Robert Juillard

Art Direction: Christian Bérard

Music: Renzo Rossellini

Editing: Eraldo Da Roma

Cast: Anna Magnani

Producer: Roberto Rossellini for Tevere Film (Rome)

Availability: North America/video (Italian with English subtitles)

Roberto Rossellini: *Joan of Arc Burned at the Stake (Giovanna d'Arco al rogo*, 1954)

Scenario: from Paul Claudel

Screenplay: Roberto Rossellini

Assistant Director: Marcello Caracciolo Di Laurino

Photography: Gabor Pogany

Art Direction: Carlo Maria Cristini

Costumes: Adriana Muojo

Music: Arthur Honegger

Editing: Jolanda Benvenuti

Main Cast: Ingrid Bergman (Joan), Tullio Carminati (Fra Domenico), Giacinto Prandelli (Procus)

Producers: Giorgio Criscuolo and Franco Francese for Produzioni Cinematografiche Associate (Roma), Franco-London Film (Paris)

Availability: Italy/private or institutional collections only

Roberto Rossellini: *Fear (Paura*, 1954–55)

Scenario: from Stefan Zweig

Screenplay: Sergio Amidei, Franz Treuberg

Assistant Directors: Franz Treuberg, Pietro Servadio

Photography: Carlo Carlini

Costumes: Jacques Griffe

Music: Renzo Rossellini

Editing: Jolanda Benvenuti, Walter Boos

Main Cast: Ingrid Bergman (Irene Wagner), Kurt Kreuger (Enrico Stoltz), Renate Mann-hart (Johanna Schultze), Mathias Wieman (Alberto Wagner)

Producers: Aniene Film (Rome), Ariston Film (Munich)

Availability: Italy/public media libraries

Roberto Rossellini: *Vanina Vanini* (1961)

Scenario: Franco Solinas and Antonello Trombadori, from Stendhal

Screenplay: Diego Fabbri, Jean Gruault, Monique Lange, Roberto Rossellini, Franco Solinas, Antonello Trombadori

Assistant Directors: Renzo Rossellini (Jr.), Franco Rossellini, Philippe Arthuys

Photography: Luciano Trasatti

Art Direction: Luigi Scaccianoce

Costumes: Danilo Donati

Music: Renzo Rossellini (Sr.)

Editing: Daniele Alabiso, Mario Serandrei

Main Cast: Martine Carol (Countess Vitelleschi), Isabelle Corey (Clelia), Sandra Milo (Vanina Vanini), Antonio Pierfederici (Livio Savelli), Paolo Stoppa (Prince Asdrubale Vanini), Carlo Tamberlani (*Monsignor* Benini), Laurent Terzieff (Pietro Missirilli)

Producer: Moris Ergas for Zebra Film (Rome), Orsay Film (Paris)

Availability: North America/video (Italian with English stubtitles)

Ettore Scola: *The Most Exciting Evening in My Life (La più bella serata della mia vita*, 1972)

Scenario: from Friedrich Dürrenmatt

Screenplay: Sergio Amidei, Ettore Scola

Assistant Director: Giorgio Scotton

Photography: Claudio Cirillo

Art Direction and Costumes: Luciano Ricceri

Music: Armando Trovajoli

Editing: Raimondo Crociani

Main Cast: Janet Agren (Simonetta), Pierre Brasseur (Count La Brunetière, attorney), Claude Dauphin (Bouisson, chancellor), Giuseppe Maffioli (Pilet), Michel Simon (Zorn, prosecutor), Alberto Sordi (Alfredo Rossi), Charles Vanel (Dutz, head justice)

Producer: Dino De Laurentiis for De Laurentiis Cinematografica, Inter. Ma. Co. (Rome), Columbia (Paris)

Availability: Italy/public media libraries

Ettore Scola: *The Terrace (La terrazza,* **1980)**

Scenario and Screenplay: Age (Agenore Incrocci), Furio Scarpelli, Ettore Scola

Photography: Pasqualino De Santis

Art Direction: Luciano Ricceri

Costumes: Ezio Altieri

Music: Armando Trovajoli

Editing: Raimondo Crociani

Main Cast ("Fracassa" episode): Mino Monicelli (president of RAI TV), Serge Reggiani (Dr. Sergio Stiller, TV administrator). Other episodes: Ombretta Colli (Enza, Amedeo's wife), Vittorio Gassman (Mario, PCI senator), Carla Gravina (Carla, Luigi's wife), Marcello Mastroianni (Luigi, journalist), Stefania Sandrelli (Giovanna, Mario's mistress), Stefano Satta Flores (Tizzo, film critic), Jean-Louis Trintignant (Enrico, scenarist), Ugo Tognazzi (Amedeo, film producer), Milena Vukotic (Emanuela, Enrico's wife)

Producers: Pio Angeletti and Adriano De Micheli for Dean Film (Rome), Film Marceau-Cocinor (Paris)

Availability: Italy/video (Italian)

Ettore Scola: *The New World* **a.k.a.** *The Night of Varennes (Il mondo nuovo* **a.k.a.** *La nuit de Varennes,* **1982)**

Scenario and Screenplay: Sergio Amidei, Ettore Scola

Assistant Director: Paola Scola

Assistant for Historical Matters: Claude Manceron

Photography: Armando Nannuzzi

Art Direction: Dante Ferretti

Costumes: Gabriella Pescucci

Music: Armando Trovajoli

Editing: Raimondo Crociani

Main Cast: Jean-Louis Barrault (Restif de la Bretonne), Laura Betti (Italian soprano), Andréa Ferréol (Mme. Adelaïde Gagnon), Enzo Jannacci (crier on the barge), Harvey Keitel (Tom Paine), Marcello Mastroianni (Giacomo Casanova), Hanna Schygulla (Countess Sophie de la Borde), Jean-Louis Trintignant (M. Sauce)

Producer: Renzo Rossellini for Opera Film (Rome), Gaumont, FR 3 (Paris)

Availability: North America/video (French with English subtitles)

Ettore Scola: *What Time Is It (Che ora è,* **1989)**

Scenario: Ettore Scola

Screenplay: Beatrice Ravaglioli, Ettore Scola, Silvia Scola

Assistant Director: Franco Angeli

Photography: Luciano Tovoli

Art Direction: Luciano Ricceri

Costumes: Gabriella Pescucci

Music: Armando Trovajoli

Editing: Raimondo Crociani

Main Cast: Lou Castel, Marcello Mastroianni (Marcello, the father), Renato Moretti, Anne Parillaud (Loredana), Massimo Troisi (Michele, the son)

Producers: Mario and Vittorio Cecchi Gori for C.G. Group, Tiger Cinematografica, Studio EL (Rome), Gaumont (Paris)

Availability: Italy/video (Italian)

Ettore Scola: *The Voyage of Captain Fracassa (Il viaggio di Capitan Fracassa,* **1990)**

Scenario: from Théophile Gautier

Elaboration: Vincenzo Cerami, Fulvio Ottaviani, Silvia Scola

Screenplay: Furio Scarpelli, Ettore Scola

Assistant Director: Franco Angeli

Photography: Luciano Tovoli

Art Direction: Luciano Ricceri, Paolo Biagetti

Costumes: Odette Nicoletti

Music: Armando Trovajoli

Editing: Raimondo Crociani, Franco Malvestiti

Main Cast: Emmanuelle Béart (Isabella), Tosca d'Aquino (Zerbina), Ciccio Ingrassia (Pietro, Sigognac's servant), Lauretta Masiero (Madama Leonarda), Ornella Muti (Serafina), Vincent Perez (Sigognac), Jean-François Perrier (Matamoro), Massimo Troisi (Pulcinella), Toni Ucci (the tyrant), Massimo Wertmüller (Leandro)

Producers: Franco Committeri (Mass Film) and Luciano Ricceri (Studio EL) for Cecchi Gori Group (Rome), Gaumont (Paris)

Availability: Italy/video (Italian)

Ettore Scola: *The Novel of a Young Man in Poverty (Romanzo di un giovane povero,* **1995)**

Scenario: Ettore Scola

Screenplay: Giacomo Scarpelli, Ettore Scola, Silvia Scola

Assistant Director: Amanzio Todini

Photography: Franco Di Giacomo

Art Direction: Luciano Ricceri

Costumes: Simonetta Leoncini, Enrico Sabbatini

Music: Armando Trovajoli

Editing: Raimondo Crociani

Main Cast: Aida Billardelli (Ms. Bartoloni), Renato De Carmine (Cantini, lawyer), André Dussolier (Moscati, prosecutor), Isabella Ferrari (Andreina), Sara Franchetti (Vincenzo's mother), Gea Martire (deranged neighbor), Rolando Ravello (Vincenzo Persico), Gloria Sirabella (owner of the deli shop), Alberto Sordi (Bartoloni)

Producers: Franco Committeri and Luciano Ricceri for Massfilm-Studio EL, Matopigia, Istituto Luce, RAI (Rome), Les Films Alain Sarde (Paris)

Availability: Italy/video (Italian)

Mario Soldati: *Eugenie Grandet (Eugenia Grandet*, 1946)

Scenario: from Honoré de Balzac

Screenplay: Emilo Cecchi (unacknowledged), Aldo De Benedetti, Mario Soldati

Assistant Director: Marino Girolami

Photography: Vaclav Vich

Art Direction: Maurice Colasson, Gastone Medin

Costumes: Gino C. Sensani

Music: Renzo Rossellini

Editing: Eraldo Da Roma

Main Cast: Giorgio De Lullo (Carlo Grandet, Eugenia's cousin), Pina Gallini (Nanon), Giuditta Rissone (Mme. Grandet), Gualtiero Tumiati (Felix Grandet, Eugenia's father), Alida Valli (Eugenia Grandet)

Producer: Excelsa Film

Availability: Italy/public media libraries

Silvio Soldini: *The Clear Skies of the West (L'aria serena dell'ovest*, 1990)

Scenario: Paola Candiani, Silvio Soldini

Screenplay: Silvio Soldini, Roberto Tiraboschi

Assistant Directors: Isabella Cagnardi, Giorgio Garini

Photography: Luca Bigazzi

Art Direction and Costumes: Daniela Verdenelli

Music: Giovanni Venosta

Editing: Claudio Cormio

Main Cast: Roberto Accornero (Mario), Fabrizio Bentivoglio (Cesare), Olga Durano (Rosa), Antonella Fattori (Irene), Ivano Marescotti (Tobia), Patrizia Piccinini (Veronica), Silli Togni (Clara)

Producers: Monogatari (Milan), Pic Film (Lugano), SSR-Radio Televisione della Svizzera Italiana

Availability: Italy/public media libraries

Paolo and Vittorio Taviani: *Saint Michael Had a Rooster (San Michele aveva un gallo*, 1971)

Scenario: from Leo Tolstoy

Screenplay: Paolo and Vittorio Taviani

Assistant Director: Renzo Micheletti

Photography: Mario Masini

Art Direction: Giovanni Sbarra

Costumes: Lina Nerli Taviani

Music: Vincenzo Bellini, Pyotr Ilich Tchaikovsky, Benedetto Ghiglia

Editing: Roberto Perpignani

Main Cast: Giulio Brogi (Giulio Manieri), Virginia Ciuffini (Virginia), Daniele Dublino (the jailer)

Producer: Giuliani G. De Negri for Ager Film (Rome), RAI

Availability: North America/video (Italian with English subtitles)

Paolo and Vittorio Taviani: *The Meadow (Il prato*, 1978)

Scenario and Screenplay: Paolo and Vittorio Taviani

Assistant Director: Marco De Poli

Photography: Franco Di Giacomo

Art Direction: Gianni Sbarra

Costumes: Lina Nerli Taviani, Renato Ventura

Music: Ennio Morricone

Editing: Roberto Perpignani

Main Cast: Giulio Brogi (Sergio, Giovanni's father), Saverio Marconi (Giovanni), Michele Placido (Enzo), Isabella Rossellini (Eugenia)

Producer: Giuliani G. De Negri for Filmtre (Roma)

Availability: Italy/public media libraries

Paolo and Vittorio Taviani: *The Night Sun (Il sole anche di notte*, 1990)

Scenario: from Leo Tolstoy

Screenplay: Tonino Guerra, Paolo and Vittorio Taviani

Assistant Director: Mimmola Girosi

Photography: Giuseppe Lanci

Art Direction: Gianni Sbarra

Costumes: Lina Nerli Taviani

Music: Nicola Piovani

Editing: Roberto Perpignani

Main Cast: Massimo Bonetti (prince Santobuono), Teresa Brescianini (Concetta), Charlotte Gainsbourg (Matilda), Nastassja Kinski (Cristina), Margarita Lozano (Sergio's mother), Patricia Millardet (Aurelia), Lorenzo Perpignani (Sergio as a child), Matilde

Piana (the peasant woman), Salvatore Rossi (Eugenio), Julian Sands (Sergio Giuramondo), Pamela Villoresi (Giuseppina, Sergio's sister), Rüdiger Vogler (King Carlo)

Producer: Giuliani G. De Negri for Filmtre, RAI 1 (Rome), Capoul—Interpool—Sara Film (Paris), Direkt Film (Munich)

Availability: North America/video (Italian with English subtitles)

Paolo and Vittorio Taviani: *Elective Affinities (Le affinità elettive*, 1996)

Scenario: from Johann Wolfgang von Goethe

Screenplay: Paolo and Vittorio Taviani

Assistant Director: Mimmola Girosi

Photography: Giuseppe Lanci

Art Direction: Gianni Sbarra

Costumes: Lina Nerli Taviani

Music: Carlo Crivelli

Editing: Roberto Perpignani

Main Cast: Jean Hugues Anglade (Edoardo), Fabrizio Bentivoglio (Ottone), Marie Gillain (Ottilia), Isabelle Huppert (Carlotta)

Producer: Grazia Volpi for Filmtre, Gierre Film, RAI (Rome), Jean-Claude Cécile for Florida Movies, France 3 Cinema, Canal + (Paris)

Availability: Italy/video (Italian)

Luchino Visconti: *White Nights (Le notti bianche,* 1957)

Scenario: from Fyodor Dostoyevsky

Screenplay: Suso Cecchi D'Amico, Luchino Visconti

Assistant Directors: Nando Cicero, Albino Cocco

Photography: Giuseppe Rotunno

Art Direction: Mario Chiari, Mario Garbuglia

Costumes: Piero Tosi

Music: Nino Rota

Editing: Mario Serandrei

Main Cast: Clara Calamai (prostitute), Jean Marais (tenant), Marcello Mastroianni (Mario), Corrado Pani (young-man-about-town), Marcella Rovena (owner of the boardinghouse), Dick Sanders (dancer), Maria Schell (Natalia)

Producers: Franco Cristaldi for Vides (Rome), Jean-Paul Guibert for Intermondia Films (Paris)

Availability: North America/video (Italian with English subtitles)

Luchino Visconti: *Rocco and His Brothers (Rocco e i suoi fratelli,* 1960)

Scenario: Suso Cecchi D'Amico, Vasco Pratolini, Luchino Visconti

Screenplay: Suso Cecchi D'Amico, Pasquale Festa Campanile, Massimo Franciosa, Enrico Medioli, Luchino Visconti

Assistant Director: Rinaldo Ricci

Photography: Giuseppe Rotunno

Art Direction: Mario Garbuglia

Costumes: Piero Tosi

Music: Nino Rota

Editing: Mario Serandrei

Main Cast: Claudia Cardinale (Ginetta Giannelli), Max Cartier (Ciro Parondi), Nino Castelnuovo (Nino Rossi), Alain Delon (Rocco Parondi), Spiros Focas (Vincenzo Parondi), Annie Girardot (Nadia), Roger Hanin (Duilio Morini), Corrado Pani (Ivo), Katina Paxinou (Rosaria Parondi, the mother), Renato Salvatori (Simone Parondi), Paolo Stoppa (Cerri), Rocco Vidolazzi (Luca Parondi)

Producer: Goffredo Lombardo for Titanus (Rome), Films Marceau (Paris)

Availability: North America/video (Italian with English subtitles)

Luchino Visconti: "The Job" ("Il lavoro)," in *Boccaccio '70* (1962)

Scenario: from Guy de Maupassant

Screenplay: Suso Cecchi D'Amico, Luchino Visconti

Photography: Giuseppe Rotunno

Art Direction: Mario Garbuglia

Music: Nino Rota

Editing: Mario Serandrei

Main Cast: Tomas Milian (Ottavio), Romy Schneider (Pupe), Paolo Stoppa and Romolo Valli (lawyers)

Producers: Carlo Ponti and Tonino Cervi for Concordia, Cineriz (Rome), Francinex, Gray Films (Paris)

Availability: North America/video (Italian with English subtitles)

Luchino Visconti: *The Stranger (Lo straniero*, 1967)

Scenario: from Albert Camus

Screenplay: Suso Cecchi D'Amico, Georges Conchon, Emmanuel Roblès, Luchino Visconti

Assistant Directors: Rinaldo Ricci, Albino Cocco

Photography: Giuseppe Rotunno

Art Direction: Mario Garbuglia

Costumes: Piero Tosi

Music: Piero Piccioni

Editing: Ruggero Mastroianni

Main Cast: Alfred Adam (prosecutor), Bernard Blier (defense lawyer), Bruno Cremer
(chaplain), Georges Geret (Raymond), Anna Karina (Marie Cardona), Marcello Mastroianni (Meursauls, Georges Wilson (judge)

Producer: Dino De Laurentiis for Dino De Laurentiis Cinematografica, Master Film
(Rome), Marianne Productions (Paris), Casbah Film (Algiers)

Availability: Italy/private or institutional collections only

Luchino Visconti: *Death in Venice (Morte a Venezia*, 1971)

Scenario: from Thomas Mann

Screenplay: Nicola Badalucco, Luchino Visconti

Assistant Director: Albino Cocco

Photography: Pasqualino De Santis

Art Direction: Ferdinado Scarfiotti

Costumes: Piero Tosi

Music: Gustav Mahler

Editing: Ruggero Mastroianni

Main Cast: Carole André (Esmeralda), Björn Andresen (Tadzio), Marisa Berenson (Aschenbach's wife), Dirk Bogarde (Gustav von Aschenbach), Mark Burns (Alfried), Leslie
French (the employee at Cook's), Sergio Garfagnoli (Jaschu), Silvana Mangano (Tadzio's mother), Nora Ricci (Tadzio's governess), Romolo Valli (the hotel director)

Producer: Mario Gallo for Alfa Cinematografica (Rome), Editions Cinématographiques
Françaises (Paris)

Availability: North America/video (Italian with English subtitles)

Maurizio Zaccaro: *The Stone Valley (La valle di pietra*, 1992)

Scenario: from Adalbert Stifter

Screenplay: Ermanno Olmi, Maurizio Zaccaro

Assistant Director: Piergiorgio Gay

Photography: Pasquale Rachini

Art Direction: Carlo Simi

Costumes: Simonetta Leoncini

Music: Claudio Capponi, Alessio Vlad

Editing: Paolo Cottignola, Maurizio Zaccaro

Main Cast: Aleksander Bardini (the parish priest), Fabio Bussotti (the assistant), Charles
Dance (the surveyor)

Producers: Mario and Vittorio Cecchi Gori for Penta Film, Roberto Cicutto and Vincenzo
De Leo for Aura Film (Rome), Marcello Siena for Produzioni SIRE (Milan)

Availability: Italy/video (Italian)

For ongoing updates, see the following Web sites:

http://www.imdb.com/ (Internet Movie Database)
http://kwcinema.play.kataweb.it (Kataweb Cinema)

Indications on availability are given in order of *easiest access* to North American viewers. Thus, "North America/video (Italian with English subtitles)" does not imply that the film cannot *also* be found in Italy on Italian video, that no videos are held in Italy in public media libraries, and so on. On a less positive note, the indication that a film has been distributed on video does not—alas— necessarily mean that it will be possible to purchase it from a commercial outlet; videos do tend to go out of print much faster than books.

Bibliography

HISTORY

General

Bloch, Marc. *Apologie pour l'histoire, ou Métier d'historien.* Paris: Armand Colin, 1949.
———. *Apologie pour l'histoire: Or, The Historian's Craft.* Trans. Peter Putnam. New York: Knopf, 1963.
Carr, Edward Hallett. *What Is History?* London: Macmillan, 1986 [1961].
"European Unemployment: Fiddling." *The Economist,* 4 October 1997, pp. 54–57.
Goez, Werner. *Translatio Imperii. Ein Beitrag zur Geschichte des Geschichtdenkens und der politischen Theorien im Mittelalter und in der frühen Neuzeit.* Tübingen: J. C. B. Mohr (Paul Siebeck), 1958.

Germany

Vann, James A., and Steven W. Rowan. *The Old Reich: Essays on German Political Institutions, 1495–1806.* Brussels: Editions de la Librairie Encyclopédique, 1974.

Italy

"Berlusconi: An Italian Story." *The Economist,* 28 April 2001, pp. 17–18, 23–28.
D'Alema, Massimo. *Un paese normale: La sinistra e il futuro dell'Italia.* Milan: Mondadori, 1995.
Eco, Umberto. "L'egemonia fantasma nella scuola." *la Repubblica,* 15 November 2000, p. 1.

Esposito, Marco. "Disoccupazione salita al 12,5%." *la Repubblica*, 26 June 1997, p. 30.

Gundle, Stephen. *I comunisti italiani tra Hollywood e Mosca: La sfida della cultura di massa (1943–1991)*. Florence: Giunti, 1995. (Original publication in Italian).

Gundle, Stephen, and Simon Parker, eds. *The New Italian Republic: From the Fall of the Berlin Wall to Berlusconi*. London: Routledge, 1996.

Ignazi, Piero. *Dal PCI al PDS*. Bologna: Il Mulino, 1992.

Lonardi, Giorgio. "La nuova frontiera: Tirana, la Taiwan oltre l'Adriatico." *la Repubblica*, 30 December 1996, p. 20.

Lumley, Robert. *States of Emergency: Cultures of Revolt in Italy from 1968 to 1978*. London: Verso, 1990.

Spotts, Frederic, and Theodor Wieser. *Italy, a Difficult Democracy: A Survey of Italian Politics*. Cambridge: Cambridge University Press, 1986.

Turone, Sergio. *Politica ladra: Storia della corruzione in Italia, 1861–1992*. Rome and Bari: Laterza, 1992.

Urban, Joan Barth. *Moscow and the Italian Communist Party: From Togliatti to Berlinguer*. London: I. B. Taurus, 1983.

Willan, Philip. *Puppetmasters: The Political Use of Terrorism in Italy*. London: Constable, 1991.

Further Works Relevant to Italian History and Society

General

Berta, Giuseppe. *Mirafiori*. Bologna: Il Mulino, 1998.

Campi, Alessandro. *Mussolini*. Bologna: Il Mulino, 2001.

Candeloro, Giorgio. *La fondazione della Repubblica e la ricostruzione: Considerazioni finali (1945–1950)*. Vol. 11 of his *Storia dell'Italia moderna*. Milan: Feltrinelli, 1986.

Carocci, Giampiero. *Storia d'Italia dall'unità ad oggi*. Milan: Feltrinelli, 1975.

Castronovo, Valerio. "La storia economica." In Ruggiero Romano and Corrado Vivanti, general eds., *Storia d'Italia*, vol. 4, part 1. Turin: Einaudi, 1976.

———. *L'eredità del Novecento*. Turin: Einaudi, 2001.

Clark, Martin. *Modern Italy 1871–1995*. London: Longman, 1996 [1984].

De Bernardi, Alberto. *Una dittatura moderna*. Milan: Bruno Mondadori, 2000.

De Bernardi, Alberto, and Luigi Ganapini. *Storia d'Italia 1860–1995*. Milan: Bruno Mondadori, 1996.

Dorfles, Piero. *Carosello*. Bologna: Il Mulino, 1998.

Follini, Marco. *La DC*. Bologna: Il Mulino, 2000.

Galli Della Loggia, Ernesto. *L'identità italiana*. Bologna: Il Mulino, 1998.

Gambino, Antonio. *Inventario italiano: Costumi e mentalità di un paese materno*. Turin: Einaudi, 1998.

Ginsborg, Paul. *Storia d'Italia dal dopoguerra a oggi: Società e politica 1943–1988*. Turin: Einaudi, 1989.

———. *A History of Contemporary Italy: Society and Politics 1943–1988*. Harmondsworth, U.K.: Penguin, 1990.

Graziani, Augusto. *Lo sviluppo dell'economia italiana: Dalla ricostruzione alla moneta europea*. Turin: Bollati Boringhieri, 1998.

Isnenghi, Mario, ed. *I luoghi della memoria. Personaggi e date dell'Italia unita.* Rome and Bari: Laterza, 1997.

King, Bolton, and Thomas Okey. *L'Italia d'oggi.* Rome and Bari: Laterza, 2001. [Anastatic rpt. of 1904 ed.].

Lanaro, Silvio. *Storia dell'Italia repubblicana: Dalla fine della guerra agli anni novanta.* Venice: Marsilio, 1999 [1992].

Lepre, Aurelio. *Storia della prima repubblica: L'Italia dal 1945 al 1998.* Bologna: Il Mulino, 1999 [1993].

Mack Smith, Denis. *Storia d'Italia dal 1861 al 1997.* Bari and Rome: Laterza, 1997. (Original edition *Modern Italy: A Political History.* London: Yale University Press, 1997).

Mainardi, Roberto. *L'Italia delle regioni: Il Nord e la Padania.* Milan: Bruno Mondadori, 1998.

Ottaviano, Chiara, and Peppino Ortoleva, eds. *I giorni della storia d'Italia dal Risorgimento a oggi.* Novara: Istituto Geografico De Agostini, 1997 [1991].

Podbielski, Gisele. *Italy: Development and Crisis in the Post-War Economy.* Oxford: Oxford University Press, 1974.

Putnam, Robert D., with Robert Leonardi and Raffaella Y. Nanetti. *Making Democracy Work: Civic Traditions in Modern Italy.* Princeton, N.J.: Princeton University Press, 1993.

Rossi, Salvatore. *La politica economica italiana 1968–1998.* Rome and Bari: Laterza, 1998.

Sapelli, Giulio. *Storia economica dell'Italia contemporanea.* Milan: Bruno Mondadori, 1997.

Schiavone, Aldo. *Italiani senza Italia: Storia e identità.* Turin: Einaudi, 1998.

Unification and Its Discontents

Abba, Giuseppe Cesare. *Da Quarto al Volturno: Noterelle d'uno dei Mille.* Bologna: Zanichelli, 1909.

———. *The Diary of One of Garibaldi's Thousand.* Trans. E. R. Vincent. London: Oxford University Press, 1962.

Banti, Alberto M. *La nazione del Risorgimento: Parentela, santità e onore alle origini dell'Italia unita.* Turin: Einaudi, 2000.

Bianciardi, Luciano. *Antistoria del Risorgimento (Dàgliela avanti un passo!).* Milan: Tascabili degli Editori Associati, 1995 [1992, 1969].

Bocca, Giorgio. *La disunità d'Italia.* Milan: Garzanti, 1990.

Cafagna, Luciano. *Nord e Sud. Non fare a pezzi l'unità d'Italia.* Venice: Marsilio, 1994.

———. *Cavour.* Bologna: Il Mulino, 1999.

Del Boca, Lorenzo. *Maledetti Savoia.* Casale Monferrato: Edizioni Piemme, 1998.

Mack Smith, Denis. *Garibaldi: Una grande vita in breve.* Milan: Mondadori, 1993. (Original edition *Garibaldi: A Great Life in Brief.* Englewood Cliffs, N.J.: Prentice-Hall, 1969 [1956]).

———. "Regionalismo e patriottismo nel Risorgimento." *Bollettino della Società di Studi Politici* 3 (July 1970): 9–32.

Scirocco, Alfonso. *In difesa del Risorgimento.* Bologna: Il Mulino, 1998.

Sereni, Emilio. *Il capitalismo nelle campagne (1860–1900).* Turin: Einaudi, 1968 [1947].

Villari, Rosario, ed. *Il Sud nella storia d'Italia: Antologia della questione meridionale.* 2 vols. Bari: Laterza, 1974.

Brigandism

Del Carria, Renzo. *Proletari senza rivoluzione: Storia delle classi subalterne italiane dal 1860 al 1950.* 2 vols. Rome: Savelli, 1975. [Milan: Edizioni Oriente, 1970].

De Matteo, Giovanni. *Brigantaggio e Risorgimento: Legittimisti e briganti tra i Borbone e i Savoia.* Naples: Alfredo Guida Editore, 2000.

Hobsbawm, Eric J. *Primitive Rebels: Studies in Archaic Forms of Social Movement in the 19th and 20th Centuries.* Manchester: Manchester University Press, 1959.

———. *Bandits.* London: Weidenfeld and Nicolson, 1969.

Molfese, Franco. *Storia del brigantaggio dopo l'Unità.* Milan: Feltrinelli, 1964.

Pezzino, Paolo. "Risorgimento e guerra civile: Alcune considerazioni preliminari." Chapter 3 of *Guerre fratricide: Le guerre civili in età contemporanea.* Ed. Gabriele Ranzato. Turin: Bollati Boringhieri, 1994.

The 1960s

Balestrini, Nanni, and Primo Moroni. *L'orda d'oro, 1968–1977: La grande ondata rivoluzionaria e creativa* [. . .]. Ed. Sergio Bianchi. Milan: Feltrinelli, 1997 [1988].

Capanna, Mario. *Lettera a mio figlio sul Sessantotto.* Milan: Rizzoli, 1998.

Flores, Marcello, and Alberto De Bernardi. *Il Sessantotto.* Bologna: Il Mulino, 1998.

Longo, Antonio, and Giommaria Monti. *Dizionario del '68: I luoghi, i fatti, i protagonisti, le parole e le idee.* Rome: Editori Riuniti, 1998.

Paolini, Marco, and Gabriele Vacis. *Il racconto del Vajont.* Milan: Garzanti, 1997.

Radi, Luciano. *Tambroni trent'anni dopo: Il luglio 1960 e la nascita del centrosinistra.* Bologna: Il Mulino, 1990.

Scalfari, Eugenio, and Giuseppe Turani. *Razza padrona: Storia della borghesia di Stato e del capitalismo italiano, 1962–1974.* Milan: Baldini e Castoldi, 1998 [1974].

Terrorism and Other Threats

Bettin, Gianfranco, and Maurizio Dianese. *La strage. Piazza Fontana: Verità e memoria.* Milan: Feltrinelli, 1999.

Cederna, Camilla. *Pinelli: Una finestra sulla strage.* Milan: Feltrinelli, 1971.

Ferraresi, Franco. *Minacce alla democrazia.* Milan: Feltrinelli, 1995.

———. *Threats to Democracy: The Radical Right in Italy After the War.* Princeton, N.J.: Princeton University Press, 1996. See author's preface for relation to the preceding entry.

La strage di Stato: Controinchiesta. Rome: La Nuova Sinistra/Samonà e Savelli, 1970.

Zavoli, Sergio. *La notte della Repubblica.* Rome: Nuova ERI; Milan: Mondadori, 1995 [1992].

The 1980s

Barca, Luciano, and Sandro Trento, eds. *L'economia della corruzione.* Rome and Bari: Laterza, 1994.

Fiori, Giuseppe. *Il venditore: Storia di Silvio Berlusconi e della Fininvest.* Milan: Garzanti, 1995.

Lodi, Mario. *La TV a capotavola.* Milan: Mondadori, 1994.

Novelli, Edoardo. *Dalla TV di partito al partito della TV: Televisione e politica in Italia, 1960–1995.* Florence: La Nuova Italia, 1995.

Fin de Siècle—Opportunities Found and Lost

"Another Italian Debt Problem." *The Economist*, 1 July 1995, p. 68.

Barbagli, Marzio. *Immigrazione e criminalità in Italia*. Bologna: Il Mulino, 1998.

Bardi, Luciano, and Martin Rhodes, eds. *Politica in Italia: I fatti dell'anno e le inter-pretazioni. Edizione 98*. Bologna: Il Mulino, 1998.

Bocca, Giorgio. *Il sottosopra*. Milan: Mondadori, 1994.

Caciagli, Mario, and David I. Kertzer, eds. *Italian Politics: The Stalled Transition*. Boulder, Colo.: Westview Press, 1996.

Di Pietro, Antonio. *Memoria: Gli intrighi e i veleni contro "Mani pulite."* Milan: Kaos Edizioni, 1999.

———. *Intervista su Tangentopli*. Ed. Giovanni Valentini. Rome and Bari: Laterza, 2000.

Ginsborg, Paul. *L'Italia del tempo presente: Famiglia, società civile, Stato 1980–1996*. Turin: Einaudi, 1998.

Pansa, Giampaolo. *I bugiardi*. Milan: Sperling & Kupfer, 1992.

Pasquino, Gianfranco. *La transizione a parole*. Bologna: Il Mulino, 2000.

Rumiz, Paolo. *La secessione leggera*. Milan: Feltrinelli, 2001.

Sapelli, Giulio. *L'Italia di fine secolo. Economia e classi dirigenti: un capitalismo senza mercato*. Venice: Marsilio, 1998.

Travaglio, Marco, and Elio Veltri. *L'odore dei soldi: Origini e misteri delle fortune di Silvio Berlusconi*. Rome: Editori Riuniti, 2001.

LITERATURE, SEMIOTICS

Theory

Conger, Syndy M., and Janice R. Welsch, eds. *Narrative Strategies*. N.p. [Macomb, Ill.]: Western Illinois University, 1980.

Genette, Gérard. *Palimpsestes: La littérature au second degré*. Paris: Seuil, 1982.

———. *Palimpsests: Literature in the Second Degree*. Trans. Claude Doubinsky and Channa Newman. Lincoln: University of Nebraska Press, 1997.

Lessing, Gotthold Ephraim. *Laokoon: Oder Über die Grenzen der Malerei und Poesie* (1766). Vol. 5, part 2 of his *Werke und Briefe in zwölf Bänden*. Ed. Wilfried Barner. Frankfurt am Main: Deutscher Klassiker Verlag, 1990.

Lotman, Jurij M. *La semiosfera: L'asimmetria e il dialogo nelle strutture pensanti*. Ed. Simonetta Salvestroni. Venice: Marsilio, 1992 [1985].

———. *Il girotondo delle Muse. Saggi sulla semiotica delle arti e della rappresenta-zione*. Ed. Silvia Burini. Bergamo: Moretti e Vitali, 1998.

Lotman, Yurii M. *Universe of the Mind: A Semiotic Theory of Culture*. Trans. Ann Shukman. Intro. Umberto Eco. London and New York: I. B. Tauris, 1990.

———. "Tekst v tekste." *Trudy po znakovym sistemam* 14 (1981): 3–18.

———. "K postroeniiu teorii vzaimodeistviia kul'tur (Semioticheskii aspekt)." *Trudy po romano-germanskoi filologii* (1983): 92–113.

———. "O semiosfere." *Trudy po znakovym sistemam* 17 (1984): 5–23.

———. *Vnutri mysliashchikh mirov: Chelovek—Tekst—Semiosfera—Istoriia*. Moscow: Yazyki Russkoi Kul'tury, 1996.

Matejka, Ladislav, and Krystyna Pomorska, eds. *Readings in Russian Poetics: Formalist and Structuralist Views*. Ann Arbor: Michigan Slavic Publications, 1978.

Mikiel [?], M., De. "O vospriiatii rabot Yu. M. Lotmana v Italii." In *Lotmanovskii sbornik*. Vol. 1. Ed. E. V. Permyakov. Moscow: ITs Garant, 1995. Pp. 294–306.

Moretti, Franco. *Atlante del romanzo europeo: 1800–1900*. Turin: Einaudi, 1997.

Pagnini, Marcello. *Semiosi: Teoria ed ermeneutica del testo letterario*. Bologna: Il Mulino, 1988.

Striedter, Jurij, ed. *Texte der russischen Formalisten*. 2 vols. Munich: Wilhelm Fink Verlag, 1969.

Devil in Literature

Testa, Carlo. *Desire and the Devil: Demonic Contracts in French and European Literature*. New York: Peter Lang, 1991.

FILM STUDIES

Theory

Bordwell, David. *Making Meaning: Inference and Rhetoric in the Interpretation of Cinema*. Cambridge, Mass.: Harvard University Press, 1989.

Casetti, Francesco. *Teorie del cinema 1945–1990*. Milan: Bompiani, 1994 [1993].

———. *Theories of Cinema: 1945–1995*. Trans. Francesca Chiostri et al. Austin: University of Texas Press, 1999.

Mitry, Jean. *Esthétique et psychologie du cinéma*. 2 vols. Paris: Editions Universitaires, 1963–65.

———. *The Aesthetics and Psychology of the Cinema*. Trans. Christopher King. Bloomington: Indiana University Press, 1997.

Stam, Robert. *Film Theory: An Introduction*. Oxford: Blackwell, 2000.

General

Bordwell, David. *Narration in the Fiction Film*. London: Methuen, 1985.

Èizenshtein, Sergei. *Izbrannye proizvedeniia y shesti tomakh*. 6 vols. Moscow: Iskusstvo, 1964–1971.

Sorlin, Pierre. *The Film in History: Restaging the Past*. Oxford: Basil Blackwell, 1980.

Further Works Relevant to Film Studies

Adorno, Theodor W. "Filmtransparente." In *Ohne Leitbild*. In *Kulturkritik und Gesellschaft I*, vol. 10, part 1 of his *Gesammelte Schriften*. Frankfurt am Main: Suhrkamp, 1977. Pp. 353–61.

Allen, Robert C., and Douglas Gomery. *Film History: Theory and Practice*. New York: Knopf, 1985.

Andrew, J. Dudley. *The Major Film Theories: An Introduction*. London: Oxford University Press, 1976.

————. *Concepts in Film Theory*. London: Oxford University Press, 1984.

Arnheim, Rudolf. *Film as Art*. Berkeley: University of California Press, 1964.

Aumont, Jacques, et al. *L'esthétique du film*. Paris: Nathan, 1983.

Bazin, André. *Ontologie et langage*. Vol. 1 of his *Qu'est-ce que le cinéma?* Paris: Editions du Cerf, 1958.

Bernardi, Sandro. *Introduzione alla retorica del cinema*. Florence: Le Lettere, 1994.

Bordwell, David, and Noël Carroll, eds. *Post-Theory: Reconstructing Film Studies*. Madison: University of Wisconsin Press, 1996.

Bordwell, David, Janet Staiger, and Kristin Thompson, eds. *The Classical Hollywood Cinema: Film Style and Mode of Production to 1960*. New York: Columbia University Press, 1985.

Branigan, Edward. *Point of View in the Cinema: A Theory of Narration and Subjectivity in Classical Film*. Berlin: Mouton, 1984.

Costa, Antonio. *Saper vedere il cinema*. Milan: Bompiani, 1985.

Geduld, Harry M., ed. *Authors on Film*. Bloomington: Indiana University Press, 1972.

Ivanov, Viacheslav Vs. "Fil'm v fil'me." *Trudy po znakovym sistemam* 14 (1981): 19–32.

Jameson, Fredric. *The Geopolitical Aesthetic: Cinema and Space in the World System*. Bloomington: Indiana University Press; London: BFI, 1992.

Kracauer, Siegfried. *Theory of Film: The Redemption of Physical Reality*. New York: Oxford University Press, 1960.

Metz, Christian. *Essais sur la signification au cinéma*. 2 vols. Paris: Klincksieck, 1968–73.

————. *Le signifiant imaginaire: Psychanalyse et cinéma*. Paris: Union Générale d'Editions, 1977.

————. *L'énonciation impersonnelle, ou le site du film*. Paris: Méridiens Klincksieck, 1991.

Nichols, Bill. *Movies and Methods: An Anthology*. Berkeley: University of California Press, 1976.

Stam, Robert. *Subversive Pleasures: Bakhtin, Cultural Criticism, and Film*. Baltimore: Johns Hopkins University Press, 1989.

Stam, Robert, Robert Burgoyne, and Sandy Flitterman-Lewis. *New Vocabularies in Film Semiotics: Structuralism, Post-Structuralism and Beyond*. London: Routledge, 1992.

Whittock, Trevor. *Metaphor and Film*. Cambridge: Cambridge University Press, 1990.

Film and Literature

Aycock, Wendell, and Michael Schoenecke, eds. *Film and Literature: A Comparative Approach to Adaptation*. Lubbock: Texas Tech University Press, 1988.

Bazin, André. *Le cinéma et les autres arts*. Vol. 2 of his *Qu'est-ce que le cinéma?* Paris: Editions du Cerf, 1959.

Bluestone, George. *Novels into Film*. Berkeley: University of California Press, 1966.

Brady, Ben. *Principles of Adaptation for Film and Television*. Austin: University of Texas Press, 1994.

Brunetta, Gian Piero, ed. *Letteratura e cinema*. Bologna: Zanichelli, 1976.

Cartmell, Deborah, and Imelda Whelehan, eds. *Adaptations: From Text to Screen, Screen to Text*. London: Routledge, 1999.

Chatman, Seymour. "What Novels Can Do That Films Can't (and Vice Versa)." *Critical Inquiry* 7, no. 1 (Autumn 1980): 121–40.

———. *Coming to Terms: The Rhetoric of Narrative in Fiction and Film*. Ithaca, N.Y.: Cornell University Press, 1990.

Clerc, Jeanne-Marie. *Littérature et cinéma*. Paris: Nathan, 1993.

Cohen, Keith. *Film and Fiction: The Dynamics of Exchange*. New Haven, Conn.: Yale University Press, 1979.

Deltcheva, Roumiana. "Literature-Film Relations: Selected Bibliography (1985–1996)." In *Literature and Film: Models of Adaptation*. Special issue of *Canadian Review of Comparative Literature/Revue Canadienne de Littérature Comparée* 23, no. 3 (September 1996): 853–71.

Griffith, James. *Adaptations as Imitations: Films from Novels*. Newark: University of Delaware Press, 1997.

Horton, Andrew, and Joan Magretta, eds. *Modern European Filmmakers and the Art of Adaptation*. New York: Frederick Ungar, 1981.

Jenkins, Greg. *Stanley Kubrick and the Art of Adaptation: Three Novels, Three Films*. Jefferson, N.C.: McFarland, 1997.

Mast, Gerald. "Literature and Film." *Interrelations of Literature*. Ed. Jean Pierre Barricelli and Joseph Gibaldi. New York: MLA, 1982. Pp. 278–306.

McDougal, Stuart Y. *From Literature to Film*. New York: Holt, Rinehart and Winston, 1985.

McFarlane, Brian. *Novel to Film: An Introduction to the Theory of Adaptation*. Oxford: Clarendon Press, 1996.

Miller, Gabriel. *Screening the Novel: Rediscovered American Fiction in Film*. New York: Frederick Ungar, 1980.

Naremore, James. *Film Adaptation*. New Brunswick, N.J.: Rutgers University Press, 2000.

Orr, John, and Colin Nicholson, eds. *Cinema and Fiction: New Modes of Adapting, 1950–1990*. Edinburgh: Edinburgh University Press, 1992.

Shklovskii, Viktor. *Literatura i kinematograf*. Berlin: Russkoe Universal'noe Izdatel'stvo, 1923.

Testa, Carlo. "Dalla letteratura al cinema: Adattamento o ri-creazione?" *Bianco & Nero* 62, no. 1–2 (April 2001): 37–51.

Further Works Relevant to Film and Literature

Albersmeier, Franz-Josef, and Volker Roloff, eds. *Literaturverfilmungen*. Frankfurt am Main: Suhrkamp, 1989.

Bauschinger, Sigrid, Susan L. Cocalis, and Henry A. Lea, eds. *Film und Literatur: Literarische Texte und der neue deutsche Film*. Bern: Francke, 1984.

Beja, Morris. *Film and Literature*. New York: Longman, 1979.

Bisztray, George. "Cinema e letteratura: Le prospettive aperte dallo studio comparato delle arti." *I Quaderni di Gaia. Rivista di letteratura comparata* 5-6-7 (1992–93): 49–57.

Gallagher, Brian. "Film Imagery, Literary Imagery: Some Distinctions." *College Literature* 5, no. 3 (Fall 1978): 157–73.

Gaudreault, André. *Du littéraire au filmique: Système du récit.* Montreal: Presses de l'Université Laval; Paris: Klincksieck, 1988.

Goodwin, James. "Film Study in a Literature Program?" *College Literature* 5, no. 3 (Fall 1978): 174–82.

Gould Boyum, Joy. *Double Exposure: Fiction into Film.* New York: New American Library/Plume, 1985.

Kotzin, Miriam. "A Bibliographic and Filmographic Guide to Teaching Literature/Film." *College Literature* 5, no. 3 (Fall 1978): 249–62.

Marcus, Fred H. *Film and Literature: Contrasts in Media.* Scranton, Pa.: Chandler, 1971.

Marcus, Millicent. "Who Owns Film Studies?" *Romance Languages Annual* 5 (1993): 239–45.

Paech, Joachim. *Literatur und Film.* Stuttgart: Metzler, 1988.

Peary, Gerald, and Roger Shatzkin, eds. *The Modern American Novel and the Movies.* New York: Frederick Ungar, 1978.

Sinyard, Neil. *Filming Literature: The Art of Screen Adaptation.* London: Croom Helm, 1986.

Wagner, Geoffrey. *The Novel and the Cinema.* London: Tantivy Press/Fairleigh Dickinson University Press, 1975.

Italy

General

Aristarco, Guido. *Neorealismo e nuova critica cinematografica. Cinematografia e vita nazionale negli anni quaranta e cinquanta: Tra rotture e tradizioni.* Florence: Nuova Guaraldi, 1980.

———. *Il cinema fascista: Il prima e il dopo.* Bari: Dedalo, 1996.

Bertelli, Sergio. *I corsari del tempo: Gli errori e gli orrori dei film storici.* Florence: Ponte alle Grazie, 1995.

Bondanella, Peter. *Italian Cinema from Neorealism to the Present.* New York: Continuum, 1991 [1983].

Brunetta, Gian Piero. *Storia del cinema italiano.* 4 vols. Rome: Editori Riuniti, 1993 [1982].

———, ed. *L'Europa: Miti, luoghi, divi.* Vol. 1, part 1 of his *Storia del cinema mondiale.* Turin: Einaudi, 1999.

Canova, Gianni. *L'occhio che ride: Commedia e anti-commedia nel cinema italiano contemporaneo.* Milan: Editoriale Modo, 1999.

Cappabianca, Alessandro. *Il cinema e il sacro.* Recco: Le Mani, 1998.

Chiarini, Luigi. *Arte e tecnica del film.* Bari: Laterza, 1962.

Chiti, Roberto, Enrico Lancia, Andrea Novarin, Mario Pecorari, and Roberto Poppi, eds. *Dizionario del cinema italiano.* 4 vols. Rome: Gremese, 1991–1996. *I film dal 1930 al 1944,* vol. 1, ed. Chiti and Lancia, 1993; *I film dal 1945 al 1959,* vol. 2, ed. Chiti and Poppi, 1991.

D'Agostini, Paolo. "Il cinema ritorna agli anni di piombo." *la Repubblica,* 4 July 1992, p. 29.

Di Giammatteo, Fernaldo. *Nuovo dizionario universale del cinema: I film*. 2 vols. Rome: Editori Riuniti, 1994 [1984].

———. *Nuovo dizionario universale del cinema: Gli autori*. 2 vols. Rome: Editori Riuniti, 1996 [1985].

———. *Lo sguardo inquieto: Storia del cinema italiano 1940–1990*. Florence: La Nuova Italia, 1994.

Di Giammatteo, Fernaldo, and Cristina Bragaglia. *Dizionario del cinema italiano*. Rome: Editori Riuniti, 1995.

Faldini, Franca, and Goffredo Fofi, eds. *L'avventurosa storia del cinema italiano raccontata dai suoi protagonisti: 1935–1959*. Milan: Feltrinelli, 1979.

———. *L'avventurosa storia del cinema italiano raccontata dai suoi protagonisti: 1960–1969*. Milan: Feltrinelli, 1981.

———. *Il cinema italiano d'oggi 1970–1984 raccontato dai suoi protagonisti*. Milan: Mondadori, 1984.

Fofi, Goffredo. *Capire con il cinema: Duecento film prima e dopo il '68*. Milan: Feltrinelli, 1971.

———. *Il cinema italiano: Servi e padroni*. Milan: Feltrinelli, 1971.

———. *Dieci anni difficili: Capire con il cinema parte seconda, 1975–1985*. Florence: La Casa Usher, 1985.

Gieri, Manuela. *Contemporary Italian Filmmaking: Strategies of Subversion*. Toronto: University of Toronto Press, 1995.

Hay, James. *The Passing of the Rex: Popular Film Culture in Fascist Italy*. Bloomington: Indiana University Press, 1987.

Landy, Marcia. *Italian Film*. Cambridge: Cambridge University Press, 2000.

Liehm, Mira. *Passion and Defiance: Film in Italy from 1942 to the Present*. Berkeley: University of California Press, 1984.

Marcus, Millicent. *Italian Film in the Light of Neorealism*. Princeton, N.J.: Princeton University Press, 1986.

Marrone, Gaetana, ed. *New Landscapes in Contemporary Cinema*. Thematic issue of *Annali d'Italianistica* 17 (1999).

Martini, Giulio, and Guglielmina Morelli, eds. *Patchwork due: Geografia del nuovo cinema italiano*. Milan: Il Castoro, 1997.

Micciché, Lino. *Cinema italiano: Gli anni '60 e oltre*. Venice: Marsilio, 1995 [1975].

———. *Cinema italiano degli anni '70: Cronache 1969–1979*. Venice: Marsilio, 1989 [1980].

Micciché, Lino, ed. *Il neorealismo cinematografico italiano*. Venice: Marsilio, 1999 [1978, 1974].

———, ed. *Il cinema del riflusso: Film e cineasti italiani degli anni '70*. Venice: Marsilio, 1997.

———, ed. *Schermi opachi: Il cinema italiano degli anni '80*. Venice: Marsilio, 1998.

Pasolini, Pier Paolo. *I film degli altri*. Ed. Tullio Kezich. Parma: Guanda, 1996.

Quaglietti, Lorenzo. *Storia economico-politica del cinema italiano 1945–1980*. Rome: Editori Riuniti, 1980.

Sesti, Mario. *Nuovo cinema italiano*. Rome: Theoria, 1994.

———. *La "scuola" italiana: Storia, strutture e immaginario di un altro cinema (1988–1996)*. Venice: Marsilio, 1996.

Sorlin, Pierre. *Italian National Cinema 1896–1996*. London and New York: Routledge, 1996.

Tassone, Aldo. *Parla il cinema italiano*. 2 vols. Milan: Il Formichiere, 1980.

Tinazzi, Giorgio, ed. *Il cinema degli anni '50*. Venice: Marsilio, 1979.

Viganò, Aldo, *Storia del cinema storico in cento film*. Recco: Le Mani, 1997.

Zagarrio, Vito. *Cinema italiano anni novanta*. Venice: Marsilio, 1998.

———, ed. *Il cinema della transizione: Scenari italiani degli anni novanta*. Venice: Marsilio, 2000.

Further Works Relevant to Italian Cinema

Bazin, André. *Une esthétique de la réalité: Le néo-réalisme*. Vol. 4 of his *Qu'est-ce que le cinéma?* Paris: Editions du Cerf, 1962.

Bertetto, Paolo. *Il più brutto del mondo: Il cinema italiano oggi*. Milan: Bompiani, 1981.

Bondanella, Peter. "Recent Work on Italian Cinema." *Journal of Modern Italian Studies* 1, no. 1 (Fall 1995): 101–23.

Brunetta, Gian Piero. *Identikit del cinema italiano oggi: 453 storie*. Venice: Marsilio, 2000.

———, ed. *Spari nel buio. La letteratura contro il cinema italiano:* settant'anni di stroncature memorabili. Venice:Marsilio, 1994.

———, ed. *Identità italiana e identità europea nel cinema italiano: Dal 1945 al miracolo economico*. Turin: Edizioni della Fondazione Giovanni Agnelli, 1996.

Buache, Freddy. *Le cinéma italien 1945–1990*. Lausanne: L'Age d'Homme, 1992.

Castello, Giulio Cesare. *Il cinema neorealistico italiano*. N.p.: Edizioni Radio Italiana, 1956.

Dalle Vacche, Angela. *The Body in the Mirror: Shapes of History in Italian Cinema*. Princeton, N.J.: Princeton University Press, 1992.

D'Amico, Masolino. *La commedia all'italiana: Il cinema comico in Italia dal 1945 al 1975*, Milan: Mondadori, 1985.

Ferrero, Adelio, ed. *Storia del cinema: Autori e tendenze negli anni cinquanta e sessanta*. 3 vols. Venice: Marsilio, 1978.

Ferrero, Adelio, Giovanna Grignaffini, and Leonardo Quaresima. *Il cinema italiano degli anni '60*. Rimini and Florence: Guaraldi Editore, 1977.

Fofi, Goffredo. "Il cinema italiano dopo il '45." In his *I grandi registi della storia del cinema*. Rome: Donzelli, 1995.

Giacovelli, Enrico. *La commedia all'italiana*. Rome: Gremese, 1990.

Lizzani, Carlo. *Il cinema italiano dalle origini agli anni ottanta*. Rome: Editori Riuniti, 1982 [1979].

Pintus, Pietro. *Storia e film: Trent' anni di cinema italiano (1945–1975)*. Rome: Bulzoni, 1980.

Schifano, Laurence. *Le cinéma italien de 1945 à nos jours: Crise et création*. Paris: Nathan, 1995.

Tinazzi, Giorgio, and Marina Zancan, eds. *Cinema e letteratura del neorealismo*. Venice: Marsilio, 1983.

Viganò, Aldo. *Commedia italiana in cento film*. Recco: Le Mani, 1995.

Vitti, Antonio, ed. *Italian Cinema*. Special anniversary issue of *Canadian/American Journal of Italian Studies* 20, no. 54 (1997).

Film and Literature

Attolini, Vito. *Storia del cinema letterario in cento film*. Recco: Le Mani, 1998.

Bernardi, Sandro, ed. *Storie dislocate*. San Miniato: Edizioni ETS, 1999.

Bragaglia, Cristina. *Il piacere del racconto: Narrativa italiana e cinema (1895–1990)*. Florence: La Nuova Italia, 1993.

Cortellazzo, Sara, and Dario Tomasi. *Letteratura e cinema*. Rome and Bari: Laterza, 1998.

Costa, Antonio. *Immagine di un'immagine: Cinema e letteratura*. Turin: UTET, 1993.

Marcus, Millicent. *Filmmaking by the Book: Italian Cinema and Literary Adaptation*. Baltimore: Johns Hopkins University Press, 1993.

Micciché, Lino. "Cinema e letteratura." In his *La ragione e lo sguardo: Saggi e note sul cinema*. Cosenza: Lerici, 1979. Pp. 147–77.

Moscariello, Angelo. *Cinema e/o letteratura*. Bologna: Pitagora Editrice, 1981.

Nuvoli, Giuliana, and Maurizio Regosa. *Storie ricreate: Dall'opera letteraria al film*. Turin: UTET, 1998.

Testa, Carlo. *Masters of Two Arts: Re-creation of European Literatures in Italian Cinema*. Toronto: University of Toronto Press, 2002.

DIRECTORS AND ACTORS

Amelio

Amelio, Gianni. *Lamerica: Film e storia del film*. Ed. Piera Detassis. Turin: Einaudi, 1994.

Amelio, Gianni, and Vincenzo Cerami. *Colpire al cuore: Trattamento e sceneggiatura*. Mantua: Circolo del Cinema, 1996.

Amelio, Gianni, Andrea Porporati, and Alessandro Sermoneta. *Lamerica. Sceneggiatura originale*. Mantua: Circolo del Cinema, 1999.

Albano, Lucilla, ed. *Il racconto tra letteratura e cinema*. Rome: Bulzoni, 1997.

Cattini, Alberto. *Le storie e lo sguardo: Il cinema di Gianni Amelio*. Venice: Marsilio, 2000.

Fofi, Goffredo. "Gianni Amelio." In his *Come in uno specchio: I grandi registi della storia del cinema*. Rome: Donzelli, 1995. Pp. 260–62.

———, ed. *Amelio secondo il cinema: Conversazione con G. F.* Rome: Donzelli, 1994.

Martini, Emanuela, ed. *Gianni Amelio: Le regole e il gioco*. Turin: Lindau, 1999.

Sesti, Mario, and Stefanella Ughi, eds. *Gianni Amelio*. Rome: Dino Audino Editore, n.d. [1995?].

Volpi, Gianni, ed. *Gianni Amelio*. Turin: Edizioni Scriptorium, 1995.

Antonioni

Antonioni, Michelangelo. *Quel bowling sul Tevere*. Turin: Einaudi, 1995 [1983].

———. *Fare un film è per me vivere*. Ed. Carlo di Carlo and Giorgio Tinazzi. Venice: Marsilio, 1994.

———. *The Architecture of Vision: Writings and Interviews on Cinema*. Ed. Carlo di Carlo and Giorgio Tinazzi. Trans. Marga Cottino-Jones. New York: Marsilio, 1996.

Brunetta, Gian Piero. *Forma e parola nel cinema: Il film muto, Pasolini, Antonioni.* Padua: Liviana, 1970.

Brunette, Peter. *The Films of Michelangelo Antonioni.* Cambridge: Cambridge University Press, 1998.

Chatman, Seymour. *Antonioni: Or, the Surface of the World.* Berkeley: University of California Press, 1985.

Pasolini, Pier Paolo. "Moravia e Antonioni" and "Difendo *Deserto rosso.*" In his *I film degli altri.* Ed. Tullio Kezich. Parma: Guanda, 1996. Pp. 75–81.

Peavler, Terry J. "Blow-Up: A Reconsideration of Antonioni's Infidelity to Cortázar." *PMLA* 94, no. 5 (October 1979): 887–93.

Ranieri, Nicola. *Amor vacui: Il cinema di Michelangelo Antonioni.* Chieti: Métis Editrice, 1990.

Rohdie, Sam. *Antonioni.* London: British Film Institute, 1990.

Tassone, Aldo. *I film di Michelangelo Antonioni.* Rome: Gremese, 1990.

Tinazzi, Giorgio. *Michelangelo Antonioni.* Florence: La Nuova Italia, 1994 [1989, 1974].

Wenders, Wim. *Avec Michelangelo, Antonioni: Chronique d'un film.* Trans. Henri Christophe et al. Paris: L'Arche Editeur, 1995.

———. *Il tempo con Antonioni: Cronaca di un film.* Trans. Silvia Bortoli. Rome: Edizioni Socrates, 1995.

———. *Die Zeit mit Antonioni: Chronik eines Films.* Frankfurt am Main: Verlag der Autoren, 1995.

———. *My Time with Antonioni.* Trans. Michael Hofmann. London and New York: Faber and Faber, 2000.

Bellocchio

Bellocchio, Marco. *Nel nome del padre.* Ed. Goffredo Fofi. Bologna: Cappelli, 1971.

———. *Il principe di Homburg di Heinrich von Kleist: Sceneggiatura.* Ed. Giovanni Spagnoletti. Milan: Baldini e Castoldi, 1997.

Bernardi, Sandro. *Marco Bellocchio.* Milan: Il Castoro, 1998 [1978].

Bertuzzi, Laura. *Il cinema di Marco Bellocchio.* Castelsangiovanni: Pontegobbo, 1996.

Malanga, Paola, ed. *Marco Bellocchio: Catalogo ragionato.* Milan: Edizioni Olivares, 1998.

Nicastro, Anita, ed. *Marco Bellocchio: Per un cinema d'autore.* Florence: Ferdinando Brancato Editore, 1992.

Bertolucci

Campani, Ermelinda M. *L'anticonformista: Bernardo Bertolucci e il suo cinema.* Fiesole: Cadmo, 1998.

Campari, Roberto, and Maurizio Schiaretti, eds. *In viaggio con Bernardo: Il cinema di Bernardo Bertolucci.* Venice: Marsilio, 1994.

Costa, Francesco. *Bernardo Bertolucci.* Rome: Dino Audino Editore, n.d. [1995?].

Kline, T. Jefferson. *I film di Bernardo Bertolucci: Cinema e psicanalisi.* Rome: Gremese, 1994. Translation of *Bertolucci's Dream Loom: A Psychoanalytic Study of Cinema.* Amherst: University of Massachusetts Press, 1987.

Pasolini, Pier Paolo. *"Partner."* In his *I film degli altri.* Ed. Tullio Kezich. Parma: Guanda, 1996. Pp. 84–88.
Socci, Stefano. *Bernardo Bertolucci.* Milan: Il Castoro, 1996.
Wicks, Ulrich. "Borges, Bertolucci, and Metafiction." In *Narrative Strategies.* Ed. Syndy M. Conger and Janice R. Welsch. N.P. [Macomb, Ill.]: Western Illinois University, 1980. Pp. 19–36.

Brass

Codelli, Lorenzo. *Nerosubrass.* Rome: Dino Audino Editore, 1996.
Iori, Stefano. *Tinto Brass.* Rome: Gremese, 2000.
Tentori, Antonio. *Tinto Brass: Il senso dei sensi.* Alessandria: Edizioni Falsopiano, 1998.

Camerini

Grmek Germani, Sergio. *Mario Camerini.* Florence: La Nuova Italia, 1980.

Comencini

Comencini, Luigi. *Infanzia, vocazione, esperienze di un regista.* Milan: Baldini e Castoldi, 1999.
Gosetti, Giorgio. *Luigi Comencini.* Florence: La Nuova Italia, 1988.

Freda

Freda, Riccardo. *Divoratori di celluloide: Cinquanta anni di memorie, cinematografiche e non.* Milan: Emme Edizioni/Edizioni del Mystfest, 1981.
———. *Riccardo Freda: Un pirate à la caméra. Entretiens.* Ed. Eric Poindron. Arles: Institut Lumière/Actes Sud, 1994.
Della Casa, Stefano. *Riccardo Freda.* Rome: Bulzoni, 1999.

Gassman

Gassman, Vittorio. *Bugie sincere.* Milan: Longanesi, 1997.
Kezich, Tullio. "Vittorio fra i tromboni." In *Vittorio Gassman: L'ultimo mattatore.* Ed. Fabrizio Deriu. Venice: Marsilio, 1999. Pp. 51–60.

Lattuada

Lattuada, Alberto. *La tempesta.* Ed. Filippo M. De Sanctis. Bologna: Cappelli, 1958.
———. *La steppa.* Ed. Franco Calderoni. Bologna: Cappelli, 1962.
———. *L'occhio di Dioniso: Racconti, ricordi, lettere d'amore.* Florence: La Casa Usher, 1990.
———. *Il mio set: Qualche sogno, qualche verità, una curiosità illimitata.* Ed. Vito Zagarrio. Ragusa: Libroitaliano, 1995.

Bruno, Edoardo. *Alberto Lattuada*. Rome: Edizioni Cinecittà International, 1993.
Bulgakov, Mikhail Afanas'evich. *Cuore di cane: Il romanzo e la sceneggiatura di Alberto Lattuada*. Bari: De Donato, 1975.
Camerini, Claudio. *Alberto Lattuada*. Florence: La Nuova Italia, 1982.
Cosulich, Callisto. *I film di Alberto Lattuada*. Rome: Gremese, 1985.

Luchetti

Luchetti, Daniele, Sandro Petraglia, and Stefano Rulli. *Il portaborse*. Milan: Feltrinelli, 1993.

Martone

Martone, Mario, and Fabrizia Ramondino. *Morte di un matematico napoletano*. Milan: Ubulibri, 1992.
Ranucci, Georgette, and Stefanella Ughi, eds. *Mario Martone*. Rome: Dino Audino Editore, n.d. [1996?].

Mastroianni

Mastroianni, Marcello. *Mi ricordo, sì, io mi ricordo*. Ed. Francesco Tatò. Milan: Baldini e Castoldi, 1997.
Biagi, Enzo, ed. *La bella vita: Marcello Mastroianni racconta*. Rome: RAI-ERI; Milan: Rizzoli, 1996.
Costantini, Costanzo. *Marcello Mastroianni: Vita, amori e successi di un divo involontario*. Rome: Editori Riuniti, 1996.

Moretti

Bernardi, Sandro, et al. *Nanni Moretti*. Turin: Paravia Scriptorium, 1999.
De Bernardinis, Flavio. *Nanni Moretti*. Milan: Il Castoro, 1998.
Ranucci, Georgette, and Stefanella Ughi, eds. *Nanni Moretti*. Rome: Dino Audino Editore, n.d. [1995?].
Testa, Carlo. "From the Lives of Underground Men: Dostoevsky, Moretti's *Bianca*, and the Italian Revolution." *Romance Languages Annual* 8 (1996): 328–34.

Olmi

Dillon, Jeanne. *Ermanno Olmi*. Florence: La Nuova Italia, 1985.
Kezich, Tullio, and Piero Maccarinelli, eds. *Da Roth a Olmi: La leggenda del santo bevitore*. Siena: Nuova Immagine Cinema, 1988.
Rossi, Flavia. *La leggenda del santo bevitore: Roth e Olmi*. Rome: Edav, 1993.
Viganò, Dario E., ed. *Il cinema delle parabole*. Vol. 1. Cantalupa (Turin): Effatà Editrice, 1999.

Pasolini

Pasolini, Pier Paolo. *Teorema*. Milan: Garzanti, 1974 [1968].

Ceccatty, René de. *Sur Pier Paolo Pasolini*. Le Faouët: Editions du Scorff, 1998.

De Giusti, Luciano. *I film di Pier Paolo Pasolini*. Rome: Gremese, 1983.

Greene, Naomi. *Pier Paolo Pasolini: Cinema as Heresy*. Princeton, N.J.: Princeton University Press, 1990.

Lawton, Ben. "The Evolving Rejection of Homosexuality, the Sub-Proletariat, and the Third World in the Films of Pier Paolo Pasolini." *Italian Quarterly* 82–83 (Fall 1980–Winter 1981): 167–73.

Marchesini, Alberto. *Citazioni pittoriche nel cinema di Pasolini (da* Accattone *al* Decameron). Florence: La Nuova Italia, 1994.

Moscati, Italo. *Pasolini e il teorema del sesso. 1968: dalla mostra del cine al sequestro. . . .* Milan: Il Saggiatore, 1995.

Murri, Serafino. *Pier Paolo Pasolini*. Milan: Il Castoro, 1994.

Naldini, Nico. *Pasolini: Una vita*. Turin: Einaudi, 1989.

Rumble, Patrick. *Allegories of Contamination: Pier Paolo Pasolini's Trilogy of Life*. Toronto: University of Toronto Press, 1996.

Siciliano, Enzo. *Vita di Pasolini*. Florence: Giunti, 1995 [1978].

———. *Pasolini: A Biography*. Trans. John Shepley. New York: Random House, 1982.

Spila, Piero. *Pier Paolo Pasolini*. Rome: Gremese, 1999.

Viano, Maurizio. *A Certain Realism: Making Use of Pasolini's Film Theory and Practice*. Berkeley: University of California Press, 1993.

Rosi

Guerra, Tonino, and Francesco Rosi. *Tre fratelli: Sceneggiatura*. Mantua: Circolo del Cinema, 1999.

Bolzoni, Francesco. *I film di Francesco Rosi*. Rome: Gremese, 1986.

Ciment, Michel. *Le dossier Rosi*. Paris: Ramsay, 1987 [1976].

Gesù, Sebastiano, ed. *Francesco Rosi*. Acicatena: Incontri con il Cinema, 1991.

Giacci, Vittorio, ed. *Francesco Rosi*. Rome: Cinecittà International, 1994.

Mancino, Anton Giulio, and Sandro Zambetti. *Francesco Rosi*. Milan: Il Castoro, 1998 [1977].

Testa, Carlo, ed. *Poet of Civic Courage: The Films of Francesco Rosi*. Trowbridge, U.K.: Flicks Books, 1996.

Rossellini

Rossellini, Roberto. *Il mio metodo*. Ed. Adriano Aprà. Venice: Marsilio, 1987.

———. *My Method*. Trans. Annapaola Cancogni. New York: Marsilio, 1992.

———. *Quasi un'autobiografia*. Ed. Stefano Roncoroni. Milan: Mondadori, 1987.

Baldelli, Pio. *Roberto Rossellini*. Rome: Samonà e Savelli, 1992.

Bondanella, Peter. *The Films of Roberto Rossellini*. Cambridge; Cambridge University Press, 1993.

Brunette, Peter. *Roberto Rossellini*. New York: Oxford University Press, 1987.

Forgacs, David, Sarah Lutton, and Geoffrey Nowell-Smith, eds. *Roberto Rossellini: Magician of the Real*. London: British Film Institute, 2000.

Guarner, José Luis. *Roberto Rossellini*. New York: Praeger, 1970.

Masi, Stefano, and Enrico Lancia. *I film di Roberto Rossellini*. Rome: Gremese, 1987.

Rondolino, Gianni. *Roberto Rossellini*. Florence: La Nuova Italia, 1974.

———. *Roberto Rossellini*. Turin: UTET, 1989.

Serceau, Michel. *Roberto Rossellini*. Paris: Les Editions du Cerf, 1986.

Verdone, Mario, ed. *Roberto Rossellini*. Paris: Seghers, 1963.

Sandrelli

Alberione, Ezio, et al., eds. *Stefania Sandrelli*. Palermo: Edizioni Papageno, 1998.

Scola

Scola, Ettore. *Il cinema e io*. Ed. Antonio Bertini. Rome: Officina Edizioni, 1996.

Scola, Ettore, Beatrice Ravaglioli, and Silvia Scola. *Che ora è: Sceneggiatura*. Mantua: Circolo del Cinema, 1989.

Amidei, Sergio, and Ettore Scola. *Il mondo nuovo: Sceneggiatura*. Mantua: Circolo del Cinema, 1989.

De Santi, Pier Marco, and Rossano Vittori. *I film di Ettore Scola*. Rome: Gremese, 1987.

Ellero, Roberto. *Ettore Scola*. Florence: La Nuova Italia, 1996.

Reynaud, Patricia. "De la nuit de Varennes à la terreur: Le voyage de la mystification." *Canadian/American Journal of Italian Studies* 20, nos. 55–56 (1997): 221–34.

Scarpelli, Furio, and Ettore Scola. *Il viaggio di Capitan Fracassa: Trattamento e sceneggiatura originali*. Mantua: Circolo del Cinema, 1992.

Soldati

Barberi Squarotti, Giorgio, et al., eds. *Mario Soldati: La scrittura e lo sguardo*. Turin: Museo Nazionale del Cinema/Lindau, 1991.

Ioli, Giovanna, ed. *Mario Soldati: Lo specchio inclinato*. San Salvatore Monferrato (Alessandria): Edizioni della Biennale Piemonte e Letteratura, 1999.

Soldini

Soldini, Silvio, and Roberto Tiraboschi. *L'aria serena dell'ovest: Sceneggiatura originale*. Mantua: Circolo del Cinema, 1995.

Audino, Emilia, and Francesco Medosi, eds. *Silvio Soldini*. Rome: Dino Audino Editore, 2000.

Malanga, Paola, ed. *Silvio Soldini: Nella città dell'anima*. Bologna: Alphabet, 1998.

Paolo and Vittorio Taviani

Accialini, Fulvio, and Lucia Coluccelli. *Paolo e Vittorio Taviani*. Florence: La Nuova Italia, 1979.

Ambrosini, Maurizio, and Ignazio Occhipinti. *Le affinità elettive di Paolo e Vittorio Taviani*. Milan: Sapiens, 1996.

Aristarco, Guido. *Sotto il segno dello scorpione: Il cinema dei fratelli Taviani*. Messina and Florence: G. D'Anna, 1978. Pp. 101–52. Repr. as *"San Michele aveva un gallo."* In his *I sussurri e le grida: Dieci letture critiche di film*. Palermo: Sellerio, 1988. Pp. 173–206.

De Santi, Pier Marco. *I film di Paolo e Vittorio Taviani*. Rome: Gremese, 1988.

Ferrucci, Riccardo, and Patrizia Turini. *Paolo e Vittorio Taviani: La poesia del paesaggio*. Rome: Gremese, 1995. With parallel English ed. *Paolo and Vittorio Taviani: Poetry of the Italian Landscape*.

Gili, Jean A., ed. *Paolo et Vittorio Taviani: Entretien au pluriel*. Arles: Institut Lumière/ Editions Actes Sud, 1993.

Spila, Piero. "La fine delle 'utopie' nel cinema dei Taviani." In *Il cinema del riflusso*. Ed. Lino Micciché. Venice: Marsilio, 1997. Pp. 154–62.

Torri, Bruno, ed. *Il cinema dei Taviani*. Roma: Ministero degli Affari Esteri, Direzione Generale Relazioni Culturali, 1989.

Visconti

Visconti, Luchino. *Rocco e i suoi fratelli*. Ed. Guido Aristarco and Gaetano Carancini. Bologna: Cappelli, 1978 [1960].

———. *Three Screenplays: White Nights, Rocco and His Brothers, The Job*. Trans. Judith Green. New York: Orion Press, 1970.

Aristarco, Guido. *Su Visconti: Materiali per una analisi critica*. Rome: La Zattera di Babele, 1986.

Baldelli, Pio. *Luchino Visconti*. Milan: Gabriele Mazzotta Editore, 1973.

Bencivenni, Alessandro. *Luchino Visconti*. Milan: Il Castoro, 1999 [1994, 1982].

Bruni, David, and Veronica Pravadelli, eds. *Studi viscontiani*. Venice: Marsilio, 1997.

D'Amico de Carvalho, Caterina. *Life and Work of Luchino Visconti*. Rome: Cinecittà International, n.d. [1998].

De Franceschi, Leondrdo. *Il film Lo straniero di Luchino Visconti: Dalla pagina allo schermo*. Rome: Scuola Nazionale di Cinema/Biblioteca di Bianco & Nero, 1999.

———. "Piccola storia di un film dimenticato: *Lo straniero*." *Bianco & Nero* 60, no. 2 (March–April 1999): 68–89.

De Giusti, Luciano. *I film di Luchino Visconti*. Rome: Gremese, 1985.

Micciché, Lino. *Luchino Visconti: Un profilo critico*. Venice: Marsilio, 1996.

Nowell-Smith, Geoffrey. *Luchino Visconti*. New York: Viking Press, 1973 [1967].

Pravadelli, Veronica, ed. *Il cinema di Luchino Visconti*. Rome: Scuola Nazionale di Cinema, Biblioteca di Bianco & Nero, 2000.

Renzi, Renzo. *Visconti segreto*. Bari: Laterza, 1994.

Rohdie, Sam. *Rocco and His Brothers (Rocco e i suoi fratelli)*. London: British Film Institute, 1992.

Rondolino, Gianni. *Luchino Visconti*. Turin: UTET, 1981.

Sanzio, Alain, and Paul-Louis Thirard. *Luchino Visconti cinéaste*. Paris: Persona, 1984.

LITERATURE AND OTHER ARTS

France

Artaud

Artaud, Antonin. *Le théâtre et son double*. Paris: Gallimard, 1964 [1938]. Also in vol. 4 of his *Oeuvres completes*. Paris: Gallimard, 1976–1982.
———. *The Theater and Its Double*. Trans. Mary Caroline Richards. New York: Grove Press, 1958.

Balzac

Balzac, Honoré de. *La Comédie humaine*. Ed. Pierre-Georges Castex. Paris: Gallimard Pléiade, 1976. *Eugénie Grandet* in *Scènes de la vie de province*, ed. Pierre Barbéris et al., vol. 3.
———. *Eugenie Grandet*. Trans. Marion Ayton Crawford. London: Penguin, n.d. [1955].

Baudelaire

Baudelaire, Charles. *Oeuvres complètes*. Ed. Claude Pichois. Vol. 1. Paris: Gallimard Pléiade, 1975.

Beckett

Beckett, Samuel. *En attendant Godot*. Paris: Les Editions de Minuit, 1990 [1952].
———. *Waiting for Godot: Tragicomedy in Two Acts*. New York: Grove Press, 1954.

Claudel

Claudel, Paul. *Jeanne d'Arc au bûcher*. In his *Théâtre*. Ed. Jacques Madaule and Jacques Petit. Vol. 2. Paris: Gallimard Pléiade, 1965. Pp. 1215–42.

Cocteau

Cocteau, Jean. *La voix humaine*. In his *Oeuvres complètes*. Vol. 7. Geneva: Marguerat, 1948.
———. *The Human Voice*. Trans. Carl Wildman. London: Vision Press, 1951.
Knapp, Bettina L. *Jean Cocteau*. Boston: Twayne, 1989 [1970].

Dumas

Dumas, Alexandre, *père*. *Kean ou Désordre et génie* (1836). In his *Théâtre complet*. Vol. 5. Paris: Calmann-Lévy, n.d. [ca.1866]. Pp. 101–212.
———. *Kean*. In his *The Great Lover and Other Plays*. Adapted by Barnett Shaw. New York: Frederick Ungar, 1979. Pp. 73–162.
Stowe, Richard S. *Alexandre Dumas père*. Boston: Twayne, 1976.

Flaubert

Flaubert, Gustave. *Oeuvres complètes*. Ed. Jean Bruneau and Bernard Masson. Paris: Seuil Intégrale, 1964. *Un Coeur simple* in vol. 2.
———. *Correspondance*. Ed. Jean Bruneau. Vol. 3. Paris: Gallimard Pléiade, 1991.

———. *A Simple Heart.* In his *Three Tales.* Trans. A. J. Krailsheimer. Oxford: Oxford University Press, 1991. Pp. 3–40.

Gautier

Gautier, Théophile. *Le Capitaine Fracasse.* In his *Oeuvres complètes.* Vol. 6. Geneva: Slatkine Reprints 1978 [Paris: Charpentier, 1889].

Hugo

Hugo, Victor. *Les misérables.* Vol. 2 of his *Romans.* Paris: Seuil Intégrale, 1963.
———. *Les Miserables. The Works of Victor Hugo.* Trans. Isabel F. Hapgood et al. Vols. 4, 5, and 6a. New York: Kelmscott Society, 1887.
———. *Les Miserables.* London: D. Campbell, 1998.

Ionesco

Ionesco, Eugène. *Le nouveau locataire.* In his *Théâtre.* Vol. 2. Paris: Gallimard, 1967 [1958].

Mallarmé

Mallarmé, Stéphane. *Poésies.* Vol. 1 of his *Oeuvres complètes.* Ed. Carl Paul Barbier and Charles Gordon Millan. Paris: Flammarion, 1983.
———. *Oeuvres complètes.* Ed. Bertrand Marchal. Paris: Gallimard Pléiade, 1998.

Maupassant

Maupassant, Guy de. "Au bord du lit." In his *Contes et nouvelles (1875–1884).* Ed. Louis Forestier. Vol. 1. Paris: Gallimard Pléiade, 1974. Pp. 1040–46.

Nerval

Nerval, Gérard de [Gérard Labrunie]. *Oeuvres.* Ed. Henri Lemaitre. Paris: Garnier, 1966.

Queneau

Queneau, Raymond. *Exercices de style.* Paris: Gallimard, 1964 [1947].
———. *Exercises in Style.* Trans. Barbara Wright. London: Gaberbocchus Press, 1958.

Radiguet

Radiguet, Raymond. *Le diable au corps.* In his *Oeuvres complètes.* Ed. Chloé Radiguet and Julien Cendres. Paris: Stock, 1993.
———. *The Devil in the Flesh: A Novel.* Trans. A. M. Sheridan Smith. London: Calder and Boyars, 1968.

Restif de la Bretonne

Restif de la Bretonne, Nicolas-Edmé. *Les nuits de Paris.* Ed. Henri Bachelin. Vol. 1. Paris: Editions du Trianon, 1930.
———. *Les nuits de Paris.* Paris: Hachette, 1960.
———. *Les Nuits de Paris: Or The Nocturnal Spectator.* Trans. Linda Asher and Ellen Fertig. New York: Random House, 1964.
Rétif [*sic*] de la Bretonne. "Mes ouvrages." In *Monsieur Nicolas.* Ed. Pierre Testud. Vol. 2. Paris: Gallimard, 1989.

Blanchot, Maurice. *Sade et Restif de la Bretonne*. Paris: Editions Complexe, 1986.

Coward, David. *The Philosophy of Restif de La* [sic] *Bretonne*. Oxford: Voltaire Foundation, 1991.

Graitson, Jean-Marie, ed. *Sade, Retif* [sic] *de la Bretonne et les formes du roman pendant la Révolution française: Actes du 3e Colloque International des Paralittératures de Chaudfontaine*. Liège: C.L.P.C.F., 1992.

Rimbaud

Rimbaud, Arthur. *Les déserts de l'amour*. In his *Oeuvres*. Ed. Suzanne Bernard and André Guyaux. Paris: Garnier, 1987 [1983].

————. *Complete Works, Selected Letters*. Ed. and trans. Wallace Fowlie. Chicago: University of Chicago Press, 1975 [1966].

Robbe-Grillet

Robbe-Grillet, Alain. *Les gommes*. Paris: Editions de Minuit, 1953.

Sartre

Sartre, Jean-Paul. *Kean*. Paris: Gallimard, 1954. With Dumas's text in appendix.

————. *Kean: Disorder and Genius*. Trans. Kitty Black. London: Hamish Hamilton, 1973 [1954].

————. *Kean*. Ed. David Bradby. Oxford: Oxford University Press, 1973.

————. *Les séquestrés d'Altona: Pièce en cinq actes*. Paris: Gallimard, 1960.

————. *The Condemned of Altona: A Play in Five Acts*. Trans. Silvia Leeson and George Leeson. New York: Vintage, 1961.

Teroni, Sandra, and Andrea Vannini. *Sartre e Beauvoir al cinema*. Florence: La Bottega del Cinema, 1987.

Stendhal

Stendhal [Henri Beyle]. *La Chartreuse de Parme*. Ed. Ernest Abravanel. Vols. 24–25 of his *Oeuvres complètes*. Ed. Victor Del Litto. Geneva: Cercle du Bibliophile, 1969.

————. *The Charterhouse of Parma*. Trans. C. K. Scott Moncrieff. London: Zodiac Press, 1980.

Verne

Verne, Jules. *Michel Strogoff*. In his *Les oeuvres*. Ed. Gilbert Sigaux. Paris: Hachette, 1978.

————. *Michel Strogoff*. Evry: Editions Carrefour, 1998.

————. *Michael Strogoff: The Courier of the Czar*. In his *Works*. Ed. Charles F. Horne. Vol. 8. New York and London: Vincent Parke, 1911. Pp. 143–396.

German Area

Brecht

Brecht, Bertolt. *Gedichte 4: Gedichte und Gedichtfragmente 1928–1939*. Vol. 14 of his *Werke*. Ed. Werner Hecht et al. Berlin-Weimar: Aufbau; Frankfurt am Main: Suhrkamp, 1993.

————. *Poems 1913–1956*. Ed. John Willett et al. New York: Methuen, 1976.

Broch

Broch, Hermann. *Die Schlafwandler.* Vol. 1 of his *Kommentierte Werkausgabe.* Ed. Paul Michael Lützeler. Frankfurt am Main: Suhrkamp, 1978.
———. *The Sleepwalkers.* Trans. Willa Muir and Edwin Muir. London: Quartet, 1986.

Dürrenmatt

Dürrenmatt, Friedrich. *Die Panne. Eine noch mögliche Geschichte.* (Short story, 1955). In his *Gesammelte Werke in sieben Bänden.* Vol. 5. Zürich: Diogenes Verlag, 1988. Pp. 267–326.
———. *Die Panne.* (Radio drama, 1956). In his *Werkausgabe in dreißig Bänden.* Vol. 16. Zürich: Diogenes Verlag, 1980. Pp. 9–56.
———. *Die Panne.* (Comedy, 1979). In his *Werkausgabe in dreißig Bänden.* Vol. 16. Zürich: Diogenes Verlag, 1980. Pp. 57–173.

Goethe

Goethe, Johann Wolfgang von. *Sämtliche Werke nach Epochen seines Schaffens.* Münchner Ausgabe. Ed. Karl Richter et al. Munich: Carl Hanser, 1987. *Zum Schäkespears* [sic] *Tag* and *Die Leiden des jungen Werthers* in *Der junge Goethe: 1757–1775,* ed. Gerhard Sauder et al, vol. 1, part 2: *Faust I* in *Weimarer Klassik: 1798–1806,* ed. Victor Lange, vol. 6, part 1; *Die Wahlverwandtschaften* in *Epoche der Wahlverwandtschaften: 1807–1814,* ed. Christoph Siegrist et al., vol. 9; *Shakespear* [sic] *und kein Ende!* in *Divan-Jahre: 1814–1819,* ed. Johannes John et al., vol. 11, part 2.
———. *Die Wahlverwandtschaften: Ein Roman.* Ed. Erich Trunz and Benno von Wiese. Munich: Deutscher Taschenbuch Verlag, 1980 [1977].
———. *Collected Works.* Ed. Victor Lange et al. Princeton, N.J.: Princeton University Press, 1994. "Shakespeare: A Tribute" in *Essays on Art and Literature,* ed. John Gearey, trans. Ellen von Nardroff and Ernest H. von Nardroff, vol. 3; *The Sorrows of Young Werther, Elective Affinities, Novella,* ed. David E. Wellbery, trans. Victor Lange and Judith Ryan, vol. 11.
———. *Elective Affinities.* Trans. Elizabeth Mayer and Louise Bogan. Chicago: Henry Regnery, 1963.
———. *Faust: A Tragedy.* Trans. Bayard Taylor. New York: Modern Library, 1967 [1870].
———. "Shakespeare *Ad Infinitum.*" In *Goethe's Literary Essays.* Ed. J. E. Spingarn. New York: Frederick Ungar, 1964 [1921]. Pp. 174–89.
———. *The Sufferings of Young Werther* and *Elective Affinities.* Ed. Victor Lange. New York: Continuum, 1990.

Kafka

Kafka, Franz. *In der Strafkolonie.* In *Ein Landarzt und andere Drucke zu Lebzeiten.* Vol. 1 of his *Gesammelte Werke in zwölf Bänden.* Ed. Hans-Gerd Koch. Frankfurt am Main: Fischer, 1994.
———. *The Penal Colony, Stories and Short Pieces.* Trans. Willa Muir and Edwin Muir. New York: Schocken, 1995 [1961].

Müller-Seidel, Walter. *Die Deportation des Menschen: Kafkas Erzählung* In der Strafkolonie *im europäischen Kontext*. Frankfurt am Main: Fischer, 1989 [1986].

Kleist

Kleist, Heinrich von. *Werke und Briefe in vier Bänden*. Ed. Siegfried Streller. Berlin: Aufbau, 1978. *Prinz Friedrich von Homburg* in vol. 2.
———. *Prince Frederick of Homburg*. In his *Five Plays*. Ed. and trans. Martin Greenberg. New Haven, Conn.: Yale University Press, 1988.
Allan, Seán. *The Plays of Heinrich von Kleist: Ideals and Illusions*. Cambridge: Cambridge University Press, 1996.
Hackert, Fritz, ed. *Heinrich von Kleist. Prinz Friedrich von Homburg: Erläuterungen und Dokumente*. Stuttgart: Reclam, 1979.
Hinderer, Walter, ed. *Kleists Dramen: Neue Interpretationen*. Stuttgart: Reclam, 1981.
Lukács, Georg. "Die Tragödie Heinrich von Kleists" [1937]. In his *Deutsche Realisten des 19. Jahrhunderts*. Bern: Francke; Berlin: Aufbau, 1951. Pp. 19–48. Repr. in his *Deutsche Literatur in zwei Jahrhunderten*. Neuwied: Luchterhand, 1964. Pp. 201–31.
Müller-Seidel, Walter, ed. *Kleists Aktualität: Neue Aufsätze und Essays 1966–1978*. Darmstadt: Wissenschaftliche Buchgesellschaft, 1981.
Neumann, Gerhard, ed. *Heinrich von Kleist: Kriegsfall—Rechtsfall—Sündenfall*. Freiburg im Breisgau: Rombach Verlag, 1994.
Sembdner, Helmut. *In Sachen Kleist: Beiträge zur Forschung*. Munich: Carl Hanser, 1974.
Stephens, Anthony. *Heinrich von Kleist: The Dramas and Stories*. Providence, R.I.: Berg, 1994.
Wichmann, Thomas. *Heinrich von Kleist*. Stuttgart: Metzler, 1988.

Mann

Mann, Thomas. *Gesammelte Werke in dreizehn Bänden*. Frankfurt am Main: S. Fischer, 1974. *Der Tod in Venedig* in *Erzählungen. Fiorenza. Dichtungen*, vol. 8.
———. *Death in Venice*. Ed. and trans. Clayton Koelb. New York: Norton, 1994.

Nietzsche

Nietzsche, Friedrich. *Sämtliche Werke: Kritische Studienausgabe in fünfzehn Einzelbänden*. Ed. Giorgio Colli and Mazzino Montinari. Munich: dtv; Berlin: De Gruyter, 1988. *Jenseits von Gut und Böse* in vol. 5.
———. *Complete Works*. Ed. Oscar Levy. New York: Russell and Russell, 1964 [1909–11]. *Beyond Good and Evil*, trans. Helen Zimmern, vol. 12.

Roth

Roth, Joseph. *Die Legende vom heiligen Trinker*. In *Romane und Erzählungen*. Vol. 6 of his *Werke*. Ed. Fritz Hackert. Cologne: Kiepenheuer und Witsch, 1991.
———. *The Legend of the Holy Drinker* Trans. Michael Hofmann. London: Chatto and Windus, 1989.
Magris, Claudio. "Il tempo non è denaro. Note sull'anticapitalismo nella letteratura austriaca." *Nuova Antologia* 2205 (January–March 1998): 32–42.

Schnitzler

Schnitzler, Arthur. *Doktor Gräsler, Badearzt*. In his *Gesammelte Werke: Die erzählenden Schriften*. Vol. 2. Frankfurt am Main: S. Fischer, 1961.
———. *Dr. Gräsler [Health-Resort Physician]*. Trans. E. C. Slade. New York: Thomas Seltzer, 1923.
———. *Reigen*. In his *Gesammelte Werke: Die dramatischen Werke*. Vol. 1. Frankfurt am Main: S. Fischer, 1962.
———. *La Ronde*. In his *Plays and Stories*. Ed. Egon Schwarz. Trans. Eric Bentley. New York: Continuum, 1982.
Koebner, Thomas, ed. *Arthur Schnitzler*. Reigen: *Erläuterungen und Dokumente*. Stuttgart: Reclam, 1997.
Schneider, Gerd K., ed. *Die Rezeption von A. S.s* Reigen, *1897–1994*. Riverside, Calif.: Ariadne Press, 1995.

Stifter

Stifter, Adalbert. *Kalkstein*. In *Bunte Steine*. Vol. 2, part 2 of his *Werke und Briefe: Historisch-kritische Gesamtausgabe*. Ed. Alfred Doppler and Wolfgang Frühwald. Stuttgart: Kohlhammer, 1982.
———. *Brigitta*. With *Abdias, Limestone*, and *The Forest Path*. Trans. Helen Watanabe-O'Kelly. London: Angel Books; Chester Springs, Pa.: Dufour Editions, 1990.

Italy

Leopardi

Prete, Antonio. *Finitudine e infinito: Su Leopardi*. Milan: Feltrinelli, 1998.

Montale

Montale, Eugenio. *Ossi di seppia*. In his *L'opera in versi*. Ed. Rosanna Bettarini and Gianfranco Contini. Turin: Einaudi, 1980.
———. *Cuttlefish Bones (1920–1927)*. Trans. William Arrowsmith. New York: Norton, 1992.

Moravia

Moravia, Alberto. *L'uomo che guarda*. Milan: Fabbri, Bompiani, Sonzogno, Etas, 1985.
———. *The Voyeur: A Novel*. Trans. Tim Parks. London: Secker and Warburg, 1986.

Vittorini

Vittorini, Elio. *Conversazione in Sicilia*. Milan: Bompiani, 1941.

Russia

Bulgakov

Bulgakov, Mikhail Afanas'evich. *Sobach'e serdtse*. In *Povesti*. Vol. 3 of his *Sobranie sochinenii*. Ed. Ellendea Proffer. Ann Arbor, Mich.: Ardis, 1983.

Bulgakov, Mikhail. *The Heart of a Dog.* Trans. Michael Glenny. New York: Harcourt, Brace and World, 1968.

Levin, Volker. *Das Groteske in Michail Bulgakovs Prosa.* Munich: Otto Sagner, 1975.

Milne, Lesley. *Mikhail Bulgakov: A Critical Biography.* Cambridge: Cambridge University Press, 1990.

Natov, Nadine. *Mikhail Bulgakov.* Boston: G. K. Hall, 1985.

Proffer, Ellendea. "Predislovie." In *Povesti.* Vol. 3 of *Sobranie sochinenii.* By Bulgakov. Pp. xix–xxx.

———. *Bulgakov: Life and Work.* Ann Arbor, Mich.: Ardis, 1984.

Sacharov, Vsevolod. *L'addio e il volo: Biografia letteraria di Michail Bulgakov.* Venice: Il Cardo, 1995. Original publication in Italian.

Wright, Anthony Colin. *Mikhail Bulgakov: Life and Interpretations.* Toronto: University of Toronto Press, 1978.

Chekhov

Chekhov, Anton Pavlovich. *Polnoe sobranie sochinenii i pisem.* Moscow: Nauka. *Step',* in *Sochineniia 1888–1891,* vol. 7 (1977); *Uchitel' slovesnosti* in *Sochineniia 1892–1894,* vol. 8 (1977); *Chaika* in *Sochineniia: P'esy 1895–1904,* vol. 13 (1978).

———. *The Oxford Chekhov.* Ed. and trans. Ronald Hingley. Oxford: Oxford University Press. *The Seagull* in vol. 2 (1967); *The Steppe* in *Stories 1888–1889,* vol. 4 (1980), *The Schoolteacher,* here as *The Russian Master,* in *Stories 1893–1895,* vol. 7 (1978).

Johnson, Ronald L. *Anton Chekhov: A Study of the Short Fiction.* New York: Twayne, 1993.

Magarshack, David. *The Real Chekhov: An Introduction to Chekhov's Last Plays.* London: George Allen and Unwin, 1972.

Dostoyevsky

Dostoevskii, Fëdor Mikhailovich. *Polnoe sobranie sochinenii v tridsati tomakh.* Leningrad: Nauka, 1972. *Dvoinik* in vol. 1; *Belye nochi* in vol. 2; *Zapiski iz podpol'ia* in vol. 5.

Dostoyevsky, Fedor. *Notes from Underground. The Double.* Trans. Jessie Coulson. Harmondsworth, U.K.: Penguin, 1972.

Dostoevsky, Fyodor. *Notes from Underground.* Ed. and trans. Michael R. Katz. New York: Norton, 1989.

———. *White Nights.* Trans. Constance Garnett. New York: Macmillan, 1923 [1918].

Gogol

Gogol', Nikolai Vasil'evich. *Polnoe sobranie sochinenii.* Moscow and Leningrad: Izdatel'stvo Akademii Nauk SSSR. *Povest' o tom, kak possorilsya Ivan Ivanovic s Ivanom Nikiforovichem* in *Mirgorod,* vol. 2 (1937); *Mërtvye dushi 2,* vol. 7 (1951).

Gogol, Nikolai. *The Complete Tales.* Trans. Constance Garnett. Ed. Leonard Kent. Vol. 2. Chicago: University of Chicago Press, 1985.

Driessen, F. C. *Gogol as a Short-Story Writer: A Study f His Technique of Composition.* Trans. Ian F. Finlay. The Hague: Mouton, 1965.

Pasternak

Pasternak, Boris Leonidovich. *Doktor Zhivago*. Ann Arbor: University of Michigan Press, 1959 [1958].

──────. *Doktor Zhivago: Roman*. Paris: Société d'Edition et d'Impression Mondiale, 1959.

──────. *Doktor Zhivago: Roman*. Vol. 3 of his *Sobranie sochinenii v piati tomakh*. Moscow: Khudozhestvennaia Literatura, 1990.

Pasternak, Boris. *Doctor Zhivago*. Trans. Max Hayward and Manya Harari. New York: Ballantine Books, 1981.

Pushkin

Pushkin, Aleksandr Sergeevich. *Polnoe sobranie sochinenii*. Moscow and Leningrad: Izdatel'stvo Akademii Nauk SSSR. "Dubrovskii" and *Kapitanskaia dochka* in *Romany i povesti*, vol. 8, part 1.

Pushkin, Alexander. *The Captain's Daughter and Other Stories* [incl. "Dubrovsky"]. Trans. Natalie Duddington. London: Dent; New York: Dutton, 1961.

Tolstoy

Tolstoi, Lëv Nikolaevich. *Polnoe sobranie sochinenii*. Moscow and Leningrad: Khudozhestvennaia Literatura. *Smert' Ivana Il'icha* in vol. 26 (1936); *Bozheskoe i chelovecheskoe* in vol. 42 (1957).

Tolstòj, Lëv. *La morte di Ivàn Il'ích*. Trans. Serena Prina. In his *Tutti i racconti*. Ed. Igor Sibaldi. Vol. 2. Milan: Mondadori, 1998 [1991]. Pp. 330–401.

Tolstoy, Leo. *The Works of Leo Tolstoy*. *Tolstoy Centenary Edition*. Trans. Louise Maude and Aylmer Maude. London: Tolstoy Society/Oxford University Press, 1929. *The Death of Ivan Ilich*, vol. 15 (1934).

──────. *The Divine and the Human and Other Stories: A Volume of Stories on Revolution; Crime and Death; Regeneration; Love and Eternal Life*. Christchurch, U.K.: Free Age, 1900 [?].

OTHER FIELDS

Psychiatry

Basaglia, Franco. *L'istituzione negata*. Turin: Einaudi, 1968.

──────. *La maggioranza deviante*. Turin: Einaudi, 1971.

Laing, Ronald David. *The Divided Self: An Existential Study in Sanity and Madness*. Baltimore: Penguin, 1959.

Sèchehaye, M.-A. *Journal d'une schizophrène: Auto-observation d'une schizophrène pendant le traitement psychothérapique*. Paris: Presses Universitaires de France, 1987 [1950].

Sèchehaye, M. R. *Diary of a Schizophrenic Girl*. New York: Grune and Stratton, 1951.

──────. *Autobiography of a Schizophrenic Girl: The True Story of "Renee."* Trans. Grace Rubin-Rabson. New York: Penguin Meridian, 1994.

Index